CW01367295

IBERIAN AND LATIN AMERICAN STUDIES

The Other Catalans

Series Editors

Professor David George (Swansea University)
Professor Paul Garner (University of Leeds)

Editorial Board

Samuel Amago (University of Virginia)
Roger Bartra (Universidad Autónoma de México)
Paul Castro (University of Glasgow)
Richard Cleminson (University of Leeds)
Catherine Davies (University of London)
Lloyd H. Davies (Swansea University)
Luisa-Elena Delgado (University of Illinois)
Maria Delgado (Central School of Speech and Drama, London)
Will Fowler (University of St Andrews)
David Gies (University of Virginia)
Gareth Walters (Swansea University)
Duncan Wheeler (University of Leeds)

Other titles in the series

Postcolonial Spain: Coloniality, Violence and Independence
Edited by Helena Miguélez-Carballeira
The Space of Latin American Women Modernists
Camilla Sutherland
Paradise in Hell: Alcohol and Drugs in the Spanish Civil War
Jorge Marco
Motherhood and Childhood in Silvina Ocampo's Works
Fernanda Zullo-Ruiz
Jesus of Nazareth in the Literature of Unamuno
C. A. Longhurst
Latin America and Existentialism: A Pan-American Literary History (1864–1938)
Edwin Murillo
Spain is different? Historical memory and the 'Two Spains' in turn-of-the-millennium Spanish apocalyptic fictions
Dale Knickerbocker
Blood, Land and Power: The Rise and Fall of the Spanish Nobility and Lineages in the Early Modern Period
Manuel Perez-Garcia
Fantastic Short Stories by Women Authors from Spain and Latin America: A Critical Anthology
Patricia Gracía and Teresa López-Pellisa
Carmen Martín Gaite: Poetics, Visual Elements and Space
Ester Bautista Botello
The Spanish Anarchists of Northern Australia: Revolution in the Sugar Cane Fields
Robert Mason
Paulo Emilio Salles Gomes: On Brazil and Global Cinema
Maite Conde and Stephanie Dennison

IBERIAN AND LATIN AMERICAN STUDIES

The Other Catalans
Representations of Immigration in Catalan Literature

Edited by

JOSEP-ANTON FERNÀNDEZ

UNIVERSITY OF WALES PRESS
2024

© The Contributors, 2024

All rights reserved. No part of this book may be reproduced in any material form (including photocopying or storing it in any medium by electronic means and whether or not transiently or incidentally to some other use of this publication) without the written permission of the copyright owner. Applications for the copyright owner's written permission to reproduce any part of this publication should be addressed to the University of Wales Press, University Registry, King Edward VII Avenue, Cardiff CF10 3NS.

www.uwp.co.uk

British Library CIP
A catalogue record for this book is available from the British Library.

ISBN   978-1-83772-156-6
e-ISBN 978-1-83772-157-3

The rights of the Contributors to be identified as authors of this work have been asserted in accordance with sections 77 and 79 of the Copyright, Designs and Patents Act 1988.

MIX
Paper | Supporting responsible forestry
FSC® C013604

Typeset by Geethik Technologies, India

Printed by CPI Antony Rowe, Melksham

Contents

Series Editors' Foreword   vii

Acknowledgements   ix

Notes on Contributors   xi

Introduction   xv
Josep-Anton Fernàndez

Part I Otherness and Representational Authority

1. On Masks and Cracks: Positions of Authority in the Portrayal of the Migrant Phenomenon in Catalan Literature   3
   Mercè Picornell

2. Egalitarian Aesthetics and the Literary Representation of Immigration: The Work of Julià de Jòdar   33
   Àlex Matas Pons

3. The Representation of the *forasters* by the Majorcan Literary Generation of the 1970s   57
   Guillem Colom-Montero

Part II Spaces, Borders and Memory

4. To Speak the Unspeakable: Francesc Candel and the Trespass of Borders   81
   Olga Sendra Ferrer

5. The Ego-History of Valencian Immigration: Julià Guillamon's *El barri de la Plata*   105
   Teresa Iribarren

6 'Catalunya termina aquí. Aquí comença Vietnam':
   Urbanism, Migration and Spatial Immunity in
   Jordi Puntí's *Els castellans*   129
   William Viestenz

Part III Disidentification, Dislocation and Mourning

7 'Te deix, mare, un fill com a penyora':
   Disidentificatory Intertextuality in Najat El
   Hachmi's *La filla estrangera*   155
   Natasha Tanna

8 Limits and Borders in *No*, by Saïd El Kadaoui   181
   Roger Canadell Rusiñol

9 Mourning, Trauma and Ambivalence in the
   Catalan Literature of the Argentine Diaspora:
   Silvana Vogt's *La mecànica de l'aigua*   204
   Josep-Anton Fernàndez

Bibliography   233

Index   247

Series Editors' Foreword

Over recent decades the traditional 'languages and literatures' model in Spanish departments in universities in the United Kingdom has been superseded by a contextual, interdisciplinary and 'area studies' approach to the study of the culture, history, society and politics of the Hispanic and Lusophone worlds – categories that extend far beyond the confines of the Iberian Peninsula, not only in Latin America but also to Spanish-speaking and Lusophone Africa.

In response to these dynamic trends in research priorities and curriculum development, this series is designed to present both disciplinary and interdisciplinary research within the general field of Iberian and Latin American Studies, particularly studies that explore all aspects of Cultural Production (inter alia literature, film, music, dance, sport) in Spanish, Portuguese, Basque, Catalan, Galician and indigenous languages of Latin America. The series also aims to publish research in the History and Politics of the Hispanic and Lusophone worlds, at the level of both the region and the nation-state, as well as on Cultural Studies that explore the shifting terrains of gender, sexual, racial and postcolonial identities in those same regions.

Acknowledgements

The project for this book originated at a one-day conference on immigration in Catalan literature, organised by the LiCMES research group of the Universitat Oberta de Catalunya (UOC) and held at the Sala Beckett in Barcelona on 22 November 2019. I am grateful to the organiser, Teresa Iribarren, for inviting me to develop a publication project out of this conference, and to the speakers at the event, who provided three of the chapters for this book. I would also like to express my gratitude to the members of the LiCMES and IdentiCat research groups at the UOC, who create a lively, stimulating and convivial environment for intellectual discussion.

This volume would not have been possible without a generous grant from the Arts and Humanities Department of the Universitat Oberta de Catalunya. My heartfelt gratitude goes to Joan Fuster-Sobrepere, who believed in this project from the beginning and agreed to support it, and to Glòria Pujol. I would like to extend my thanks to the editorial team of the University of Wales Press, and especially to Sarah Lewis, Head of Commissioning, for her enthusiasm about the project, her help preparing this book for publication and her patience. Thanks are also due to the contributors to the volume for their knowledge and generosity. I am grateful to the anonymous readers who reviewed both the proposal and the book for their feedback.

I dedicate this volume to the memory of Ferran Miquel Benaiges (1989–2023).

Notes on Contributors

Roger Canadell Rusiñol is associate professor (*professor agregat*) in Catalan literature at the Universitat Oberta de Catalunya. He has published extensively on nineteenth and twentieth-century Catalan literature and culture. Roger is the author of *Josep Anselm Clavé: una vida al servei de la cultura i la llibertat* (2016), the editor of *Premsa i literatura en el vuit-cents: Vuit estudis* (2020) and *Et devia una carta. Correspondència Miquel Martí i Pol – Joan Oliver (1961–1983)* (2020), and co-editor of *Narratives of Violence* (2021, with Teresa Iribarren and Josep-Anton Fernàndez). He is also a member of the LiCMES research group.

Guillem Colom-Montero is a lecturer in Hispanic studies at the University of Glasgow. He specialises in contemporary Hispanic literary and cultural studies, with a particular focus on Catalan culture and on the intersections between tourism and cultural production in Spain. Guillem is the author of *Quim Monzó and Contemporary Catalan Culture (1975–2018): Cultural Normalization, Postmodernism and National Politics* (Legenda, 2021). He has also published academic articles in the *Bulletin of Hispanic Studies* and *Studies in Comics*, as well as pieces in *Brave New Europe* and the Catalan magazine *Núvol*. He is a member of the committee of the Modern Humanities Research Association.

Josep-Anton Fernàndez is Head of the Language and Universities Department at the Institut Ramon Llull (Barcelona). Until 2023 he was associate professor (*professor agregat*) in Catalan studies and director of the BA in Catalan language and literature at the Universitat Oberta de Catalunya. He specialises in contemporary

Catalan literature and culture, gender and sexuality studies, queer studies, and psychoanalytic criticism. Among other publications, Josep-Anton is the author of *Another Country: Sexuality and National Identity in Catalan Gay Fiction* (2000) and *El malestar en la cultura catalana* (2008), and co-editor of *Funcions del passat en la cultura catalana: Institucionalització, representacions i identitat* (2015, with Jaume Subirana) and *Narratives of Violence* (2021).

Teresa Iribarren is associate professor (*professora agregada*) at the Universitat Oberta de Catalunya, where she specialises in contemporary Catalan literature, translation studies and gender studies. She is the author of *Literatura catalana i cinema mut* (2012) and co-editor of *Constel·lacions variables: Literatura en la societat de la informació* (2012), *Cultura i tecnologia: Els reptes de la producció cultural en l'era digital* (2014), *Narratives of Violence* (2021) and *Literatura i violències masclistes: Guia per a treballs acadèmics* (2023). Teresa is the leading investigator of the LiCMES research group.

Àlex Matas Pons is associate professor (*professor agregat*) of literary theory at the University of Barcelona. He is the author of *La ciudad y su trama: Literatura, modernidad y crítica de la cultura* (2010), *En falso: Una crítica cultural del siglo XX* (2017) and *Els marges dels mapes: Una geografia desplaçada* (2021).

Mercè Picornell is associate professor (*professora titular*) of Catalan literature and literary theory at the University of the Balearic Islands. Her most recent books are *Sumar les restes: Ruïnes i mals endreços en la cultura catalana postfranquista* (2020) and *Continuïtats i desviacions. Debats crítics sobre la cultura catalana en el vèrtex 1960/1970* (2013).

Olga Sendra Ferrer is an associate professor of Spanish at Wesleyan University. She specialises in modern Spanish and Catalan culture, with a particular focus on the intersections of urbanism, architecture, literature and photography. Her book *Barcelona, City of Margins*, on the urban (re)construction of the Barcelona of the dictatorship, seen through literary and photographic production between 1950 and 1970, was published in 2022 by the University of Toronto Press.

Natasha Tanna is a lecturer in world literature at the University of York. Previously, she held a Leverhulme Trust Early Career Research Fellowship at University College London, and she was lecturer in Spanish at Christ's College, University of Cambridge. Natasha specialises in modern Latin American, Spanish and Catalan culture, with a particular focus on contemporary literary engagements with queer theory, decolonial theory and critical race theory. She is the author of *Queer Genealogies in Transnational Barcelona* (Legenda, 2019).

William Viestenz is an associate professor at the University of Minnesota, where he specialises in modern Iberian literature and culture. His most recent book is *By the Grace of God: Francoist Spain and the Sacred Roots of Political Imagination* (University of Toronto Press, 2014), and he is co-editor of *The New Ruralism: An Epistemology of Transformed Space* (2012). He is the editor-in-chief of the *Catalan Review* and vice-president of the North American Catalan Society.

Introduction

Josep-Anton Fernàndez

Immigration is a crucial fact in the history of Catalonia, one that has massively influenced the shape of Catalan society. It is an old phenomenon: in the seventeenth century one in five men in Catalonia were born in Occitania and other parts of France.[1] However, it was in the nineteenth and twentieth centuries, under the aegis of industrialisation, that successive migratory waves decisively transformed Catalan society: population movements first went from the Catalan countryside to the cities; then, migrants arrived from neighbouring territories such as Aragon and Valencia; later, in the 1920s, they came from Murcia and eastern Andalusia; in the 1950s and 1960s, from all over Spain; and in the twenty-first century, from the entire world, particularly northern and sub-Saharan Africa, Latin America, Asia and eastern Europe.

The two most prominent Catalan demographers, Anna Cabré and Andreu Domingo, give us an idea of the dimensions of this phenomenon. In her influential book *El sistema català de reproducció* ('The Catalan System of Reproduction', 1999), published just before the latest wave of incoming population, Cabré states that immigration is part and parcel of the system of social reproduction in Catalonia, whereby a very low birth rate throughout the nineteenth century (among the lowest in Europe) was compensated by the arrival of immigrants.[2] These phenomena, argues Cabré, emerged as a consequence of industrialisation and the crisis of the traditional system of patrimonial transmission, organised around the figure of the *hereu*, the first-born son who would inherit all family assets (Cabré, *El sistema*, pp. 213–14). Starting with migrations from Catalan rural areas to cities and industrialised areas, the attraction of a quickly developing Catalonia soon extended beyond its borders (Cabré, pp. 215–16). As Andreu Domingo points out, most of the first wave of non-Catalan migration, between 1901 and 1930, originated in Valencia, Aragon and Murcia, and by 1930 almost 20 per cent of the population was born outside Catalonia.[3] This figure is comparable to Argentina's demography during the same period (Cabré, p. 178). The second wave of migration, approximately between 1951 and 1975, entailed an enormous demographic transformation, with almost 2 million people moving from Andalusia and other rural areas of Spain, bringing the total proportion of the population born outside Catalonia to 36.5 per cent (Domingo, *Catalunya al mirall*, p. 26).

For the next twenty-five years the total population remained largely stable at 6 million, a figure that was soon incorporated into the Catalan imagination. With the advent of the twenty-first century, however, a new, massive wave was set in motion, prompting the arrival of more than 2 million immigrants, 66.9 per cent of which were born outside Spain (Domingo, p. 29). Statistics reflect the sheer scale of this population influx: in 2000 Catalonia had just over 6 million inhabitants, 2.9 per cent of which were foreigners; by 2010 the total population was 7.5 million, and the foreign contingent had increased to 15.95 per cent.[4]

The impact of immigration has been such that, as Anna Cabré has famously claimed, without these migratory waves Catalonia today would have had less than half its current population and a weak economy (Cabré, p. 26). The demographic, social and cultural transformation brought about by immigration has been staggering, to the extent that by the end of the twentieth century only 25 per cent of Catalans had all four grandparents born in Catalonia, or to put it another way, three-quarters of the Catalan population had an immigrant origin (Cabré, p. 164); and yet, Catalan society saw and to this day sees itself as a distinct nation. As some scholars have pointed out, however, this rich migratory history stands in stark contrast with the poverty of its literary representations in Catalan: considering the social, cultural and political impact of immigration, it is surprising that in twentieth-century Catalan literature there are relatively few texts portraying this experience. No doubt this was due in part to the structural weakness of the Catalan literary system and to the lack of a language policy and the absence of the Catalan language from schools until the 1980s; but there were ideological causes too. Sociologist Salvador Cardús has attributed the relative invisibility of immigration in Catalan literature to an effect of the subaltern position of Catalan nationalism during Franco's dictatorship, leading to a defensive reaction that stressed the trope of cultural roots in the discourses about Catalan identity.[5] Discussing this same phenomenon, Josep-Anton Fernàndez has alluded to the 'process of national deconstruction' resulting – as an unintended consequence – from the policies of 'cultural normalisation' deployed in the 1980s and 1990s, whereby 'the categories that defined Catalan identity . . . experienced a process of fragmentation and redefinition that dissolved the consensus over what being Catalan was', and limited the capacity of Catalan society 'to represent itself' in all its diversity and complexity.[6]

The latest migratory wave, between 2000 and 2012 approximately, has had two major effects. On the one hand, its massive proportions have given rise once again to profound changes in Catalan society and identity. It has transformed the linguistic landscape of Catalonia, which is no longer a 'bilingual' society, but one where more than 200 languages are spoken, thus setting out a new scenario for a long-standing language conflict. It has also put to the test the welfare system built during the 1980s and 1990s as well as the language and education policies of the Catalan government, and has underscored the limitations of Catalan self-government, devoid of any real powers to regulate immigration fluxes. Moreover, it has prompted the production of discourses aimed at reconciling diversity and Catalan national identity by adopting immigration as a foundational myth of Catalan society (Domingo, p. 303), but it has also been met by increasing levels of xenophobia and racism.

On the other hand, it has triggered a wave of new literary representations, in terms both of a memorial drive regarding the Spanish migrations of the twentieth century, and of the incorporation of 'new Catalans' to Catalan literature as authors and intellectuals. Building on the conditions created both by an educational system aimed at guaranteeing equal access to the Catalan language and by a growing awareness of 'els fonaments migratoris de la nació' ('the migratory foundations of the nation'), this latest influx of foreign populations has encouraged 'l'emergència d'una generació d'autors que es puguin reconèixer ells mateixos com a deutors de la immigració familiar o que la immigració va marcar el seu espai i infància (tot i que ells no fossin migrants)' (Domingo, p. 290) ('the emergence of a generation of authors who will recognise themselves as a product of their families' immigration, or whose environment and childhood were impacted by immigration, even though they were not migrants themselves').[7]

The case of the Balearic Islands is somewhat different from that of the mainland. Shielded by insularity, Majorcan society retained for the most part its traditional, rural ways of life until the 1960s, when mass tourism propelled deep economic and socio-cultural transformations. A key element of these changes was the arrival of thousands of migrants from impoverished, Castilian-speaking areas of Spain (mostly from Andalusia, Extremadura and Castile La Mancha) who moved to the island to work in the rising tourism industry. Catalan, the island's vernacular language, was in a minoritised position due to Francoist laws proscribing its use in most public domains, reinforcing the diglossia historically operative on the island. In spite of this, the majority of the Majorcan population spoke Catalan in their day-to-day life and had only basic knowledge of Spanish. As a result, the influx of Castilian-speaking newcomers in the Francoist context radically altered the social, linguistic and cultural fabric of the island. The local population othered these migrants through offensive sociocultural constructions focusing on their poverty, deficient education and alleged laziness and lack of manners, as well as emphasising linguistic and cultural difference. The derogatory term *foraster* ('foreigner') came to be widely used to refer to any deprived, Castilian-speaking migrant, encapsulating the narratives of alterity generated in that historical juncture. These profound social and cultural transformations, examined by Guillem Colom-Montero in Chapter 3, have been an important element of the literature in Catalan produced in Majorca since the 1970s.

The Other Catalans is the first book published in any language (even in Catalan) offering a comprehensive account of immigration in Catalan literature – that is, literature produced in the Catalan language – since the 1930s until the present day. The book does not focus on 'migrant literature' *per se*, but rather on literary representations of immigration; some of the authors discussed have a migrant origin, while others do not. In this sense, we are echoing recent debates in Germany, Scandinavia and other European countries around the concept of 'postmigration', a perspective that seeks to move away from what Regina Römhild calls a 'migrantology' that makes migration itself the object of study and reproduces 'the image of the ethnicised, racialised, religiously connoted "Other", defining migrants as foreign minorities on the margins of society'.[8] Postmigration proposes instead working 'towards research that examines and analyses society from the perspective of migration'.[9] This perspective entails observing society 'from the margins it has itself created', in order to generate 'new insights into the contested arenas of "society" and "culture"',[10] taking as its starting point societal conflicts and negotiations over migration. As literary scholar Roger Bromley suggests, postmigration is 'a useful concept for exploring the conflicts and contradictions, the dialectic of belonging and unbelonging, the split subjectivities which, in many cases, are a feature of postmigrant belonging'.[11]

Our focus on representations and not on the solidification of a subgenre of 'migrant literature' (and the fixed identity it would entail) is, I believe, consistent with the perspective I have just outlined. It allows us to examine the conflicts, the blind spots, the ambivalences and ambiguities, and the impasses in the negotiations over identity and otherness in Catalan culture as they are deployed in literary texts. Indeed, the literature of immigration challenges binarisms such as us/them or foreign/native, and problematises concepts such as origin, roots, home, authenticity, citizenship, sameness and difference. This problematisation is even more probing in the context of a stateless nation such as Catalonia, where the concepts and binarisms outlined above often become sites for dissent and contestation.

Furthermore, the literature of migration treats in very specific ways certain fundamental issues that deserve close analytical attention: the construction of national identity; the role played in it by cultural memory; and how a culture narrates the past and connects it to the future. These issues are intertwined with the construction of subjectivity through gender and sexuality and in relation to experiences such as the trauma of losing one's native country or seeing one's environment profoundly altered by social change, as well as the pain caused by racism, racialisation and social exclusion, and the work of mourning. The literary texts discussed in this book thus bring to the fore questions that are crucial to understanding contemporary Catalan culture: how has immigration shaped the discourses about identity and otherness in Catalan culture over time? Who may claim the authority of representing Catalan society in literary texts, and how is this authority constructed? How are class inequalities, power differentials and the transformation of the urban space represented in the texts? How do authors portray the consequences of racialisation and xenophobia? How is the dialectic between identification and disidentification played out in Catalan subjects of migrant origin? How does immigration interlink with an existing language conflict? In what ways is the work of mourning articulated in migrant literature, and to what effect? What role does the subject of immigration play in the political conflict between Catalonia and Spain? How is the literary production of the 'new Catalans' transforming existing discourses of Catalan identity? What relationship does it establish with the Catalan literary tradition?

By posing these questions and discussing the selected literary texts in their light, this book seeks to shed new light on a crucial aspect of Catalan society and culture, contribute to a deeper understanding of the complexities of the social context of Catalonia, and provide new elements for conceptualising national identity and belonging in the increasingly diverse societies of southern Europe, especially in stateless nations like Catalonia. More specifically, through a series of detailed analyses of Catalan literary texts portraying the experience of migration in Catalonia and the Balearic Islands, and its social, cultural and subjective impact, *The Other Catalans* aims to provide a comprehensive view of the subject, not limited to the most recent migratory waves, but covering a wider historical scope, from the 1930s to the present. Furthermore, this book seeks to situate the literature of migration in Catalan within the context of the demographic, political and cultural history of Catalonia, in order to show how these texts both portray and contribute to shape the internal tensions in Catalan society and the political conflict between Catalonia and Spain. Finally, it intends to explore the various links between the representation of immigration in Catalan literature and other issues such as representational authority, symbolic power, citizenship and otherness, gender and sexuality, subjectivity, and the construction of national identity.

From Fear of the Other to a Shared Memory

The title of this book is a gesture towards one of the most important texts dealing with the consequences of Spanish-speaking immigration for Catalan society and identity: *Els altres catalans* ('The Other Catalans', 1964), by Francesc Candel, which Mercè Picornell and Olga Sendra Ferrer analyse in Chapters 1 and 4, and whose cultural impact has been gigantic and durable. With this gesture we not only aim to acknowledge the existence of otherness at the core of Catalan identity, but also, and mainly, we wish to situate the reflection on the current conditions of diversity in Catalan society both within the context of the history of immigration (which, as sociologist Salvador Cardús has argued, is the history of the Catalans of the twentieth and the twenty-first centuries) and in relation to changing discourses and representations of the migratory phenomenon. In this section of the introduction, we will look into some of these discourses and briefly examine relevant literary texts that have not been discussed in detail in the chapters of this book.

Cultural debates and literary representations of immigration in Catalonia have been forcefully marked by two authors from the 1930s: journalist Carles Sentís and demographer Josep Antoni Vandellós. In 1932 and 1933 Sentís published a series of feature articles in the weekly magazine *Mirador* that gave rise to an intense public debate. At this time the effects of the first wave of migration (originating in Aragon, Valencia, Murcia and eastern Andalusia, but inscribed in the popular imagination as that of the *murcianos*) were apparent in the wake of Barcelona's 1929 Universal Exposition. Sentís investigates the causes and circumstances of the migration of the *murcianos* and echoes concerns over the impact of these demographic changes on the future of Catalan society. In his features, the budding journalist travels to the poorest towns of Murcia, joins a group of migrants in their journey to Catalonia on the crowded bus dubbed 'el Transmiserià' ('Poverty Express') and describes the appalling living conditions in the shanty towns of Barcelona and adjoining cities. But Sentís's narrative voice is certainly not objective: it painstakingly engages in the xenophobic othering of the *murciano* migrants, presented as dirty, loud, untrustworthy savages, prone to crime or, worse, to the revolutionary radicalism of the anarchist union Confederación Nacional del Trabajo (CNT). Sentís also insists on the high prevalence of trachoma among *murcianos*, expressing a fear of contamination whereby immigration is equated with a dangerous infection that threatens to damage the foundations of Catalan society. These articles, compiled in book format in 1994, are discussed by Mercè Picornell in Chapter 1.

Sentís's controversial journalistic intervention found an academic counterpart in two works by demographer Josep Antoni Vandellós, *Catalunya, poble decadent* ('Catalonia, a Nation in Decline') and *La immigració a Catalunya* ('Immigration in Catalonia'), both published in 1935. The author argued that Catalonia was at risk of becoming 'denationalised' because of the combined action of two factors: on the one hand, a declining birth rate resulting from the access of women to the labour market, Catholicism's loss of influence and the 'Malthusian propaganda' that encouraged couples to have fewer children;[12] on the other, a strong influx of immigrants, presented as an 'invasió pacífica' ('peaceful invasion') that threatened to turn 'els veritables catalans' ('true Catalans') into a minority in their own country:[13] 'Plana damunt de la gent de llengua catalana una fonda amenaça, la importància de la qual ningú no ha de desconèixer perquè pot representar l'anul·lació d'una cultura' ('Over the Catalan-speaking people looms a serious threat whose importance nobody must ignore, for it might entail the extinction of a culture').[14] While Vandellós acknowledges the importance and necessity of immigration in order to sustain population levels and identifies it as a systemic phenomenon, at the same time he sees it as the cause of denationalisation and moral chaos and as a threat of revolutionary upheaval.[15]

The echoes of Vandellós's ambivalence can be heard in one of the main reformulations of Catalan identity after the debâcle of the Civil War: Jaume Vicens Vives's *Notícia de Catalunya* ('An Account of Catalonia', 1954/1960). In this historical essay Vicens formulated a project for the reconstruction of Catalanism in order to attempt, once again, the modernisation of Spain while preserving the specificity of the national culture of the Catalans. The clarity and ambition of this project was one of the reasons for its enormous influence in the decades following its publication, through to the end of the twentieth century. Another reason was that Vicens posited immigration as a foundational myth of the Catalan nation. In his account of the Catalan 'mentality' the historian presents 'mestissatge' ('miscegenation') as a constant force in Catalonia's history. Indeed, Catalonia is 'un lloc de pas' ('a land of passage') that has favoured the mixing of populations. As Vicens famously proclaimed: 'Som fruit de diversos llevats i, per tant, una bona llesca del país pertany a una biologia i a una cultura del mestissatge' ('We are the product of various ferments, and therefore a good slice of the country belongs to a biology and a culture of miscegenation').[16] Yet precisely when Catalonia was receiving a new, massive wave of Spanish-speaking migrants, Vicens warns against the moral and psychological pitfalls of hybridity, often characterised by 'un orgull a vegades insuportable i una vanitat pueril' ('a sometimes insufferable pride and a puerile vanity'), a 'ressentiment primari' ('primal resentment') and 'un sentimentalisme torbador' ('a disturbing sentimentality').[17] In fact, throughout his book Vicens Vives manifests his deep ambivalence *vis-à-vis* immigration and suggests that the most turbulent moments in the history of Catalonia (notably the revolution and Civil War of 1936–9) are a direct consequence of hybridity.[18]

In Francesc Candel's hugely influential *Els altres catalans* (1964) we also find resonances of Vandellós's argument, as Olga Sendra Ferrer shows in Chapter 4, but this time to present a contrary position from the perspective of the migrant. Candel, who was born in the Spanish-speaking area of the Valencia region, describes in his quirky, colloquial style the living conditions, the social problems and the everyday life in the shanty towns of Catalonia, and introduces all sorts of characters from the neighbourhoods who offer their points of view in their own voices, thus humanising them. At the same time, Candel stresses the importance of the Catalan language in the socialisation of the migrants. In doing so, Candel promotes the visibility of the 'other Catalans', whose claim to belonging to Catalan culture is explicitly made, and draws a social horizon in which immigrants incorporate themselves into Catalan society.

Otherwise, the presence of Spanish-speaking migrants in the literature of the 1950s and 1960s is rather limited and focuses on the depiction of social conditions along the lines of the 'historical realism' of the period. As Julià Guillamon and Maria Dasca indicate, authors such as Concepció G. Maluquer, Robert Saladrigas or Lluís Ferran de Pol tend to highlight the otherness of the immigrants, whose presence contrasts with the habits of the native working classes.[19]

The periods of the resistance against Franco's dictatorship and the 'cultural normalisation' process (after the restoration of democracy in 1976 and the return of self-government for Catalonia in 1980) were characterised by a tension between the hope for the integration of Spanish-speaking migrants into Catalan culture and the ambivalences already expressed by Vandellós and Vicens Vives. A suspicion that the Francoist regime had intentionally promoted immigration to dilute Catalan identity and denationalise Catalonia was frequently voiced, but historian Martí Marín convincingly argues that, quite the contrary, Francoism made it difficult for people to move from rural areas to the cities in its efforts to control the population and prevent further revolutionary movements.[20] Jordi Pujol's *La immigració, problema i esperança de Catalunya* ('Immigration: Catalonia's Problem and Hope', 1976) is a good example of how the tensions mentioned above were negotiated on the eve of the political changes to come; here the fear of denationalisation expressed by Vandellós gives way to the ghost of a Catalonia traumatically split into two communities.[21] Pujol, who would later become president of the Catalan government between 1980 and 2003, presents immigration as both a problem and a cause for hope: it infuses new blood, talent and energy into the Catalan social body, but it also leaves the community vulnerable to divisive populist discourses. For this reason, in order to ensure social cohesion and conviviality, the 'integration' of immigrants is required. Pujol states that 'els immigrats volen ser catalans' ('the immigrants want to be Catalans'),[22] and rejects assimilation in favour of a process of integration that would result in a single community, organised around the nucleus of the 'native' Catalans.[23] It is in this context that Pujol formulates his famous definition of Catalan identity: 'català és tot home que viu i treballa a Catalunya, i que amb el seu treball, amb el seu esforç, ajuda a fer Catalunya' ('a Catalan is any man who lives and works in Catalonia, and who contributes to build it with his work and effort').[24]

Pujol's definition was quickly adopted by a majority of Catalan society, but despite its good intentions, it has been criticised for its reduction of identity to residence, emptying Catalan identity of its attributes and concealing the conditions necessary for subjects to obtain social recognition as Catalan, while forcing this status on people who might not desire it.[25] It could be argued that this definition is an effect of the political weakness of Catalan nationalism, unable to establish and sustain a proper hegemony in order to bring its political vision to fruition. For this reason, the process of linguistic normalisation launched in 1983, although instrumental in spreading knowledge of the Catalan language and its social use, was from the outset challenged by Spanish-speaking sectors reluctant to yield their dominant position, and thus immigration became a site of social antagonism and an arena of symbolic struggles throughout the 1980s and 1990s, with the Andalusian diaspora acting as the locus of intense political and symbolic competition.[26] It was also during this period that Anna Cabré conducted her demographic research. The publication in 1999 of her book *El sistema català de reproducció*, discussed earlier, was a decisive intervention in the debates around demography and identity that clarified the crucial role of immigration in Catalan history: while showing it as a systemic, endogenous phenomenon, Cabré presented immigration as the condition of possibility of Catalan modernity and dispelled the fears of demographic decline that Vandellós had expressed sixty-five years earlier.

Surprisingly, Catalan literature of the 1970s and 1980s did not pay a great deal of attention to the demographic reality of the country, with two exceptions. One is the narrative of Majorcan authors of the 1970s that Guillem Colom-Montero examines in Chapter 3; these texts portray critically the othering of Spanish-speaking migrants who had moved to Majorca in order to work in the tourist industry and display the anxieties regarding the rapid linguistic, social and cultural changes the island was experiencing. The other exception is Montserrat Roig's novel *L'òpera quotidiana* ('The Everyday Opera', 1982), which engages with the deconstruction of Catalan identity prompted by Pujol's definition, by means of a multi-perspective narrative typical of postmodern aesthetics. This novel, built around operatic conventions and the myth of Pygmalion, dramatises both nationalist resistance and the integration of immigrants. It presents the interlinking stories of a lower-middle-class nationalist activist, his Andalusian lover, who has embraced the Catalan cause, and a Spanish-speaking girl who seeks a sense of identity and belonging through sexual fulfilment. Roig problematises the notion of integration and sets out a dialectic between national and gender subordination. Moreover, *L'òpera quotidiana* questions the established grand narratives of Catalan identity through its fragmentary structure and its emphasis on performativity and the body. In this sense, Roig's novel becomes an emblem of the paradoxes of the period of cultural normalisation, in which the institutional promotion of Catalan language and culture coexists with and in fact triggers a crisis of identity discourses.[27]

The latest wave of immigration (2000–12), originating mostly in Africa, Latin America and eastern Europe, had a significant impact in discursive production, which was substantially transformed. The main interventions during this period were by sociologist Salvador Cardús and demographer Andreu Domingo, both on the eve of the failed self-determination process that would culminate in 2017. Cardús's contribution is twofold. First, having spelled out the economic, demographic and political importance of immigration for Catalan society, Cardús explores the causes of the 'invisibility' of the 'migrant condition', which he attributes to Catalonia's lack of 'the mechanisms that permit nation states to engage in the sort of invisible coercion that facilitates adherence to the nation-cum-political community'.[28] He also proposes the transformation of immigration into a 'memory place' or a foundational myth of origin in order to conceive of Catalonia as a 'country of immigrants'.[29] Secondly, Cardús has been instrumental in rethinking the metaphors on which Catalan identity discourses are built. He has proposed to think of the metaphor of the roots not in terms of the past, but of the future, since 'allò que proporciona futur és la capacitat d'arrelar, independentment de l'origen' ('what makes future possible is the capacity to take roots, independently of one's origin').[30] He further proposes to adopt the metaphor of grafting, which permits a figuration of the new migrants incorporating themselves into the shared tree that is the 'country of immigrants', and invigorating it. This, argues Cardús, would facilitate the '*dissolució* de la condició d'immigrant' ('dissolution of the immigrant condition').[31] Finally, the third metaphor Cardús rewrites is that of the skin as a figure of identity. The skin, he argues, 'és el territori més social del cos' ('the body's most social territory'), the locus of relationality and interaction with the other where the social construction of identity takes place: 'la pell – la identitat – té per missió ocultar i protegir els teixits i els fluids interns. I és que la identitat, si bé sembla que serveix per dir què som, en realitat té un paper social encara més decisiu: estalviar-nos de precisar els continguts concrets que amaga' ('the skin – that is, identity – conceals and protects the inner tissues and fluids. For identity, while it seems to simply say what we are, in reality plays an even more decisive social role: to relieve us from having to spell out the specific contents it conceals').[32] The imaginary concealment of the contents of identity, argues Cardús, facilitates the process of recognition on which identity depends. The play of these metaphors would be the necessary condition for a rewriting of Catalonia as a nation of immigrants.

Andreu Domingo's seminal *Catalunya al mirall de la immigració: Demografia i identitat nacional* ('Catalonia in the Mirror of Immigration: Demography and National Identity', 2014) is the most comprehensive analysis of the discourses on immigration in Catalonia, the legislation and policies that these discourses have underpinned since the 1930s and the power dynamics that have legitimated in each historical period the othering of immigrants. Domingo shows how Vandellós's ambivalence was reproduced throughout the rest of the twentieth century, but he also detects a significant transformation of national identity discourses along the lines described by Cardús: in the twenty-first century, 'ja no és la nostra identitat la que veiem reflectida a l'espill de la immigració. En travessar-lo, ens hem convertit nosaltres mateixos en immigrants, la nostra memòria i la nostra herència, i la migració com a recurs per a la supervivència' ('it is no longer our identity that we see reflected in immigration's mirror. In crossing to the other side of the looking glass, we ourselves have become immigrants, and immigration is now our memory, our heritage and a means of survival').[33] Domingo confirms Cabré's analysis of the role of immigration in the Catalan system of social reproduction, outlines the threats and attacks on this system coming from Spanish state nationalism (Domingo, pp. 286–7) and stresses the role that the Catalan language plays in it as an 'element estructurador' ('structuring element') of a society whose reproduction depends on the incorporation of migrants (p. 327). However, Domingo warns us that the future success of this system cannot rely on discourses from the nineteenth and twentieth centuries or on individual initiatives. Rather, it demands the creation of 'una memòria social compartida' ('a shared social memory') that requires 'una redefinició dels fonaments comuns, que faci comprensible la identitat a aquells que s'adhereixen [*sic*] i a aquells que se'n situen fora, articulant sobre aquest fonament tot un sistema de creences de diferents orígens culturals, geogràfics i socials, de classe' (Domingo, pp. 330–1) ('a redefinition of the common foundations that would make identity comprehensible to those who adhere to it and to those who remain outside of it, thus articulating on these foundations a whole belief system about different cultural, geographical and class origins').

The creation of a shared memory and the representation of diverse origins is one of the most remarkable developments in Catalan literature of the past twenty years. This period has seen the emergence into the literary field of a new contingent of writers of foreign origin. Some of them offer autobiographical accounts of their migration experiences, like Laila Karrouch's *De Nador a Vic* ('From Nador to Vic', 2004), Matthew Tree's *Memòries!* ('Memoirs!', 2004), Agnès Agboton's *Més enllà del mar de sorra: Una dona africana a la nostra terra* ('Beyond the Sea of Sand: An African Woman in Our Country', 2005), Pius Alibek's *Arrels nòmades* ('Nomadic Roots', 2010) and Saïd El Kadaoui's *Cartes al meu fill: Un català de soca-rel, o gairebé* ('Letters to My Son: A Catalan Born and Bred, almost', 2011). In other cases they represent the effects of migration in their novels, such as Salah Jamal's *Lluny de l'horitzó perfumat* ('Far from the Perfumed Horizon', 2004), Patrícia Gabancho's *La neta d'Adam* ('Adam's Granddaughter', 2012), El Kadaoui's *No* (2016) or Silvana Vogt's *La mecànica de l'aigua* ('The Mechanics of Water', 2016). Among these authors, Najat El Hachmi has perhaps achieved the highest critical success and public recognition with her novels *L'últim patriarca* ('The Last Patriarch', 2008), *La filla estrangera* ('The Foreign Daughter', 2015) and *Mare de llet i mel* ('Mother of Milk and Honey', 2018). El Hachmi's first book, the autobiographical essay *Jo també soc catalana* ('I Am also Catalan', 2004) reflects on the conflicts and difficulties experienced by the Moroccan postmigrant generation in Catalonia as they try to define a sense of belonging and negotiate a plural identity. El Hachmi questions the rosy narratives of integration put forward by Catalan nationalism, describes intergenerational conflicts and posits a postmigrant identity based on a 'border thinking' that reflects the migrant subject's complex position.[34]

Catalan culture's need to come to terms with the consequences of the profound changes resulting from the latest migration wave encouraged the elaboration of a shared memory of the Spanish-speaking migration of the 1950s to 1970s, until then left largely unrepresented in Catalan literature. Novelist Maria Barbal – whose *Pedra de tartera* ('Stone in a Landslide', 1985) acknowledged the migration from the Catalan Pyrenees to Barcelona in the post-Civil War period – presents in *Carrer Bolívia* ('Bolivia Street', 1999) the story of Lina and Néstor, an Andalusian couple who settle in Barcelona in the 1960s. The novel, fully immersed in the integration discourse prevalent before the turn of the century, reconfirms some of the myths of Catalanism: Lina participates in the life of her community in the periphery of Barcelona, learns Catalan and progressively adopts a Catalan identity, whereas her husband Néstor becomes involved in the communist struggle against Franco and is ambivalent about Catalonia. At the same time, however, Barbal problematises these myths, showing them as a site of conflict and presenting immigration as a process of subjective transformation.[35]

Barbal's precedent in the creation of a shared migratory memory has been followed by other authors in the past twenty years. For instance, novelists Francesc Serés and Jordi Puntí, and Sergi Belbel in the field of theatre, do not have (to our knowledge) a migrant origin but depict the transformations of the social environment caused by immigration, past and present. Others, such as Julià de Jòdar and Julià Guillamon, are descendents of Spanish-speaking migrants, and in their works fictionalise or document the confluence of native and immigrant working classes in the periphery of Barcelona. Belonging to this second group are two other authors worth mentioning here. Bel Olid's *Una terra solitària* ('A Solitary Land', 2011) features the story of three generations of women: the grandmother's life in a poor Andalusian village, the migration of the daughter to a Catalan coastal city, and the granddaughter's process of social promotion and adoption of both Catalan identity and lesbian desire. Olid thus brings together an intergenerational memory and a discourse about gender and queer sexuality, turning immigration into an experience that cracks open the possibility of fashioning one's identity. Finally, in *Un home que se'n va* ('A Man who Goes Away', 2014) novelist Vicenç Villatoro documents the life of his grandfather Vicente Villatoro, who having suffered for years the repression inflicted by the victors of the Civil War, left his village in the Andalusian province of Córdoba to start a new life in the industrial town of Terrassa, in Catalonia. In his moving account, Villatoro travels to the village and to the various prisons where his grandfather had been jailed, searches archives, speaks to witnesses, speculates about the motivations and emotions of his grandfather, and documents his narrative with a wealth of photographs. In this way, Villatoro constructs a memory of immigration that is at the same time discursive and sensual, as an emblem of the trajectories of so many Catalans of Andalusian origin.

Representing Immigration in Catalan Literature

The literary works we have just reviewed underscore the link between the representation of immigration and wider issues of subjectivity, class, gender, sexuality and the body that often frame the construction of discourses about otherness and (national) identity. These issues prompt us to interrogate Catalan literature, culture and society from the perspective of immigration as one of their constitutive factors, rather than focus on 'migrant literature' as a separate category. In this sense, this book aims to avoid and redress some of the shortcomings of the critical coverage of the subject so far. By examining a representative sample of the literary series, from the 1930s to the present day, and covering a range of genres (narrative fiction, autobiography, journalism, essay), we have attempted to historicise the representation of immigration, place it into its discursive contexts and recognise the place of authors of migrant origin in the history of Catalan literature. Indeed, we have sought to take stock of the complex historical experience of immigration in the Catalan-speaking territories: some chapters deal with the memory of the migration from Valencia to Barcelona or with the social transformations experienced in Majorca as an effect of mass tourism, while others examine the consequences of the large migratory waves from Spanish-speaking parts of Spain, and finally, we have devoted a great deal of attention to the narratives produced by Catalan authors born in other continents.

Moreover, the categories of 'migrant literature' and 'migrant author' are often naturalised by the critics, thus promoting a fixed identity that contradicts the very mobility on which migration depends, and making it more difficult to obtain full recognition as a Catalan author. By contrast, the book's focus on representations of subjective experiences and social changes has allowed us to examine texts by non-immigrant authors (Guillem Frontera, Maria Antònia Oliver, Jordi Puntí, Carles Sentís, Francesc Serés, Antònia Vicens, and others), authors of Spanish-speaking background (Francesc Candel, Julià Guillamon, Julià de Jòdar), and Catalan authors of recent migrant origin from northern Africa (Najat El Hachmi, Saïd

El Kadaoui) and Latin America (Silvana Vogt). In this way we are acknowledging that the choice of Catalan for literary expression both manifests a desire to belong to a chosen tradition and entails consequences in terms of the definition of authorship in the Catalan literary institution, the positions of authority derived from it, and, given the subaltern position of Catalan literature in the market, the social effectiveness of the discourses it conveys.

This being said, the critical coverage of this subject often displays a problematic slippage from a reflection on otherness and identity to a discourse about the vitality of Catalan literature, as though the texts studied were in the end simple instrumental markers of such vitality, not agents that affect and actively transform Catalan literature and society. For example, Maria Dasca claims that the literature of immigration demonstrates 'la vitalitat de la narrativa catalana a l'hora de tractar temes d'actualitat' ('the vitality of Catalan fiction when it comes to treating topical subjects'), while Aitana Guia Conca states that the works by migrant writers show 'que la cultura catalana, contràriament al que proclamen les veus més derrotistes, és dinàmica, saludable i . . . capaç d'atreure l'interès dels escriptors nouvinguts en un context de conflicte lingüístic' ('that Catalan culture, contrary to defeatist views, is dynamic, healthy and . . . capable of attracting the interest of newcomer writers in a context of language conflict'), and Isabel Marcillas-Piquer argues that the success of the literature of immigration is a sign 'del camí cap a la normalitat cultural, pel que fa a l'àmbit literari, i cap a la normalitat social, pel que té a veure amb la tasca d'integració dels nous catalans d'ara' ('of the path towards cultural normality with regards to literature, and towards social normality as far as the integration of today's new Catalans is concerned').[36] In other cases, a rather uncritical adoption of a postcolonial framework is adopted, together with a multiculturalist approach that does not take into account the subordinate position of Catalan culture: this perspective is problematic because it contributes to fix the identities of migrants and ignores the existence of a political conflict between Spain and Catalonia that conditions the representations of immigration and complicates the position of writers of migrant origin in the literary field.[37] Contrary to these critical positions, the essays in this book assume that immigration is a force that profoundly transforms not only subjects but also the entire Catalan society, and place conflict and dislocation at the centre of their arguments.

The Other Catalans comprises nine chapters organised in three parts. The first section of the book, 'Otherness and Representational Authority', centres around the conditions of representation of immigration in Catalan literature, focusing specifically on issues of authorship and authority, of difference and otherness, and of aesthetics and politics. In Chapter 1, 'On Masks and Cracks: Positions of Authority in the Portrayal of the Migrant Phenomenon in Catalan Literature', Mercè Picornell argues that critical attention to the issue of migration in Catalan literature has tended to focus on thematic analyses of its representations and its intersections with gender, identity and interculturality, and on how immigration has affected the Catalan cultural field. The works studied within this framework are often selected in terms of the foreign origin of the author, whose voice and experience would be determined by hybridisation and nomadism. Picornell proposes an alternative perspective, shifting the focus from the works themselves to the construction of a specific authorial position. More precisely, she analyses how the fact of both representing and being in contact with what is perceived as foreign – and often, too, as subaltern – tends to activate various authorial mechanisms, ranging from Carles Sentís's xenophobic distancing in *Viatge en Transmiserià* ('A Journey on the Poverty Express'), to Francesc Candel's well-intentioned condescension in *Els altres catalans*, to Francesc Serés's questioning of the author's own position in *La pell de la frontera* ('The Skin of the Border', 2014). Picornell reads these and other non-fiction works not as witnesses to an occurrence of the foreign to be added to Catalan literature and culture in greater or smaller degrees of hybridisation, but as active agents in the revision and reformulation of the very position of the writer as an author in contemporary Catalan culture.

In Chapter 2, 'Egalitarian Aesthetics and the Literary Representation of Immigration: The Work of Julià de Jòdar', Àlex Matas Pons focuses on the aesthetic choices made by this author in *L'atzar i les ombres* ('Chance and Shadows', 1997–2006), his narrative trilogy set in a working-class suburb in the vicinity of Barcelona. These novels deal with the phenomenon of immigration in Catalonia during the entire twentieth century and the first years of the twenty-first century, and depict the dynamics of inclusion and exclusion that have shaped the metropolitan area of Barcelona. The narrative model of progressive historiography, Matas argues, cannot properly account for the dialectical complexity of these dynamics, which simultaneously subject different groups to multiple forms of repression and exploitation (in terms of class, gender, language, etc.). The author shows how, for this reason, Julià de Jòdar adheres to Walter Benjamin's poetics of history and chooses a narrative time that is incompatible with a linear and progressive sequence. Similarly, the techniques of representation in the novels are consistent with the social and political complexity of the metropolitan space. The movements through the various spaces and the relationships between the characters are not organised according to the official distribution of roles, territories and languages, says Matas, but are represented through aesthetic choices that suggest what Jacques Rancière calls a new 'distribution of the sensible', which enables an egalitarian understanding of the community.

The first section of the book closes with Guillem Colom-Montero's analysis of the dialectic of otherness and subalternity experienced by both migrants and local populations in 1970s Majorca. The transformation of this island due to tourism-led dynamics was masterfully represented in a series of novels published by a generation of young authors emerging in the late 1960s and early 1970s, known as the Majorcan Generation of the 1970s. In his chapter, Colom-Montero examines the representation of the *forasters* ('foreigner', the term associated since the 1960s with Spanish-speaking migrants) in five of the most representative novels of the period: Antònia Vicens's *39° a l'ombra* ('39° in the Shade', 1968), Guillem Frontera's *Els carnissers* ('The Butchers', 1969), Maria Antònia Oliver's *Cròniques d'un mig estiu* ('Chronicles of a Half Summer', 1970), Gabriel Tomàs' *Corbs afamegats* ('Starving Raven', 1972) and Jaume Santandreu's *Camí de Coix* ('Limping Walk', 1980). Colom-Montero shows how these texts critically depict the othering of the *forasters*, while at the same time portray the anxieties associated with the rapid de-Catalanisation process derived from the demographic, linguistic and cultural changes. Ultimately, argues the author, these novels emphasise the shared class interests between local and migrant workers in the context of the mass-tourism revolution, thus aiming to offer alternative possibilities for their interrelations.

The essays in the second part of this volume, titled 'Spaces, Borders and Memory', focus on the spatial dimension of migration, including the transformations of the urban landscape, the social boundaries dividing native and migrant populations and the reconstruction of the memory of working-class neighbourhoods. Olga Sendra Ferrer, writing on Francesc Candel's work (notably *Els altres catalans*, but also his novels, which he wrote in Spanish), considers how Candel's representation of the city defines an interstitial space that questions dominant notions of national identity. Sendra argues that this author, instead of defining a new idea of what Catalunya or Barcelona are, ruptures the idea of borders, establishing the possibility of a plural identity not limited to one single national allegiance. Thus, Candel's books are full of transitions and transgressions – geographic, visual, cultural and linguistic – that destabilise the idea of frontier, creating an interstice that, as he follows the development of the Catalan city through the decades, redefines existing ideas of Spanish and Catalan identity, and forging a contact zone that, years later, will set the stage for the work of authors like Najat El Hachmi.

In 'The Ego-History of Valencian Immigration: Julià Guillamon's *El barri de la Plata*' Teresa Iribarren analyses the role of literary texts in constituting immigration as a place of memory of the lived experience of working-class areas. Guillamon's book is an original contribution in this respect, as it delves into a migratory process originating in the Valencia region that has been largely unexamined. Iribarren contexualises this work within the demographic research conducted in recent years on Valencian migration, and following Enzo Traverso presents Guillamon's autobiographical narrative as an example of 'ego-history', the subjectivist turn in historical writing. Iribarren argues that in his reconstruction of his family history and his neighbourhood's social history, Guillamon presents himself both as a model of a successful integration and as the interpreter of the urban landscape where Valencian immigrants first settled, thus appearing as a 'narcissist historian' (using Traverso's term) who makes significant contributions to the understanding of the social history of immigration in Catalonia, notably in his depiction of a mixed marriage and in the visibility that he lends to a hitherto overlooked Valencian migration. Iribarren further analyses the different roles played in Guillamon's narrative by his eccentric, bullfight-loving, Spanish-speaking father and his hard-working, selfless, Catalan-speaking mother: the writer's identity is presented as the dialectical synthesis of these two conflicting positions.

Finally, in Chapter 6, '"Catalunya termina aquí. Aquí comença Vietnam": Urbanism, Migration, and Spatial Immunity in Jordi Puntí's *Els castellans*', William Viestenz reads Puntí's memoir in the light of Roberto Esposito's negative biopolitics, Peter Sloterdijk's theorisation of the apartment block and immunitary alliances and Michel Serres's concept of parasitism, in order to analyse how in *Els castellans* ('The Castilians', 2011) urbanism and immunitary social mechanisms to preserve identity boundaries work hand in hand. Examining Puntí's depiction of the apartment blocks that housed Spanish-speaking migrants in the town of Manlleu and the author's memory of his childhood perceptions of them, Viestenz argues that Puntí's book, while displaying the processes of subjectivation experienced by a group of children on the brink of adolescence, allows readers to perceive how different concepts of the immunological are inseparable from understanding the spatiality of migration, especially with respect to urban planning, during Francoism and in present-day Catalonia. At the same time, according to Viestenz, this book constitutes a valuable archive of the histories, cultures and populations that inhabited those spaces.

The last part of the book, 'Disidentification, Dislocation and Mourning', turns its attention to Catalan authors of foreign origin, in this case from Morocco and Argentina. Here we concentrate on the subjective and intersubjective impact of migration and its articulation in literary texts, exploring issues such as the dialectic of identification and disidentification in the authors' engagement with literary traditions, cultural logics and gender norms; the negotiations over postmigrant dislocated identities and the place of writing and the sexual in them; and the work of mourning and its relevance for the production of new, complex identities.

In Chapter 7, '"Te deix, mare, un fill com a penyora": Disidentificatory Intertextuality in Najat El Hachmi's *La filla estrangera*', Natasha Tanna examines El Hachmi's intertextual engagements with literary foremothers within and beyond the Catalan tradition through the lens of José Esteban Muñoz's theory of 'disidentification', which describes the survival strategies through which 'outsiders' negotiate more 'mainstream' cultural forms. Tanna argues that El Hachmi's engagement with literary inheritance is a textual correlate for her ambivalent negotiation with Catalan and Amazigh culture and involves a seemingly paradoxical invocation of closeness and estrangement. The 'filla estrangera' ('foreign daughter') of the novel's title resonates with Maria Mercè Marçal's *La germana, l'estrangera* ('Sister, Foreigner', 1981/1984), which, in turn, echoes Audre Lorde's *Sister Outsider* (1984). However, these and other intertexts are altered in a process of disidentification, thematising dislocation and desire between women. In this regard, El Hachmi disidentifies with authors who themselves disidentify with dominant cultural norms and forms, even while they have become increasingly incorporated into them, thus enacting neither a process of assimilation nor complete opposition to dominant cultural forms, but a way of transforming cultural logics and exploring new possibilities of selfhood beyond normative citizenship.

In Chapter 8, 'Limits and Borders in *No*, by Saïd El Kadaoui', Roger Canadell Rusiñol analyses how in his work the Moroccan-Catalan author and psychoanalyst takes his own experience as a migrant as a starting point for a discourse around the protagonists' dislocated identities. Canadell argues that, in the novel *No* (2016), an explicit theoretical reflection on otherness, difference and the idea of the border prompts the narrator to engage in a metaliterary reflection about the crossing of borders, the transgression of limits, the negotiation of an identity dislocated between two cultures, and the interplay between the servitudes of male sexuality and writing as a creative act in the sphere of subjectivity. By means of this reflection, the book itself becomes, as El Kadaoui puts it, 'the space of infeasible possibilities', making fiction the only possible homeland.

In the final chapter, Josep-Anton Fernàndez considers how Silvana Vogt articulates the work of mourning of the Argentine diaspora after the *corralito* financial crisis of 2001 in her novel *La mecànica de l'aigua* ('The Mechanics of Water', 2016). Vogt's moving narrative contains some elements that make it eminently relevant for an analysis of the vicissitudes of mourning: a traumatic scene that causes the loss of the protagonist's country, an original transgression that leads to deep ambivalence with regard to the lost country, and the occurrence of repetition both of traumatic experiences in the diegesis and in the text's narrative devices. In his chapter Fernàndez examines these elements from a psychoanalytic point of view, drawing on Sigmund Freud, Darian Leader, Laurie Laufer and other authors. In particular, the author shows how Vogt's novel highlights the importance of the social dimension of mourning in terms of the symbolisation of loss, how it articulates the work of mourning by means of what Leader calls a 'dialogue of mournings', and how the text works through ambivalence to constitute the object (the native country) as effectively lost, in order to register an empty space that allows for a new subjective narrative to be created.

The book's closing focus on mourning is important because the issues raised by the chapters – the questioning of narrative authority, the transformations of urban space and the resulting social changes, the elaboration of memory, the dislocation of the migrants' identity, and so on – suggest that the study of the representations of immigration demands the acknowledgement of negativity and ambivalence. As a site of conflict and opportunity, of uncertainty and negotiation, immigration promotes a conception of subjectivity based on emptiness, absence, separation and loss that not only transforms the identity of the migrant subject but also that of the reception society. Earlier in this introduction I referred to the defensive role played by the trope of cultural roots in Catalan cultural discourse, as a defence mechanism against the risk of dissolution of Catalan identity. The epitome of this position is the famous line in a song by Raimon, the most prominent songwriter of anti-Franco resistance: 'Qui perd els orígens, perd identitat' ('he who loses his origins, loses his identity'). Yet as Salvador Cardús claims, this idea is false, for identity is always contingent and thrives only if origins are subject to constant revision.[38] Indeed, losing one's origins is an integral part of the migrant experience; it is the condition that grants access to the possibility of rewriting one's identity. For loss makes subjectivity possible, and emptiness permits the creation of something new. If immigration is an experience of loss for both the migrants and the society that receives them, then the work of mourning offers the opportunity to build new identifications, new narratives of identity and a new, shared memory.

For Catalan culture and society, then, the task of mourning would require working through the loss of its attachment to the idea of an identity centred on a full, substantive origin. From this standpoint, *The Other Catalans* pursues an overarching aim: to participate in the project of instituting immigration into a place of memory in Catalan society, and to assess the consequences of this project for the definition of (Catalan) national identity. The promise of a new beginning that arises from loss suggests that our analyses of Catalan identity must consider the place and the role of mourning in its discursive constitution. This invites us, I would argue, to explore the possibilities of conceiving (Catalan) national identity as an empty place – or to use Ernesto Laclau's term, an empty signifier – no longer centred on an idea of origin but dislocated and constituted on the basis of an empty origin shared by the citizens of a polity defined as a nation of immigrants. Based on this idea, whose social, political and cultural potential must be deployed, the essays in this book seek to conceptualise Catalan identity as radically open to construction and redefinition by all those interpellated by it, regardless of their origin or ethnic background.

Notes

1 Daniele Conversi, *The Basques and the Catalans: Alternative Routes to Nationalist Mobilisation* (London: C. Hurst, 1997), pp. 189–9.
2 Anna Cabré, *El sistema català de reproducció* (Barcelona: Proa, 1999), pp. 211–12.
3 Andreu Domingo, *Catalunya al mirall de la immigració: Demografia i identitat nacional* (Barcelona: L'Avenç, 2014), pp. 24 and 41.
4 Institut d'Estadística de Catalunya (Idescat), *Població a 1 de gener: Total i estrangera* (28 February 2022), *www.idescat.cat/poblacioestrangera/?b=0*.
5 Salvador Cardús i Ros, 'The Memory of Immigration in Catalan Nationalism', *International Journal of Iberian Studies*, 18/1 (2005), 39–42.
6 Josep-Anton Fernàndez, 'Impossible Sutures: Loss, Mourning, and the Uses of Catalonia's Past in TV3's *La Mari*', in Xabier Payá and Laura Sáez (eds), *National Identities at the Crossroads: Literature, Stage and Visual Media in the Iberian Peninsula* (London: Francis Boutle, 2018), p. 134. See also Fernàndez, *El malestar en la cultura catalana: La cultura de la normalització 1976–1999* (Barcelona: Empúries, 2008), pp. 232–50.
7 All translations from Catalan are mine, unless indicated otherwise.
8 Regina Römhild, 'Postmigrant Europe: Discoveries beyond Ethnic, National and Colonial Boundaries', in Anna Meera Gaonkar, Astrid Sophie Øst Hansen, Hans Christian Post and Moritz Schramm (eds), *Postmigration: Art, Culture, and Politics in Contemporary Europe* (Bielefeld: Transcript, 2021), p. 46.
9 Römhild, 'Postmigrant Europe', p. 46.
10 Regina Römhild, 'Beyond the Bounds of the Ethnic: For Postmigrant Cultural and Social Research', *Journal of Aesthetics and Culture*, 9/2 (2017), 69–70.

11 Roger Bromley, 'A Bricolage of Identifications: Storying Postmigrant Belonging', *Journal of Aesthetics and Culture*, 9/2 (2017), 36.
12 Josep Antoni Vandellós, *Catalunya, poble decadent* (Barcelona: Edicions 62, 1985), pp. 103–39.
13 Vandellós, *Catalunya, poble decadent*, pp. 54–5.
14 Vandellós, *Catalunya, poble decadent*, p. 58.
15 For a detailed analysis of Vandellós's discourse, see Domingo, *Catalunya al mirall*, pp. 60–78.
16 Jaume Vicens Vives, *Notícia de Catalunya* (Barcelona: Edicions 62, 1999 [1954/1960]), p. 26.
17 Vicens Vives, *Notícia*, pp. 26–7.
18 See, for example, Vicens Vives, *Notícia*, pp. 27, 149 and 171. For an analysis of Vicens Vives's ambivalence regarding immigration, see Josep-Anton Fernàndez, '"Virilitat del país": Gender, Immigration, and Power in Jaume Vicens Vives's *Notícia de Catalunya*', *Hispanic Research Journal*, 21/2 (2020), 143–58.
19 See Julià Guillamon, 'La novel·la catalana de la immigració', *L'Avenç*, 298 (2005), 46–9; and Maria Dasca, 'La immigració com a fenomen en la literatura catalana', *Cercles: Revista d'Història Cultural*, 18 (2015), 61–78.
20 Martí Marín, 'Ritmes i composició migratoris: Les xifres d'un fenomen complex', *L'Avenç*, 298 (2005), 28.
21 Jordi Pujol, *La immigració, problema i esperança de Catalunya* (Barcelona: Nova Terra, 1976), p. 48.
22 Pujol, *La immigració*, p. 29.
23 Pujol, *La immigració*, pp. 34–6.
24 Pujol, *La immigració*, p. 42.
25 Fernàndez, *El malestar*, pp. 258–61.
26 See, for example, Lluís Cabrera, Pedro Morón, Marta Riera et al., *Els altres andalusos: La qüestió nacional de Catalunya* (Barcelona: L'Esfera dels Llibres, 2005).
27 See Josep-Anton Fernàndez, 'Thou Shalt Not Covet Thy Roots: Immigration and the Body in Novels by Roig, Barbal, and Jaén', *Romance Quarterly*, 53/3 (2006), 225–9.
28 Salvador Cardús i Ros, 'The Memory of Immigration in Catalan Nationalism', *International Journal of Iberian Studies*, 18/1 (2005), 41.
29 Cardús, 'The Memory of Immigration', 42–3.
30 Salvador Cardús i Ros, *Tres metàfores per pensar un país amb futur: Discurs de recepció de Salvador Cardús i Ros com a membre numerari de la Secció de Filosofia i Ciències Socials, llegit el dia 12 de novembre de 2009* (Barcelona: Institut d'Estudis Catalans, 2009), p. 11.
31 Cardús, *Tres metàfores*, p. 15; emphasis in the original.
32 Cardús, *Tres metàfores*, p. 18.
33 Domingo, *Catalunya al mirall*, p. 316.

34 On El Hachmi's book and other autobiographical writing by Catalan writers of migrant origin, see for example: Ernest Carranza Castelo, '¿Integración o desintegración?: El cuestionamiento de Cataluña como tierra de acogida en textos de ficción y no ficción de Najat El Hachmi', *Journal of Catalan Studies*, 1/20 (2017); Margarida Castellano Sanz, *Les altres catalanes: Memòria, identitat i autobiografia en la literatura d'immigració* (Valencia: Tres i Quatre, 2018); Aitana Guia Conca, 'Molts mons, una sola llengua: La narrativa en català escrita per immigrants', *Quaderns de Filologia: Estudis literaris*, 12 (2007), 229–48; and Isabel Marcillas-Piquer, 'Veus de frontera: Els *altres catalans* d'ara', *Caplletra*, 65 (2018), 177–89.
35 See Fernàndez, 'Thou Shalt Not Covet Thy Roots', 229–31.
36 Dasca, 'La immigració com a fenomen', 76; Guia Conca, 'Molts mons, una sola llengua', 246; Marcillas-Piquer, 'Veus de frontera', 188.
37 See, for example, Stewart King, 'Inmigración y literatura nacional en Cataluña: Una lectura periférica', *Journal of Iberian and Latin American Research*, 27/2 (2021), 357–63.
38 Cardús, *Tres metàfores*, p. 11.

Part I
Otherness and Representational Authority

Chapter 1

On Masks and Cracks: Positions of Authority in the Portrayal of the Migrant Phenomenon in Catalan Literature

Mercè Picornell

In the Catalan literary sphere today, the dividing line between original works in Catalan and in Spanish has become somewhat blurred. In recent years, bilingualism has been justified in stylistic terms, or as the basis of the verisimilitude of Catalan-language works when portraying scenes of obvious multilingualism. Moreover, it is a part of the publishing world, where the most visible works are published simultaneously in both Catalan and Spanish. When commenting on *El barri de la plata* ('The Silver District', 2008), by Julià Guillamon, Amadeu Cuito asserts that it is the 'drama of a bilingual family' that Josep Pla failed to bring to Catalan literature.[1] The book was published in both Catalan and Spanish. In the Catalan edition, the cover is illustrated with the initials of the Catalan mother, embroidered on a linen sheet. This contrasts sharply with the cover of the Spanish edition, which features the red and yellow of the father's bullfighting cape. These two textures were carefully selected by the author, who translated the work into Spanish so that it would also form part of his 'father's world', as he put it. The contrast between the two speaks of a conflict that is relevant to the story of the novel, yet which inevitably, through the two editions, is projected onto the very borders of current Catalan literature, where phenomena such as self-translation and simultaneous publication in Catalan and Spanish have not been sufficiently assessed.

The literature-migration pairing has been the subject of many studies within the context of Catalan literature. The process, as explored by Pilar Arnau in her doctoral dissertation, is both similar to and different from what has been observed in Italian, German and French literature.[2] It is similar in certain generic and thematic developments – from the memoir to the novel, from the travel log to the hybridisation process – and different in the critical response, which in our case is marked by the celebration of the incorporation of Catalan voices into a literature that is still viewed as lacking or weak. Generally speaking, and at the risk of oversimplification, it could be said that the academic study of the issue has given rise to two types of approach. On the one hand, there is the analysis of migration as a theme found in the works of both native Catalan authors and those of migrant origin, in studies such as the initial one carried out by Julià Guillamon and later by Maria Dasca and Andreu Domingo.[3] On the other hand, there is the approach that focuses more on the detailed study of the production of these writers, covering thematic connections, aspects of identity and comparative perspectives. In the latter group of studies, the terms associated with the aim of the analyses are both varied and problematic. Diego Muñoz speaks of 'xenographics', Isabel Marcillas and Marta Segarra discuss 'migrant literatures', Miquel Pomar-Amer makes reference to 'diasporic literature', Katiuscia Darici uses the term 'transnational literature', Margarida Castellano coins the term 'migration literature' and Aitana Guia describes the phenomenon as 'Catalan narrative written by immigrants'.[4] Within our field, Arnau, who has explored this discussion in German literature, explains that there has never been a debate in Catalan studies on the term to be used to describe this corpus, though there has been a push to label it and thus to segment it within the literary field. Josep-Anton Fernàndez challenges the use of these labels in his analysis of *L'últim patriarca* as 'a Catalan novel', with no other name to define a corpus that in fact belongs to a Catalan society in which 75 per cent of the people are of migrant origin; for Fernàndez, there is no reason for such literature.[5] In any case, we will not discuss the debate on terminology in this chapter. Rather, the point here is to note that most of these taxonomies are determined by the apparent foreignness of the author of the book. Hence, in this fashion, the focus on the writer's origins justifies a particular type of analysis.

Without underrating the importance of the studies carried out from these perspectives, in this chapter we examine the literature-migration coupling from a different point of view. We are interested in analysing the way in which attention placed on migration that is perceived as an alterity transforms the author's position. Hence, we also look closely at the author, not so much from the standpoint of a presupposition of a work, but rather as a projection of the text. This shift in focus does not negate the empirical figure or the social function of the writer, but instead places it in a different context: the author's origin is important because it can determine the distance between them and what they portray. As a result, 'foreignness' is in the gaze and is therefore performative insofar as it depends on an action rather than an essence. On the other hand, in this chapter we are interested in the works that fall into an ambiguous category between the essay and the memoir. Generic segmentation is justified by the fact that the distance between the narrator and the author is appreciably smaller than the distance found in novels. In factual narration, 'l'autor assumeix la plena responsabilitat de les seves afirmacions' ('the author takes full responsibility for his/her statements').[6] Here it is not the moral implications of this assumption that interest us, but rather the fact that there is an implied mutual identification between the narrator and the author. In the cases addressed in this article, such identification is not intended to explain the author's life, as in the classical autobiography, but rather to reflect on the lives of others from the viewpoint of the author. In short, the texts discussed here do not adhere to either the expression model typical of the essay (where the author and narrator are one and the same) or the autobiographical model (where the main character is included as part of the author-narrator voice). Instead, they combine the two in a distinctive fashion, particularly insofar as the main character is slightly outside the realm of the author, whether they are speaking *for* or *about* others.

Our theoretical point of departure relates to the debate that followed the publication of Gayatri Spivak's essay 'Can the Subaltern Speak?'.[7] As has been noted, the response to Spivak's text was determined by an excessive focus on the question that serves as its title and that appears to promise a clear answer as a conclusion. That answer is no; however, this denial is not the only objective of the article. Spivak in fact builds an in-depth critique of the concept of representation based on the dialogue between Gilles Deleuze and Michel Foucault on power, in its two senses: as a delegation of some form of power from one person to another or from a group to an individual (i.e., political representation); and as a product that presents a prior reference (i.e., theatre or pictorial representation). In its simplest form, we could say that in the first of these senses, Spivak concludes that the Western intellectual tends to assert themselves by creating a homogeneous oppressed 'other' from whom to set themselves apart. In the second sense, where, in the act of portraying an individual, the intellectual can never be transparent, they are always conditioned by what they portray. To overcome the radical negation in Spivak's article, Fernando Coronil proposes a redefinition of the subaltern as a relational subject that can create spaces that move them away from the place of silence to which they were relegated previously.[8] This redefinition opens up the possibility of assessing the shift from silence to the voice as a process consisting of many small steps.

One of the first steps could be the phase that spurs the shift in the writer's authorship in order to confront otherness. From this perspective, listening to the subaltern can also mean reading differently, not by inventing meanings for a silence, but rather by attempting to decipher the way that the author repositions themselves in order to either convey or mask the voice of the other. All literary portrayals are ideological constructions, and as such, they also involve the creation of a position of authorship and authority. As Mieke Bal notes regarding the artist, in the very act of portraying a world, the writer also exposes themselves to the world.[9] This self-exposure entails a risk that authors may try to prevent, either by creating masks that protect them or by inserting themselves into a space of doubt where the responsibility for what they have said becomes blurred. Alternatively, they can do the opposite and expose their fragility to the world. In the forthcoming pages, we will analyse the logic behind this authorial alteration by examining four different cases that have often been positioned in a logic of continuity. Those works are *Viatge en transmiserià* ('Journey on the Poverty Express', 1994; originally published as articles in 1932–3) by Carles Sentís; *Els altres catalans* ('The Other Catalans', 1964) by Francesc Candel; *Els castellans* ('The Castilians', 2011) by Jordi Puntí; and *La pell de la frontera* ('The Skin of the Border', 2014) by Francesc Serés. Our observations will be additionally supported with the examples of other works to which less attention will be devoted.

Carles Sentís: The Fake Infiltrator

We will begin with *Viatge en Tranmiserià*, as the very name of Carles Sentís and his articles on migration from the Spanish region of Murcia frequently mark the start of the genealogies of literary discourses on immigration in Catalonia.[10] This starting place is also a blind spot that occasionally elicits in-depth studies. Sentís's texts on migration have not been studied independently, with the exception of an unpublished master's degree thesis written by Miguel Díaz.[11] In contrast to this academic neglect, the compilation of the original articles in the book *Viatge en Transmiserià* in 1994 enjoyed a spectacular critical reception in terms of both the number of reviews and the positive ratings of the book. Sentís presents himself as a pioneer of testimonial and investigative journalism. According to Valentí Puig, he is a good example of the 'ganas de hacer las cosas bien' ('desire to do things properly').[12] Most of the reviews mention the introduction of the infiltrator technique to carry out the reports, which, according to Josep Losada, he would produce by 'fent-se passar per un immigrant' ('pretending to be an immigrant').[13] Moreover, according to Isabel Torras, he did so through a 'camaleònic exercici de camuflatge' ('chameleon-like exercise in camouflage').[14] This is expressed in a book that perfectly combines what Julià Guillamon describes as 'lo ligero y lo patético' ('the light-hearted and the pathetic'), a combination that according to Teresa Pàmies includes 'tendresa, compassió i rigor periodístic' ('tenderness, compassion and journalistic rigour').[15] We do not agree with any of these descriptions.

As has been explained on many occasions, in 1933 Just Cabot accepted Carles Sentís's proposal to draw up some reports on Murcian immigration for the weekly publication *Mirador*. The then twenty-two-year-old student formed part of the intellectual groups frequented by older thinkers such as Manuel Brunet and Josep M. de Sagarra. Miguel Díaz insinuates that the commission was fuelled by the desire within this group to spur public debate on the need to regulate the arrival of migrants to Catalonia. If this was the case, young Sentís most likely took it on with an assured degree of controversy: his xenophobic discourse sparked reactions in the left-wing media and among circles of the Casa de Múrcia in Barcelona, leading Sentís's patrons – by then on their own behalf – to take to the stage to defend him or support his theses. This would occur in articles such as 'El problema de la immigració' ('The Immigration Problem'), by Just Cabot, which proposed restrictive immigration, and 'Poesia murciana' ('Murcian Poetry'), by Sagarra, which alerted readers to an invasion that had already taken root, *even* in the Jocs Florals, the Catalan poetry competition.[16] This facilitated receptiveness to the views of the demographer Josep Antoni Vandellòs, who on 11 May 1934, alongside intellectuals such as J. M. Batista Roca and Pompeu Fabra, signed the manifesto 'Per preservar la raça catalana' ('To Preserve the Catalan Race'), a document that advocated the creation of a Catalan Eugenics Society, in which Vandellòs would serve as secretary.[17]

Much has been said about the modernity of Sentís's reporting, where he engages in an infiltration journalism that some consider to be the result of a New Journalism *avant la lettre*. If we examine the reports, the journalist's 'infiltration' into what he intends to study only takes place in two of the articles. Moreover, even in those cases, he does so from a position of distance that makes complete immersion impossible. The camouflage that critics have sought to underscore is not only denied by Sentís himself – 'no em vaig disfressar mai' ('I never disguised myself'), he asserts – but it is also refuted throughout the text.[18] Here we find the first authorial inconsistency that characterises his story: he authorises himself by inserting himself in the milieu – Sentís performs 'la proesa' ('the feat') of getting into a bus that is taking people from Murcia to Catalonia – yet with no desire to form part of the group he is describing. In a text that criticises the general inability of the Murcian people to integrate into the Catalan community – Sentís writes that 'mentre l'italià s'assimila al medi, el murciano-almerià és refractari a l'assimilació' (*Viatge en transmiserià*, p. 99) ('whereas the Italian becomes part of the community, the Almerian-Murcian is resistant to assimilation') – he himself is incapable of assimilating, not from the standpoint of disguise, but simply in order to understand the people who are travelling with him. On the journey, he does not take part in the shared activities. Instead, he observes them from a place of privilege: because he knows how to write, he is part of what he ironically refers to as the 'high life' of the expedition and ends up sitting next to the wealthy drivers, in relative isolation from the others. The infiltration only manifests at certain times when he lies, somewhat gratuitously, such as when he feigns familiarity with the Murcia Football Club to please a few men who ask about his opinion, and when he masquerades as the clerk of a lawyer who wishes to buy houses in La Torrassa (a district of L'Hospitalet de Llobregat, in the vicinity of Barcelona). In the latter case, his false position does not place him at the same level as the migrants, who, according to his chronicle, rent the homes they live in and often fail to pay the rent. The alleged infiltration does not give rise to knowledge or understanding, but rather to a measured opposition between the image of the young, attractive, polished, well-informed and ironic reporter and the poverty of the migrants he depicts. The photograph that appears in the 1994 edition leaves no room for doubt: the modernity of Barcelona, embodied by a polished, well-groomed and well-dressed Sentís, contrasts with the backwardness of the Murcians, which is as contagious as the trachoma that he obsessively describes.

Sentís's authority to draw categorical conclusions about Murcia and the migrants is founded on the fact that he has been there. Nevertheless, his description could never stem from what he has seen on a journey of just a few days. What he sees on a single occasion is built into his story as a general and irrefutable truth. Hence, his statements are often not about a specific person but about 'these people', 'the Murcians' or 'those men'. For example, he writes that Múrcia 'És un país . . . on tothom, rics i pobres, té dues coses: tracoma als ulls i parents a Barcelona' (*Viatge*, p. 32) ('[Murcia] is a country . . . where everyone, both rich and poor, has two things: trachoma in the eyes and relatives in Barcelona'). The migrants who travel in the bus share common savage behaviours: *all* the children are ill-mannered; *all* the women are selfish gossips; and *all* the men take advantage of others. As a group, for example, they enjoy insulting those that they see along the road and they get off the bus to steal food from vegetable patches. Moreover, the *Murcians* have no name. Only one of them, Cañizares, is individualised to serve as an emblem: he is an ignorant man and a thief who attempts to create an alliance with Sentís. When conveying his opinions about them, the author rarely employs a direct style, and when he does, it is often to ridicule the incorrect and vulgar speech of the Murcian people. The voice is generally not heard, but rather shown through a collective diegetic summary and through subjects who arbitrarily decide when to speak and when to remain silent: the men talk when they drink harsh wine – 'una conversa plena d'al·lusions poc falagueres per a algunes mares' (p. 25) ('a conversation full of allusions that are rather unflattering for certain mothers') but then they suddenly quiet down. He writes impersonally that on the bus, '[s]ense que *se'n puguin* esbrinar les causes exactes . . . alternaven els períodes de xerrameca i xerinola general, amb els de postració més aclaparada' (p. 47, emphasis added) ('the phases of chatter and general merriment alternated with moments of a more subdued prostration *for no particular identifiable reason*'). Hence, they speak, though uncontrollably and without saying anything important.

All in all, the shift from the individual experience to the generalised assertion is underpinned by two rhetorically effective yet documentarily forced resources of verisimilitude. The first consists of the references to the intended objectivity of a text that stems from personal observation. 'Situem-nos, com sempre, objectivament' (p. 68) ('Let us take an objective perspective, as always'), Sentís writes. He also cites 'la importància de la qüestió . . . procurarem que es desprengui de l'exposició objectiva dels fets' (p. 83) ('the importance of the matter . . . we shall try to ensure that it stems from the objective presentation of the facts'). Finally, at the end of the series of articles he writes: 'No he pretès per a aquests meus articles res més que un valor informatiu, i creient que aquest resideix en la veracitat i l'objectivitat, m'he esforçat sempre a no apartar-me'n gens' (p. 123) ('My sole aim in writing these articles was to provide information, and because I believe information resides in veracity and objectivity, I have always strived not to stray from them at all'). The second strategy is the extensive use of numbers and data, often of undetermined origin, which lend the author expert status. For example, the evidence that leads him to general conclusions regarding the abandonment of young children can be very specific: 'he vist la carta d'una família de la província d'Almeria, responent una altra carta exhortant-la a recollir una criatura de l'hospital, que s'excusava en la manca de diners per al viatge' (p. 77) ('I saw a letter from a family from the province of

Almeria, replying to another letter that urged them to fetch a child from hospital. In their letter, their excuse was a lack of money for the trip'). Alternatively, the evidence may be vague and generalising: 'en qualsevol tractat de pediatria trobareu que és Múrcia la primera regió espanyola en aquest aspecte [mortalitat infantil]' (p. 75) ('in any paediatrics treatise you will see that Murcia is the number one region in Spain in this aspect [infant mortality]'). The data often come from what we could describe as 'faceless voices', in other words, anonymous informants, such as an 'advocat i escriptor lorquí' (p. 26) ('lawyer and writer from Lorca'), 'un funcionari del govern civil' (p. 35) ('a civil servant') or 'un natural de Vélez Rubio' (p. 37) ('a native of Vélez Rubio').

We will not reiterate the xenophobia that permeates the entire text. There is virtually no positive mention of the community under study and even his reference to the 'amusing' bodies of some of the Murcian children appears only after he has compared them to pigs.[19] There has already been coverage of the controversy caused by the publication of these articles and reinforced by the denigrating caricatures of the satirical weekly *El Be Negre*. The regional centre known as the Casa Regional de Murcia y Albacete published a letter in *Solidaridad Obrera* arguing that Sentís's slanderous tone was a discredit to the author himself, and cited the contradictory nature of some of the most egregious insults in the work, such as the allegations about the incestuous nature of the relationships among the Murcians and the frivolity of the ties between parents and their children.[20] The members of the Casa de Murcia requested from Sentís the only thing that could justify his accusations (that is, supporting evidence), and recommended that he read Josep Maria de Sagarra's scandalous novel *Vida privada* ('Private Life', 1932) if he was so interested in moral and sexual depravity, thereby demonstrating their knowledge of the literature written in Catalan. In the 1994 prologue to *Viatge en Transmiserià*, Sentís asserts that due to the controversy, the articles were never published in book form (p. 12).

In any case, these chronicles marked the beginning of Sentís's journalistic career, which would continue until he was ninety-nine years old. He would hold important posts both during the Franco regime – as director of the EFE agency, *Tele/eXprés* and Ràdio Barcelona – and later, as the Dean of the Col·legi de Periodistes (Journalists' Association). We believe that his public prominence may have predetermined the rating of *Viatge en Transmiserià*, the story of a fake infiltrator who wears the mask of modern journalism to promote a political discourse on immigration.

Paco Candel: The Chameleon's Writing

If Sentís was a false infiltrator, Francesc Candel was more of a chameleon. The origins of *Els altres catalans* ('The Other Catalans', 1964) can be traced back to an article in Spanish published in 1959 in the magazine *La Jirafa*, which prompted the commissioning of a book for Edicions 62, promoted by Josep Benet. The title proposed to Candel was *Nosaltres, els immigrants* ('We, the Immigrants'), calling to mind the essay by Joan Fuster, *Nosaltres, els valencians* ('We, the Valencians'), which had essentially launched the publishing house.[21] The interplay among the titles is interesting, as Candel's refusal to echo Fuster's title establishes a space of inclusiveness that, as Andreu Domingo has observed, can be linked to a certain discourse on integration that was also defended by Jordi Pujol.[22] Candel refused to adopt the first-person 'nosaltres' ('we') perspective of a migrant and created a slogan that would stir up controversy at the time, as can be seen, for example, in Manuel Cruells's emphatic reaction in *Els no catalans i nosaltres* ('The Non-Catalans and Us').[23] Nevertheless, the 'other Catalans' paraphrase would continue to emphasise the identity of those who were not *one* but *the other*, based on the differences of origin. Reissued six times in 1964, *Els altres catalans* would become an almost unprecedented best seller since the start of the post-war period. Even the Franco regime's censoring, which would cut twenty-two pages out of it, would rate the book favourably, believing that there was 'no hint of separatism' in it.[24]

As Domingo explains, it is believed that one of the reasons for the book's success is that it is written in the first person, from the perspective of a migrant.[25] However, we do not entirely agree with this assertion. It may be that Candel, who came to Barcelona at the age of two, was of migrant origin, yet the authority of the book does not stem from this position alone. We believe that the authorial focus that gives rise to *Els altres catalans* is unstable. The entire book is structured from a shifting position that is fostered by generic ambiguity. At different points in the same work, Candel reflects on the complex literary nature of his writing: 'De vegades, quan escrivim, ens deixem portar per un cert lirisme, pel gust de fer frases, per la "literatura", diguem-ho d'un cop. Nosaltres no ho voldríem pas. Sempre hem desitjat una literatura aliterària . . . És tanmateix difícil. La ploma ens domina' ('Sometimes, when we write, we allow ourselves to be carried away by a certain lyricism, by the pleasure of producing phrases, by "literature". For once and for all, let's just say it. We wouldn't want that. We have always longed for a non-literary literature . . . Yet it's difficult. We are ruled by the pen and ink').[26] In an interview, Victòria Hita asked him: '*Els altres catalans* és un llibre frontera, que es troba a mig camí entre el reportatge periodístic i l'assaig social?' ('Is *Els altres catalans* a border book that falls somewhere between the journalistic report and the social essay?'). In reply, Candel answered: 'Sí, podrien ser les dues coses' ('Yes, it could be both').[27] Implicit in this 'it could be both' is a variety of formalisations that also include memories, interviews and expert discourses. The variability in genre enables him to speak from different positions on the continuum marked by two connected lines. The first refers to the degree of objectivity or subjectivity of the discourse. Candel writes:

> M'és difícil escriure aquest llibre. Tot és massa complicat. Et penses que saps molt d'una cosa, i no en saps res. O al revés . . . Les coses, en abstracte són blanques o negres. En detall, admeten tons intermedis. I allò que és, no és, i allò que no és, és . . . Personalment, endut per un objectivisme particular que per a molts altres no ho serà, trobo que l'assumpte és complex, bigarrat, amb ramificacions. Sempre veiem més l'arbre que no pas el bosc. Ens falta perspectiva. Per això recorrerem el paisatge així, d'arbre en arbre i no de bosc en bosc. (*Els altres catalans*, p. 91)

> It is hard for me to write this book. It's all too complicated. You think you know a lot about something, but you don't know anything. Or the other way round . . . In the abstract, things are either black or white. But in detail, they can take on in-between shades. And that which is, is not, and that which is not, is . . . Personally, led by a particular objectivism that for many others will not be so, I find the issue to be complex, multi-coloured, with ramifications. We don't see the forest for the trees. We lack perspective. That is why we go through the landscape this way, from tree to tree rather than from forest to forest.

This shift from the tree to the landscape throughout the text translates into an odd combination of individual cases and impersonal generalisations. It also allows for the expression of doubt: 'potser tenen raó' (p. 7) ('maybe they're right'), 'Els uns diuen . . . i els altres [diuen]' (p. 9) ('Some say . . . and others [say]'), etc. The second and more explicit line refers to the transit of many different possible identifications between the 'we' and the 'others'. Throughout the book, there are Catalan people who pejoratively refer to the migrants as *xarnegos* (loosely meaning 'unadapted Spanish-speaking transplants'), and others who treat them with respect. Some migrants are 'other Catalans', while others are known as 'non-Catalans' who have 'settled here'. Many of the characters who serve as informants are in fact ambiguous. One such example is Enrique, who 'no sap si se sent català o no' (p. 67) ('doesn't know whether he feels Catalan or not'). Another example is the strange case of 'un senyor' ('a gentleman'), whose attitude is described ironically:

> Em diu un senyor que és català que, quan veu un foraster, sense voler-ho, s'indigna . . . És una cosa més forta que ell, una cosa instintiva. Comprèn que no ha de ser així. Per això, quan ho rumia bé, ofega aquest sentiment perniciós. Aleshores s'indigna contra la seva pròpia indignació. Però no pot evitar de pensar que Catalunya va deixant d'ésser Catalunya. El cas curiós, com reconeix ell mateix – i graciós, trobo jo – és que la seva mare era andalusa. (p. 177)

> A Catalan gentleman tells me that when he sees a non-Catalan outsider, he unintentionally becomes outraged . . . It's more powerful than he is, it's instinctive. He knows it shouldn't be that way. So, when he really thinks it over, he buries that destructive feeling. And then he is outraged at his own outrage. But he cannot help but feel that Catalonia is gradually ceasing to be Catalonia. The odd thing, as he himself admits – and the funny thing, I think – is that his own mother was Andalusian.

He would write in the prologue: 'Tota aquesta gent no s'adona de la seva aclimatació. "Són" catalans fins a cert punt. "No" són catalans també fins a cert punt. Ho són i no ho són sense adonar-se'n. Es van fusionant amb els seus germans' (p. 19) ('All these people don't realise they're adapting. To a certain extent they "are" Catalans. And to a certain extent they "are not" Catalans. They are and are not without even realising it. They are gradually blending in with their brothers'). And he added, calling to his model Catalan reader: 'No tingueu por, que de tot això no en sortirà pas una Catalunya híbrida o succedània' (p. 19) ('Don't be afraid, this won't lead to a hybrid or ersatz Catalonia').

According to Candel, the very writing of the book was transformational for the author's own identity, as is apparent in his preface to *Els altres catalans vint anys després* ('The Other Catalans, Twenty Years Later', 1985): 'acabava de trobar la meva catalanitat i la raó de ser d'aquesta catalanitat definitivament' ('I had just finally discovered my Catalanness and the *raison d'être* of that Catalanness').[28] From this chameleon-like authorship, Candel reveals in practice the myriad possible positions from which *one may or may not be* a migrant or a Catalan. Those positions are not placed within a dichotomic framework, but rather along a continuum of choices that are made in practice. In other words, like all identities, they are performative. Such performativity challenges the very title of the book, which suggests that there are *both* 'Catalans' *and* 'Catalans who are branded with the sign of otherness'. From this shift in identity, any stability in the authorial position that constructs the discourse is impossible. The identity of the migrants who have arrived in Catalonia and their relations with 'pure-blood, native' Catalans is thus portrayed through authorial positions that range from testimonials to expert discourse, at times all on the same page. Candel first establishes his authority as a migrant through his own life story. He 'has been' in the position that he describes. Yet by describing it to us in Catalan and through a publishing house, he is obviously no longer in the same position. In a report published in 1965 in *Serra d'Or*, a photograph displayed him in a shantytown, dressed in a black jacket and holding a sombre leather briefcase in his hand, as though he were an intellectual visiting the slums. Second, through direct and indirect reported speech, the author cites the statements of family and acquaintances and such utterances often become maxims. In order of their closeness, those individuals are: 'el meu oncle Esteban' (*Els altres*, pp. 52 and 54) ('my uncle Esteban'), 'un senyor conegut meu que viu a la Torrassa' (p. 26) ('an acquaintance of mine who lives in Torrassa'), 'el padrí d'un bon amic nostre'(p. 26) ('the godfather of a good friend of ours') and 'un català' (p. 57) ('a Catalan'). Among these descriptions and the general discourse, there are also sentimental voices and shared places that can contradict each other in terms of the experience and at the same time serve as aphorisms about the reality of life. Those sayings are expressed through the impersonal voice – 'es diu que' (p. 42) ('it is said that') – or by quoting Vandellòs, Fàbregues or statistical sources.

Over the course of time, Candel has become a symbol. His personal and political trajectory makes him a valuable figure in different social and political sectors. We believe that the value of *Els altres catalans* resides in the way the text itself challenges the dichotomy inherent in the title. Candel aims to serve as a narrator, and as Edward Said asserts regarding this figure in the colonial world,[29] he makes an effort to fit into a place from which he can present a discourse 'for the Catalan people'. Nevertheless, in his text, both migrants and 'pure-blood Catalans' form a 'they' opposite an 'I'. When the 'I' becomes a 'we' it is not in order to acknowledge the existence of a group, but rather to attempt to make the results of the testimonial appear more objective. Quoting Lacan, Homi Bhabha spoke of camouflage to support the theory of mimetics, which, through its ambivalence, reveals the excess of what cannot be totally identical.[30] Candel can be neither Catalan nor immigrant. He himself acknowledges that he writes from a place 'entremig de dos focs' (*Els altres*, p. 9) ('between the devil and the deep blue sea'), yet his own ambivalence does not appear through the imposed presence of a mask, but rather by virtue of the diverse positions through which he constructs a performative, heterogeneous and involuntarily paradoxical discourse on identity, between conviction and doubt.

Els castellans, and 'our' Memory

In the cases of Sentís and Candel, the specific circumstances surrounding the production of their works are important. In 2007, the magazine *L'Avenç* commissioned novelist Jordi Puntí to write a series of stories about childhood. This proposal gave rise to the publication of *Els castellans* ('The Castilians', 2012), a book in which the construction of personal memory is based on the opposition to 'others' who become so important that they lend the book its title. Here we will cite only the distance between the two purposes, which we will resume at the end of this section. On the whole, the critics' response to *Els castellans* was highly positive. Guillamon felt that the book handled a taboo topic with a 'tacto de terciopelo' ('velvety touch').[31] The interviews and reviews described Puntí's boldness in discussing an identity clash between Catalans and outsiders that many people would undoubtedly recognise or remember. In our analysis, we will explain that this 'boldness' is nevertheless masked throughout the entire book, with a recurrent appeal to the impossibility of placing the story's content within the realm of reality. This is justified by two different means. The first method, as stated in each chapter, reminds us that 'la infantesa és una ficció' ('childhood is a fiction') and therefore anything that is told comes from children's partial understanding.[32] The book asserts that children experience reality by transposing their imagination into their experience; therefore, film stories now serve to explain a clash between Catalans and 'Castilians' (the term that was widely used in the twentieth century to refer to Spaniards settled in Catalonia) that is fuelled by the biases of adults. The second is the ambiguous generic attribution of the stories. Jordi Puig states that 'combinen l'autobiografia, el reportatge i la literatura' ('they combine autobiography, journalism and literature').[33] Puntí refers to them as 'memòries de ficció' ('fictional memories') and describes the text typology as an intentional 'trick' that 'frees' the text from the need to be politically correct. He asserts: 'Si hi entres des de l'assaig, has de ser políticament correcte. En la ficció, com que només has de passar comptes amb la versemblança del llibre, pots jugar amb més llibertat' ('If you come from the essay, you have to be politically correct. In fiction, because you only have to take verisimilitude into account, you have got greater freedom').[34]

Ambiguity can serve as a shield against those who might identify in the childhood memory of the past the prejudices of an adult and present-day world. Moreover, the very need to display the defensive tactic throughout the text suggests a double strategy. This is not only because the literary filter is not an antidote to the ideological judgement of what it depicts, but also because the shield it constructs, in fact, has several cracks. Those breaches are manifest, for example, when the explicit uncertainty is contradicted by the present certainty of past judgements. For example, he writes: 'Donàvem per descomptat que pel fet de ser castellans eren antibarcelonistes i, probablement, madridistes. Per arbitrària que fos, l'equació solia funcionar' (Puntí, *Els castellans*, p. 80) ('We assumed that because they were Castilians they were against Football Club Barcelona and probably fans of Real Madrid. As arbitrary as it was, the equation used to work'). The childhood prejudice is contradicted by the statement in the subsequent sentence, which claims that 'it used to work', an assertion that does not correspond to the view of the child, but instead to the adult's ulterior judgement. The story 'Trampolí' ('Springboard') begins with the following statement: 'A vegades els records pugen a la superfície perquè una arbitrarietat els ha conservat intactes al llarg dels anys' (p. 91) ('Sometimes memories surface because some arbitrary thing has kept them intact through the years'). However, childhood memories are constructed when one is no longer a child and therefore cannot keep a remote past intact. From the subjective point of view of childhood, Puntí creates images of the others' opposition to an unequivocal 'us'. The Castilians *are* poor, crude and neglected by their families. The only two Catalans who 'mix in' with the Castilians are confused because they are ill-mannered or because they are in some way mentally lacking. 'Estic segur' – he writes in the present tense and goes on without the filter of the memory – 'que això de voler ser castellà i català alhora, el governava i el feia parar boig' (p. 97) (I'm sure that his obsession with this thing of wanting to be Castilian and Catalan at the same time drove him mad'). The intermingling of the communities begins in high school and is completed with the arrival of a new other, 'els moros' ('the Moors'), in a bilingual and repetitive utterance: 'Condueixen sense carnet – deien catalans i castellans –, *si veis un moro con un coche, apartad a las criaturas*' (p. 115) ('They drive with no driving licence – said Catalans and Castilians – if you see a Moor with a car, get the kids out of the way').

In a word, Puntí describes his experience of migrants through the prism of his childhood prejudices. His gaze, however, adapts to the contemporary moment at some points in the book, and particularly when the writer presents it as a provocation in the face of the well-intentioned images of the history of Spanish migration to Catalonia or the 'political' readings of his text. He asserts, 'El que vull és provocar reaccions i pensaments, sempre des d'una mirada incorrecta, amb una barreja d'ingenuïtat i perversió' ('What I want to do is provoke reactions and thought, but always from an incorrect point of view, with a mixture of naïveté and perversion').[35] In an interview with Pere Antoni Pons, he further explains the issue:

> Com que explico les coses sense el filtre del que és políticament correcte, pot haver-hi lectures literals que distorsionin el sentit dels textos... De fet, quan varen sortir els primers textos a la revista, un individu del qual no en diré el nom es va dedicar a copiar al seu blog un dels articles tot substituint catalans per nazis i castellans per jueus. Jo li vaig escriure dient-li que era demagògia pura, i que es podia fer la substitució a l'inrevés i que funcionaria igual. A més, aquest no és el tema.[36]

> Because I explain things without the filter of what is politically correct, there may be literal readings that distort the meaning of the texts... In fact, when the first texts were published in the magazine, an individual whose name I won't tell you copied one of the articles into his blog, replacing Catalans with Nazis and Spaniards with Jews. I wrote to him saying that this was pure demagogy, and that he could have replaced them the other way round and that the effect would have been the same. Besides, that is not the point.

In any case, once the work has been read, it is no longer up to the author to determine the theme of the work. The provocation of those who attempt to equate it with Nazi rhetoric is pernicious at every level. At the very least, however, it is not interchangeable, as Pons says. Puntí cannot overlook the fact that the strict dichotomy that the book presents not only pits Catalans and Castilians against each other, but also establishes a rivalry between docile, well-fed, polite, white individuals and uneducated, darker-skinned, uncivilised others. There is no equalling balance, nor is there any attempt at such. Rather, the book deliberately creates a positioned view of the other and provides an explanatory context to justify it. As we have seen, it loses meaning when its 'truth' is projected into the present.

This stated 'incorrectness' of the book contradicts the repeated placement of the text in the genre of memoirs and the connection between childhood and fiction. Why should the portrayal of children's prejudices necessarily defy 'politically correct' depictions? What are these portrayals in the Catalan context? How is Puntí's title – as he claims – a politically incorrect reply to Candel's title?

Regardless of the author's intention, the ambiguity of his piece is based on the complex genre filiation with the political function of the book. For the purposes of this chapter, what most interests us in Puntí's writing is neither the content of the children's prejudices nor the more or less fictionalised form of the memory from which they are evoked. To evaluate the authorial construction of those prejudices, we must take a step back and consider once again the origin of the book and ask why the call for a narrative of childhood memories ultimately becomes a description of migrants. Puntí answers this question in an interview with Pere Antoni Pons: 'Em va semblar que el contrapunt dels castellans m'aniria bé per compensar l'exhibicionisme personal' ('The inclusion of the Castilians seemed like a good contrast to offset my personal exhibitionism').[37] As Puntí explains, the elements intended to serve as a 'contrast' would become the focus of the most detailed descriptions of the story: the names and surnames of the Castilian antagonists are explicitly discussed and their houses are also described. In contrast, the 'Catalans' are an integral 'we' that is often identified with the pluralised projection of the narrator's 'I', which rarely appears in the singular form. From this perspective, the entire book becomes the outcome of an *altered* memory, that of an identity that is sustained only if it can show that the other justifies a less specific, less described unity. Moreover, that united 'we', identifies with the standard reader of the book, a Catalan – and, dare we say, male – reader who can easily recall his own childhood prejudice from the blameless patina of nostalgia. Hence, *Els castellans* is not just a book about outsiders. Nor is it a book about a real conflict experienced through the eyes of childhood fantasy. Rather, it is a book about the need to affirm, through the memory and in the present, a uniform Catalan identity that feels threatened, and it uses the most efficient means to reconstruct itself: the creation of a constitutive difference from the sense of self.

At the same time, we are not ignoring the fact that many readers undoubtedly identify with Puntí's story. Moreover, we cannot deny the existence of an antagonism between Catalans and Castilians, which in fact justifies the creation of the very term 'Castilians' to denote a certain foreignness. The proposal is probably necessary, and in literary terms, it has its place and serves a purpose. Yet in this dichotomy, it is similarly true that the 'Catalans' also reaffirm themselves as a target of opposition. Fortunately, the Catalan literature of the twenty-first century admits the coexistence of contradictory narratives that together portray us as heterogeneous, as we are. In this case, two subsequent books by Vicenç Villatoro and Julià Guillamon follow a similar strategy to that of Puntí, as they weave a story from the perspective of migrants in order to discuss their own identity. Those works are *Un home que se'n va* ('A Man Goes Away', 2014) and *El barri de la plata* ('The Silver District', 2018). The space for difference constructed by Puntí's story is impossible here, as these are tales told by the sons and daughters of families that include migrant family members. They necessarily paint a more complex and nuanced picture than that of the town of Manlleu in *Els castellans*, partially because the two latter works are written with the intention of understanding the past in order to explain the present-day identity. In that present, a character speaking in the first-person endeavours to re-create the life of his ancestors and his own childhood to better understand himself. In Villatoro's work, the story is structured around the search for the reasons that led the grandfather – a victim of reprisals and financial ruin after the Civil War – to leave his Andalusian village in Cordova and settle in Terrassa. This enquiry constantly turns to reflect the narrator's own identity crisis: 'Per què va marxar? I potser d'aquesta pregunta en pengen d'altres, de seves i de mon pare i dels meus fills. De meves també. Sobre qui soc i qui no soc. Sobre quina és la meva tribu, si és que en tinc alguna' ('Why did he leave? And maybe this question leads to others, those of his own and those of my father and my children. And my own questions too. About who I am and who I am not. About who my tribe is, if in fact I have one').[38] The tone of the question also takes root in the recovery of a fragmentary past about which there is not always certainty. Hence, the 'maybe' marks the reconstruction of a world and a journey through the figure of the migrant grandfather. This contrasts with the direct dialogues in Spanish, which give the story greater authenticity and lend voices to the grandfather and his family, as is particularly apparent in the last chapter, when the narrator describes a cassette tape recorded by the grandfather. In this manner, the journey becomes a metaphor for the search for the meaning of a life that brings about a contrast between opposing worlds whose differences go beyond the origins of their inhabitants. The difference is determined by the historical and political context, as well as by the contrasts between the rural world of the family's origins and the industrial city of their later arrival.

This also occurs in *El barri de la plata* (2018), by Julià Guillamon, which, like *Els castellans*, was initially written as a sequence of articles in *L'Avenç*. As we have seen, Amadeu Cuito defined it as 'el drama d'una família bilingüe' ('the drama of a bilingual family'). This description could evoke an anecdote about the contrast between two linguistic and cultural worlds that appear in the story, yet are not always a source of conflict or the main focus of the narrative. Instead, Guillamon reconstructs the history of an entire milieu: that of the streets of Poblenou in Barcelona, which have been repopulated by Valencian migrants. Those streets are differentiated from the setting of the author's mother: a family from Gràcia, a lower-middle-class district of Barcelona, which still sharply contrasts with the working-class status of Poblenou, and a hotel in the mountain village of Arbúcies. The narrator reconstructs the past to reflect on the way in which each person invents his or her own identity from the references available to them. The selection of his parents' references opens up a space of freedom for the construction of his own identity. Guillamon's text differs from that of Puntí in terms of the sources of authority employed in the story, which are characterised by a referential and creative use of archival sources.[39] Memory and space are two common threads of a quest that requires a documentary framework in which to be rooted. That framework consists of images from the period, family photos and demographic and commercial data from different documentary archives. As a result, there is no place here for past or present prejudice, but rather for an emotional gaze that is at once personal and collective.

Francesc Serés and the Ambiguous Role of the Writer

While the results are very diverse, the texts studied thus far have all used the first-person ('I') identity of the author and narrator as a locus for the authentication of a story about the lives of others. There is still another type of non-fiction book on immigration in Catalonia that would fit in with the model that we have set out to study here, though where the author acts as a mediator of the migrant's voice. These works take on diverse formats, which often arise from a sequence of prior conversations that empower the author to serve as a conveyor of the experience of others. Only in some cases, such as *Nosaltres, els catalans* ('We, the Catalans', 2008), by Víctor Alexandre, the work takes on the form of an interview. In most of the texts we have managed to consult, the writer disappears, giving way to a story about the other. In those cases, the stories feature a heterodiegetic narrator that nevertheless looks inward; in other words, a narrative voice that does not intervene in the action yet is capable of explaining the thoughts, motivations and feelings of the other. The degree of the writer's intrusiveness and, therefore, the extent to which his or her persona disappears varies from book to book. In *El somni català* ('The Catalan Dream', 1997), by Gabriel Pernau, the sixteen 'stories of settlement' are told as tales of life around the settling of the newcomers into the environment around them, which is not without its difficulties. What is more interesting is the format of Toni Sala's *Un relat de la nova immigració africana* ('A Tale of Recent African Immigration', 2004), and Mariona Masferrer's *Origen: Tambakunda* ('Origin: Tambakunda', 2013). Sala's book describes a weekend in the life of Alí, a Gambian who works the fields in the Alt Maresme region. In contrast, in Masferrer's work, the writer is a character described in the third person in the story who at the same time writes a story about Samba, with an internal focus. In all these stories, the writer serves as a mediator; while they enable migrants to express themselves, the author's presence in the paratexts – the name on the cover and the copyright, the photos of the author or the author's signature in the forewords – is necessary to authenticate the others' discourse. By virtue of the author's social and political involvement and interest in the inclusion of the migrant experience in Catalan culture, they inadvertently reveal the inability of migrants to gain access to a space of self-expression as individuals with a name and voice of their own, as well as their lack of access to a copyright.

La pell de la frontera, by Francesc Serés, was born out of the inability to undertake the position of the mediator.[40] Like those we have seen thus far, this book is also difficult to categorise in terms of genre, with a story based on a search for the self that starts within the region of childhood and upbringing, a place that has later become inhabited by people from other countries. Our interest in this work resides in its reading as a process of investigation of the literary mechanisms used to resolve a conflict of portrayal. Specifically, we are interested in those that stem from the difficulty of speaking of an *other* without *othering* them; in other words, without defining them as different, which necessarily creates a distance and leads to the risk of generalisation and objectification when that *other* is a group.[41] Through both theory and ethnographic accounts, dialogical and reflexive anthropology have sought strategies to avoid this othering, yet they have not completely resolved the conflict. Dialogues continue to use marks (typographic, modal, linguistic) that indicate where the other's speech begins. In self-reflective stories, we simply have open access to the position from which the difference is constructed. Serés's story draws on mechanisms that can be identified in different anthropological studies while at the same time refuting the theory. Theory is of no use to him, as it marks a distance that his point of view cannot allow:

> Teoritzem i llegim els metres de prestatgeria d'antropologia postmoderna que calgui, ens empassem coll avall la societat líquida, la pluriculturalitat i tots i cadascun dels neologismes que s'encunyen, però, després, un home et dona el passaport que porta dins dels pantalons embolicat amb una bossa de plàstic, suada, una bossa que put perquè la suor put, la roba put i l'herba i els camps puden. I la teoria falla... I tota la teoria i les bones intencions les carreguen dos nois que van quasi nus per la vora del camí del Riu, amb un farcell de canyes tallades sobre el cap per fer-se una cabana i, de sobte, tot és clar, i els gèneres confusos i tota la faramalla teòrica desapareixen: tot és nítid, dos nois, suats, que pateixen i carreguen canyes per fer-se una cabana, de Mali a Alcarràs, aquesta és la conclusió, que encara no ho sabem, però de Mali a Alcarràs, la distància és mínima. No hi ha teoria perquè no hi cap, no hi ha distància i la conclusió és clara: demà podem ser nosaltres els que carreguem les canyes, i també portarem un núvol de mosquits que no ens deixaran viure.[42]

> We theorise and read shelf after shelf of all the postmodern anthropology we can find, we gobble down the liquid society, pluriculturalism and each and every neologism they mint, but then a man gives you the passport he's been carrying in his trousers inside a plastic bag, a bag that smells because sweat smells, clothes smell and grass and fields smell. And theory fails... And two young lads carry all the theories and good intentions with them as they walk almost naked along the verge of the river path, a bundle of cut cane on their heads

to make a hut, and, suddenly, everything is clear, and all the hybridity and that theoretical palaver disappear: all is crystal clear, two young lads, sweating, toiling, and carrying reeds to make huts, from Mali to Alcarràs, that is conclusive, though we don't realise that yet: the distance from Mali to Alcarràs is minimal. There is no theory because there is no need, the distance is nil and the conclusion is crystal clear: tomorrow we could be the ones carrying those reeds, when we too will attract a swarm of mosquitoes to make our lives unbearable.

The insistence on the smells and sensations is essential when it comes to justifying the proximity of the narrator, a presence speaking in the first person, 'I', who, at the end of the passage, speaks as part of a 'we' who could someday be 'them'. The path that leads from the 'I' to the 'we' and from the 'we' to the 'they' runs through the physical contact with the grime, burden and suffering of the others. Rosi Braidotti has noted the importance of the experience of the other's condition as a mechanism for the transformation of the canonical subject into a nomadic subject, one that is defined through the process of becoming and by changing the limits that define one's individuality and uniqueness from others.[43] In Serés's work, the permeable skin of the portrayed author's self is a space of friction. The body of the portrayed author does not disappear from the scene to create distance or to yield his voice to another. Rather, it is displayed precisely through the passage towards this other, through the physical contagion stemming from the contact with the other's space.

As we have shown thus far, authorial loci are constructed spaces that afford access to a position of power. In other words, the subject of enunciation is transformed as they construct an object of enunciation; they are affected by the depiction of *what* the *subject described* intends to *say*. As of the very title, *La pell de la frontera* questions the definition of that something and its relationship with the subject that enunciates it, by evoking the skin virtually as a border, the sensitive limit that demarcates the line of one's own body, and, territorialising it, invites us to venture out towards others. In the book, the very concept of the border has different meanings. The most obvious one relates to the fact that most of the stories are set in the Franja de Ponent, the territory within the autonomous community of Aragon that borders Catalonia and where Catalan is spoken; a border inhabited by different 'skins'. At the same time, it evokes the borders that many of the book's main characters have crossed, taking us to Nigeria, Guinea and Bulgaria.

Serés's stories present the contrast of a radical distance from the others (which marks not only the cultural difference but also and above all, the poverty in which many of the migrants live) and the mention of the places of friction with the newcomers, who share spaces, experiences and work with those who were already there. In this friction, 'the others' become 'some others' with whom they coexist until they eventually become part of the place and transform its identity and its memory. Serés does not aim to lend a voice to these 'others'. Instead, he sets out to redefine the 'own' space of enunciation through the process of his attempt to speak of them. In fact, in interviews following the publication of the book, Serés emphasises his own presence as a focal point of the book: 'El que m'interessa és l'impacte d'aquesta gent, com m'ha modificat a mi' ('What interests me is the impact these people have had, how that has changed me').[44] According to Serés, the book also draws a personal boundary within the work itself: 'No tornaré a parlar ni d'aquest tema ni d'aquella zona. Ja no puc explicar més, el proper que escrigui d'aquesta terra que sigui un altre' ('I will not speak again about this or about that area. I can't tell about it anymore, the next one to write about this place will be someone else').[45] He also notes, 'No sé qui ho descriurà, tot això, els fills de l'Andrei i de tants d'altres algun dia donaran l'altra versió de la seva vida aquí. Algú altre ho haurà d'explicar' (Serés, *La pell*, p. 92) ('I don't know who will describe it all; Andrei's children and those of so many others will one day offer another version of their lives here. Somebody else will have to describe it').

Here, therefore, there is neither an infiltrator nor a chameleon nor any attempt to explain a distance. The writer's first-person persona is central, yet he portrays himself as taking a step backwards that should allow for the opening of a position of enunciation for the other. In *La pell de la frontera*, that opening never occurs, as this would entail writing *as the other*, either through fiction or through the guise of the ventriloquist;[46] yet the terrain is prepared through the disclosure of doubts about the very role as a writer to tell the stories of the lives of others. This occurs in two contrasting stories: 'Avions que entren per la finestra' ('Planes that Come in through the Window') and 'Cada ocell és una illa' ('Every Bird is an Island'). In the former, Serés describes his stay at a writers' residence in the United States, where there were frequent conversations about what could 'sell' in literature and about the training of writers in expensive and promising master's degree programmes. The publishing system collapses when, in 'Cada ocell és una illa', the writer must explain his work in a bar full of Senegalese, Gambian and Guinean migrants. Here, the writer is an outsider. This alienness gives rise to the stories that make up the book.

In fact, in *La pell de la frontera*, Serés the writer appears to be passing through a landscape that is at once familiar and foreign to him. It is familiar because it evokes his childhood and adolescent memories. Yet it is also distant in that both he and the landscape have changed. He recognises the scents and sensations of the place from his past experience and they foster an identification with the people who now live there – peasants and migrants – and who no longer recognise him as one of them. He therefore explores the coordinates of a well-known space that is clearly outlined on the maps featured at the start of the book, yet where he has become a stranger who moreover has no clear purpose at the moment. Both the police forces patrolling the area and the migrants with whom he wishes to speak are suspicious of his intentions, and claiming to be a 'writer' seems inappropriate in both cases. He tells the Mossos (Catalan police force) that he is looking for Majeed, an Algerian who will be the main character in one of his stories. The migrants think he's a plainclothes policeman. Faced with the difficulty of telling the truth and sounding believable, he comes up with an outright lie: '¿Què vol? Em dic Josep i busco finques – mentir . . . Anem per zones i a mi em toca aquesta. Hem de mirar el registre de la propietat i revisar molta paperassa. – Mentir, mentir, mentir' (*La pell*, p. 64) ('What do you want? My name is Josep and I'm looking for properties – I lie . . . We go by zones and I was assigned to this one. We've got to check the land registry and go over a lot of paperwork – I lie, and lie and lie').

The writer's authority is thus eroded when he appears on the scene, alongside the others and with no clear role in the setting around him. If there is no displacement, Serés writes, there is no literature. And the word 'displacement' here can mean both movement and detachment from the place from which, as a writer, it seems he should be instilling authority into his story. In *La pell de la frontera* the author has not died; nevertheless, his authority is presented as fragile and tainted by the inability to distance himself from it. The writer's skin is not an impermeable membrane. The act of writing is performed from this vulnerable self that is moreover constantly exposed throughout the story. Even in chapters structured in the form of a dialogue, the interviewer's self does not lose its prominence. There is neither objectivity nor a desire to conceal, yet nor is there any stable perspective from which to paint a portrait of what happens 'elsewhere' or 'to others'.

Conclusion

Thus far, we have refrained from identifying the evolutionary lines in the framework of a sequence of books that we have nevertheless presented in chronological order and that gives us a certain image of the process: from the non-critical distance of Sentís to the erosion of the authorial space in Serés. We could explain this progression by appealing to both evolution in the sense of what it means to be Catalan and in sense of the role of the intellectual, as explained by Víctor Martínez-Gil while applying Bauman's categories to the Catalan context, ranging from the position of a lawmaker who controls what he wants to explain, to that of the interpreter of a culture with vague borders.[47] The works studied here share a hazy genre location, which, regardless of whether it is explicitly placed in the realm of the documentary or fiction, needs to buttress its setting with explicit references to objectivity; in the case of fiction, references are made to the writer's personal creativity. Oddly, and with the exception of *Els altres catalans*, all the works mentioned above include documentary photographs. We have already discussed the cover of *Viatge en Transmiserià*, which at once depicts the verisimilitude and presents evidence of the impossibility of being an infiltrator. Each chapter of *Els castellans* includes photographs of either the setting that the writer wishes to depict or the everyday scenes of the era. In the works of Villatoro and Guillamon, family photographs are paired with archival images or even with objects that have been found. *El somni català* also contains family album photos. In *Nosaltres els catalans*, the faces of the informants replace their names on the cover, and in *Un relat de la nova immigració africana*, the smiling photograph of Toni Sala and Alí suggests a cordial relationship between informant and mediator. Serés's book provides photographic documentation of the settings visited. The images reinforce the verisimilitude of a story that emerges from an authorship that has been exposed to otherness. According to Ileana Rodríguez, that exposure is essential in the portrayal of the subaltern voice because it determines the act of listening.[48] However, it is not always a comfortable position. It forces the writer to struggle to uphold an objective appearance, to move among different identities, to disguise what he wishes to say as fiction, to draw on a particular memory to reinforce the shared past, and finally, to refrain from speaking of others as such. All in all, we have endeavoured to present the voice and the experience of migration as a place of transformation in Catalan literature, which is so deeply rooted that it serves to transform authorial voices and to bring about innovations in the conventional structures of the genres. From this standpoint, 'migrant' writing *must* yet *cannot be* a label for a specific set of texts, an independent sub-system for an intercultural audience at a food fair. Rather, it is a place of conflict and contact, a place of innovation and transformation of the writing itself, and with such transformation, it is a place for the Catalan culture and for any nation that identifies with it.

Notes

1. See this and other information on the response to the book in the media package of the publishing house *L'Avenç*, *www.lavenc.cat/index. php/index.php?/cat/layout/set/print/Els-Llibres-de-L-Avenc/Que-han-dit-dels-nostres-llibres/El-barri-de-la-Plata-Julia-Guillamon-2018*. Unless otherwise stated, translations from Catalan are mine.
2. Pilar Arnau, 'Literatura i immigració internacional a la cultura catalana del segle XXI: Conceptualització i recepció crítica', unpublished PhD thesis, Universitat de les Illes Balears, 2023.
3. Julià Guillamon, 'La novel·la catalana de la immigració', *L'Avenç*, 298 (2005), 46–9; Maria Dasca, 'La immigració com a fenomen en la literatura catalana', *Cercles: Revista d'Història Cultural*, 18 (2015), 61–78; Andreu Domingo, 'La literatura sobre la immigració al segle XXI', *L'Avenç*, 408 (2015), 28–34.
4. See the following references: Diego Muñoz Carrobles, 'Xenografías femeninas en la literatura catalana contemporánea: Laila Karrouch y Najat El Hachmi, integración e identidad', *Revista de Lenguas y Literaturas Catalana, Gallega y Vasca*, 22 (2017), 207–20; Isabel Marcillas-Piquer, 'Veus de frontera: *Els altres catalans* d'ara', *Caplletra*, 65 (2018), 177–89;

Marta Segarra, 'Literatures migrants: *Jo també soc catalana* de Najat El Hachmi', *Mètode: Science Studies Journal*, 4 (2014); Miquel Pomar-Amer, 'Voices Emerging from the Border: A Reading of the Autobiographies by Najat El Hachmi and Saïd El Kadaoui as Political Interventions', *Planeta Literatur: Journal of Global Literary Studies*, 1 (2014), 33–52; Katiuscia Darici, 'Literatura transnacional en Cataluña: *La filla estrangera* de Najat El Hachmi', *Diablotexto Digital*, 2 (2017), 106–34; Margarida Castellano, 'La construcció del subjecte autobiogràfic femení en la literatura catalana de la immigració' (unpublished PhD thesis, Universitat de València, 2013); Aitana Guia Conca, 'Molts mons, una sola llengua: La narrativa en català escrita per immigrants', *Quaderns de Filologia: Estudis literaris*, 12 (2007), 229–48.

5 Josep-Anton Fernàndez, 'Dislocated Temporalities: Immigration, Sexuality, and Violence in Najat El Hachmi's *L'últim patriarca*', in Teresa Iribarren, Roger Canadell and Josep-Anton Fernàndez (eds), *Narratives of Violence* (Venice: Edizioni Ca' Foscari, 2021), p. 210.

6 Gonçal López-Pampló, 'L'assaig català en l'època postmoderna: Funció social i especificitat estètica' (unpublished PhD thesis, Universitat de València, 2015), 32.

7 Gayatri C. Spivak, 'Can the Subaltern Speak?', in Cary Nelson and Lawrence Grossberg (eds), *Marxism and the Interpretation of Culture* (Urbana IL: University of Illinois, 1988), pp. 271–313.

8 Fernando Coronil, 'Listening to the Subaltern: The Poetics of Neocolonial States', *Poetics Today*, 15/4 (1994), 643–58.

9 Mieke Bal, *Double Exposures: The Subject of Cultural Analysis* (London and New York: Routledge, 1996), p. 2.

10 Carles Sentís, *Viatge en Transmiserià* (Barcelona: La Campana, 1995).

11 Miguel Díaz Sánchez, '"Viaje en Transmiseriano": Moviments socials a l'Espanya Contemporània' (unpublished master's thesis, Universitat Autònoma de Barcelona, 2014).

12 Valentí Puig, 'Del tracoma a la FAI', *ABC Cataluña* (25 November 1994), x.

13 Josep Losada, 'Mor Carles Sentís', *El Punt Avui* (20 July 2011), 30.

14 Isabel Torras, 'Emigrar: L'única sortida', *Foc nou* (January 1995), 32.

15 Julià Guillamon, 'El sistema murciano en Cataluña', *La Vanguardia* (18 November 1994), 33. Teresa Pàmies, 'El reportatge triomfant', *Avui* (14 November 1994), 72.

16 Just Cabot, 'El problema de la immigració', *Mirador* (26 January 1933), 3. Josep Maria de Sagarra, 'Poesia murciana', *Mirador* (10 August 1933), 2.

17 Anonymous, 'Para preservar la raza catalana', *La Vanguardia* (3 May 1934), 8.

18 Ignasi Aragay, 'Sentís reviu el Transmiserià', *Avui* (18 October 1994), B1.

19 'Furgant per la brossa o xipollejant pel fang, hi havia dues espècies d'éssers. D'una banda porcs, truges i porcells; de l'altra, criatures en l'adolescència o la infància. Els primers no s'atipen tal com desitgen, són magres i negrosos, de lluny semblen senglars. Els altres seleccionen material i cerquen petits tresors. Van espellifats i bruts, però sota la crosta es descobreixen sovint figures gracioses' (Sentís, *Viatge en Transmiserià*, p. 71) ('Scavenging through the weeds or wading through the mud, there were two species of creatures. On the one hand, pigs, sows and piglets; on the other hand, adolescent or young kids. The former do not eat the way they wish, they are lean and black, and from afar they look like boars. The others select material and search for small treasures. Their clothes are shabby and dirty, but under the crust you'll often discover amusing figures').
20 Junta Directiva de la Casa Regional de Murcia y Albacete, 'Carta abierta a Carlos Sentís', *Solidaridad Obrera* (27 January 1933), 4.
21 Francesc Candel, *Els altres catalans vint anys després* (Barcelona: Edicions 62, 1985), p. 20. Jaume Vicens Vives had previously attempted to publish *Notícia de Catalunya* under the title *Nosaltres, els catalans*, and was prohibited from doing so by the state's censorship.
22 Andreu Domingo, *Catalunya al mirall de la immigració: Demografia i identitat nacional* (Barcelona: L'Avenç, 2014), pp. 79–97.
23 Manuel Cruells, *Els no catalans i nosaltres* (Barcelona: Edicions d'Aportació Catalana, 1965).
24 Jordi Amat, 'Nota a l'edició: *Els altres catalans* a censura', in Francesc Candel, *Els altres catalans* (Barcelona: Edicions 62, 2008), p. 16.
25 Andreu Domingo, 'La literatura sobre la immigració al segle XXI', *L'Avenç*, 408 (2015), 29.
26 Francesc Candel, *Els altres catalans* (Barcelona: Edicions 62, 1964), p. 33.
27 Victòria Hita, '"Ho he publicat tot, he publicat massa": Entrevista a Paco Candel, escriptor', *Capçalera* (July 2005), 25.
28 Francesc Candel, *Els altres catalans vint anys després* (Barcelona: Edicions 62, 1985), p. 21.
29 Edward Said, 'Representing the Colonized: Anthropology's Interlocutors', *Critical Inquiry*, 15/2 (1989), 205–25.
30 Homi Bhabha, *The Location of Culture* (London and New York: Routledge, 2004 [1994]), p. 128.
31 Julià Guillamon, 'Las dos culturas', *La Vanguardia* (27 April 2011), 11.
32 Jordi Puntí, *Els castellans* (Barcelona: L'Avenç, 2011), p. 13.
33 Jordi Puig, 'Catalans i castellans ara fan front comú contra la nova migració', *El 9 nou* (26 March 2011), https://el9nou.cat/osona-ripolles/cultura-i-gent/catalans-i-castellans-ara-fan-front-comu-contra-la-nova-immigracio/
34 Puig, 'Catalans i castellans'.

35 Puig, 'Catalans i castellans'.
36 Pere Antoni Pons, 'Jordi Puntí, escriptor: Vull explicar la immigració afrontant-ne els tabús', *Diari de Balears* (21 May 2011), 3.
37 Pons, 'Jordi Puntí, escriptor', 3.
38 Vicenç Villatoro, *Un home que se'n va* (Barcelona: Proa, 2014), p. 33.
39 The author also complements these archival sources with guided tours through the district and the use of audiovisual material to accompany the book, *www.elsllibresdelavenc.cat/?p=3617* and *llegirencata la.cat/activitats/ruta-pel-barri-de-la-plata-amb-julia-guillamon/*.
40 The following pages include, with only a few changes, my recent discussion of other aspects of Serés's book. See Mercè Picornell, *Sumar les restes: Ruïnes i mals endreços en la cultura catalana postfranquista* (Barcelona: Publicacions de l'Abadia de Montserrat, 2020), pp. 205–32.
41 Johannes Fabian, *Time and the Other: How Anthropology Makes its Object* (New York: Columbia University Press, 2002 [1983]).
42 Francesc Serés, *La pell de la frontera* (Barcelona: Quaderns Crema, 2014), pp. 73–4.
43 Rosi Braidotti, *Metamorphoses: Towards a Materialist Theory of Becoming* (Cambridge: Polity, 2002), p. 19.
44 Anna Ballbona, 'Francesc Serés: "Tens possibilitat de literatura quan hi ha un desplaçament"', *El Temps* (16 December 2014), 64.
45 Roger Maiol, 'La fricció amb la immigració és una crònica social del nostre país', *El País*, suplement *Quadern* (24 October 2014), 8.
46 Clifford Geertz, *Works and Lives* (Stanford CA: Stanford University Press), p. 145.
47 Víctor Martínez-Gil, 'Els escriptors com a intel·lectuals postmoderns', in Ramon Panyella and Jordi Marrugat (eds), *L'escriptor i la seva imatge* (Barcelona: L'Avenç, 2006), 299–322.
48 Ileana Rodríguez, 'Hegemonía y dominio: Subalternidad, un significado flotante', *Estudios: Revista de investigaciones literarias*, 14–15 (2000), 35–50.

Chapter 2

Egalitarian Aesthetics and the Literary Representation of Immigration: The Work of Julià de Jòdar

Àlex Matas Pons

L'atzar i les ombres ('Chance and Shadows') is the most well-known work of writer Julià de Jòdar (Badalona, 1942). Consisting of the novels *L'àngel de la segona mort* ('The Angel of the Second Death', 1997), *El trànsit de les fades* ('The Movement of Fairies', 2001) and *El metall impur* ('The Impure Metal', 2006), this trilogy recounts the social history of the Catalan working classes and the disappearance of their industrial world. The main characters are the residents of Gorg-Progrés, a working-class district of the city of Badalona, which in the trilogy is known as Guifré i Cervantes, taking the names of two central streets of the fictitious neighbourhood.

Nestled amid the factories, this neighbourhood in the city of Badalona is the birthplace and hometown of Julià de Jòdar, who was born into two migrant families – his mother's from Murcia and his father's from Andalusia. Like many other neighbourhoods around the Besòs River and in the Metropolitan Area of Barcelona as a whole, the population of the Gorg-Progrés district grew rapidly with the arrival of workers from all around the Iberian Peninsula and their families. Such was the case of the writer's family, who arrived in Catalonia around the time of the 1929 Barcelona Universal Exposition, years before the Spanish Civil War broke out, and decades before the arrival of new waves of migrants, who would make their way to the Catalan capital's industrial centre during the 1960s and 1970s.

The *L'atzar i les ombres* trilogy tells the collective story of the district's residents: families like that of the author himself, who had come to settle in a working-class neighbourhood far from the city centre. In this community, Catalan families who had lived there for a long time mixed with newcomers. One such case was that of Julià de Jòdar's father, a worker who, as the writer himself explains, 'es va catalanitzar en el sentit sociològic i de llengua a la fàbrica' ('was sociologically and linguistically Catalanised in the factory') where he worked, in Poblenou, an industrial district of the city of Barcelona.[1] The trilogy in particular recalls a period spanning from the 1950s to the 1970s and reveals the way in which the defeat of the Republicans and the subsequent repression under the Franco dictatorship shaped the blue-collar life of this Catalan industrial area.

The first book of the trilogy, *L'àngel de la segona mort*, depicts the life of a district that still clearly feels the scars of the Spanish Civil War, with vivid memories of those who died during the war, the neighbours who were executed and the exile of the few who survived. At the same time, the community continues to suffer the daily humiliation inflicted by the social forces of the Franco regime that control the district. The second novel, *El trànsit de les fades*, recreates the emotional life of the neighbourhood and connects the sentimental and sexual education of the residents with the cultural climate and moral hypocrisy of the Franco regime, while at the same time coalescing the world of the factory with the world of theatre and popular entertainment. Finally, the third novel, *El metall impur*, chronicles Gabriel Caballero's arrival to the factory, which takes place in the 1960s. The trilogy concludes with the end of Gabriel Caballero's learning process, spanning from his childhood to his incorporation into the workforce.

In much the same manner that the trilogy presents a cohesive chronological framework (the Franco dictatorship during the 1950s and 1960s) and a unified spatial milieu, consisting of the working-class district of Gorg-Progrés in Badalona, the role of Gabriel Caballero as the main character also lends a sense of cohesion to the three books. The trilogy essentially tells the story of the upbringing of the son of Angustias Pacheco and Bonifacio Caballero, the owners of the local grocery store known as El Rancho Grande. Nevertheless, this educational process does not follow the progressive line that has characterised the well-known European genre of the *Bildungsroman*. This progressive sequence of events is in fact an identifying feature of the literature about immigration written in Spanish in Catalonia, which frequently adopts the linear narrative model of the *Bildungsroman*, together with other elements of the Spanish tradition that derive originally from the picaresque novel. Such is the case of well-known novels including those written by Eduardo Mendoza and Juan Marsé, among others, which have customarily excluded Catalan workers from working-class settings and have tended to identify the Catalan characters with the industrialist and bourgeois elites of the Franco regime. However, the neighbourhood of Gabriel Caballero's childhood does not admit such a simple spatial segregation, and the diverse social relations make it impossible to ascribe a strict class identity to any given national or linguistic community.

In the novel's Guifré i Cervantes district (known in real life as the district of Gorg-Progrés, in Badalona), there is a definite sense of tension, conflict and mistrust between the newcomers and the original inhabitants. Yet despite everything, the collective memory of all the working classes who were defeated during the Spanish Civil War continues to be very much alive. This is in part possible thanks to Gabriel's storyline, which neither unfolds in a linear fashion nor simplifies the portrayal of the spaces and the social and class relations that comprise them, as is noted below. The formation of the collective memory is also possible because it is precisely Gabriel Caballero who lends his voice as the ambiguous narrator of the novel. At times, the story is told through the voice of a third person who takes the perspective of the character; other times we are met by an intermediate narrative figure, that of 'el noi que va prendre el relleu de l'Eulògia' ('the boy who took over from Eulògia'), which can be identified with the voice of Gabriel Caballero.[2]

The Pitfalls of Integration

In addition to Gabriel Caballero, another key character in the trilogy is Gregori Salicrú. As the neighbourhood's anarchist teacher and revolutionary prophet in the years preceding the Spanish Civil War, he encouraged the young neighbours, including Boni and Gabriel's father, to revolt. Once the war was over, however, Salicrú returned to the neighbourhood as a catechist: 'ratificant una depressió general i massiva. El Boni va saber que les coses no tornarien mai més a ser com abans' ('ratifying a general and massive depression. Boni knew things would never be the same again').[3]

It is noteworthy that in 2018 Julià de Jòdar published a novel, *Els vulnerables* ('The Vulnerable Ones'), bringing back this emblematic character from the trilogy. This novel tells the story of Gregori Salicrú's arrival in Barcelona in the days prior to the 1929 Universal Exposition, under the dictatorship of Primo de Rivera. According to the first volume of the trilogy, *L'àngel de la segona mort*, Salicrú's experiences take the reader to the Bon Pastor district before he would ever become the Guifré i Cervantes district's 'mestre de tots els revolucionaris del barri' (*L'àngel*, p. 95) ('master of all the neighbourhood's revolutionaries'), and long before he would also become the catechist of the children who were orphaned during the post-war period.

This 'futur doctrinari àcrata'[4] ('future anarchist doctrinaire') is embodied by one of the many workers who came to Catalonia from elsewhere in mainland Spain as part the great resettlement that took place in the first decades of the twentieth century. *Els vulnerables* recreates the construction of what were popularly dubbed the Cases Barates ('Cheap Houses'). Formally named Milans del Bosch, the Cases Barates area would later become known as Bon Pastor. This was one of the neighbourhoods that were erected primarily to house and improve the living conditions of many of these immigrants, who were barely surviving in the shantytowns around the city. Milans del Bosch was one of the four groups of houses – alongside Eduard Aunós, Ramon Albó and Baró de Viver – that formed a palpable clean-up project conceived by Primo de Rivera and his representatives in Barcelona, in anticipation of the forthcoming celebration of the 1929 Barcelona Universal Exposition.

The names of these four neighbourhoods correspond to four members of the Patronato Municipal de la Vivienda ('Municipal Housing Board'), who promoted their construction on rezoned land only to generate private economic income once they were urbanised through public resources. The novel recounts the founding of the neighbourhood that belonged to Milans del Bosch, a government delegate and trusted confidant of Primo de Rivera's regime in Catalonia, who was building on the right bank of the Besòs River, outside the administrative limits of Barcelona. As a result, the mayor of the neighbouring town of Santa Coloma de Gramenet was perplexed to see that the orchards and trees that administratively depended on his municipality had suddenly been transformed into a small neighbourhood full of outsiders, despite the fact that such land formed part of the right bank of the Besòs River.

The selection of the Cases Barates quarter is significant because the river, which cuts off part of the town of Santa Coloma de Gramenet, clearly reveals the arbitrary nature of the jurisdictional and administrative limits that determine the different forms of coexistence and sociability. Thus, when the Republic was proclaimed in 1931, the town's mayor made an initial attempt to drive away the outsiders, demanding that the city of Barcelona assume the administrative responsibility for the new neighbourhood. However, this demand would finally be met in 1945, under the Franco regime, thereby making it clear that it would ultimately be the mechanisms of real estate speculation and economic profit that would separate the right bank of the Besòs from the old town of Santa Coloma. The administrative border of Barcelona would annex a neighbourhood, and a substantial part of a neighbouring town, based on a precise calculation made in around 1929 on the profitability of regenerative urban development. As can be read in *Els vulnerables*:

> Aquests són dies de preparació de la gran Exposició Internacional a l'altre vessant de la muntanya . . . Per tal d'evitar que les barraques facin mal als ulls dels visitants . . . a fi d'erradicar la degeneració dels individus sense socialitzar, descentrats i degradats per la voràgine de la urbanització empesa per la ciutat – una situació causada per les depravacions que acompanyen la promiscuïtat que impera a *Barracòpolis*.[5]

> These are the days of preparation for the great International Exposition on the other side of the mountain . . . To keep the shacks from being such an eyesore for visitors . . . to put a stop to the degeneration of unsocialised individuals, people cast aside and demeaned by the rampant urban sprawl driven by the city – a situation caused by the depravities that accompany the promiscuity that rules the shanty town of *Barracòpolis*.

Hence, through the figure of Gregori Salicrú, in *Els vulnerables* Julià de Jòdar recounts the history of this border area of the Besòs River that straddles Barcelona and Santa Coloma de Gramenet to the west, and Sant Adrià del Besòs and Badalona to the east, forming the backdrop of the well-known trilogy, *L'atzar i les ombres*. It is these streets that will watch Boni's son Gabriel Caballero grow up. In this case, it can be asserted that the promise of integration underlying the urban and social reform initiative will simply consist of a redistribution of the powers of economic production and reproduction within the liminal space of the Besòs river basin, which will never have a stable physical appearance of its own. This explains the matter that shapes Julià de Jòdar's literary imagination, which consists of political conflicts, workers' revolts and democratic resistance. Exploring and understanding the history of this area at the edge of the Besòs River means not betraying its liminal nature with a narrative construction that simply draws up a chronological sequence of events, in keeping with the hegemonic model of integration. In fact, a narrative order of that sort would be incompatible with the border-like nature of the Besòs River, as it would dissolve any ambiguity through a moral significance that would neatly organise all that is derelict or unfinished under the guise of a meaning: the redemption of the defeated, by bringing them into prosperity, for example, or the reception of the newcomers, by naturalising them.

This desire for events to reveal a sense of cohesion, integrity and a conclusion that are completely alien to them is an invention of the historicist narrative and its keenness to pass moralising judgements. Indeed, historicism, as we shall see later, is defined precisely because it goes beyond strict chronology when it ascribes a value to the chronological sequence of events. However, unlike the old stories told in past annals or chronicles, there is no longer an important or momentous principle that dictates the chronology. Instead, the source of authority in charge of the distribution and classification of the events in moral terms is a governmental body. The states are the new social core that guarantee the existence of a legal system. The cartographers under their administrations are responsible for defining the borders of a region, which in turn are bound by parliamentary legislation that dictates what is allowed and what is forbidden.

The promise of integration and the goal of prosperity derive from this successful spirit of enlightenment, and the new statewide governmental instruments in fact aim to prevent any foreigner from being treated as an enemy ever again. This explains the influential conceptual discovery of Kant, who, in his book *Perpetual Peace*, suggested the formula of cosmopolitan law, which would elevate the hospitable attitude of a hypothetical ideal host country to a legal and political category. Cosmopolitan law sought to reconcile the territorial ownership of states with the individual freedoms of the people, although the strictly economic spirit underlying that proposal, in which free trade was virtually a metaphor for benevolent cosmopolitanism, is now evident.

Kant promoted an incipient capitalism that in fact only took into account the rights of the foreigner as a citizen of another state. In other words, hospitality was provided strictly within the confines of citizenship, as noted in *Of Hospitality* by Derrida where the author explores Kant's aporetic proposal.[6] The protection of newcomers' rights is therefore the same institutional violence that sentences them to assimilation by means of an oath of official loyalty in the host country. An oath that states moreover renew by default when they validate birth as a signature of this contract that ensures the inclusion of the *citizens* in the community.

Hence, the progressive narrative, which is structured around a dialectics that pits exclusion against integration and backwardness against prosperity, also makes it possible to reproduce the economistic logic of nation states, which are built on structural imbalances that must be preserved in order to obtain the returns envisaged by the capitalist logic that inspires them. As Ferran Muñoz Jofre rightly suggests, this explains why the predominant literary imagery of immigration in Catalonia has shown a tendency towards the antinomy of the Catalan bourgeoisie and the working class: 'caldria, però, revisar no tan sols si només existien dos únics grups socials, sinó també si el model de convivència plantejat és l'únic possible' ('However, it would be important to reconsider not only whether there were only two social groups, but also whether the proposed model of coexistence was the only possible option').[7]

The Chronicle of Defeats and the Denial of Linear Time

Such a reassessment would have to consider the narrative elements that break down the linear time of the continuum, as can be seen in *L'àngel de la segona mort* (1998), the first book of the *L'atzar i les ombres* trilogy. Here, we read of Gregori Salicrú's return to the Guifré i Cervantes area, after having lived in Madrid during the years of the Spanish Civil War. As mentioned above, Salicrú had been a leader for the young militiamen in the neighbourhood in the years preceding the war, yet, unlike most of them, he had neither died at the front, nor been shot at Camp de la Bota, nor gone into exile.

Salicrú returns to teach catechism to the young people of the area and from the perspective of the storyline, his reappearance is interwoven into a narrative structure that revolves around the accidental death of Àngel Cucharicas, Gabriel Caballero's friend. Salicrú had undertaken the task of leaving on the railway track the lifeless body of the boy who had died in Quimet Font's furnace: 'En aquesta via del tren descobreix que l'anar i venir de la memòria no està regulat per la mesura del temps' (Jòdar, L'àngel, p. 234) ('On these railway tracks, he discovers that the ebb and flow of memory is not regulated by the measure of time'), we read. He discovers this because at the very same moment he recalls the murder in Madrid of a young paper boy who died under the fire of fascist bullets:

> Va ser al Madrid assetjat pels feixistes, un dia que ell havia baixat de la Sierra amb permís. Acostumat a les alarmes, el petit venedor de diaris de la plaça del Callao va voler comprovar que, com al cine, la sort somriu als audaços. Els obusos dels rebels arribaven a intervals irregulars des de Cerro Garabitas perquè la gent, confiada que tot havia passat, sortís dels refugis, moment que aprofitaven els criminals feixistes per descarregar canonades sense treva i matar-los com mosques. Aquell dia dels volts de Nadal del trenta-vuit, un full de diaris que solia cridar al pas dels vianants ('*El Heraaaaldo*', '*La Naciooóon*') va servir per tapar els ulls del petit venedor, esbalaïts contra un cel on la trajectòria del projectil que venia per esventrar-lo ja traçava el rètol de la seva mort.
>
> Amb tu ha estat menys magnànima, que no s'ha conformat amb un sol cop de dalla, podia haver pensat el Salicrú vint anys després, mentre contempla el rostre de l'Àngel Cucharicas a la llum de la lluna sota el pont de Can Clos. (*L'àngel*, pp. 234–5)

> It was in Madrid that he was attacked by the fascists, on a day when he had been given permission to come down from the mountains. Accustomed to alarms, the little boy who sold newspapers in Plaza del Callao wanted to prove that luck shined on the audacious, as it always

did in the movies. The rebel gunfire arrived at irregular intervals from Cerro Garabitas so that the people, believing that everything had passed, would then leave the shelters. That was when the fascist criminals took the opportunity to shoot them down with cannons and kill them like flies. That day around Christmas time of 1938, a newspaper headline page that used to call out to the passers-by ('*El Heraaaaldo*', '*La Nacioooón*') served to cover the young vendor's eyes, which were open with fright against a sky where the trajectory of the shot that was coming to blow him up was already tracing out the notice of his death.

'With you she has been less magnanimous, she was not satisfied with just a single strike of the scythe', Salicrú may have thought twenty years later, while contemplating the face of Angel Cucharicas in the moonlight under the bridge of Can Clos.

Hence, in that instant, Salicrú thus illustrates one of the contentions which, according to Walter Benjamin's 'Theses on the Philosophy of History', might make it feasible to remove linear time from the continuum of history. In his Sixth Thesis, Walter Benjamin corrects historicism's pretension of knowing the past 'the way it really was' and instead suggests that historicising the past would mean 'to seize hold of a memory, as it flashes up at a moment of danger'.[8] There would therefore be no real, genuinely unique fact that we could preserve against the passage of time or that we could make become identical to itself: the way it was. However, we can bring it back as an image, fleeting or spectral, in a given constellation or framing of time. All that remains are snapshots of time that are organised into constellations of scattered moments, the sediments of which settle in things, revealing the non-linear connection between what once was and what now is. This is in fact reflected by the narrator of *L'àngel de la segona mort* in his folk ballad about Salicrú's return to the Badalona neighbourhood of Guifré i Cervantes, as Salicrú, the former advocate of anarchism who is now a catechist, lays the lifeless body of Àngel Cucharicas to rest on the train tracks:

> Havia trencat tots els ponts entre el passat i el present, els distints moments de la seva vida eren com les capes superposades d'un jaciment a l'aire lliure, on els objectes apareixien trencats i desordenats sense que ningú mostri interès a recompondre'ls per explicar-ne bellesa i utilitat, calibrar-ne necessitat i usura. (*L'àngel*, p. 245)

He had broken all the bridges between the past and the present, the different moments of his life were like the overlapping layers of an outdoor anthropological site, where the objects lay broken and in disarray and where there was no interest in putting them back together to illustrate their beauty and utility, to gauge the need for them and their usury.

This is just one of the ways in which *L'àngel de la segona mort* approaches the collective history of the working-class neighbourhood of Guifré i Cervantes, through cyclical repetitions and falsely repressed returns. The novel deliberately makes a legend of the death of Àngel, which unleashes a storyline that in turn brings to light the defeat of the anarchists of the CNT and the Federación Anarquista Ibérica (FAI), as well as the post-war oppression of the Republican survivors, their widows and children, and against the district's Catalan craftspeople. This is also the case of the second novel in the trilogy, *El trànsit de les fades* (2001), in which the legendary death is that of Boni, Gabriel's father. He is stabbed to death with a knife on Easter Sunday, in Garrofers, to protect Lilà, his employee at El Rancho Grande, against the attacks of Chuti, one of the fearsome young louts of the neighbourhood. In this case, it is the vaudevillian language that opens the door to the long and squalid decade of the 1950s, the years of 'la brutal autoconservació obligada per la derrota' (Jòdar, *El trànsit de les fades*, p. 111) ('brutal self-preservation forced by defeat'). Finally, the third volume of the trilogy, *El metall impur* (2006), revolves around the death in 1962 of Marià Castells, the assistant to the chief engineer of La Farga, a foundry near the mouth of the Besòs River. The occupational accident is an example of the infamous Francoist developmentalism of the 1960s, just as mesocracy was emerging during the years of the scientific organisation of labour. This spurred a pragmatic and individualised conduct under the rubric of productivity and competitiveness, leaving little room for niceties or shared co-operative work.

The chronicle of the three deaths never illustrates any evolutionary process that could be construed as reasonably sequenced by means of an historiographic arrangement of the periods, as the vision of *L'atzar i les ombres* totally opposes the evolutionist vision of history. Rather than following the model of cumulative conquests as a means to progress towards freedom, democracy or civilisation, this story emphasises the record of defeats and the rightful remembrance deserved by those who were defeated. This entails a departure from a materialist hegemonic narrative of history, which, in its most orthodox version, appears to believe that it is the *laws of history* that will necessarily lead to the ultimate crisis of capitalism and bring about a reparatory destiny through the final victory of the proletariat or at the very least, a sufficiently thorough reform for the gradual change of society. This narrative of *mechanical* materialism depends on a specific conception of time that Walter Benjamin accurately summed up in his Thirteenth Thesis: 'The concept of the historical progress of mankind cannot be sundered from the concept of its progression through a homogenous, empty time.'[9] In this light, the ideology of progress took on the pre-eminent conception of time of the modern age: the mere laicisation of Christianity's linear and irreversible notion of time, having removed from it any notion of a *telos* beyond a process structured in keeping with a before and an after.

Views that are critical of the notion of progress (such as those of Walter Benjamin and Julià de Jòdar) aim to establish a link between history and politics by linking the past and the present in a manner that is compatible with historical discontinuity. In other words, they experiment with narrative lines that break away from the notion of a sequentially structured process in keeping with a *before* and an *after*. In the case of *L'atzar i les ombres*, the legendary account of the three deaths illustrates the connection between remembrance and the redemption of a historical poetics that aims to keep alive the conscious awareness of the injustice of the past, generation after generation.

To re-establish the revolutionary force of historical materialism, while simultaneously remaining faithful to the premises expounded by Walter Benjamin, the chronicle of the Guifré i Cervantes district attempts to mediate between the secular, historical and liberating struggles of humanity, and the fulfilment of a messianic promise. It is in this sense that, for example, the timeline of *L'àngel de la segona mort* must be interpreted. In this novel, the narrative time is organised around the death of Àngel Cucharicas and is rhythmically arranged in keeping with the model of the psalmody and its usual litanies, as it aims to promote the solace of memory without allowing the narrative logic of oblivion, inherent to the novel, to offset the accident of Gabriel's friend. For this reason, the storyline is developed in keeping with a legendary chronology around the reiterated death of an innocent child: 'El primer dissabte després de la mort de l'Àngel Cucharicas' (*L'àngel*, p. 289) ('The first Saturday after the death of Àngel Cucharicas'); 'El matí del sisè dissabte després de la mort de l'Àngel Cucharicas' (p. 328) ('The morning of the sixth Saturday after the death of Àngel Cucharicas'); 'El vespre del sisè dissabte després de la mort de l'Àngel Cucharicas' (p. 346) ('The night of the sixth Saturday after the death of Àngel Cucharicas'); 'La matinada del setè dissabte després de la mort de l'Àngel Cucharicas' (p. 353) ('The wee hours of the morning of the seventh Saturday after the death of Àngel Cucharicas'); and so on.

As is well-known, both in his 'Theses on the Philosophy of History' and in his famous text 'The Storyteller', Walter Benjamin called on the return of the chronicler. Nevertheless, he sought the return of a chronicler 'in changed form, secularized, as it were', who did not adhere to any sort of reactionary or theologically restorative spirit.[10] A new storyteller who was more interested in freeing himself from the burden of explaining what could be demonstrated than in recovering the chronological order of the story of his ancient predecessors. Thus, unlike the narrative model of historicism, where virtually everything that occurs benefits the information, the art of the chronicler would be 'to keep a story free from explanation as one reproduces it' (Benjamin, 'The Storyteller', p. 89). In fact, Walter Benjamin did not seek the restoration of a theological order, although he did not consider historical materialism to be entirely incompatible with theological thought; nor did he feel the instrumental distinction between reason and religion to be necessary. In fact, given the results of the enlightenment project and the ongoing need to combat the rise of fascism, the philosopher held that Marxism had not achieved its objectives partly because it had relegated religion to the private sphere and had positioned reason – detached from religion and from any form of mystery – as the sole instrument to bring about justice in the world. For him, the revolutionary role of prophetic discourse and the messianic promise were not to be underestimated. In fact, according to him, the Messianic face would have to be returned to the concept of a society free of class differences.

Hence, the presence of the two childhood friends in *L'àngel de la segona mort*, the deceased Àngel Cucharicas and Gabriel Caballero, could not go unnoticed among the crowd of children who gathered around Aunt Eulògia while she told her stories,[11] for after her death, the new voice that would ensure that the traditional stories would be passed down would be the ambiguous voice of Gabriel, who became known as 'the boy who took over from Aunt Eulògia'. The language of chronicles and legends would thus feed Julià de Jòdar's literary recreation of this working-class area of Badalona, adopting Walter Benjamin's poetics of history: his critique of bourgeois civilisation and his distrust of the hopes for progress. The chronicler is not necessarily the paradigmatic figure who writes from the point of view of the victors, princes, emperors or kings. Rather, as we read in *The Storyteller*, the chronicler would be an exemplary figure capable of undertaking a portrayal that would not exclude any details or events, regardless of how insignificant they might be. In fact, Walter Benjamin revisits this crucial definition of the chronicler in his Third Thesis in the 'Theses on the Philosophy of History', when he says: 'A chronicler who recites events without distinguishing between major and minor ones acts in accordance with the following truth: nothing that has ever happened should be regarded as lost for history.'[12]

This is undoubtedly the vocation that fuels the literary project of *L'atzar i les ombres*, where it is plain to see that the author avoids psychologism and appears to share the same distinction that Walter Benjamin made between the story and the novel. If the former was the literary form of traditional craft societies in an era before the invention of the printing press, where the story was shared in community, the stories that spread through the novel would rather belong to modern technological societies, where reading is an individual and solitary activity. The boy who took over from Eulògia wished to retake the old 'ritual contra la desmemòria' (*L'àngel*, p. 17) ('ritual against oblivion') of his old and blind Aunt Eulògia, a ritual that had been efficient partially because it accompanied him through the routine time of his mechanical activity. Lacking the psychological nuances characteristic of novels, the events recounted found in those circumstances a place in the listener's memory, and it was entirely feasible that sooner or later they would be told again.

Nevertheless, according to Walter Benjamin, this optimal narrative liturgy against oblivion must have ultimately come to an end, making it utterly impossible to gain knowledge of an authentic experience of time (*Erfahrung*), based on the memory of a cultural tradition. Now it was only possible to live the immediate experience (*Erlebnis*), which led to reactive behaviours typical of the machines that 'han esborrat per complet la seva memòria' ('have completely erased their memory').[13] It therefore comes as no surprise that the temptation of the boy who took over from Eulògia to revive that old ritual would be met with the mistrust and suspicion of a neighbour who did not believe that it was realistic for anyone to 'reviure els fantasmes' ('revive ghosts') as Eulògia did, who 'no esperava diners ni fama. Es limitava a recordar-nos d'on veníem i on havíem arribat' (*L'àngel*, p. 245) ('expected neither money nor fame. She limited herself to reminding us of where we had come from and what we had come to').

Aunt Eulògia and Gabriel Caballero, the boy who took over from Eulògia, make *L'atzar i les ombres* a pleasant story to be remembered. They make it a narrative conducive to a memory that is capable of opening up the archives that historicism believes to have been closed and buried away, if not entirely destroyed. This is how the third book of the trilogy, *El metall impur*, is to be understood. In it, we find an expressly recreated search for authenticating documents stored in official archives and a reproduction of photographs of people, objects and buildings that purport to be genuine. Through a manuscript found in Barcelona's historic second-hand flea market, Els Encants, the reader follows the plot of the novel about the death of Marià Castells at the La Farga foundry. At the same time, however, a second plot emerges and develops, relating to the narrator's search for and verification of the facts. At the end of the story, the narrator admits that he is 'insuficient d'ingenu cercador de la *veritat* entre els plecs de la història col·lectiva i la memòria particular' ('insufficient and ingenuous in his search for the truth amidst the folds of collective history and private memory').[14] Hence, there is no complete clarity regarding an occupational accident caused by the greed of Josep Massarré, a factory foreman. Massarré is thought to have exploited the ineptitude and needs of Marià Castells, the assistant to the chief officer of the electric furnace at La Farga (the hypothetical foundry in the Catalana district of Sant Adrià de Besòs), who was allegedly swept away towards Camp de la Bota by a flood in 1962.

Nevertheless, the inaccuracy regarding the location of the foundry is not compelling enough evidence to deny the crime to which Marià Castells fell victim. His death is similarly irreparable and comes to form part of the collective history of the Besòs River precisely because the novel clearly shows that memory is more than mere data in an objective archive that can serve as the basis for a scientific and well-founded history of events. It is not something that is found and compiled in the archives, but rather something that is constantly made and re-made. This explains the inclusion of the archival documents and graphic materials that the narrator consults during his research, not so much to disprove the legendary imagination of the chronicle of the boy who took over from Eulògia, but to illustrate the mechanisms used by historicism to provide itself with legitimacy, authority and approval.

As a product of a *social magic*, the archive is certainly a supreme shrine of verification; yet the transformation of documents into monuments cannot drive the memory to forget that it is in fact the law of the land that determines what can be said and what cannot even be thought or imagined. The investigation of the mystery around the unregistered death of Marià Castells enables us to understand the mechanisms by which the truths archived in the Franco regime's official versions were fabricated, written by technicians, civil servants, inspectors or union representatives after interrogating witnesses with vested interests or who were intimidated and coerced. This is how the murder of the Poblenou-born trainee has a place among the interstices of history's great monuments and acts as a revolutionary messianic outbreak capable of disrupting the continuum of historicism.

This is precisely its role in *El metall impur*, much like the roles of the deaths of Àngel Cucharicas and Boni Caballero in *L'àngel de la segona mort* and *El trànsit de les fades*, respectively. Yet this role not only applies to the deaths of these three characters, but also to those of all the other residents of the Besòs River who are continually remembered because their names have ended up in Camp de la Bota, the vast archive made up of ruins and refuse piled up by the storm of progress at the Besòs River: from the fourteen young men from Boni's town who were executed by the fascists,[15] to Torva, the Gypsy woman who lived in the shantytown, who exclaims, 'Quants cops ens han passat pel damunt!' (*L'àngel*, p. 257) ('We've been knocked around so much') and who, while playing with Gabriel, tells him:

Aquí afusellaven gent des que tu i jo vam néixer, i a la nostra barraca he ajudat la meva mare a rentar un germanet mort. Plàcido i Simón, diu que es deien els dos últims afusellats, però el meu germà no va arribar a tenir nom. En moren molts, de nadons, aquí, rere el mur on afusellaven gent. (p. 257)

Here they've been executing people since you and I were born, and in our shack, I helped my mother to clean up my dead little brother. They say Plàcido and Simón were the last two to be killed, but my brother never even had a name. Many new-borns die here, behind the wall where they used to execute people.

Excess Words and the Poetics of Non-adhesion

There is a particular image of *L'àngel de la segona mort* that confirms the chronicle's resistance of linear time: the seashell. At the end of the novel, Gabriel Caballero returns to the Guifré i Cervantes district at the request of the town council, after construction work on a new car park next to the town cemetery has led to the collapse of a wall of niches. Accompanied by former members of the neighbourhood, Gabriel Caballero – who was expected to be 'l'únic noi del barri que no haurà de portar granota' (p. 367) ('the only lad in the neighbourhood who won't have to wear overalls') – would have to help the civil servants with the task of identifying the remains of the families. In this way, Gabriel expresses his resentment that reveals his status as an outsider: 'no em vau consentir de viure entre vosaltres i us he portat a viure amb mi' (p. 367) ('you didn't allow me to live among you and I've taken you to live with me'). Invited to work with the other residents in repairing the destruction caused by progress (the construction of the car park), Gabriel mocks the wilful intention of the relatives, forensic experts and anthropologists to classify, distribute and sort out the collective corpse of a defeated neighbourhood like Guifré i Cervantes. And it is precisely in the face of the absurd desire to separate what has been mixed and to hierarchise the confusion when the powerful image of the seashell reappears: '¿Va ser llavors, que va començar a sentir les veus del passat com el so de les ones d'una cargola?' (p. 367) ('Was it then that he began to hear the voices of the past like the sound of the waves in a seashell?').

Angustias, Gabriel's mother, had already dreamt of the image of the seashell. Following the death of Àngel Cucharicas, she dreamt that Gabriel would undertake exactly the same journey that he was now taking as an adult, as he returned to the neighbourhood, having already left behind the cemetery and the duties of the municipal officers. According to Angustias's dream, at that very moment, Gabriel:

> desembolica el paquet i deixa caure a plom el peu de l'Àngel en el llenç d'aigua, on s'enfonsa girant entorn d'ell mateix mentre el remolí blauverdós li esfilagarsa la mortalla vegetal i li'n teixeix una de nova i de més subtil amb tots els colors de l'aigua. Un breu esclat de llum és l'últim senyal deixat per la resta pelegrina, abans que les ombres l'embolcallin per sempre, quan, en el centre de l'embut que es tanca com una cargola al voltant de la massa blava i negra, apareix, en darrer comiat, la imatge refractada del rostre de l'Àngel: un somriure capciós d'invitació al viatge, que els rínxols de la superfície converteixen en una altra imatge més inquietant, un rictus d'amargura de qui sembla que retreu a l'amic que no es guardi el peu com a penyora per tal de restar sempre plegats. (p. 63)

> he opens the package and drops Àngel's foot into the water, where it sinks to the bottom, swirling as the blue-green whirlpool strips away the plant veil, weaving a new, subtler one with all the colours of the water. A brief flicker of light is the last trace left behind by the remains of the foot before it is forever engulfed by the depths of the water. In that instant, the refracted image of Àngel's face appears in the centre of the swirl, which closes up like a seashell around the black and blue mass: a false smile beckoning travel, which the curves of the water's surface transform into another, more disturbing image, a bitter grimace of someone who seems to be reproaching the friend who has not kept his foot, as a pledge to remain together forever.

Hence, the seashell, which had appeared in his mother's dream while Gabriel was saying goodbye to his friend Àngel Cucharicas, now reappears in the cemetery and opens up the 'ritual against oblivion'. Following the outlandish attempt of the relatives, forensic experts and anthropologists, the scene continues and Gabriel discreetly withdraws from the group, when he sees a forgotten grave that has been uncovered by the collapse of the niche wall.

Inside, he sees a coffin containing an intact skeleton. It is difficult to make out the initials of the name of the deceased resident, as they have been erased by the passage of time. Nevertheless, he goes down into the hole of the grave and wraps the bones of the right foot in a makeshift cone of newspaper. In this manner, he identically reproduces the juvenile impulse that inspired Angustias' dream. That dream had hypothetically led him years before to rescue the foot of the deceased Àngel Cucharicas, which, covered by the brushwood of a hole, was never seen by either the judge or the police officers who were supposed to have taken his body away in two pieces. As we have seen, it is the same foot that, in the dream, Gabriel drops straight down into the water, generating on the surface the image of 'un rictus d'amargura de qui sembla que retreu a l'amic que no es guardi el peu com a penyora' ('a bitter grimace of someone who seems to be reproaching the friend who has not kept his foot as a pledge').

In this manner, the reader discovers that Gabriel Caballero's gesture is more of a reparation than a repetition. Here it becomes clear that no foot was ever missing from the body of his childhood friend, Àngel Cucharicas, at the time of his burial. Rather, it was Gabriel's imagination that had created a fiction that would enable him to overcome his indecision and pay homage to his departed friend by throwing his foot into the sea along the shores of Badalona, near the Pont del Petroli bridge. It is significant that this return of Gabriel's past takes place in the specific setting of a cemetery, which, due to the collapse caused by progress, has become an open-air archaeological site. As we have seen, this is precisely the manner in which the return of Gregori Salicrú's past has been described, at the very moment in which he leaves the corpse of the ill-fated Àngel Cucharicas on the train tracks: 'Havia trencat tots els ponts entre el passat i el present, els distints moments de la seva vida eren com les capes superposades d'un jaciment a l'aire lliure, on els objectes apareixien trencats i desordenats' (*L'àngel*, p. 245) ('He had broken all the links between the past and the present, the different moments of his life were like the overlapping layers of an open-air archaeological site, where the objects lay broken and in disarray').

As is well known, the cemetery is one of the heterotopias cited by Michel Foucault in his 1967 lecture, 'Des Espaces Autres' ('Of Other Spaces'). In his lecture, Michel Foucault recalls a word, 'heterotopia', which he previously defined in *The Order of Things*, based on a story by Jorge Luis Borges in which the Argentinian writer uses the parable of a Chinese encyclopaedia to illustrate the insufficiency of an arbitrary system such as that of the alphabet to put into order and make sense of the abundance of a totally inaccessible animal reality. This is the point of departure of Michel Foucault's well-known epistemological theory. Herein resides his suspicion that any other taxonomy will be equally implausible, for the very idea of a shared space into which reality can coherently fit, has been shattered. It is in this sense that the French philosopher asserted the disquieting power of heterotopias:

> because they secretly undermine language, because they make it impossible to name this and that ... because they destroy 'syntax' in advance, and not only the syntax with which we construct sentences but also that less apparent syntax which causes words and things (next to and also opposite one another) to 'hold together'.[16]

This is how Gabriel's subversion in the cemetery, disobeying the hygienic and social codes of the individualising practices of the anthropologists and forensic doctors, suggests one of the still-viable pathways of the weak messianic force. The heterotopic space of the cemetery makes the coexistence of heterogeneous temporalities viable, which, according to Jacques Rancière, is typical of the aesthetic regime of the arts. According to Rancière's well-known thesis expressed in *The Distribution of the Sensible*, the aesthetic regime would overwhelm the frames of mimetic representation by inverting the traditional hierarchies of representation, which have historically favoured storylines and themes to the detriment of description or a modality of fragmented focalisation. In fact, the rational linkage of history would have been one of the factors conducive to this traditional hierarchy that has now been destroyed. Once the aesthetic regime has shattered the mimetic representation, the assignment of functions and the distribution of traditional spaces is annulled. The French theoretician categorically asserts this in *The Lost Thread*: 'It is the great democracy of sensible coexistences that revokes the narrowness of the old order of causal consequences and narrative and social proprieties.'[17]

In the case of Julià de Jòdar's novel, the theft of the bones of the foot of an anonymous corpse marks the start of the new calendar of redemption that will hinder the intended orderly assignment of identities by the municipal forensic services. Making it difficult to restore order to the cemetery also implies making it difficult to assign papers on the basis of the condemnatory dialectic between exclusion and integration. As the novel reads, in the centre of the town 's'imposa la voluntat de separar cossos i espais per dur els esperits formalment lliures al recinte on els sentiments hauran de ser compassats amb els interessos particulars' (*L'àngel*, p. 251) ('there is a prevalent desire to separate bodies and spaces in order to bring the formally free spirits to the enclosure where feelings must be weighed up against private interests'). In *L'atzar i les ombres*, the memory of a Catalan working-class neighbourhood that has suffered the repressions of the Franco regime is invoked against this will, with no recognisable strict antinomy between Castilian immigrants and native Catalans that would dissolve or cover up the bourgeois and Francoist status of some and the working-class and anarchist status of others.

Therefore, the image of the open-air archaeological site speaks of a ritual against oblivion that aims to prevent precisely these restitutions that are made thanks to the above-mentioned antinomies of the 'inegalitarian' order, as Jacques Rancière cites: the logic of this unequal order is the explicatory logic that finds a root cause that puts everyone and everything in its place; a reductive cause that provides an understanding and a clarity that is often interpreted as a form of democratic equality, even though it may be nothing more than a self-serving delimitation of time and space, of the visible and the invisible, of speech and noise. In other words, the distribution of the sensible.

As we have seen above, from the perspective of historicism, that basic root cause is determined by the ideology of progress, which, through the criterion of mimetic verisimilitude, forces intelligibility to rest on the rational concatenation of history. The disarray of the corpses that have fallen from their respective niches now reveals everything that can no longer remain hidden. Benjamin updates his statement on the angel of history in his Ninth Thesis: 'Where we perceive a chain of events, he sees one single catastrophe which keeps piling wreckage and hurls it in front of his feet' (Benjamin, 'Theses', p. 257).

Julià de Jòdar himself has explained how his literary project on the memory of the Gorg-Progrés district is a reaction to this rational chain of historicism and its invisibilising effects:

Aquí la qüestió rau en la utilització de les memòries (la individual i la col·lectiva) en la lluita contra l'oblit, o sigui, la mort, com a alçaprem per aixecar la identitat literària, bastida sobre el mite recreat, a la manera del protagonista de la *Recherche*, en competència amb la veritat històricament (col·lectivament) establerta i personalment (míticament) inacceptable . . . La versemblança històrica del projecte literari no seria gaire distinta d'una successió de moments encadenats pel mateix teixit narratiu, defensa i justificació última contra aquella 'arrogància de la Història', que, segons Günter Grass, 'fixa, retrunyent, les seves dates'.[18]

Here the issue resides in the use of memories (individual and collective) in the fight against oblivion. In other words, the struggle to defy death, as a means of leverage to elevate the literary identity, which is founded on the recreated myth, much like the main character of *À la recherche du temps perdu*, in competition with the (collectively) historically established and personally (mythically) unacceptable truth . . . The historic verisimilitude of the literary project would not be very different from a sequence of moments linked together by the same narrative fabric, the ultimate justification and defence against that 'arrogance of History' which, according to Günter Grass, 'sets its dates, by echoing them'.

Gabriel's impulsive gesture of stealing the foot of the corpse at the cemetery is far more than a mere anecdotic mishap. Rather, it is the equivalent of the redemptive eruption of Messianic time that Walter Benjamin called for. The disappearance of the bones from the foot of the corpse that will never completely return to its grave marks a new calendar where time will no longer have the mechanical quality of calculation or computation. Walter Benjamin's 'time of the now' no longer allows the postponement of a future of liberation, but rather enables the co-presence of heterogeneous temporalities in the same present. The cadavers, which are ultimately unclassifiable thanks to Gabriel, will not find a single source of authoritative language that enables them to be conceived as a single, homogeneous, collective body. Now, as occurred in the story of Aunt Eulògia, these bodies will exist in the political realm, in the form of enunciations. However, such enunciations, deprived of legitimate parents, as Rancière suggests, will instigate breach lines, points of disincorporation, in the imaginary collective bodies: 'Ils dessinent ainsi des communautés aléatoires qui contribuent à la formation des collectifs d'énonciation qui remettent en question la distribution des rôles, des territoires et des langages – en bref, de ces sujets politiques qui remettent en cause le partage donné du sensible' ('They form uncertain communities that contribute to the formation of enunciative collectives that call into question the distribution of roles, territories and languages – in a word, the predetermined distribution of the sensible').[19]

This notion of a narrative from the bottom up, as Julià de Jòdar would perhaps put it, is consistent with Rancière's other conviction, according to which the voices of the poor and working classes would be democratic bodies precisely by virtue of their disincorporation, their non-adhesion to the imaginary collective body. They speak outside of an assigned place; they use a language that has not been ascribed to them and they inscribe their actions into a temporality that does not grant them any order other than their own experience of time. They live and express realities and qualities that cannot be interpreted in terms of time or the measures of exceptionality, as required by the ideology of progress and the account of history to make them intelligible: moments in a relentless evolution of capitalism.

Rancière explains all this while contradicting the work of historians. Moreover, in another book, *The Philosopher and His Poor* he additionally disputes the task of sociologists, calling into question the method of the surveys; specifically, the self-serving questions put forth by sociologists. He believes that they simply and repeatedly reinstate the difference between those who 'do not know' and those who 'know' through the methodical suppression of the 'points of meeting and exchange between the people of reproduction and the élite of distinction'.[20] Gabriel, on the other hand, would like to avoid just that. It had been said that he 'seria l'únic noi del barri que no haurà de portar granota' (*El trànsit de les fades*, p. 169) ('would be the only lad in the neighbourhood who will not have to wear overalls'). Additionally, he reproaches his neighbours for treating him as an outsider, as he stands in front of the open-air archaeological site: 'no em vau consentir de viure entre vosaltres i us he portat a viure amb mi' ('you didn't allow me to live among you and I've taken you to live with me'). He, who thought he heard the reproof of the residents of the working-class district of Guifré i Cervantes because he has taken over for Aunt Eulògia, 'que no esperava diners ni fama perquè es limitava a recordar-nos d'on veníem i on havíem arribat' (*L'àngel*, p. 375) ('who expected neither money nor fame, for she limited herself to reminding us of where we had come from and what we had come to'). Hence, Gabriel's voice as an outsider stands up to the view of historians and sociologists precisely because he experiences a fundamental concern about otherness that Jacques Rancière aptly sums up in the preface of *The Philosopher and His Poor*. A preoccupation triggered by a virtually fatal sentence that renders the workers and the poor, those who 'do not know', invisible. Sometimes, because it is said that the 'dominated' class theoretically cannot *on their own* break away from the way of being and thinking that the system of domination has assigned to them. Other times, the condescension manifests itself in the form of prohibition, because they are not allowed to give up their identity and their culture by appropriating the culture and way of thinking of the others. One way or another, historians and sociologists, who are the effective agents of this 'impossibility' and this 'prohibition', have traditionally made it unfeasible to depict a model of coexistence which, far from the logic of integration, is expressed *through the excess of words*: through a different *distribution of the sensible*.

Notes

1 Josep Maria Muñoz, 'Julià de Jòdar o la construcció literària de la memòria', *L'Avenç*, 284 (2003), 59. Unless otherwise stated, all translations from Catalan are mine.
2 Julià de Jòdar, *L'àngel de la segona mort* (Barcelona: Quaderns Crema, 1998), p. 173. See María Dasca, 'Confused Otherness: A Reading of the *L'atzar i les ombres* (1997–2005) trilogy by Julià de Jòdar', in Xabier Payá and Laura Sáez (eds), *National Identities at the Crossroads: Literature, Stage and Visual Media in the Iberian Peninsula* (London: Francis Boutle, 2018), p. 58.
3 Julià de Jòdar, *El trànsit de les fades* (Barcelona: Quaderns Crema, 2001), p. 111.
4 Julià de Jòdar, *Els vulnerables* (Barcelona: Comanegra, 2018), p. 154.
5 Jòdar, *Els vulnerables*, pp. 79–80.
6 Jacques Derrida, *La hospitalidad* (Buenos Aires: Ediciones de la Flor, 2000), pp. 69–75.
7 Ferran Muñoz Jofre, 'Més enllà del Pijoaparte: La ciutat dels marges', *L'Avenç*, 485 (2021), 52.

8   Walter Benjamin, 'Theses on the Philosophy of History', in *Illuminations* (New York: Schocken, 1968), p. 255.
9   Benjamin, 'Theses on the Philosophy of History', p. 261.
10 Walter Benjamin, 'The Storyteller', in *Illuminations* (New York: Schocken, 1968), p. 96.
11 This elderly resident of the neighbourhood, Aunt Eulògia, evokes the mythical figure of the rhapsode. The trilogy begins precisely with a scene in which she is surrounded by the children of Guifré i Cervantes, as she recounts the destruction of the house of El Sorral by the bombs of Italian fascist fighter planes during the Spanish Civil War. The plot of land of El Sorral was later used for the construction of the building that would house El Rancho Grande, the shop owned by Gabriel Caballero's parents. In the very first pages of the book, the relationship between Aunt Eulògia and Gabriel Caballero is established: 'el noi que va prendre el relleu de la tia Eulògia' ('the boy who took over from Aunt Eulògia'): 'La tia Eulògia resta en silenci, i el silenci de la parròquia li retorna la presència de les ombres compartides. Molts anys després, un dels nens que se l'escolten aquest matí xafogós de finals de juny visitarà els fantasmes de la Casa del Sorral per prendre el relleu del record' ('Aunt Eulògia remains silent, and the silence of the parish church returns to her the presence of the shared shadows. Many years later, one of the children who listened to her on that muggy late-June morning would visit the ghosts of the Casa del Sorral to take over the memory'). Julià de Jòdar, *L'àngel de la segona mort*, p. 18.
12 Benjamin, 'Theses', p. 254.
13 Michael Löwy, *Walter Benjamin: Avís d'incendi* (Barcelona: Flâneur, 2020), p. 33.
14 Julià de Jòdar, *El metall impur* (Barcelona: Proa, 2006), p. 423.
15 In an interview, Julià de Jòdar explains that he had based his calculation on the work of historians, and that 60 per cent of the people of Badalona who had been executed at Camp de la Bota were people from his father's town, Vélez de Rubio. Josep Maria Muñoz, 'Julià de Jòdar o la construcció literària de la memòria', *L'Avenç*, 284 (2003), 57–65.
16 Michel Foucault, *The Order of Things: An Archaeology of the Human Sciences* (New York: Vintage, 1994), p. xviii.
17 Jacques Rancière, *The Lost Thread: The Democracy of Modern Fiction* (London: Bloomsbury, 2017), p. 13.
18 Julià de Jòdar, 'Notes sobre memòria col·lectiva i identitat literària', in *Literatura, territori i identitat: La gestió del patrimoni literari a debat* (Girona: Curbet, 2011), p. 129.
19 Jacques Rancière, *Le partage du sensible* (Paris: La Fabrique, 2000), p. 63. My translation.
20 Jacques Rancière, *The Philosopher and His Poor* (Durham NC and London: Duke University Press, 2003), p. 189.

Chapter 3

The Representation of the *forasters* by the Majorcan Literary Generation of the 1970s

Guillem Colom-Montero

When in Majorca, I usually take my bike out with a group of friends to cycle around the island. On a windy yet sunny afternoon in December 2021, we were touring the Pla, a rural county right in the middle of the island, and took a rest in Santa Eugènia, a small town of 1,600 inhabitants. Drinking a bit of water by the village church, one of my friends made friendly chit-chat with an old man, who answered him in Catalan packed with Spanish words, clearly making an effort to speak the island's vernacular language. After a couple of interactions, another friend asked the gentleman in Spanish, with a big smile, '¿de dónde es usted?' ('where are you from?'). The man looked half surprised, half unsurprised, opened his eyes wide, cracked a smile and answered, as though stating the obvious, 'yo . . . yo soy un *foraster*' ('I . . . I'm a *foraster*'). He went on to recount how he had arrived from Extremadura with his parents in 1944 at the age of nine, and settled on the island, forming his own family and working until his retirement in the early 2000s. Despite having spent most of his life in Majorca, the term *foraster* still (self-)defined him. In the Catalan language, *foraster* literally means 'foreigner', as in someone from outside the community, though in Majorca *foraster* is a polyvalent, fluid and historically loaded term with highly relevant sociocultural ramifications.

On the island, *foraster* has traditionally been used to refer to the Castilian language and, by extension, to a Castilian-speaking person.[1] For instance, the *Diccionari Català-Valencià-Balear* states in its third entry that, specifically in Majorca, a *foraster* is a 'Castellà de nació o de llenguatge' ('Castilian by birth or a native Castilian speaker').[2] This particular use of the term *foraster* encapsulates some of the tensions and complexities that define Majorca's cultural identity and its interrelations with Catalonia and Spain. On the one hand, it shows a typical islander tendency to divide people following in-group versus out-group dynamics, which places the island at the centre of a specific worldview. On the other hand, the term *foraster* has not been applied traditionally to Catalan speakers from outside the island, who are generally described by using the generic term 'catalans' or the pertinent demonym, be it 'catalans', 'valencians', 'menorquins', 'eivissencs' or 'formenterencs'.[3] This reveals the pivotal role played by the vernacular language in how Majorcans have historically (self-)defined their cultural identity and the various layers of alterity developed: the in-group are Majorcans, that is, the locals who speak Majorcan Catalan; after this come Catalan speakers from other Catalan-speaking areas; and, finally, those who speak Castilian in its diverse varieties. In the first decades of the twentieth century, a further layer of alterity was developed in relation to Majorca's emerging tourism industry, and the term *estranger* ('foreigner') came to be widely used to refer to someone from outside Spain, usually a tourist or a floating resident.[4]

From the late 1950s onwards, Majorca went through deep economic and sociocultural transformations propelled by the advent of mass tourism. Some 98,081 tourists arrived on the island in 1950, the numbers rose to 361,000 in 1960, to then dramatically increase all through the decade thanks to the Stabilisation Plan approved by the Francoist regime in 1959, reaching 2,849,632 in 1973.[5] Since the local population could not fill all the jobs that the rising tourism industry was creating, thousands of migrants from impoverished, Castilian-speaking areas of Spain (mostly from Andalusia, Extremadura and Castile-La Mancha) relocated to the island to work on tourism-related jobs. Between 1955 and 1975, 82,657 Castilian-speaking migrants arrived in Majorca, whose population rose in the same period from 345,208 to 492,257 inhabitants; in the period 1960–75, migrants accounted for 57 per cent of the Majorcan absolute population growth rate.[6] The exodus of Castilian-speakers to the island in the Francoist context rapidly, radically and unexpectedly reshaped the social and linguistic fabric of the island, in what is one of the most relevant sociocultural changes triggered by the tourist revolution. At the time, the Catalan language was in a minoritised position due to Francoist laws proscribing its use in most public domains and a diglossia that operated historically on the island. Although Castilian was used in formal settings and, therefore, was the language of social development, the majority of the Majorcan population spoke Catalan in their day-to-day life and had only a basic knowledge of Spanish.[7] While Majorcans were used to coexisting with the historically established Castilian-speaking civil servants, high-ranking members of the Spanish army and state security forces, Spanish had not been a commonly spoken language on the island on an everyday basis and, furthermore, incoming migration had not been a feature in Majorca's history.[8] In light of such overwhelming transformations, a process of othering was developed by the local population, who talked about and represented Castilian-speaking migrants through offensive sociocultural constructions focusing on their poverty, deficient education, alleged laziness and lack of manners, as well as emphasising the cultural and linguistic differences. The word *foraster*, which had remained stable until then as a purely descriptive word to signal a geocultural difference with Castilian-speaking Spain, came to be used widely as a derogatory term to refer to any deprived, Castilian-speaking migrant arriving to work in the tourism industry, thus encapsulating the narratives of alterity generated in the context of Majorca's demographic shift.

The transformation of the island due to tourism-orientated dynamics was represented masterfully in a series of novels published by a generation of young authors emerging in the late 1960s and early 1970s, known as the Majorcan Literary Generation of the 1970s. Their novels had an enormous impact and modernised Majorcan literature at a time of rapid social change. The blossoming of a new generation of authors is strongly connected to the overarching impacts of mass tourism on the island; as Pilar Arnau notes, 'la narrativa mallorquina dels setanta neix d'una crisi socioeconòmica de la qual els autors són totalment conscients' ('the Majorcan narrative of the 1970s originates in a socio-economic crisis of which the authors are totally aware').[9] This chapter will focus on the representation of the *forasters* in five of the most emblematic novels of the period: Antònia Vicens's *39° a l'ombra* ('39° in the Shade', 1968), Guillem Frontera's *Els carnissers* ('The Butchers', 1969), Maria Antònia Oliver's *Cròniques d'un mig estiu* ('Chronicles of a Half Summer', 1970), Gabriel Tomàs' *Corbs afamegats* ('Starving Raven', 1972) and Jaume Santandreu's *Camí de Coix* ('Limping Walk', 1980 [written between 1972 and 1978]). These novels offer some of the best accounts to analyse the narratives, tropes and metaphors built around the Castilian-speaking migrants who relocated to Majorca between the mid-1950s and the mid-1970s. To show this, I will first discuss the way in which the texts represent the challenging experience of uprooting their lives and the terrible working and living conditions that the migrants endured. The second part will explore the derogatory discourses and vocabularies deployed against these migrants, as well as the ways in which members of both communities moved beyond such dichotomous constructions and engaged in fulfilling relationships. The final section will focus on the role that language and cultural difference played in the othering of the *forasters*, and I will close the chapter reflecting on how the politics of alterity developed at that historical juncture still condition Majorcan society today.

Forasters: Uprooting, Labour Exploitation and Deplorable Housing Conditions

Antònia Vicens's *39° a l'ombra* was published in 1968. It was awarded the prestigious Premi Sant Jordi de Novel·la in 1967 and was considered the Generation of the 1970s' inaugural novel. Its protagonist, Miquela, is a young woman of humble origin who lost her parents as a child and now lives with her aunt, uncle and cousin Maria in an unnamed Majorcan village in the centre of the island. Miquela and Maria experience an oppressive atmosphere in the house due to the couple's constant fighting and the staunchly religious auntie who is constantly reminding the girls that their role in life is to become suffering wives and mothers. While Maria finds solace in prayers and religion, Miquela is more rebellious and moves to the coast to work in a souvenir shop right in front of a recently built hotel. Told in the first person from Miquela's perspective, the novel focuses on her coming of age and juxtaposes both spaces, 'la vila' and 'la Cala' ('the village and the bay'), combining different moments of the past. Through the contrasting narration of Miquela's experiences, the text relates the poor, depressing and tradition-anchored ethos defining Miquela's village as well as the harsh conditions, exclusions and persistent sexism endured by those working in the tourism industry.

39° a l'ombra opens with Miquela elaborating on how she likes her job at the souvenir shop because she gets to talk with a diverse array of curious people. One such group are the hotel cleaners, who, as the narrative voice tells us on the second page, 'panteixoses de cansament i de calorassa, venien a prendre un refresc... La majoria eren fadrines i forasteres, un poc curtes, treballadores, bones al·lotes' ('breathless due to the exhaustion and high temperatures, came to grab a cold drink . . . Most were single and *forasteres*, a bit dull, hard-working, good girls').[10] Beyond the expression 'un poc curtes', which in Majorca is generally used in a rather affectionate manner, the first sentence describing Castilian-speaking migrants displays a tender instance of female solidarity, highlighting as it does that the young women are nice and hardworking, pointing out the physical harshness of their jobs and the high summer temperatures that they endure. The novel's sensitivity towards migrants' vulnerability is not restricted to these women, as later in the novel Miquela recounts the frustration felt by a group of migrant men who had just arrived in the bay looking for work and were told that all jobs had already been filled. They were totally disheartened, particularly those who had secured contracts the previous year at one of the hotels but, since it was under new management, these were no longer valid – '[n]egocis, paranys' (Vicens, *39° a l'ombra*, p. 35) ('deals, scams'), Miquela adds critically. After this, she elaborates on the men's anguish, on how they were spending their days drinking wine purchased at the souvenir shop '[p]erquè se n'havien de tornar a la seva terra miserable, poblets perduts de la província d'Albaceta [*sic*], havent gastant tot quan tenien. Essent homes, essent forts, i a penes sabent llegir' (p. 35) ('because, having already spent all their money, they had to return to their miserable birthplaces, little towns in the province of Albacete; they were strong men, almost illiterate').

These fragments offer some examples of how *39° a l'ombra* exposes the human pain and misery on which Spain's tourist boom is built. The Castilian-speaking migrants arriving in Majorca had no qualification and in many instances were almost illiterate, coming from the poorest Spanish regions as they did; they were relocating to a distant, linguistically and culturally different island in which they faced high levels of concealed exploitation. As Manuela Aroca Mohedano puts it, '[a] los problemas generalizados del desarraigo y la estacionalidad se añadían condiciones de trabajo casi feudales y una incapacidad para desarrollar protestas o reivindicaciones' ('alongside the generalised problems of uprooting and casual labour, they experienced almost feudal working conditions and the inability to organise protests and push for change').[11] Aroca Mohedano's research shows how their situation was, on the one hand, deliberately ignored by the Spanish Francoist institutions and, on the other, initially overlooked by trade unions, since the hospitality industry was not a traditional sector of working-class organisation in Spain (Aroca Mohedano, *Sindicatos y turismo de masas en las Baleares*, pp. 16–18). The tourist boom, therefore, caused the arrival of 'una población inmigrante desvalida y desatendida' ('a helpless and neglected migrant population'), which became 'los nuevos marginados, el nuevo sector social desfavorecido de Baleares' ('the new marginalised, disadvantaged social group in the Balearics') (p. 89).

The hardships and adversities endured by the migrants are also at the heart of Gabriel Tomàs' *Corbs afamegats* (1972), which focuses its narrative on the interpersonal and labour relations developing on the touristic beaches around Andratx, and offers what is probably the best account of the Castilian-speaking migrants' experience as depicted by the Majorcan Generation of the 1970s. Awarded the Premi Ciutat de Palma de Novel·la in 1970, the book revolves around the tangled relationship between the Majorcan male protagonist, who narrates the novel in the first person, and his Peninsular girlfriend Llúcia. Both work in hotels at the fictional Cala Dofí – he as a kitchen porter, she as a maid – and the book represents most Majorcan characters as rather selfish and unscrupulous, unsympathetic towards the migrants and their tribulations, lacking any kind of human solidarity. By focusing on Llúcia's aims and desires, *Corbs afamegats* depicts the migrants' overall experience through a sad, sombre tone and a matter-of-fact narrative voice that reproduces the locals' perspective and vocabularies in the othering of Peninsular migrants. Descriptions of the terrible working and living conditions are a constant in the novel: bosses who pay less than agreed; hotels who do not register their employees to avoid paying taxes, meaning that, as a result, workers cannot access winter subsidies; and three or four staff members living together all season in a small, unventilated basement room at the hotel where they work, given almost inedible food. At one point in the novel the protagonist relates how some years earlier 'dotzenes d'escamots de *jaeneros*' ('dozens of flocks of *jaeneros*') had formed a shanty town that he used to pass by as a teenager.[12] Describing the scene, he tells us that:

> tenien . . . la carrera bruta de restes del dinar que havien llençat als moixos o a les gallines . . . I una forta olor a bugada corrupta que inflava el nas: hi havia bassiots d'aigua de bugada, amb mosquits i abelles . . . A la porta d'una cotxeria . . . me vaig topar amb tres criatures que em miraven esporuguides, el major devia tenir tres anys, plens de miques de pa i taques negroses als vestidets, bruna la cara, untada de greixum. (Tomàs, *Corbs afamegats*, p. 65)

> the footpath was dirty, packed with the leftovers they had thrown to the cats and chickens. A terrible smell from contaminated laundry reached my nose: dirty puddles of water packed with mosquitoes and bees. By an old garage door, three frightened little ones were staring at me, the oldest must have been three years old; they were dark-skinned, with filthy faces, their small dresses covered in black stains and littered with crumbs.

Reminiscent of Camilo José Cela's *tremendismo*, the imagery deployed to describe the migrants' arrival to the area offers a compelling account of the hardships that they endured as well as of the material basis of the politics of alterity othering them. The vocabularies used to refer to these migrants are also revealing. In the earlier quotation, the narrator uses the term *jaeneros* – literally people from the Andalusian city of Jaén – which was another word used at the time to refer to Castilian-speaking migrants, as was *murcians*, that is, people from Murcia. In most novels they are also called *peninsulars*, a term still in use, which reveals the dichotomous division between Majorca and *la Península*, the latter a word that generally alludes to Castilian-speaking Spain. The migrants, for their part, usually refer to the locals as '*los mallorquines*' (p. 224, italics in original). Such charged, antithetic terms expose how both groups are reduced to their geocultural identities, ultimately revealing the sharp divide between both communities during the first decades of the tourist boom.

Jaume Santandreu's *Camí de coix*, written between 1972 and 1978 and eventually published in 1980 after having won the Premi Ciutat de Palma de Novel·la in 1979, also deploys a strong critique of the dehumanisation caused by the tourism industry. The novel revolves around Joan, a young homosexual man from Palma's upper classes who, after losing his father and later his domineering, staunchly Catholic mother, starts a path of sexual and sociopolitical (self-)exploration. Told in the first person from the protagonist's point of view, the novel is highly influenced by the psychoanalytical perspective *en vogue* during the 1970s and, for this reason, the text is rife with (self-)reflection and sociopolitical commentary. Joan initially travels to Eivissa and has a number of casual sexual encounters that leave him feeling unsatisfied and empty. On returning to Majorca, Joan joins a Catholic group offering help and support to Peninsular migrants and eventually resolves to work in the tourism industry to experience first-hand what they go through. Joan is bewildered to discover, on the one hand, their terrible hardships and, on the other, how indifferent most Majorcans and in particular his own family are towards their suffering. Like *Corbs afamegats*, *Camí de coix* is particularly critical of Majorcans and their reactions to the influx of migrants, though the latter displays better articulated sociopolitical critique. As Joan tells us, he and his parents enjoyed teasing the Peninsular waiters because, as they saw it, these migrants lived like kings, working with smart suits after having left their poor, underdeveloped regions. Right after this, however, Joan points out how wrong he was and reflects, with particularly evocative language, on the fact that, while from the outside the hotels may seem modern and stylish, 'al soterrani . . . es mouen i viuen els esclaus del nostre segle, lluny de la família, fermats dia i nit al servei dels clients, explotats en cadena, menjant les sobres, dormint en solls, cobrant una pixarada' ('the slaves of our century live in the basement, far from their families, tied day and night to serving customers, brutally exploited, eating leftovers, sleeping in pigsties, making peanuts').[13]

The critical representation of migrants' exploitation by Spain's tourism industry during the Francoist period deployed by these three novels is particularly innovative within the Catalan and Spanish cultural contexts. Justin Crumbaugh has analysed how tourism came to symbolise the modernising narratives defining official Francoist discourses about progress and economic growth from 1959 onwards. Through the analysis of 1960s Spanish mainstream cultural products, he argues that '[b]y taking on a life of its own in the cultural imaginary, tourism enabled Franco's Spain to bill itself as a paradise of prosperity, freedom, and efficient planning'.[14] Highlighting how the island of Majorca played a key role in the symbolic edifice built around tourism, Crumbaugh discusses the strong ideological interconnections between Manuel Fraga's *aperturismo* and the sociocultural shifts that tourism was prompting, which in conjunction 'emblematized the "new", "open", "tolerant" Spain promoted through the mass media' (Crumbaugh, *Destination Dictatorship*, p. 51). In contrast to the state-sanctioned cultural products analysed by Crumbaugh, *39° a l'ombra*, *Corbs afamegats* and *Camí de coix* reveal the painful reality endured by Castilian-speaking migrants relocating to Majorca to work in tourism-related jobs and, in so doing, challenge the mainstream celebratory narrative of Spain's economic miracle in the 1960s. Crumbaugh notes how critical representations of tourism were particularly scarce in Spain at the time, with few exceptions such as those by Juan Goytisolo, Max Aub and Manuel Vázquez Montalbán (*Destination Dictatorship*, pp. 3–7). Seen under this light, the novels of the Majorcan Literary Generation of the 1970s emerge as historically significant texts offering a fresh, different perspective, both more human and more humane, of the much-celebrated Spanish tourist boom. Furthermore, their naturalistic depiction of interregional migration to Majorca turns them into highly original texts within the context of Catalan literature. In an essay discussing the memory of immigration in Catalonia, Salvador Cardús finds it 'very significant that in twentieth-century Catalan literature, in particular the Catalan novel, attention is barely paid to the social issues arising from immigration'.[15] In contrast to this, while these three novels have a Majorcan-identified point of view, Castilian-speaking migrants and their experiences are central to their plots and, in the cases of *Corbs afamegats* and *Camí de coix*, migrants are the main characters of the narrative. In view of this, I wish to suggest that the novels published by the Majorcan Literary Generation of the 1970s not only offer alternative accounts of Spain's mass-tourism boom in the 1960s but are also pivotal texts within the Catalan literary system to understand and historicise the post-1950s migrant experience from Castilian-speaking regions to the Catalan countries.

Othering (and Unothering) the *Forasters*

Despite the compassionate depictions discussed above, the novels also represent the disparaging sociocultural narratives deployed against Castilian-speaking migrants. If some lower-class protagonists of *39° a l'ombra* and *Corbs afamegats* display warmth and affection towards the newcomers, Joan's wealthy mother in *Camí de coix* is particularly derogatory, continuously reminding her son that the *forasters* are 'bruts, "fanfarrons", mentiders, baralladissos, "vagos", immorals, corruptors dels nostres costums' (Santandreu, *Camí de coix*, p. 107) ('dirty, braggers, liars, aggressive, lazy, immoral, corrupters of our customs'). The affluent and propertied protagonists of Guillem Frontera's *Els carnissers* express similar ideas. Published in 1969 after having won the Premi Ciutat de Palma the previous year, *Els carnissers* represents the rise of mass tourism in Majorca from a particularly (self-)critical perspective through a Gattopardian plot focusing on the relations and clashes between the provincial landed aristocracy and the new, ascending touristic bourgeoise. Though hardly present in the novel, the *forasters* are insulted a few times by Miquelet, the son of the *nouveau riche* Miquel and Coloma. During a night out, Miquelet and his friends end up in a bar packed with Castilian-speaking migrants, whom Miquelet defines as 'colla d'idiotes alcoholitzats, sifilítics i tuberculosos' ('a gang of syphilitic, tuberculous, idiotic drunkards').[16] These two fragments exemplify how the narratives of alterity developed against Castilian-speaking migrants reproduce the discourses of disease, idleness, moral corruption and alcoholism traditionally used to represent and marginalise poverty-stricken groups.

While the novels illustrate how such discourses were most enthusiastically embraced and circulated by the upper classes, they also show that Majorcans of all social strata engaged in the othering of underprivileged migrants. In one of his deliberations, the narrator of *Corbs afamegats* reflects on the huge shock caused by the arrival of the first Castilian-speaking migrants to his native town in the early 1950s, to subsequently discuss how, twenty years later, the situation has radically changed and the sociocultural differences have been remarkably alleviated (Tomàs, *Corbs afamegats*, p. 141). Nevertheless, he observes how the sociocultural constructions still continue to operate for significant sections of the local population because '[e]ls canvis d'hàbits, però, no han esborrat gens a molta gent del poble l'estampa malanada i ferotge de la primera invasió' (p. 142) ('for many in the village, the changes in behaviour haven't at all erased the miserable and savage perception caused by the first invasion'). The vocabularies deployed here illustrate how local narratives depicted the migrant influx in terms of invasion, almost hinting at an aggression to the native community, thus fostering the dichotomous division of us versus them.

One of the ways in which this sharp divide materialised is in the local community's strong disapproval of mixed marriages, as depicted in two of the novels. The unnamed male protagonist of *Corbs afamegats* tells us that his girlfriend Llúcia is pregnant, and she wants to meet his family and eventually get married. By contrast, he is pushing for an abortion, on the one hand, because he is not in love with her but also, on the other hand, because he does not feel like introducing her to his family, friends and the wider community in his village, since 'encara al poble preval l'opinió que casar-se amb una forastera és com aplegar-se amb el més tirat que es passeja' (p. 140) ('in the town the view still prevails that marrying a *forastera* is like getting involved with the lowest of the low'). Similar narratives are presented in *39° a l'ombra*, in which a female friend of Miquela is dating a Peninsular migrant and, as she confides to her, '[m]u mare em diu: "I ara et casaries amb un foraster?, voldries mesclar-te amb aquesta xurma?" "Es forasters són persones, mu mare – li dic"' (Vicens, *39° a l'ombra*, pp. 68–9) ('my mum tells me: "Would you marry a *foraster*?, would you get involved with this riff-raff?" "The *forasters* are people, mum", I tell her'). The examples analysed in this section reveal the classism at the core of the politics of alterity affecting Peninsular migrants and hint at the uncertainty generated by a deep and rapid sociocultural change. Drawing on Homi Bhabha's *The Location of Culture* (1994),[17] I would argue that the stereotypes, images and vocabularies built around the *forasters* suggest a discursive articulation of forms of sociocultural and geographical hierarchisation which reveal the unbalanced relations of power between both social groups at that particular historical juncture. In other words, such narratives can be seen as a mode of discursive discrimination aiming to articulate enclosed sociocultural spaces by othering a specific migrant group because the stability and cultural homogeneity of the community is felt to be under threat. Ultimately, the narratives dividing *mallorquins* versus *forasters* can be seen as a way to articulate sociocultural dissimilarity as insurmountable radical difference.

Central to the anxieties about intercommunity marriages were cultural constructions about the sexuality of the female migrant. The advent of mass tourism in Majorca prompted a sexual revolution for islander men, who were able to seek sporadic romances with female tourists. In his analysis of tourism in 1960s Spain, Crumbaugh talks about the 'fixation on sexual transgression with tourists' (*Destination Dictatorship*, p. 11) and the 'mass culture cliché of freewheeling foreign women' (p. 35) deployed in Spanish films of the time, which generated the trope of the *macho ibérico*. Tellingly, in relation to cultural and identity difference between Majorca and Spain, while the *macho ibérico* motif is overwhelmingly present in Majorca's sociocultural imaginaries, the term coined on the island was not *macho ibérico* but the local *picador* – a polysemic word stemming from the verb *picar*, which in context means 'to chip off' or 'to peck at' in reference to the *picadors*' relentless attempts to pick up female tourists. Antoni Colom points out the markedly distinct differences due to gender at the time, recounting how young Majorcan women had to be back at their parents' at ten o'clock in the evening, while local men, after dropping their girlfriends off, went out to the nightclubs to try hooking up with foreign tourists.[18] The novels depict precisely how, following the patriarchal model of Francoist Spain, female sexuality was controlled by the family and local community. In *39° a l'ombra*, for instance, her aunt tells Miquela and Maria that, although young men may already be courting them, they should be good, industrious girls because '[u]n homo [*sic*], quan se vol casar, cerca una al·lota fenera [*sic*]; ara, per divertir-se, tant li fa que sia embambada' (Vicens, *39° a l'ombra*, p. 9) ('when a man wants to marry, he looks for a hard-working woman; now, when he wants have fun, he doesn't care if she's a bit woolly-headed'). This discourse contrasts with the freedoms around casual sex that the community allows for men, as represented, for example, in *Els carnissers*: the devout Coloma, Miquelet's mother, tells an acquaintance that she wants him to find a local girlfriend, but he prefers going out with tourists, and she condones it stating that 'Tanmateix ¿què li has de fer? Ara són joves, que es divertesquin' (Frontera, *Els carnissers*, p. 48) ('Oh well, anyways, what can you do? They're young now, they should have fun').

In contrast to local Majorcan women, female migrants were usually far away from their family and community and, as a result, their sexuality was not so tightly controlled. This led to narratives about them being more sexually free and transgressive, as shown in *39° a l'ombra*, in which the Majorcan female protagonist talks about Socors, a Peninsular hotel maid, and tells us, 'jo havia sentit dir que eren pocs els vespres que no es colgava amb qualque cambrer' (Vicens, *39° a l'ombra*, p. 25) ('I had heard that it was a rare night that she didn't sleep with one of the waiters'). Nonetheless, the narrator later confesses to feeling sexually constrained and self-conscious, and mulls over that 'm'he de posar bikini, he d'anar a la platja, a colrar-me, he de fer beneitures com fan les cambreres, les turistes' (p. 43) ('I should wear a bikini, go to the beach and get tanned, be frivolous like the hotel cleaners and the tourists'). Her setting apart of Majorcan women from migrants and tourists brings to the fore the limitations that the community placed on the former group of women. The male narrator of *Corbs afamegats*, for his part, observes how, from the very first day, 'Llúcia em donà proves al llit d'un geni i d'un temperament poc freqüents' ('in bed Llúcia showed a rather unusual temperament and disposition', and says that '[e]ls peninsulars de naturalesa són de casta sexual més calenta que no els mallorquins' ('Peninsulars are by their very nature sexually hotter and more passionate than Majorcans') (Tomàs, *Corbs afamegats*, p. 45). Beyond the patriarchal stereotypes, this quotation reveals the orientalising nature of the sexual discourses built around Castilian-speaking migrants, which suggests a traditional division between mind and body. Discourses around migrants' sexuality may have also contributed to the social panic felt by older Majorcans vis-à-vis intercommunity marriages, particularly given how the previously quoted excerpts about matrimony suggest a clear generational gap in the perception of family relationships between locals and migrants.

Corbs afamegats reveals how mixed marriages were key in questioning the politics of alterity dividing *mallorquins* and *forasters*. The novel comes with an epilogue narrating how a local Majorcan male character confronts his family and marries a Castilian-speaking migrant, thus offering a particularly relevant fictional chronicle of the tropes built around such unions and how younger generations challenged them. The couple are Pere, the only son of a small landowner family in Andratx, and the Murcian Amàlia, the young widow of a Castilian-speaking migrant. Whereas his family wanted him to study, Pere had always preferred to work the land and meets Amàlia precisely in the mountains, where she lives in a little hut with her sister's family and works at a bar in Cala Dofí during the summer period. Pere and Amàlia start dating and the news quickly reaches the ears of Madò Magdalena, Pere's mother, who feels dismayed and soon starts pulling strings to stop the relationship. Despite her efforts, Pere and Amàlia fall in love and relish every minute that they spend together. Months later, Amàlia's sister gives birth to a daughter and her baptism celebration is attended by numerous migrant acquaintances as well as by three Majorcans: Pere and two female friends of Amàlia – as pointed out by the narrative voice, 'eren els tres únics mallorquins a la festa; la resta del batalló eren *jaeneros*' (Tomàs, *Corbs afamegats*, p. 222) ('they were the only three Majorcans at the party; the others were all *jaeneros*'). This illustrates how, beyond working together in the tourism industry, Majorcans and migrants lived rather segregated lives, generally not sharing common social spaces or joining in celebrations together. At the same time, it exemplifies how certain individuals from the local community challenged such a sharp divide. On discovering that Pere had attended the christening ceremony, Madò Magdalena is enraged and feels utterly ashamed. Days later she discovers that Amàlia is a widow and faints out of shock. When she comes round, Madò Magdalena recounts to her husband and son how, in her dream, an angel has told her that, after the marriage, the *jaeneros* are plotting to kill Pere and all his family in order to 'fer-se amb les terres i els diners' (p. 234) ('get hold of the lands and money'). Madò Magdalena's worries suggest that the tensions and anxieties among Majorcan wealthy classes were not only cultural but also, or even ultimately, material. Although his mother repeatedly begs Pere to end the relationship, he defies her and a few months later they get married, spending their honeymoon travelling through Majorca because Amàlia does not have any family left 'a la península' (pp. 236–7) ('in the Peninsula').

The book's closing scene depicts the newly married couple lying in a fresh-grass field, kissing and embracing each other. As the narrator describes, the lively smell 'restituïa en Pere a una infantesa llunyana i oberta, a un món on tot podia recomençar.

Un món divers, renovellat' (p. 239) ('made Pere recall a distant, open childhood, a world in which everything could start again. A diverse, reinvigorated world'). By way of contrast to the sad, depressing stories told in the book, the epilogue and its ending are particularly uplifting, which suggests two interrelated readings. First, it shows that, beyond the suffering and exploitation, Castilian-speaking migrants in general were steadily able to build a new life on the island, eventually improving their living conditions. In relation to this, it is significant that Amàlia has no family left in mainland Spain, her sister also lives in Majorca, both of them now permanently established on the island, which clearly indicates that they will not return to Murcia. Second, and relatedly, it illustrates how both communities were gradually intermingling and, in so doing, calling into question, even leaving behind, the stereotypes that othered Castilian-speaking migrants. Tellingly, the novel's closing sentences hint at narratives of renewal, openness and diversity, which celebrate the intermixing of both communities. Similar narratives are deployed in *Camí de coix*, wherein a key thread running through the plot is the protagonist's joining of a Catholic sociopolitical group to support those working in the tourism industry. As Aroca Mohedano has noted, these groups were key to the improvement of the labourers' conditions. One of their main projects was the *acolliments*, a kind of social centre where workers could rest and socialise after their shifts, as well as discuss their work concerns and organise activities to demand improvements.[19] In his *acolliment*, the main character in *Camí de coix* meets socially and politically minded people, both local Majorcans and Castilian-speaking migrants who engage together in sociopolitical activism. These projects were strictly controlled and in some instances repressed by the Francoist police forces (Aroca Mohedano, *Sindicatos y turismo de masas*, pp. 112–23, 163–73), a point that emerges as particularly relevant for this chapter because historian David Ginard has recently argued that Francoist laws and restrictions preventing workers and community organisation favoured, even promoted, the social and cultural division between *mallorquins* and *forasters*.[20] Accordingly, *Camí de coix* illustrates, on the one hand, how the lack of strong sociopolitical and community organisations was a key hindrance to articulating shared spaces and narratives between locals and migrants and, on the other hand, how despite the repression, some individuals engaged in such activism and, consequently, contributed to questioning the politics of alterity dividing both communities.

Forasters: Language and Cultural Difference

While class difference was probably the key factor in the othering of the *forasters*, there is little denying that the linguistic and cultural difference between Majorcans and incoming Castilian-speaking migrants should be considered in order to fully grasp the politics of alterity. The tourism-led demographic transformation taking place in Majorca from the early 1960s onwards is considered the starting point of the still-ongoing decline experienced by the Catalan language on the island. The historically diglossic situation was quickly followed by a unidirectional bilingualism in which Spanish was the language to be used with anyone who was not a native Catalan speaker, whether they were a Castilian-speaking migrant or a tourist.[21] This state of affairs stemmed from Majorcans' alienation from their vernacular language as a result of Spain's history of enforced monolingualism and the Francoist veto on the use of Catalan language in public and formal settings. Moreover, Castilian-speaking migrants in general were not particularly willing to learn Catalan, due in no small part to Francoist public discourses on regional vernacular languages. As Arnau concludes, '[l]a gran onada immigrant no feu més que accentuar una situació sociolingüística molt favorable al castellà i força negativa al català. L'actitud d'autòctons i immigrants contribuí a la substitució lingüística' ('the great migrant influx only accelerated a sociolinguistic situation very favourable to Castilian and significantly negative for Catalan. Locals' and migrants' attitudes contributed to the process of language substitution').[22]

The tensions and anxieties stemming from Majorca's linguistic shift are present in all the novels that I consider here. Maria Antònia Oliver's *Cròniques d'un mig estiu*, published in 1970, tells the story of a twelve-year-old boy of humble background from the island's interior, whose mother passes away and who is sent by his father to work as a bellboy in a hotel on the coast. Told as a first-person interior monologue in the present tense from the boy's naïve perspective, the novel narrates the sociocultural shock experienced by the young protagonist, and language difference emerges as a pivotal element of this shock. Even as early as on the second page, the boy relates how he struggles to express himself in Spanish with the hotel workers: 'No en sé, de parlar foraster, jo, sa llengua se me trava, i no hi ha manera, m'embull i m'embull' ('I can't speak *foraster*, I get tongue-tied and I stumble over my words again and again, I just can't do it).[23] On the next page, the boy ingenuously dreams about his plan to become rich with the money that he is making. Then, as he tells us, 'aprendré a parlar castellà, millor que es senyor de Son Vall, i podré anar a Barcelona i a Madrid com ell, a passejar, i entendré tothom i tothom m'entendrà' (Oliver, *Cròniques d'un mig estiu*, p. 9) ('I'll learn to speak Spanish, I'll speak it better than the *senyor* of Son Vall, and then I'll be able to travel and stroll through Barcelona and Madrid as he does, and I'll understand everybody and everybody will understand me'). The boy's reflections illustrate, on the one hand, the huge challenge that speaking Spanish posed to most Majorcans, who were almost monolingual in Catalan and had to quickly adapt to the new sociolinguistic situation; on the other hand, his awareness of the connection between the ability to speak Spanish and social progression exposes the historical oppression of the Catalan language on the island.

The protagonist of *Camí de coix* also reflects on his language experience in Majorca's tourism industry. Not a single word of Catalan is heard on the bus that he takes to go to his first work interview and, in the hotel's kitchen, '[c]om a l'autobús, seguia imperant la llengua oficial' (Santandreu, *Camí de coix*, pp. 106–10) ('just like on the bus, the official language prevailed'). In the interview, he introduces himself in Catalan and, since the head chef was a local Majorcan, the conversation continues in Catalan. The chef, however, 'quan digué "lavaplatos", es passà al castellà. Llengua que no abandonà durant tota l'estalviadora xerrada, tot i que jo lo seguia servint el meu mot en mallorquí' (p. 113) ('on saying "kitchen porter" turned to Spanish and continued with the pointless interview in that language, although I kept on speaking Majorcan'). These examples reveal the complex linguistic power-relations defining the tourist boom in Majorca. The island's vernacular language was a potent symbolic and affective source of cultural identity that suddenly entered into crisis due to Majorca's demographic transformation. Spanish was not only the language of the socially marginalised migrant population, but also the language that the

Francoist state was imposing on the island's native population – it is not accidental that the narrator refers to the language spoken by Peninsular migrants as 'la llengua oficial', thus bringing to the fore how complex the imbalanced relations of power between Spanish and Catalan were on the island at the time. The interview further illustrates how, for many Majorcans, the vernacular language was not considered suitable for use in tourism settings, which reveals how the tourism revolution significantly accelerated the historical alienation experienced by Majorcan speakers. Considering that tourism narratives in the 1960s powerfully promoted Spanish national-identity building,[24] there is little doubt that the tourist boom and associated migration movements turned out to be a key factor in the decline of Catalan on the island; in linguistic terms, therefore, the marginalised group were the local Majorcans. In light of this, I would like to suggest that, if Castilian-speaking migrants endured an episode of geographical and cultural displacement, the native Majorcan population, on their part, went through an experience of linguistic displacement. Such experience cannot be extricated from the distinctive characteristics that defined the demographic and language shifts following the advent of mass tourism on the island, as noted by linguist Hans-Ingo Radatz:

> la llegada del español como lengua hablada y cotidiana fue en Mallorca un proceso mucho más rápido y traumatizante que en cualquier lugar del Principado de Cataluña. Hasta bien entrados los años cincuenta del siglo XX, la proporción de peninsulares hispanohablantes era insignificante en la población de Mallorca.[25]

> the emergence of Spanish as an everyday spoken language in Majorca was a significantly quicker and more traumatising process than anywhere else in Catalonia. Until well into the 1950s, the ratio of Castilian-speakers from the Iberian Peninsula was insignificant amongst the Majorcan population.

This quotation points to two key aspects to help understand the linguistic and sociocultural ramifications of Castilian-speaking migration to Majorca. In the first place, Radatz's juxtaposition of Majorca and Catalonia is very pertinent, as both regions have an entirely different history of migration and comparing them offers a productive context through which the politics of alterity developed in Majorca can be understood. Catalonia has historically been a migration-receiving region, in particular from the late nineteenth century onwards, to the point that Cardús has defined it as 'a country of immigrants', pointing out the quantitative, temporal and qualitative effects.[26] As Francesc Candel notes in *Els altres catalans* (1964), those relocating to Catalonia in the Francoist period had previous models of integration that contributed to the development of shared narratives of belonging to the region.[27] Conversely, this chapter has shown how Castilian-speaking migration to Majorca was a sudden, quick and unexpected mass process starting only around the mid-1950s. Hence, migrants did not have access to previous models of integration and were instead met by a society feeling the threat of linguistic and cultural substitution. This takes us to another crucial difference between Catalonia and Majorca. The former was a relatively cohesive society with a strong, consolidated linguistic and cultural identity, which created the conditions for the publication of Candel's reflections on how to articulate migrants' identities and their sense of belonging to the region. In contrast, Majorca's cultural identity and sense of difference was significantly more fractured and disjointed, with conflictive debates about its linguistic and cultural tradition resulting from the competing Spanish and Catalan national(ist) discourses. It was precisely in 1964 when the politician and author Josep Melià finished the manuscript of the celebrated *Els mallorquins*, a text that offered a historic reflection on Majorcan's national identity as a Catalan-speaking region following the example of Joan Fuster's *Nosaltres els valencians* (1962). Therefore, while Catalonia was seeing debates about the importance of recognising and incorporating migrants' identities, Majorcan intellectuals were still aiming to define, historicise and articulate a cohesive sense of linguistic and cultural identity. This marked contrast helps to contextualise and explain the absence of first-hand narratives produced in Majorca about the migrant experience of the late Francoist period.

In the second instance, it is telling that Radatz uses the term 'traumatizante' to describe the linguistic impact of Castilian-speaking migration to Majorca, as I have posited elsewhere that mass tourism on the island has caused an experience of cultural trauma. Through the analysis of various cultural products, I have argued that the advent of mass tourism has been represented 'as the trigger of a sudden, comprehensive, unexpected and socially polarizing episode of sociocultural and environmental change' in ways that suggest a culturally traumatic experience.[28] Extending this line of analysis, I wish to argue that the dichotomous division between *mallorquins* and *forasters* initiated in the 1950s is a constitutive element of this ongoing cultural trauma. Although from the 1980s onwards the term *foraster* gradually lost the pejorative connotations that it had acquired during the tourist boom, the anecdote that opens this chapter illustrates that the division between *mallorquins* and *forasters* still operates on the island, socioculturally dividing its population up to the present day.

This topic has recently been discussed by a young generation of Majorcan intellectuals in the collectively authored essay *Somnis compartits: La identitat mallorquina a debat*, published in 2016 with the aim of modernising nationalist discourses on the island, which, according to the authors, is still a broken, disjointed society lacking common narratives of belonging and purpose.[29] They argue that one of the main causes behind this situation is the lack of discourses that integrate and recognise the role of Castilian-speaking migrants in Majorca's recent history, and point out how the persistent presence of the concept of *foraster* in the Majorcan imaginary is an obvious obstacle to developing common projects with the Castilian-speaking population.[30] Overall, no dynamic, bidirectional process of recognition and reckoning has been developed in Majorca and, consequently, there is no Majorcan-centred myth about the Castilian-speaking migration to the island, which is a significant hindrance and a weakness in social, cultural and political terms. In light of this, there is little denying that the novels analysed in this chapter can be seen as innovative literary creations illustrating how the authors of the Majorcan Literary Generation of the 1970s already acknowledged the relevance of integrating migrants' experiences and narratives into Majorcan culture. As such, they are essential texts that must be considered when articulating Majorca's history of migration in the Francoist period and crafting new metaphors that recognise the contribution of Castilian-speaking migrants.

Notes

1 Lucas Duane, 'Castilian Takes Backstage in the Balearic Islands: The Activation of Castilian Standardization Recursions in Facebook',

Journal of Linguistic Anthropology, 27/1 (2017), 80; Bel Peñarrubia, *Mallorca davant el centralisme (1868–1910)* (Barcelona: Curial, 2006), pp. 113–18; Hans-Ingo Radatz, '*Castellorquín*: el castellano hablado por los mallorquines', in Carsten Sinner and Andreas Wesch (eds), *El castellano en las tierras de habla catalana* (Madrid: Iberoamericana, 2008), pp. 113–14; Jackie Waldren, 'Crossing Over: Mixing, Matching and Marriage in Mallorca', in Rosemary Breger and Rosanna Hill (eds), *Cross-Cultural Marriage: Identity and Choice* (Oxford and New York: Routledge, 1998), p. 37.

2 'Foraster', in *Diccionari Català-Valencià-Balear*, Antoni Maria Alcover, Francesc de Borja Moll, Manuel Sanchis i Guarner and Aina Moll (Barcelona: Institut d'Estudis Catalans), *https://dcvb.iec.cat/*. Unless otherwise stated, all translations from Catalan and Spanish are mine.

3 Guy de Forestier, *Queridos mallorquines: Claves del trato personal en la isla de Mallorca* (Palma: La Foradada, 1995), p. 23; Guillem Frontera, 'Mallorquins, forasters i forasteristes', *Ara Balears* (24 May 2013), *www.ara.cat/opinio/mallorquins-forasters-forasteristes_129_2293407.html*; Maria de la Pau Janer, *Mallorca, l'illa de les mil i una nits: Carta a un estranger que ens visita* (Barcelona: Columna, 2011), pp. 54–6; Peñarrubia, *Mallorca davant el centralisme*, p. 83.

4 de Forestier, *Queridos mallorquines*, p. 23; Waldren, 'Crossing Over', p. 37.

5 Bartomeu Barceló, 'Història del turisme a Mallorca', *Treballs de la Societat Catalana de Geografia*, 50 (2000), 42.

6 Pilar Arnau, *Narrativa i turisme a Mallorca* (Palma: Documenta Balear, 1999), p. 46; Barceló, 'Història del turisme a Mallorca', p. 43; Radatz, '*Castellorquín*', p. 114.

7 Antoni I. Alomar, *La llengua catalana a les Balears en el segle XX* (Palma: Documenta Balear, 2002), pp. 53–5.

8 Carles Manera, 'Història del creixement econòmic a Mallorca, 1700–2000', *Anuari, Societat Catalana d'Economia* 19 (2011), 77–9.

9 Arnau, *Narrativa i turisme a Mallorca*, p. 19.

10 Antònia Vicens, *39° a l'ombra* (Barcelona: Edicions 62, 2002), p. 8.

11 Manuela Aroca Mohedano, *Sindicatos y turismo de masas en las Baleares: Del Franquismo a la democracia* (Palma: Documenta Balear, 2018), p. 42.

12 Gabriel Tomàs, *Corbs afamegats* (Palma: Nova Editorial Moll, 2020), p. 61 (italics in original).

13 Jaume Santandreu, *Camí de coix* (Palma: Editorial Moll, 1980), p. 117.

14 Justin Crumbaugh, *Destination Dictatorship: The Spectacle of Spain's Tourist Boom and the Reinvention of Difference* (Albany NY: State University of New York, 2009), p. 16.

15 Salvador Cardús i Ros, 'The Memory of Immigration in Catalan Nationalism', *International Journal of Iberian Studies*, 18/1 (2005), 41–2.

16 Guillem Frontera, *Els carnissers* (Barcelona, Club Editor, 2016), p. 134.
17 Homi Bhabha, *The Location of Culture* (London and New York: Routledge, 2004), pp. 96–9.
18 Antoni Colom Cañellas, 'Pròleg', in Toni Morlà, *Memòries d'un brusquer: Diccionari dels anys 60 i 70* (Palma: Clayton's Book, 2001), p. 11
19 Aroca Mohedano, *Sindicatos y turismo de masas*, p. 101.
20 David Ginard, 'Pròleg', in Aroca Mohedano, *Sindicatos y turismo de masas en las Baleares*, pp. 9–11.
21 Arnau, *Narrativa i turisme*, p. 51.
22 Arnau, *Narrativa i turisme*, p. 52.
23 Maria Antònia Oliver, *Cròniques d'un mig estiu* (Barcelona: Club Editor, 2006), p. 8.
24 Eugenia Afinoguénova and Jaume Martí-Olivella, 'Introduction: A Nation under Tourist's Eyes: Tourism and Identity Discourses in Spain', in Eugenia Afiguénova and Jaume Martí-Olivella (eds), *Spain is (Still) Different: Tourism and Discourse in Spanish Identity* (Lanham MD: Lexington Books, 2008), pp. xi–xv; Crumbaugh, *Destination Dictatorship*, p. 52.
25 Radatz, '*Castellorquín*', p. 114.
26 Cardús i Ros, 'The Memory of Immigration in Catalan Nationalism', 37.
27 Francesc Candel, *Els altres catalans* (Barcelona: Edicions 62, 2008), pp. 34–6, 53–5.
28 Guillem Colom-Montero, 'Mass Tourism as Cultural Trauma: An Analysis of the Majorcan Comics *Els darrers dies de l'Imperi Mallorquí* (2014) and *Un infern a Mallorca (La decadència de l'Imperi Mallorquí)* (2018)', *Studies in Comics*, 10/1 (2019), 51.
29 Joan-Pau Jordà, Joan Colom and Gabriel Mayol, *Somnis compartits. La identitat mallorquina a debat* (Palma: Documenta Balear, 2016), pp. 11–3.
30 Jordà, Colom and Mayol, *Somnis compartits*, p. 110–1.

Part II

Spaces, Borders and Memory

Chapter 4

To Speak the Unspeakable: Francesc Candel and the Trespass of Borders

Olga Sendra Ferrer

In the prologue to the 2008 edition of *Els altres catalans* ('The Other Catalans', 1964), Najat El Hachmi denounces the limited context in which Candel's work has been read. Although she seeks to show us how this book is as pertinent now as it was in the moment that it was written, El Hachmi notices how Candel's book is usually limited to 'un catalanisme reduccionista' ('a reductionist Catalanism'), characterised by a process of national identification and inclusion.[1] This critique – which she proceeds to dismantle, although not in detail, by referencing the complexities of *Els altres Catalans* – announces a conceptual rupture that Candel starts with *Donde la ciudad cambia su nombre* ('Where the City Changes Its Name', 1957) and *Han matado a un hombre, han roto un paisaje* ('A Man Has Been Killed, A Landscape Has Been Broken', 1959).[2] Instead of defining a new idea of what Catalunya or Barcelona is, he ruptures the idea of borders, establishing the possibility of a multinational identity, of an urban citizenship that starts to redefine the project of nation-building. Hence, his books are full of transitions, full of trespasses: geographic, visual, cultural and linguistic, all of which destabilise the idea of frontier, creating an interstice that redefines what it is to be Spanish and what it is to be Catalan, not only under the Franco dictatorship, but also later, as he follows the development of the Catalan city through the decades, connecting with writers like El Hachmi. In other words, Candel writes a continuous history of the city and immigration that questions and defines the limits of national and cultural construction.[3] Consequently, this chapter seeks to reframe Candel's work in a genealogical space that forges a new type of literature, a multisensorial narrative, through the direct experience of the suburban residents, becoming a contact zone that, years later, will set the stage for the work of authors like El Hachmi.[4]

There is a photograph of Francesc Candel, taken by Xavier Miserachs in 1965, that portrays Candel's trespass. In this photograph we see Candel, dressed in a suit and tie, walking through the shanties of the Riera Comtal. His clothing is elegant without being too fancy, signalling formality but by no means wealth. The ground is unpaved, and in the background we can see a shanty built with random pieces of wood and a roof made of stones and other rubbish used to hold it all in place. A child plays with a dog. In this image, as in everyday life, we have multiple levels of engagement acting simultaneously: the everyday nature of life in the suburbs; Candel's personal experience in direct contact with his surroundings and the people who live there; and the experience of the photographer as an outside entity who is behind the lens and who, although not in the photo himself, is always manifestly present by framing what does appear in the photograph. This act of framing reproduces the relationship between city and suburb, replicating how the city imposes discourses, or frames, that form and define the suburbs. Be that as it may, what I am interested in examining here is how Candel directs our gaze, makes us turn our heads and take a good look at the other side of Barcelona, the unseen side. In both this photograph as well as his own writing, Candel is the point of articulation, the trigger for a dialectical relationship that begins to take shape with the publication of *Donde la ciudad cambia su nombre* and will reach its culmination, but not its conclusion, with *Els altres catalans*.

By making us look, by directing our gaze, Candel enacts a change of register. The touristic monumentality that began to appear during the developmentalism of the 1960s is supplanted by the uncontrolled actions of the residents of the suburbs, made materially manifest like the shanties where they live, in the contradictory bits of lived experience that we see reflected in the multiple ways of viewing the image: the photograph is for us, people who do not live in the suburbs, either in terms of space or time, and it is also a critique of the polis, which both ignores and scorns urban disorder, be it physical, social, cultural or political. But more importantly still, the photograph is also for the inhabitants of the suburbs. While it is plausible to posit that, like the child playing with the dog, they are unaware of the presence of the camera, its operator and the resulting published image, this is indeed not the case. As in this photo, Candel becomes the point of connection, the interstice that opens a scar that allows us to look into that other place in the city, but more importantly, he gives residents of the suburbs a point of reference, a loudspeaker that amplifies the voices that are buried under the crushing order of the city. 'Aquests veïns m'han cridat perquè parli damunt el paper de llur situació' ('These neighbours have called on me to say it on paper'), Candel writes.[5] Perhaps the suburbs never see this particular photograph *per se*, but they do see Candel and, together with him, another way of being seen and heard: not as a visual disturbance or noise that must be silenced, but rather as a community that belongs to and builds the space of the city.[6]

And so, Candel speaks the unspeakable: it is not just a matter of what Miserachs set out to capture, or what we see, whoever we are, or how the city imposes itself on the suburbs. It is all that complexity and more, what El Hachmi calls 'les asprors' ('the brusqueness'), the confluence of tensions and contradictions created by this contact.[7] With Candel's voice and memory, just as in this photograph, the simulacrum of the contrived coherence of a unique and homogenous identity breaks down and can go no further. Moreover, the production of centralised identities that favours a political and cultural urban project later tied to the concept of Catalan identity is thrown into question, producing a conceptual rupture that redefines urban space and the identity of the suburbs, hailing the latter's potential and rejecting the social and cultural limitations forced on them by the Francoist state.[8] Here, Candel questions the idea of Catalan identity, marking how it is inextricably linked to the construction of a community-based identity manifested on multiple levels: neighbourhood, city and a new pluralistic country.

Candel's narrative, just like his physical body in this photograph, is produced against a backdrop that gives it context and must therefore be accounted for, although by no means as a way to limit our perspective when reading his work. The combination of the internal migratory movements characteristic of the population changes occurring vigorously in Spain from the 1950s onwards,[9] with a Catalan identity discourse that demographers such as Andreu Domingo even go so far as to characterise as eugenic, establishes a climate of suspicion and fear about the denationalisation of Catalunya.[10] This discourse originates before the Civil War and will continue to evolve and, of course, become ever more complex: as Domingo explains,[11] Vandellós's argument incorporates diverse traditions, spawning ambivalent attitudes, such as that of Jaume Vicens Vives, who differentiated between the Valencian and Aragonese migrants of the nineteenth century that readily accepted what the Catalan people taught them, while others, notably Murcians, were described as mass invaders.[12] Consequently, *Els altres* has been read mainly as a direct response to these questions.[13] Candel, of course, does keep these questions in the foreground, writing and structuring *Els altres* around them.[14] His direct references to Josep Antoni Vandellós (Candel, *Els altres*, pp. 74, 131 and 346) or comments that take up the nationalistic opinions of the day – 'No tingueu por, que de tot això no en sortirà pas una Catalunya híbrida o succedània' (*Els altres*, p. 38) ('Fear not; a hybrid or ersatz Catalonia will not emerge from all of this') – show how Candel dialogues directly with those interlocutors and is aware of the discursive trends that mould the idea of Catalonia and directly affect the characterisation of immigrants or suburban residents. In the context of these discussions, *Els altres* is made relevant by its reformulation of Catalan identity and its culture through the figure of the immigrant, who becomes the protagonist in the construction of said project.[15] What we are interested in highlighting here, however, is this point of convergence and dialogue, not only because of how it marks and defines the construction of Catalan identity, but also because of how it comes to represent the processes of social interaction among immigrants and inhabitants of Barcelona's suburbs, both in the 1950s and 1960s and even today. This dialogue is predicated on conflict and the dialectical structuring already built into urban organisation of Barcelona. If we approach Candel's work in terms of this dialectic, what stands out is the dissolution of borders, the creation of an interstice where diverse worlds and narratives interact. It is through this encounter that Candel initiates a process of identity construction that does not just limit itself to the 'reductionist Catalanism' referenced by

El Hachmi; rather, he focuses on the construction of a community in which suburban residents see themselves reflected. An important part of this reflection is the residents' acknowledgement of their own agency and acceptance of their own legitimate claim on their place in the city and, consequently, on the basic needs and social and civil rights that make them fully fledged citizens, a cornerstone of Candel's identity-building practice.

Identity and Space

Candel is conscious of the connection between ideology and city that takes root here, and he plays with it in both his novels and essays. Already in *Donde la ciudad cambia su nombre* he shows how the city, to borrow Manuel Delgado's words, is manipulated in order to argue for and reinforce the symbolism of an ideology of identity that is artificially propped up by the political powers that be.[16] Here we see an example:

> La populosa barriada de las Casas Baratas o Eduardo Aunós, que suena mucho mejor, consta de veintiuna calles. Así (disimulen, por favor):[17]. . . Medio aparrillada. Como un San Lorenzo del Escorial, pero menos.
> Antes estaban numeradas. Calle 1, calle 2, calle 3, calle 4, hasta 21. Sonaban a prisión o a Nueva York estos números. Ahora les han puesto nombres. Unos nombres catalanes, unos enrevesados nombres catalanes, más enrevesados aún para las estropajosas lenguas murcianas de sus moradores. (*Donde la ciudad cambia su nombre*, p. 53)

> The crowded neighbourhood of the Cheap Houses or Eduardo Aunós, which sounds much better, is made up of twenty-one streets. Like this (pretend, please) . . . Kind of like a grill. Like San Lorenzo del Escorial, but less so.
> They used to be numbered. First Street, Second, Third, Fourth, up to Twenty-first. Those numbers sounded like prison or New York. Now they have named them. Some Catalan names, some convoluted Catalan names, even more convoluted for the sticky Murcian tongues of their inhabitants.

The urbanistic discourse of the city seeks to organise the suburbs to neutralise and eliminate all complexity, reducing it to a manageable whole, as Delgado tells us by reference to Amos Rapoport: 'calmar la excitación producida por la vida urbana, y hacerlo dotando al usuario de los espacios públicos de imágenes estructuradoras' ('to calm the excitement produced by urban life while providing the user of public spaces with structuring images').[18] Urban layout silences the suburbs by means of form, and silences their residents by disconnecting them from their surroundings. However, Candel does not merely repeat this arrangement; he takes it a step further and shows us how suburban residents break away from and breathe new life into that structure:

> Ahora los nombres son: calle Ulldecona, calle Pinatell, calle Cisquer, calle Pontils, Rojals, Tragurá, Arnés, Ascó, Motrils, Riudoms, etc. Ellos, sus moradores, dicen: calle Urdecona, calle Pinatey, calle Sirqué, calle Pontís, Rochal, Traguirá, Arné, Asco, sin el acento, Motril, Rudón, etc.
>
> Algunas gitanas enturbian más las cosas. A la calle Tragurá la llaman: Trasgirá, desgrasiao, Trasgirá; ¿qué se ha creío er payo ejte? A la calle Ulldecona, Urdecoña, ¡cucha por Dios! Y así sucesivamente. (Candel, *Donde*, p. 53–4)

> Now the names are Ulldecona Street, Pinatell Street, Cisquer Street, Pontils Street, Rojals, Tragurá, Arnés, Ascó, Motrils, Riudoms, etc. They, their inhabitants, say Urdecona Street, Pinatey Street, Sirqué Street, Rochal, Traguirá, Arné, Asco, without the stress, Motril, Rudón, etc.
>
> Some gypsies make things even more complicated. They call Tragurá Street 'Trasgirá', you wretch, Trasgirá. What are they thinking? They call Ulldecona Street 'Urdecoña'. Dear God, listen! And so on.

Through everyday language, the 'sticky tongues' of suburban residents transform official denominations: they adapt them to their way of speaking and modify them according to their needs. The same happens with urban space: although planners impose an order that aims to neutralise the presence of immigrants, they resurge, assuming a new form that does not erase the original but rather modifies it, adapting it to their needs:

> De tota manera, als qui veuen aquest pisos – als del Patronat, a les dames pies, als visitadors de suburbi – se'ls eixampla el cor, i també la consciència. Per comparació amb abans, que vivien en barraques o rellogats, aquesta gent està de primera. Resolt – això pla, resolt! –; resolt, diguem, el problema del barraquisme, es va creant el del monobloc. Es viu d'esquena a la ciutat, fora de la ciutat. És un viure bigarrat, tipus rusc, tipus presó, amb sensació de poca intimitat, d'estar despullats dins aquests pisos. Tot se sent, tot es veu, es copsen totes les olors. . .
> Mossèn Jaume Cuspinera em diu: – Els primers dies t'indignes. Vols protestar. Vols que se t'adaptin a tu, als teus mètodes, al teu silenci. Però després comprens que 'ets tu qui t'has d'adaptar a ells'. (*Els altres*, pp. 267–8)

> In any case, the people who see these apartments – the people from the Board, the pious ladies, visitors of the suburbs – their hearts expand, and their conscience, too. By comparison with before, when they lived in slums or sublets, these people are well off. Problem solved – piece of cake, solved! – the problem of the shanty towns, let's say, solved, but now we've got the new problem of the tower block. They live with their backs to the city, outside the city. It's a disjointed way of living, like a beehive or a prison, with a sensation of little privacy, like being naked inside these apartments. Everything can be seen, heard and smelled. . .
> Father Jaume Cuspinera tells me: 'At first you are indignant. You want to complain. You want them to adapt to you, your ways, your silence. But then you understand that 'you are the one who has to adapt to them'.

Here Candel establishes a direct link between physical space and collective conscience, which leads him, in the first place, to alter the perception of the suburbs by levelling a critique against the physical and identity restrictions that are imposed by the city and that are clearly drawn from the concept of nation; and, second, to establish new identity possibilities precisely through urban space, which is modified by the daily use of its inhabitants. In other words,

Candel foregrounds transitions and trespassing, be they geographical, visual, cultural or linguistic, destabilising the notion of border and creating interstices that redefine the role of the suburban residents of Barcelona: they reconstruct the way in which they relate to the space in which they live, and their voices become agents of change.

In this redefinition of roles, the principal points of interaction that we find in Candel's discourse regarding the construction of a community of immigrants and suburban residents include, on the one hand, their relationships to a discourse of social and cultural definition predicated on breaking free from the stereotypes and defamatory language employed by the media and political discourse,[19] and, on the other hand, their relationships to urban space, whose shortcomings become the basis for the formation of a network of communication in the suburbs between residents and the official bodies of the city, a dialogue that will give rise to the establishment of neighbourhood associations in the 1970s.[20] Here Candel creates a physical space of representation: the neighbourhood, a geographical space without borders whose alleged boundaries shift with the incessant movement of its inhabitants. The neighbourhood, much like the figure of Candel, is the space where two distinct aspects of suburban life converge. The first layer is the spectre of origin, be it what was left behind by immigrants, or the original myth of the nation; the second part is the sediment accumulated in the wake of their arrival, which taken together creates the possibility of a place with multiple identities. In this context, the question of integration takes on a new form: it is not a matter of accepting directives imposed by the city, but rather a negotiation that reduces institutional forms and mandates to the fullest. In the suburban neighbourhood, integration takes the form of a collective coexistence capable of articulating the plurality that envelops them: 'Los barrios son como los mercados. En los buenos y abigarrados mercados todo lo encuentras. Abigarrado quiere decir reunido sin orden ni concierto' ('Neighbourhoods are like markets. In the good and crowded markets you can find it all. Crowded here meaning jumbled together without rhyme or reason').[21] Asymmetry is physical, social and economic; it is inclusive and seeks to insert the suburbs into the city's order. For this reason, even though he is speaking about the suburbs, what Candel says is applicable to all of Barcelona's neighbourhoods (*Els altres*, p. 222), creating a new denomination that questions and reformulates the idea of belonging and the idea of Catalan identity, and substitutes them with a physical space suited for identity-making in other ways. As Candel will later state: '¿Cuántas Cataluñas hay? ¿Tantas como catalanes?' ('How many Catalonias are there? As many as Catalans?'), establishing an identification between the local and the national.[22]

Interstices

Candel connects his spatially specific concept of neighbourhood, which begins to take shape in *Donde la ciudad cambia su nombre* and *Han matado a un hombre, han roto un paisaje*, to the larger question of Catalan identity with his categorisation of 'the other Catalans'. Just like in these two novels, where he constructs a genealogy of the suburbs through his characters, with 'the other Catalans' Candel establishes a connection between geographical space, the neighbourhood and the national discourse that is imposed by official discourses and practices of the dictatorship. The asymmetry and border ambiguity that we see in the neighbourhood, a space that could be anywhere in the city, can also be found in the idea of 'the other Catalans', where Candel does not reinforce limits or close off identities but rather quite the opposite: he points out the contradictory nature inherent in any political and social community and destabilises the homogeneous logic of the identity project of the state or the Catalanist cultural project. 'The other Catalans' references, like the neighbourhood, a reflection on border space; Candel establishes a point of contact and separation, a physical space where community is made and unmade.

Contradictions coexist in the very same space, just as they coexist in *Els altres* and, especially, in Candel himself: his birth in Casas Altas, Valencia; his life in Barcelona from the age of two; his education under the Republic, which provides him with formal albeit brief contact with the Catalan language; his experience under the dictatorship; his life in the suburbs and his contact with the city. Candel learns to live caught up in between the contradictory relationships that characterise him as a writer and someone whose identity is off-centre, which leads him to conclude that he is in fact not Catalan, but rather someone who is everywhere and nowhere all at once (*Els altres*, p. 30). From this de-centralised vantage point that we have located in his approach to the space of the neighbourhood or the concept of 'the other Catalans', Candel moves beyond the binary pair of centre-periphery and reveals an underlying complexity that resists canonical powers, in both his writing and the urban layout of the city. Just as we saw in his description of the Casas Baratas ('Cheap Houses') a few paragraphs earlier, where suburban residents modified and reinterpreted street names in Catalan, in the process eliminating urbanistic neutrality and using his own experience as an interstice, Candel redefines what it means to be Catalan and what it means to be/live in a neighbourhood. He incorporates the idiosyncrasies of immigrants in the national collective and in urban space – the geographical element, the border that defines identity on a very basic level. Language and space confer on the supposed immigrant minority a role in the construction of identity, breaking with classifications, making these migrants visible in their difference and agents in the construction of Catalan society: 'Aquests altres catalans, ben polits ja exteriorment, alletats com hem dit abans pel país, es veuran cridats a una curiosa tasca: la [singularització] de la novíssima Catalunya' (*Els altres*, p. 392) ('These other Catalans, now all cleaned up and nursed by the country as previously stated, will be charged with a curious task: the singularisation of the brand new Catalonia').

The same occurs with his writing. Life in the interstice explains the narrative form of many of his novels and articles, among which *Donde la ciudad cambia su nombre* stands out. Here we find a narrative that, like its author, is off-centre, which is to say, a narrative that moves beyond the tale of an individual, seeking instead a subject that does not emerge from a singular voice but rather the multiplicity of voices of those who live in the suburbs. In this approach, Candel becomes a chronicler, the voice of the neighbourhood, setting the precedent for the future establishment of neighbourhood associations. However, we must make an important distinction between the role played by Candel and the neighbourhood associations that began to appear in the 1970s in the writer's narrative, there is an essential component of critique, as there will be in neighbourhood associations, but this critique is used to develop an identity that lays out and secures the protagonism of immigrants and suburban residents in the construction of the city. The neighbourhood is, once again, a space for connection. Years later,

Candel will state as much in *Barrio* ('Neighbourhood', 1977), an essay in which he explains the experience of living in a suburban neighbourhood in the late 1970s; in this book, Candel personifies the neighbourhood as if it were a fairy tale character in order to level a critique of the structural deficiencies of the suburbs, which, in turn, gives rise to an identity:[23]

> A los animales les han dejado su voz los fabulistas y cuentistas . . . Sin embargo, a los barrios, nadie nos ha querido dejar su timbre articulado. Nadie. Los barrios no hablamos, aunque producimos ruido, y, a través de las asociaciones que nos representan, nos hacemos oír . . . Yo, para ello, para que me oigan, le he alquilado – nada de pedir prestado – su vocinglería al Candel, que no es fabulista ni cuentista, ni tampoco poeta, ni siquiera literato, dice él, únicamente escritor.[24]

> Fabulists and storytellers have lent their voices to the animals . . . However, no one has wanted to loan to us neighbourhoods their voice. No one. Us neighbourhoods don't speak, although we produce noise, lots of noise, and through the associations that represent us we make ourselves heard . . . Me, to that end, so that they hear me, I have rented – no borrowing here – Candel's boisterousness, even though he is not a fabulist or a storyteller or a poet or even a man of letters, so he says, just a writer.

First, Candel seeks neither to impose his voice nor to present a simplistic and homogeneous representation of all those who live in the suburbs; rather, he sets out to capture as many voices as he can, hence his use of the term 'vocinglería' ('boisterousness'). Candel – and here we borrow from Homi Bhabha's framework[25] – grants suburban denizens the right to narrate as a way of obtaining a communal sense of identity and, consequently, visibility, revising myths of belonging and connecting to them through his own experience: the experience in his place of origin, his journey, and having children who are disconnected from that particular experience. To establish these connections, his novels and essays are composed as a choral narrative that includes oral testimony (*Els altres*, p. 45), legends (p. 61), memories (p. 146) and/or anecdotes (p. 171). Following this general pattern, the structure of *Donde* rests on a collection of multiple stories that took place in the neighbourhood, but do not belong to him and yet are collected and presented as a chronicler would do.[26] However, Candel had to learn how to play this role: in a way, in *Donde*, the author imposes his voice on the neighbourhood by publishing these stories without their protagonists' permission. Nevertheless, his experience with this publication led him to be more aware of his role as a 'personatge solució' ('solution character'), as his biographer, Genís Sinca, calls him,[27] and he recognised his role as a point of articulation, as a meeting place, as a confluence.[28]

With his multifaceted narrative – or what he calls 'objectivisme particular' (*Els altres*, p. 106) ('particular objectivism'), a concept that seeks to avoid absolutes – Candel empowers immigrants to create an identity that also locates them squarely in the interstice, at the intersection of a mobile space of identity, in 'aquest flux i reflux de l'idioma, dels costums, dels jocs catalans, que per una banda perden i per l'altra guanyen' (p. 84) ('the ebb and flow of the Catalan language, customs and games that on one hand they lose and on the other they earn'). That in-between is an essential part of who they are, just as it is for 'el' ('the') Candel who describes himself as a writer.[29] As he explains in *Els altres*, on the one hand '[ell] no era català, no coneixia Catalunya, no sabia què dir-ne' (p. 30) ('[he] wasn't Catalan, he was unfamiliar with Catalunya and didn't know what to say about it'); on the other hand, 'no era erudit, no tractava de la literatura o de l'art català, no evocava la història del país, no n'esmentava els homes' (p. 31) ('he wasn't erudite, didn't address Catalan literature or art, didn't evoke the history of the country, didn't mention its men who made history'). Moreover, he did not write in Catalan; his essays in Catalan were translated, and the rest of his writing was done in Spanish. In this in-between, Candel sets up an aesthetic, historical and social distance, an interstitial mobility as it were, that produces a narrative that responds to his own hybridity and difference.

The language in his novels also falls into this in-between: the particular use of Catalan by suburban residents; the reproduction of neighbourhood language, labelled as crude (p. 32); the lack of technical vocabulary to engage with urbanistic subject matter.[30] This in-between quality establishes a contact zone outside of what is deemed canonical, where the concept of integration, which we have already seen modified in his use of 'neighbourhood', continues to develop within the diverse environment of the suburbs. In other words, Candel examines notions of integration through the social presence of different cultural identities, none of which can claim exclusive use of public space – turning to Delgado's words once more – which is itself the sphere of expression, visibility and the assertion of presence.[31]

In this interstice, in this neighbourhood, indeed in the very figure of Candel, we find the establishment of an essential distinction overwhelmingly presented in *Els altres*, the difference between 'trobar-s'hi' ('presence') and 'ésser' ('being'), that is, between temporality and permanence (*Els altres*, p. 88). In the citation from *Barrio* above, Candel differentiates between neighbourhood and noise, which is produced when something does not work properly, is temporarily employed to register a complaint, and carries the connotation of being bothersome. When it comes to speaking, however, Candel seeks dialogue, the elimination of stereotypes, levelling of the playing field, and the extension of time and connection, all linked to the question of belonging. He makes a distinction between the place that we inhabit and the one that defines us: it is the difference between house and home. This definitory place varies according to people's unique experiences, as many of the testimonies included in Candel's works show us. As we can see, his narratives about 'being', whether in essay or narrative form, also level a critique, but they are more about the creation of identity. Let us focus, for example, on *Han matado*, where the protagonist's story is the suburbs' history: where they come from, how they evolve, their architecture. Space and protagonist share the same destiny, mutually and simultaneously. Candel's critique is implicit, and was clearly understood by the dictatorship's censorship arm, which removed from his novel any passages on slums or shanties.[32] Their removal aside, what matters most here is how the history of the suburbs secures its presence in time and history writ large.

This 'being' comes into being physically through the space of the neighbourhood and socially through the construction of a unique history tied to the suburbs. In this construction, the city *per se* – what in *Donde* is called Barcelona, as if it were a foreign body that excludes the suburbs (*Donde*, p. 62) – and even more broadly, the nation, take on a supporting role. They are the backdrop that can be seen only from afar, even as they attempt to impose order and mould the city precisely through the presence of the suburbs. Here, Candel constructs a narration that transcends the myths of identity creation, as Homi Bhabha explains in *The Location of*

Culture, focusing on those moments and processes that arise from the articulation of cultural differences.[33] When Candel analyses concepts like 'xarnego',[34] integration, or the use of Catalan by the inhabitants of the suburbs, he articulates and creates – returning once again to Bhabha – spaces of connection or 'in-between spaces' that 'provide the terrain for elaborating strategies of selfhood – singular or communal – that initiate new signs of identity, and innovate sites of collaboration, and contestation, in the act of defining the idea of society itself'.[35] When we look at the underlying structure of *Els altres*, we can see how it responds directly to the objectives presented by Bhabha. The essay starts out by presenting the other Catalans in terms of the parameters of the established values: what it means to be Catalan; what integration is and does; what the essential elements of Catalan culture are. From there, however, Candel dives straight into the identity of immigrants and suburban residents and explores their history: where they come from; why they left their places of origin; where, how and why they live where they do. He lays out these different vectors of their identity correlatively given that, as Manuel Delgado explains when speaking on the myth of multiculturalism, heterogeneity cannot exist without standing in stark relief to homogeneity.[36] For Candel, however, these parameters are merely points of reference to guide the reader through a familiar context that he will then proceed to dismantle. The author breaks free from supposedly fixed parameters and distances himself from the cultural strictures imposed by popular folklore or a concept of nation that stereotypes and isolates residents of the suburbs, as we saw in the discourses of Vandellós or Vicens Vives. He eschews absolutes and instead presents a collective experience that can begin to be used to negotiate cultural and identity values.

In Candel's new parameters, he creates a new version of the city's history, where the suburb is replaced by the neighbourhood, with the latter cancelling out the stigmatisation of the former. The city's reprobation of the suburbs is not overlooked or eliminated; rather, it is reconsidered and given a new twist based on the residents' particular experience. Life in the city's suburbs has cornered and isolated immigrants and suburban residents, both physically and conceptually: 'El suburbi ha estat el seu corralet, el lloc on ha estat acorralat' (*Els altres*, p. 206) ('The suburb has been his corral, the place where he has been cornered'), Candel writes. Just as it happens with the use of the modernist grid in *Donde*,[37] the suburbs homogenise and eliminate the presence of immigrants and their history, which is why Candel refers to specific streets and neighbourhoods by name (*Donde*, p. 11). He relishes the use of detail since '[l]es coses, en abstracte, són blanques o negres. En detall, admeten tons intermedis. I allò que és, no és, i allò que no és, és. No solament les excepcions de què es parla sempre' (*Els altres*, p. 106) ('things, in the abstract, are black and white. In detail, they allow intermediary tones. And what they are, they aren't, and what they aren't, they are. Not just the exceptions that everybody always talks about'). Like Miserachs's camera did for him, Candel makes the city's suburbs visible; he inserts them into and makes them belong to the urban, social and cultural history of the city, forswearing the polarity and oversimplification of the city's discourse.

In this build-up, the border – between city/suburb and Catalan/not Catalan – 'is not that at which something stops but, as the Greeks recognized, the boundary is that from which something begins its presencing', as Martin Heidegger explains in his brief essay 'Building Dwelling Thinking'.[38] The notion of presence, consequently, interrogates the act of representation carried out by and from the city, its official bodies, and even concepts such as nation, identity or even the suburbs themselves, in the process uncovering the presence of a community with its own relevant protagonism and interventions in the construction of the city. In this manoeuvre, Candel manages to tear down the urbanistic barriers of the suburbs; he breaks free from the ideological barrier that expels immigrants from the city and hides them in the rubble of the tower block in order to reformulate the concept of public sphere and the role of citizens.

Citizenships

From this everyday narrative, juxtaposed against the urban or Catalan identity epic, Candel constructs a space for insurgency, where two different conceptualisations complement each other. First, we find the cultural insurgency detailed by Bhabha, according to which border limits require an encounter with something new that is not a part of their continuum between past and present, which enables the creation of an identity subject to the present and not some utopian past. In other words, this contact foments the creation of a contingent space that can renew the past from the present, and in doing so can avoid a homogeneous and therefore necessarily essentialist cultural space, which is what tends to happen with the concept of nation.[39] Second, the idea of insurgency is linked to the concept of 'insurgent citizenship' used by James Holston to highlight the opposition between urban space that absorbs citizenship-related identities under a state plan of construction, and the practices and planning generated by that space.[40] That is to say, state space creates new sources for assertion and unforeseen urban planning that can also grant legitimacy. In Candel's writing, in his project of identity construction, both assertions are made simultaneously: the construction of an urban genealogy that is predicated on the allegedly outsider perspective of the suburbs and gives rise to a new history, together with the opposition to a kind of urban planning that hides away and closes off immigrants in order to grant them visibility and the right to exist publicly.

The urban space of the tower block that Candel describes in *Donde*, and which we have seen a few lines above, imposes a new order that accentuates decontextualisation, defamiliarisation and dehistoricisation, or, in other words, a breakdown of the connections that comprise the residents' identities. Be that as it may, the suburban residents' presence makes itself manifest and in so doing it compels a negotiation with the terms of citizenship. Here Candel uses residents' insurgency to forge a community and an identity using daily practices that subvert the state's impositions, starting with a re-reading of street names or with the residents' noisy and smelly daily chores, culminating in their noisy complaints. This insurgency disinters residents from the silence that their distance from the city centre imposes as it attempts to keep them at bay. What brings about isolation here is not their traditions as immigrants but rather the space that is imposed on them. Through this anecdote, Candel reveals how the city is not a static object that contains inhabitants, but rather a living entity that expands identities and grants rights.

Candel's insurgency appears in his critique of the system, through which he makes the connections suppressed by the city reappear, underscoring their existence and challenging parameters that grant membership in a group (e.g., the law), and elaborating a concept of citizenship that recognises the need for a mechanism to facilitate adherence to the community:

Però els temps mediatitzats i burocratitzats en què ens ha tocat de viure han condemnat la caritat sense haver donat espai perquè fos substituïda per aquesta altra cosa que en diuen justícia i que no és sinó una caritat més encertada i més ben entesa. Una vegada em va venir a veure una dona, a veure què podia fer, perquè l'havien treta de la seva barraca – tot i que era una barraca 'numerada' – sense indemnització de cap mena i perdent els drets a pis, aquets drets tan problemàtics. Era un comiat per sanció. El delicte consistia a haver recollit una família que feia dies que no sabia on ficar-se. Els van considerar rellogats, i tots al carrer. S'ha arribat a un extrem en què ni la teva misèria no et deixen compartir. (*Els altres*, pp. 214–15)

But in the mediated and bureaucratised times in which we live, they have condemned charity without giving it room to be replaced by that other thing they call justice, which is just a more accurate and better understood form of charity. Once a woman came to see me, to see what I could do, because they had taken away her shack – even though it was a 'numbered' shack – without compensation and stripping her of her right of ownership, this right that is so problematic. It was a dismissal by sanction. Her crime consisted of taking in a family that for days had nowhere to stay. They considered it a sublet and threw everyone out on the street. We've reached such extremes that they won't even let you share your misery.

For Candel, citizenship is a question of opposition, of participation in urban space through social relationships developed on the neighbourhood level, a sense of belonging that is made accessible by networks of assistance that in turn generate agency. But first, he needs to rebuild these networks of almost democratic participation that had been usurped by a capitalist system that began to take shape in the 1950s: 'Però calgué animar aquells veïns a fi que reclamessin, i posar-los una mica en peu de guerra; si no, els haurien asservits' (*Els altres*, p. 246) ('those residents [in the shanties] had to be encouraged to complain and go on a war standing; if not, they would have trampled all over them'). In this way, and returning to Holston,[41] Candel suggests the possibility of a multifaceted citizenship tied to urban spaces, neighbourhoods and the individual experience of each one of their residents. Candel's and the residents' insurgency reconstruct the social identity of Barcelona not only because it considers the experience of migration in the

Catalan identity project, but also because it weighs the presence and importance of the suburbs and their inhabitants in the city project, which begets an essential quality based on the heterogeneity of lived experience.

To Speak the Unspeakable

In his narrative production under the dictatorship, starting with *Donde* and culminating with *Barrio*, Candel lays the basis for a concept of urban citizenship that emphasises a space of conflict that incorporates immigrant's presence and agency in the construction of the city and of Catalan identity, as 'founding members of society', as later sociologists like Salvador Cardús will recognise.[42] In order to do so, he seeks out a new space for representation, the neighbourhood, based on which he can portray the individual and subjective experience of residents and create a practice of citizenship founded on the notion of polymorphic community and shared experience derived from the human-scale neighbourhood itself, and not from an abstract concept of identity. In the process, he eliminates the supposed neutrality of national and urban infrastructure, focusing instead on a set of shared intentions, made palpable by their presence and immediacy, which is the principal tie here to the experience of migration. This experience spawns new morphologies (neighbourhood, suburb, migrant, resident) that underscore precisely the confrontation, transgression and role of urbanity – that is, the body of the city and the use that residents make of it. Indeed, this manifold experience becomes the source for democratic participation, rethinking and rebuilding the role of citizen participation in Barcelona.

Years later, we return to Miserachs's photograph and recover Candel's figure, voice and memory through the everyday experience of migration, specifically the multiple registers in which it plays out, then and now, as he reconfigures what it means to be one of the other Catalans. Now we see how Candel speaks the unspeakable, by recovering the role of immigration in the construction of Catalan identity. Candel's asynchronous presence, like the neighbourhood's genealogical construction in his narrative, breaks free from the abstract timelines of the notion of Catalan identity by finding a space that allows physical and temporal movement, and opens the door to an infinite exchange that undermines border, spatial and temporal dualities in favour of a complex, multifaceted identity.

Notes

1 El Hachmi, Najat, 'Pròleg: L'home que apostava pel matís', in Francesc Candel, *Els altres catalans* (Barcelona: Edicions 62, 2008), p. 7. All translations from works in Spanish and Catalan into English are my own.
2 Francesc Candel, *Els altres catalans* (Barcelona: Edicions 62, 2008); Francisco Candel, *Donde la ciudad cambia su nombre* (Barcelona: Janés, 1957); Francisco Candel, *Han matado a un hombre, han roto un paisaje* (Barcelona: Ediciones GP, 1967).
3 There is a close connection between the rise in immigration and the construction of identity and Catalan culture under the dictatorship. During this period, Spain witnessed enormous migratory waves from the countryside to the cities, exploding the urban population. Different from earlier waves of migrants, the bulk of whom hailed from Valencia and Aragon, from the 1950s onwards migrants mainly came from Andalusia and Murcia, fleeing the awful conditions of the country in search of prosperity in cities such as Barcelona. This migratory wave positioned the Catalan population as a clear minority and heightened the housing crisis in the capital city, which in turn led to an explosion in the construction of shanties and shantytowns; see José Luis Oyón and Borja Iglesias, 'Les barraques i l'infrahabitatge en la construcció de Barcelona, 1914–1950', in Mercè Tatjer i Cristina Larrea (eds), *Barraques: La Barcelona informal del segle XX* (Barcelona: Ajuntament de Barcelona, 2010), p. 32. In response, Josep Maria de Porcioles's speculative government (1957–73) focused on the eradication of shanties and urban renewal. Porcioles was the principal exponent of a new Francoist urban policy predicated on real estate and the banking sector, which led him to extol a new functionalist urban discourse couched in terms of 'sterilising' or 'modernising' the city through a series of plans that eradicated shanties and transferred their residents to remote and poorly equipped residential complexes; see Mercè Tatjer, 'Barraques i projectes de remodelació urbana a Barcelona, de l'Eixample al litoral (1922–1966)', in Tatjer i Larrea (eds), *Barraques*, pp. 54–8.
4 Indeed, Najat El Hachmi's narrative works can be read through a perspective of temporal dislocation that can be seen as the logical continuation of discontinuities, both physical and regarding identity, about which Candel spoke. For more on this matter in El Hachmi,

see Josep-Anton Fernàndez, 'Dislocated Temporalities: Immigration, Sexuality, and Violence in Najat El Hachmi's *L'últim patriarca*', in Teresa Iribarren, Roger Canadell and Josep-Anton Fernàndez (eds), *Narratives of Violence* (Venice: Edizioni Ca' Foscari, 2021), pp. 109–20; or Jessica A. Folkart, 'Scoring the National Hym(e)n: Sexuality, Immigration, and Identity in Najat El Hachmi's *L'últim patriarca*', *Hispanic Review*, 81/3 (2013), 353–76, for example.

5   Francesc Candel, 'Barraques de la riera Comtal: Uns veïns als quals ningú no fa cas', *Serra d'Or*, 7/5 (May 1965), 71.
6   For more on the relationship between Candel, urban space and dissent, see Olga Sendra Ferrer, *Barcelona, City of Margins* (Toronto: University of Toronto Press, 2022).
7   El Hachmi, 'Pròleg', p. 10.
8   The urban reforms brought about by different plans to renovate Barcelona, such as the Plan Comarcal of 1953 or specific designs such as the seaside boardwalk in the early 1960s, show the conjunction of the regime's modernising zeal with the development of a practice of social and spatial stratification predicated on segmentation, oversimplification and a supposed neutrality. Taken together, these forces correspond to the image of an official order bound by an essentialising conceptualisation of identity.
9   The regime banned foreign emigration and restricted internal migration in order to facilitate control over the populace from the immediate post-war period until 1946; see Martí Marín, *Història del franquisme a Catalunya* (Vic: Eumo Editorial, 2006), p. 231. However, from 1947 onwards, Spanish cities underwent exponential growth that forced the regime to reconsider its strict limitations, so much so that in 1957 all restrictions regarding internal and external migration were lifted. For more information, see the aforementioned Marín and also Nathan Richardson, *Constructing Spain: The Re-Imagination of Space and Place in Fiction and Film, 1953–2003* (Lewisburg PA: Bucknell University Press, 2011).
10 Andreu Domingo notes that this type of discourse can be found in influential works such as those of economist Josep Antoni Vandellós, *La immigració a Catalunya* and *Catalunya, poble decadent*, both published in 1935. Domingo cites the economist as not just a clear example of what subsequent Catalan nationalist discourse would become but also as requisite context to situate Candel's work, precisely due to the profound effect of this second wave of immigration on the Catalan population of that time; see Andreu Domingo, '"Català és. . .": El discurs sobre immigració i identitat nacional durant el franquisme: Francesc Candel i Jordi Pujol', *Treballs de la Societat Catalana de Geografia*, 75 (2013), 9–32. In Vandellós's speech marking the construction of the metro and the 1929 International Exposition, made in the con-

text of the first migratory wave of the twentieth century, we can read his suspicion of the supposed 'quality' of the newcomers, couched in racial or ethno-cultural terms, a suspicion that will grow throughout the 1950s and 1960s as migrants continue to relocate to Catalunya; see Andreu Domingo, 'L'emprenta de Candel', *Ara* (16 March 2014), 6–7. Of course, when we talk of a 'nationalist discourse' during the dictatorship, we must understand it as a Catalan cultural project without 'rojos' (communists) (Marín, *Història*, p. 191), a complex project that encompasses participants of very different political orientations, rather than one that is necessarily or exclusively anti-Francoist. However, Candel refers to the concept of a Catalanist cultural project that ties back to Vandellós.
11   Domingo, 'Català és...', 14.
12   See Josep-Anton Fernàndez, '"Virilitat del país": Gender, Immigration, and Power in Jaume Vicens Vives's *Notícia de Catalunya*', *Hispanic Research Journal*, 21/2 (2020), 153.
13   Clara Carme Parramon also explains how the Catalan debate on the second migratory wave is marked by 'fear of de-Catalanisation'; see Clara Carme Parramon, '*Els altres catalans*: entusiasme i pertorbació a la Catalunya del anys seixanta', in Andreu Domingo (ed.), *Recerca i Immigració VII: Migracions dels segles XX i XXI: Una mirada candeliana* (Barcelona: Generalitat de Catalunya, 2015), p. 43; see also Teresa Vilarós, 'The Passing of the Xarnego-Immigrant: Post-Nationalism and the Ideologies of Assimilation in Catalonia', *Arizona Journal of Hispanic Cultural Studies*, 7 (2003), 230. Indeed, this debate was still roiling in 1982 when Jacqueline Hall presented her sociological analysis of immigration to Catalunya in similar terms. For Hall, de-Catalanisation is a threat that results from the mass immigration of this period and is heaped on top of the political subordination of Catalunya, whose language and culture were reduced to the status of folklore. In fact, Hall notes the lack of studies on immigration in the 1960s and 1970s, which shows Candel's relevance to this historical moment: 'The only source of information that escapes the control of the regime are the comments on immigration written before the war by different Catalan politicians and researchers. Thus, these are, for a long time, the only sources where the problem is defined in terms of the cultural and linguistic identity of the Catalans': Jacqueline Hall, 'La bena i la mordassa: els catalans davant la immigració de l'època franquista', *Treballs de sociolingüística catalana*, 5 (1983), 74. It is surprising that Hall discredits Candel's analysis because of how he draws his observations from pre-war immigrants without accounting for the difficulties that barred the integration of later immigrants (Hall, 'La bena', 82). In spite of the incongruencies found in this study, which point towards a precarious reading of Candel, it serves in this case to

underscore an approach to immigration that continues even beyond the years of the dictatorship.
14 Even El Hachmi makes her critique within this context when she recurs to Jordi Pujol's famous turn of phrase: 'És català qui viu i treballa a Catalunya' ('Pròleg', p. 8) ('Whoever lives and works in Catalonia is Catalan').
15 See Andreu Domingo, 'Català és. . .', 29; Joan J. Gilabert, 'Francisco Candel: His Essays and the Catalan National Question', *Siglo XX*, 6/1–2 (1988), 12; and Clara Carme Parramon, '*Els altres catalans*: entusiasme i pertorbació', p. 226.
16 Manuel Delgado, *Memoria y lugar: El espacio público como crisis de significado* (Valencia: Ediciones Generales de la Construcción, 2001), p. 10.
17 Here, Candel inserts a schematic drawing of the neighbourhood, whose crude rendering denotes the inadequacy of urban space.
18 Delgado, *Memoria y lugar*, p. 11.
19 Parramon puts together a list of qualifiers used in the press to refer to immigrants, indicating the year in which they appear: '"estafadores", "ladrones" (1958–1959–1962)' ('"swindlers", "thieves" [1958–1959–1962]'), '"analfabetos" (1960)' ('"illiterate" [1960]'), '"escandalosos" . . . (1962–1964)' ('"scandalous" . . . [1962–1964]'), etc.: Carme Clara Parramon, 'El debat català sobre la immigració durant el franquisme: Integració social i adaptació cultural', *Cercles: Revista d'Història Cultural*, 18 (2015), 44. Candel is quite conscious of this discourse and attempts to refute it not just in *Els altres* but also in his earlier novels, *Donde la ciudad cambia su nombre* and *Han matado a un hombre, han roto un paisaje*. In his own words, these types of characters are 'flors que no fan estiu' (*Els altres*, p. 111) ('flowers that don't make summer').
20 For more on the neighbourhood associations and their relationship with the construction of democracy, see Carme Molinero and Pere Ysàs (eds), *Construint la ciutat democràtica: El moviment veïnal durant el tardofranquisme i la transició* (Barcelona: Icària, 2010); and Manuel Vázquez Montalbán, *Barcelones* (Barcelona: Empúries, 1990).
21 Francisco Candel, *Barrio* (Barcelona: Ediciones Marte, 1977), p. 40.
22 Francisco Candel, *Los otros catalanes veinte años después* (Barcelona: Plaza y Janés, 1985), pp. 253–4.
23 Even still, critique is always accompanied by the construction of a community (Candel, *Barrio*, p. 40).
24 Candel, *Barrio*, p. 7.
25 Homi K. Bhabha, *The Location of Culture* (London and New York: Routledge, 2004), p. xx.
26 Although Candel describes himself in *¡Dios, la que se armó!* (Barcelona: Ediciones Marte, 1964, p. 11) as 'cronista oficial de la ciudad' ('the official chronicler of the city'), the neighbours of Can Tunis

portrayed in *Donde* sued Candel for including them without permission. He tells about this experience in *¡Dios. . .!*.
27 Genís Sinca, *La providència es diu Paco: Biografia de Francesc Candel* (Barcelona: La Magrana, 2008), p. 157.
28 In his own words: 'Uno de los defectos básicos del Candel fue que escribió este libro más de cara a los plutócratas que a los miserables, olvidándose por completo que éstos también tienen su corazoncito, su amor propio y su honrilla. El libro sobre ellos no era para ellos' (*¡Dios. . .!*, p. 12) ('One of Candel's basic flaws was that he wrote this book for plutocrats rather than the poor, completely forgetting that the latter also have a heart, self-steem and pride. This book *about* them was not *for* them'). In his later writing, his tone will be very different, as we have seen in the quote from 'Barraques de la Riera Comtal': 'Aquests veïns m'han cridat perquè parli damunt el paper de llur situació' (p. 71) ('These neighbours have called on me to say it on paper').
29 In all of his novels and some of his essays, Candel is present as a background character called 'el Candel' (see, e.g., *Donde* or *Barrio*). His use of the definite article emphasises his interstitiality, as formality gives way to the everyday usage of language.
30 See, for example, Francisco Candel, 'El amazacotamiento', *CAU*, 60 (1965), 5–8.
31 Manuel Delgado, 'El mite de la multiculturalitat: De la "diversitat" cultural a la desigualtat social', *Revista Catalana de Seguretat Pública*, 2 (1998), 56.
32 It is interesting to note how the descriptions of suburban space are inserted into the narration in the same way that the suburbs are inserted into the city: suddenly, unexpectedly, breaking down orderly narration, upsetting the alleged homogeneity of the story. Likewise, Candel breaks down the space of the city, giving it a new polyhedral form, similar to how the materials used to build shanties constitute a piecemeal identity.
33 Bhabha, *Location*, p. 2.
34 'Xarnego' has no translation into English. In the 1950s and 1960s it was a derogatory term used to refer to workers that were not Catalan by origin. Candel discusses the possible origins of the term, its possible interpretations and its problematic nature in *Els altres* (p. 177).
35 Bhabha, *Location*, p. 2.
36 Delgado, 'El mite', 55.
37 Candel, *Donde*, p. 53.
38 Martin Heidegger, 'Building Dwelling Thinking', in David Farrell Krell (ed.), *Basic Writings from Being and Time (1927) to The Task of Thinking (1964)* (London and San Francisco CA: Harper Perennial, 2008), p. 356.

39 Bhabha, *Location*, p. 10.
40 James Holston, 'Spaces of Insurgent Citizenship', in James Holston (ed.), *Cities and Citizenship* (Durham NC and London: Duke University Press, 1998), pp. 157–73.
41 Holston, 'Spaces', p. 169.
42 Salvador Cardús, 'The Memory of Immigration in Catalan Nationalism', *International Journal of Iberian Studies*, 18/1 (2005), 43.

Chapter 5

The Ego-History of Valencian Immigration: Julià Guillamon's *El barri de la Plata*

Teresa Iribarren

Introduction

In 2015, the Valencian weekly publication *El Temps* reported on a study by the Centre for Demographic Studies (CED) of the Universitat Autònoma de Barcelona, titled 'Un segle de migracions valencianes a Catalunya: Població valenciana i la seva descendència a Catalunya' ('A Century of Valencian Migrations to Catalonia: Valencian Population and its Descendents in Catalonia'), based on new and surprising data.[1] After years of historical research, the CED's deputy director, Andreu Domingo, and doctoral candidate Kenneth Pitarch claimed that since the end of the nineteenth century, the largest community of Valencian immigrants concentrated in Catalonia:

> El nombre de valencians censats, que al 1920 era de 91.211 persones, al 1930 assolia el màxim de tot el segle amb 126.165 persones. Al 1970 la població encara es mantenia en 109.636. Avui en dia, però, per l'efecte de la mortalitat i les migracions de retorn, ja només representen un contingent de 61.769 persones.[2]

> The number of registered Valencians, which in 1920 was 91,211 people, reached its peak in 1930 with 126,165 people. In 1970, the pop-

ulation remained at 109,636. However, due to mortality and return migrations, nowadays the contingent of Valencians consists only of 61,769 people.

Despite its magnitude, this phenomenon had hitherto gone completely unnoticed.

Among the main discoveries of Domingo and Pitarch's research, *El Temps*'s feature highlighted that many Valencians from the first wave had settled in the Barri de la Plata ('the Silver District'), in Barcelona's working-class, industrial neighbourhood of Poblenou. However, the memory of this migration had vanished from this area due to the cultural and linguistic proximity between Valencia and Catalonia, and to the speedy integration of the Valencians into Catalan society. The article was complete with a list of twelve prominent personalities in Catalan politics and culture who briefly spoke about their Valencian ancestors. One of them was Julià Guillamon (Barcelona, 1962), a prolific writer, an influential literary critic for *La Vanguardia* and *L'Avenç*, an award-winning independent scholar and an exhibition curator for some of the most important cultural institutions in Catalonia, such as the Centre de Cultura Contemporània de Barcelona, the Centre d'Arts Santa Mònica and the Barcelona municipal libraries. In his statements to *El Temps*, Guillamon cautioned that there was no public awareness of a Valencian background among the residents of Poblenou, where his paternal grandparents had settled. He also shared with *El Temps*'s readers that he was researching his family history, which he had started publishing in the cultural magazine *L'Avenç*.

Later on, in July 2018, Pitarch defended the first doctoral thesis devoted to Valencian immigration to Catalonia, thus filling a glaring academic gap.[3] Pitarch's research, conducted using demographic techniques such as archival exploration and interviews, sought to carry out an exercise in historical memory in order to lend visibility to the Valencians who had lived or were living in Catalonia. The thesis stated that the *only* available source of biographical information about the first wave of Valencian migration and their descendants was the 1991 Sociodemographic Survey.[4] Pitarch, tracing the vicissitudes of the Valencians who settled in Barcelona from the end of nineteenth century to the twenty-first century, primarily in the Barceloneta neighbourhood, concluded that their successful integration after the three major migration waves can be explained by the historical, cultural and linguistic ties between Valencia and Catalonia.

A few months earlier, Julià Guillamon had published *El barri de la Plata* ('The Silver District', 2018). This work, previously published as a series of articles in *L'Avenç* and soon translated into Spanish by the author, was well received by the public and critics alike, and widely covered by the media. It even led to the creation of a literary route: readers could tour the neighbourhood accompanied by Guillamon himself, who acted as their guide. *El barri de la Plata* – later followed by a sequel, *El tren de la bruixa* ('The Witch's Train', 2018) – links the history of Valencian immigration with that of the author's parents, who were born in two different districts of Barcelona: his father, Julián Guillamón, was the son of immigrants from Toga (a town in the Alt Millars area of the province of Castelló, in the region of Valencia) and had grown up in Poblenou; and his mother, Maria Mota, was from a Catalan family and had been born in the district of Gràcia, in Barcelona. This autobiographical and rather unclassifiable work aimed to safeguard the past of the Poblenou industrial neighbourhood in the face of its radical urban transformation in recent decades,[5] and to counter the forgetting of Valencian identity by the descendants of the first wave of immigrants.

Based to a large extent on interviews and the exploration of the Arxiu Municipal Contemporani de Barcelona ('Modern Municipal Archive of Barcelona') and the Arxiu Municipal de Sant Martí ('Municipal Archive of the Sant Martí district'), *El barri de la Plata* aimed, albeit in a geographically partial and predominantly informative manner, to achieve the same goal as Pitarch's thesis: to reclaim the memory of the Valencians settled in the Poblenou neighbourhood and to retrace the steps of their integration into Catalan society and culture. The significant difference from Pitarch lies in the fact that Guillamon had two key sources of information for reconstructing the immigrants' biographies: the family archive and his personal memories, as well as a network of Valencian acquaintances who entrusted him with their family memories thanks to the complicity arising from shared neighbourhood experiences. In addition, Guillamon took the licences of a literary author, using historical data in service of aesthetic effects and narrative effectiveness.

In this chapter, I argue that *El Barri de la Plata*, particularly in his account of the integration of Valencians in a working-class district of Barcelona, inscribes itself into the subjectivist turn in contemporary historical narratives, which Enzo Traverso questions in *Singular Pasts: The 'I' in Historiography*.[6] I claim that Guillamon combines – in a manner somewhat comparable to that of history scholars who adopt a literary style, and writers such as W. G. Sebald, Éric Vuillard and Javier Cercas, who integrate factual history into novels – the roles, described by Traverso, of the 'Narcissistic novelist' (who combines historiographical aspirations with literary vanity) and the 'Narcissistic historian' (who delves into the lives of others in the past primarily to understand himself or herself) in exploiting the creative potential of writing the past centered around the 'I'.[7]

After describing the main elements of Guillamon's story about Valencian immigration, I will examine, following Traverso, Guillamon's alignment with the narrative mode that Pierre Nora termed 'ego-history': those narratives in which historians, displaying a strong personal involvement in the research, ultimately seek to construct their own history.[8] Furthermore, I will show how Guillamon's engagement with ego-history takes place within a work of non-fiction constructed largely through the postmemory strategies described by Marianne Hirsch in *Family Frames*.[9] Finally, I will discuss Guillamon's contribution to raising awareness of first-wave Valencian immigration and its descendants and how his aesthetic proposal takes on the micropolitical function of reparation,[10] following Xavier Pla's reflections on autofiction, literature and reality in his essay *El soldat de Baltimore*.[11]

Valencian Migrants and their Integration

El barri de la Plata begins with an autobiographical pact and an explanation of the Poblenou's historical reconstruction as a metanarrative. From the first page onwards, the reader knows that the narrative self is to be identified with the writer, Julià Guillamon. It is the awareness of writing an ego document that enables the author to reconstruct the history of the 'barri dels valencians del Poblenou' ('Valencian neighbourhood of Poblenou').[12] This neighbourhood was his home until he was almost thirty and he moved into a flat owned by his maternal Catalan grandparents in the Gràcia district of Barcelona. Guillamon's first-person testimony interweaves collective, family and personal memories, where the writer is not only a speaker but also a custodian of this place of memory, which is the neighbourhood:

> El meu amic Jordi Ribas diu que el tema de tot el que escric és la desaparició. Tot allò que va passar i que ha estat esborrat, liquidat, la memòria perduda de les coses. En recullo les restes, en col·lecciono els fragments per reconstruir un espai mental: el barri de la Plata. (Guillamon, *Barri*, p. 22)

> My friend Jordi Ribas says that everything I write is about disappearance. Everything that happened and that has been erased, cleared out, the lost memory of things. I collect the remains of it, I pick up the pieces to reconstruct a mental space: the Silver district.

Guillamon's testimonial writing recounts scenes to safeguard a historical era in much the same way as his father embalmed two bull heads in order to preserve them. Hence, we find descriptions such as, 'quan els valencians eren amos i senyors del barri de la Plata' (*Barri*, p. 186) ('when Valencians were the masters and lords of the Silver district'). It is the recovery of a world that 'només existirà dins del meu cap' (p. 219) ('will only exist in my head'), he laments, when the city gives in to the pressures of real estate and the new industrial activity, forcing the demolition of old factories and obsolete warehouses: 'Els que tinguin els maons més ben posats, *lofts*. Els altres, a terra' (p. 221) ('Those with better bricks would be converted into lofts. The rest would be demolished'). The same dynamic occurs when the footprints of the Valencians are completely erased by the overlapping footsteps of other migrations that succeeded them: the arrival of the first Chileans and Argentines in the early 1970s, followed by non-EU immigrants years later, he points out. Guillamon explains that in 2005 a group of Maghrebian people squatted in the family flat on Luchana Street. He notes that all the bullfighting bars around Marina Street are now run by Chinese people. This is also the case of the Bar Montins, which he visited in 2014 and saw it was being run by someone from an eastern European country.

In any case, he notes that the loss of the district residents' Valencian identity had already taken place when he was a child. At school, for instance, 'no es parlava mai dels avis valencians'

(p. 37) ('there was never any talk about the Valencian grandparents'). This disappearance is indicative of the extent to which the newcomers' assimilation had taken place: 'la gent havia deixat de ser i de sentir-se valenciana. Els fills, catalans o castellans, eren barcelonins. El sentiment de pertinença s'havia afeblit i ha estat molt després que hem anat reconstruint, amb amics i coneguts, una mena de xarxa' (p. 35) ('the people had ceased to be and feel Valencian. The children, whether Catalan or Spaniards, were from Barcelona. The feeling of belonging had weakened and it was much later that we began to rebuild a sort of network, with friends and acquaintances').

The seventeen chapters and epilogue that make up the book, similarly to the narcissistic trend of ego-history narratives, are always structured around self-reference. This narrative strategy is well justified: Guillamon embodies the Valencian integration that he wishes to narrate. By relying on self-referentiality, the narrative self takes the rhetorical licence of expository digression and time discontinuity. What results is an amalgam of very diverse narrative and visual material – from a photograph of the old train station in the city of Castelló or the Poblenou *trinquet* (the court used to play Valencian *pilota*, the traditional handball sport of the region), to textual quotes from his mother's diary. He even notes his auditory memory associated with Valencian immigration: 'M'he passat mitja vida sentint les pilotades d'aquest trinquet i els crits dels jugadors que salten o s'estiren per abastar la bola' (p. 223) ('For half my life I've been hearing the balls bouncing on this *trinquet* and the shouts of the players as they jump or stretch to reach the ball'). In this way, the haphazard arrangement of personal memories and emotions by the narcissistic historian, although aesthetically effective, constructs a narrative of the Valencian immigrants' community that is excessively disjointed, lacking a clear diachronic disposition.

The ensemble of highly heterogenous textual and graphic material, far removed from high culture (with a few exceptions),[13] is discursively presented through arbitrary associations that above all allow the reader to link together the experiences of family members and neighbours, while establishing connections between people of different generations and taking in their own memories and their own emotional bonds. Hence, despite the constant flashbacks and flashforwards, he weaves a fluctuating diachronic discourse that portrays the newcomers' cultural assimilation process based on very different and at times traumatic life stories over the course of several decades. Moreover, the cultural assimilation of the Valencians was viewed as less problematic than that of other groups, such as the Murcian migrants.[14] Through this kaleidoscopic composition, which prominently explores the settings of the workplace and school (spaces of socialisation par excellence), Guillamon depicts the migrant phenomenon as a complex and ever-changing symbolic reality, based on countless details that are imbued with the heartbeats of many lives.

The story of Valencian migration, which appears intermittently, is only occasionally presented in generic terms, such as when it is explained that the determination to escape poverty led many people from the province of Castelló to emigrate:

> En el pas del segle XIX al segle XX, els pobles de l'interior de la província de Castelló, lligats de manera natural amb Catalunya, van generar un flux ininterromput de gent, una gran emigració oblidada, anterior a l'emigració murciana i andalusa. (*Barri*, p. 33)

> In the transition from the nineteenth century to the twentieth century, the inland towns of the province of Castelló, which were naturally connected with Catalonia, generated a constant flow of people, a vast and long forgotten emigration, prior to the Murcian and Andalusian migration.

Although he devotes pages to the retrieval of the social, political and lifestyle aspects of the Valencians (anarchist activities, labour conditions at factories and small establishments, kinship, political and cultural associations, celebrations and recreation), the story of immigration is built primarily around the family institution. His history of immigration places the filial perspective in the foreground. Hence, from the geographical description of the Alt Millars region to the exhumation of historical demographic data, Guillamon ultimately builds his family tree.

Regarding the news of floods in October 1882 that affected several towns in Alt Millars, Guillamon speculates:

> Potser va ser el punt de partida d'una emigració que en pocs anys va esdevenir torrencial, fins al punt que el nombre de gent que es deia Guillamón es va triplicar: de seixanta-cinc a dos-cents tretze.

> Primer va venir la *tía* del meu pare, Generosa Guillamón i el seu marit, Clemente Franquero i es van instal·lar al carrer Topete. Més tard, Marcelino Andreu, el pare del Marcelino del passatge Mas de Roda, va obrir un bar al carrer Talat. El meu pare en parlava com si fossin família, i potser ho eren, de lluny. Els meus iaios no se sap exactament quan van arribar . . . El meu pare va néixer el 1929. A partir d'aquest moment es va produir un degoteig constant de gent de Toga: les germanes de la meva iaia van venir a Barcelona a servir, no es van adaptar i van tornar al poble . . . Quan els meus iaios es van instal·lar al carrer Luchana, als anys trenta, la casa va esdevenir lloc de pas per als parents, abans que trobessin feina i pis. Uns duien els altres: com fan ara els xinesos i els magribins. (p. 34; italics in the original)

> It may have been the starting point of a migration that became torrential within just a few years, to the point that the number of people called Guillamón tripled: from sixty-five to two hundred and thirteen. First came my father's aunt, Generosa Guillamón, and her husband, Clemente Franquero, who settled in Topete Street. Later, Marcelino Andreu, the father of Marcelino who lived in Passatge de Mas de Roda, opened a bar in Talat Street. My father spoke of them as if they were family, and maybe they were, from afar. No-one knows exactly when my grandparents arrived . . . My father was born in 1929. From that moment onward, there was a constant trickle of people from Toga: my grandmother's sisters came to Barcelona as servants. They didn't acclimate and went back to the village . . . When my grandparents moved to Luchana Street, in the thirties, the house became a temporary home for relatives, until they found work and a flat. Some would bring the others over, the way the Chinese and Maghrebians do today.

The emphasis on the ancestral history of grandparents, relatives and neighbours, which constitutes the initial part of the work, gradually transitions into a closer examination of both the father and the mother as the narrative unfolds. In fact, the book becomes 'el drama d'una família bilingüe' ('the drama of a bilingual family'), as Guillamon himself explained on television.[15] Julián Guillamón, who never spoke Catalan, is portrayed as a stray bullet: his great passion was bullfighting and he fashioned himself with the traits of an Andalusian man.[16] Maria Mota is presented as a level-headed, honest and overworked Catalan woman who devotes her life to the tasks of cultural propagation and family care, naturally in keeping with the patriarchal dictates of the time. The second part of *El barri de la Plata* is dedicated to portraying the constant marital conflicts, as Guillamon explained in a prime time television interview.[17] This narrative strategy means that, although the book aims to reveal the story of a relatively quick and non-traumatic cultural assimilation favored by cultural similarity and geographic proximity, in the readers' eyes the conflict between the author's parents could take on synecdochic value in terms of the exchange between the two communities.[18] After all, it must be noted that Guillamon's perspective was shaped heavily by the very fact of having grown up in the middle of the rift between two divided worlds: 'Jo vaig néixer enmig d'aquesta situació de, diguem-ne, xoc cultural. Tenia una família catalana i una família valenciana que parlava castellà. Avis i iaios. Un món a Gràcia i un altre al Poblenou' (p. 26) ('I was born in the middle of this setting of, let's say, cultural shock. I had a Catalan family and a Valencian family who were Spanish speakers. Grandparents with different names: *avis* and *iaios*. One world in Gràcia and another in Poblenou'). As often happens in ego-history texts, the problematisation of the writer's identity throughout his life trajectory, allowing him to stand as the spokesperson for a subaltern community,[19] is at the heart of *El barri de la Plata*:

> A l'Arxiu de Sant Martí he trobat alguns documents que em fan reviure aquesta sensació d'estranyesa, de no saber on ets ni quina és la norma que s'ha seguit en la construcció del lloc on et trobes, que tothom que ha viscut al Poblenou ha sentit en un moment o altre. (*Barri*, p. 44).

> I found some documents at the Municipal Archive of the Sant Martí district that have made me relive this feeling of strangeness, of not knowing where you are or what norm has been followed in the construction of the place you find yourself in. Everyone who has lived in Poblenou has felt this at some point or another.

A Work of Ego-History

The Italian historian Enzo Traverso observes in *Singular Pasts* the existence of a growing corpus of hybrid works, situated between history and narrative fiction, that subvert canonical concepts, codes and procedures of both the academic discipline and the novel. These works often focus on the study of subaltern figures, those who had been marginalised in grand historical narratives. Traverso points out that these works have in common not only the fact that they narrate the past from a homodiegetic narrative voice, but also the omnipresence of the 'I', the lack of distance between the author of the work and her object of study, as well as a self-reflexive enjoyment, a self-admiring narcissism.[20] Thus, to refer to these cultural productions he uses the term 'ego-history' coined by Nora.

Traverso, following scholar and novelist Ivan Jablonka's *History Is a Contemporary Literature*,[21] argues that the cultivation of this genre by historians has entailed the adoption of narrative strategies and styles akin to those of the novel. However, whereas Jablonka sees the literary turn in the social sciences as a highly positive development, in that it helps to reach a wider audience and allows for greater historical rigour, Traverso has a more critical perspective. The proliferation of ego-history, which enjoys great success among readers and critics alike, is changing the way that we relate to the past, warns Traverso. While acknowledging the legitimacy, interest and literary quality of many of these texts, Traverso considers several aspects of this historiographical tendency as highly problematic: the laxity with which factual reality is depicted, the magnification of detail at the expense of the bigger picture and the presentism that relinquishes the dialectic between the past and the future; all these factors militate against the creation of a horizon of expectations in the historical narrative.[22] Moreover, he regards the focus on the intimate sphere, characteristic of this tendency, as a manifestation of neoliberalism that results in the loss of a collective 'we', the pre-eminence of a subjective temporality and the depoliticisation of the past. Instead of becoming a space for generating a utopian imagination, the past tends to be commodified and turned into heritage, devoid of its political potential.[23] Thus for Traverso, in ego-history public memory is sidelined in favour of individualism, giving rise to privatised forms of memory.[24] Furthermore, this kind of work often aims to redeem or provide reparation to one or several members of a family, seeking to elicit empathetic responses from readers through a mournful discourse. Such empathetic drive is further reinforced by the fact that ego-histories often act as mirrors in which readers see themselves reflected, in consonance with a fascination with self-narration so present in our times. Traverso argues that the emphasis on individual experience and personal trauma comes at the expense of a collective understanding of history and the broader sociopolitical context.

Julià Guillamon's *El barri de la Plata* shares many of the characteristics that Traverso identifies in the narratives of the past situated within the new subjectivist paradigm that he describes. From the outset, as we have already noted, in Guillamon's book the author becomes the main protagonist. While not affording Guillamon the status of a 'hero', which Traverso attributes ironically to some authors, *El barri* does constitute a unique intellectual self-portrait in which the author recounts, with honesty but without modesty, both his school and professional experiences, his development as an adolescent writer and all sorts of personal memories and emotions. The constant presence of the narcissistic historian in this book puts on an equal footing the history of Valencian immigration and the author's account of the methods employed to research the past. In a passage in which Guillamon meets fellow writer Joan Rendé, we read:

> Hem quedat al bar del Casino de l'Aliança per parlar de les meves recerques sobre el barri. M'explica que els seus avis materns, els Matons i els Masdeus, eren drapaires i transportistes del barri del Taulat. Compraven ferros: els cèrcols de les bótes que redreçaven a mà per fer *flejes* [sic]. També portaven carbó del moll a les foneries, amb grans senalles, que carregaven en unes carretes de rodes robustíssimes. En poc temps van ser propietaris d'unes cases al carrer Major del Taulat i al carrer Odó Pinós, en un dels nuclis més antics del Poblenou: molt senzilles, amb uns pisos petits, amb uns baixos que al darrere hi tenien un hort. En una d'aquestes cases, cap a finals del segle XIX s'hi van instal·lar a viure Joaquim Monzó Vidal, bufador de vidre, valencià de Benigànim, a la vall d'Albaida: l'avi de l'escriptor Quim Monzó. (*El barri*, p. 56; italics in the original)

> We met at the bar of the Casino de l'Aliança to discuss my research on the neighbourhood. He told me that his maternal grandparents, the Matons and the Masdeus, were rag pickers and road hauliers based in the Taulat district. They would buy iron scraps: the hoops of barrels that they would straighten by hand to make bands. They

also hauled coal from the port to the foundries, using large baskets that they loaded onto sturdy wheeled carts. They quickly became the owners of some buildings on Taulat's Main Street and on Odó Pinós Street, in one of the oldest areas of the Poblenou. These were humble buildings with small dwellings and a backyard. Towards the end of the nineteenth century, writer Quim Monzó's grandfather, Joaquim Monzó Vidal, a glassblower from Benigànim in the Vall d'Albaida, Valencia, moved into one of these buildings.

In a similar vein to works mentioned by Traverso – such as *Jeanne et les siennes* by Michel Winnock, *Quelle histoire: Un récit de filiation* by Stéphane Audoin-Rouzeau, and *Landscape for a Good Woman* by Carolyn Steedman[25] – Guillamon turns the family into a privileged platform from which to contemplate history. In his case, it is the history of the Valencian immigrants who settled in Poblenou and their descendants. As evidence of the past, the author provides a plethora of textual and visual elements from his family's archive, especially private writings (letters, school notebooks) and photographs. This is the strategy that many authors have employed to shape postmemory, as argued by Marianne Hirsch. To illustrate and stress the Valencian identity of his father, Guillamon reproduces the photograph of the train station of Castelló, which his father kept until his death: 'era la porta d'entrada a un espai privat, introspectiu, un reducte ideal, on va viure el temps de la innocència, abans d'enfrontar-se al taller i a les dureses de la vida' (*El barri*, p. 42) ('it was the gateway to a private, introspective space, an ideal stronghold, where he had lived the age of innocence, before having to face the workshop and the hardships of life'). The photograph on the book cover, however, remains the most significant visual element.

This image, which occupies the entire cover in the book's Catalan version, shows a close-up of the mother's initials delicately embroidered on the white sheets of her trousseau.[26] This photograph, I would argue, is highly significant. The paratext clearly reveals that *El barri de la Plata* aims to serve as a gesture of posthumous reparation for the mother, for whom the writer feels 'un deute immens' (p. 63) ('immensely indebted'). The prominence of the embroidery on the bride's immaculate sheets, an intimate object linked symbolically to the patriarchal dictates of the time, is a public acknowledgement of the person who most suffered the consequences of the father's unruly life, which were further worsened by the social and cultural conditions of Francoism: 'L'ambient de postguerra no era gens propici a les noies' (p. 94) ('The post-war milieu was not at all favourable for girls'), he observes. The book cover is an expression of the author's gratitude to his mother, who instilled in her children a love for Catalan language and culture, thanks to her cultural authority as a mother. The photograph on the cover additionally underscores the link between women and immigration, an alliance that has been widely recognised in the Catalan literary field.[27]

In chapter 9, Guillamon reproduces a letter written in Spanish that his mother, Maria Mota, sent to her husband in August 1959, shortly after they were married, which reveals the stark differences in character between the two, while underscoring her expectations of a shared life that she will soon see thwarted:

> He recibido tu postal desde Valencia, me alegro de que te diviertas, ya que yo no puedo estar a tu lado, por lo menos que tú los pases bien, también a mí me haría muy feliz estar a tu lado paseando por Valencia, pero que [sic] le vamos a hacer, paciencia, otro año si Dios quiere. Me consuela el pensar que tenemos toda una vida por delante para ir de vacaciones juntos. (p. 101)

> I received your postcard from Valencia, I'm glad you're having fun. Since I can't be by your side, at least you're having a good time. I would also love to be by your side strolling around Valencia, but what can we do but be patient? We'll go another year, God willing. It's comforting to think that we have a whole lifetime ahead of us to go on vacation together.

The exhibition of such intimate factual material reinforces the empathetic bond between the writer and his object of study, while also seeking to appeal to the reader's sensibilities. The stimulation of a compassionate attitude from the reader is further reinforced by presenting the mother as a victim of a 'despòtic i arbitrari' (p. 95) ('despotic and arbitrary') husband, lazy, wasteful, who even resorted to physical violence against her.[28] However, Guillamon shows understanding towards his father. In fact, he expresses a strong sense of filial affection and, to a certain extent, fascination. Following Jablonka, I would argue that Guillamon formalises his emotions within the historical narrative, without compromising the rigour required to recreate the factual reality of family biographies. In fact, it would be futile and absurd to attempt to present these emotions from a distant and purely analytical objectivity.

The preponderance of emotions and intimate experiences in this work entails that the narrative presents the Valencian neighbours of Poblenou within a subjective temporality, without a well-established chronological order, always linked to the present of the narrative self and subject to his successive discoveries of the past; these are shown cumulatively filtered through the author's passion for collecting (coins, stamps, magazines, advertising, vinyls). Furthermore, the importance afforded by the author to individual portraits and emotional connections leaves no space to report on the major political events in twentieth-century Spanish history (the Second Republic, the Civil War, Francisco Franco's dictatorship), which, beyond occasional references,[29] never appear as the backdrop to biographical events. Thus, the preponderance of the expression of emotions allows the Civil War to acquire an anecdotal value:

> Quan el 1975 es va publicar el dietari de Marià Manent, *El vel de Maia*, que explicava els tres anys que Manent havia passat a Viladrau durant la guerra civil, la meva mare, que no acostumava a comprar llibres fora dels del Círculo de Lectores, el va llegir de seguida. Es va emocionar perquè en Manent esmentava la seva padrina, que va morir de part la nit de Nadal de 1937. (p. 53)

> When Marià Manent's diary, *El vel de Maia* ('Maya's Veil'), which recounted the three years he had spent in Viladrau during the Civil War, was published in 1975, my mother, who usually didn't buy books except for those from the Book Club, read it right away. She was moved because Manent mentioned her godmother, who died giving birth on Christmas Eve in 1937.

This phenomenon in which personal emotions take precedence over the large picture is actually unique, considering that the boom of memoir narratives about the Spanish Civil War still persists. Viewing it from this perspective, we could say that Guillamon's textual landscape is rather apolitical: it gets lost in biographical details and daily trivialities at the expense of developing a more sociological and historical understanding of the collective experiences of the Valencians who settled in Barcelona. By relinquishing a comprehensive view in favour of the singularisation of history, by staying within the realm of microhistory without connecting it to the grand narratives of macrohistory, Guillamon elaborates the mode of historical narrative that Traverso questions, but that it is proposed by other historians like Magnússon because of its contribution to constructing postmodern knowledge.[30]

History or Narrative Fiction?

The adoption of codes, tools and methods specific to the historian in *El barri de la Plata* – which the author, as we have seen, emphasises in the narrative – invites the reader to approach it not only as a literary text but also as a factual account. Guillamon's creative exercise – drawing both from factual reality and from a personal and collective memory infused with emotion and often formalised according to the codes of the novel, as is the case with regard to the relationship between his parents – never incorporates fiction. Thus, Guillamon stands clear from autofiction, another genre anchored in factual reality that currently enjoys great popularity. This genre has been cultivated by renowned European authors such as Annie Ernaux, the 2022 Nobel laureate, and by a considerable number of Catalan authors. Consequently, beyond paying attention to the rich compositional texture of Guillamon's prose and his stylistic treatment of language, the reader is compelled to interpret it from a historical, and even social and demographic perspective. Therefore, I would propose to examine the impact Guillamon has on both the literary field and the understanding of the history of Valencian immigration through his heterodox exercise of revisiting the past.

First and foremost, within the Catalan literary corpus that depicts Spanish inner migrations, *El barri* may well contain the most complete and accurate portrait of mixed marriages, a phenomenon of great social impact in twentieth-century Catalonia. With regard to mixed marriages, Francesc Candel had already remarked in 1964 their linguistic and social vicissitudes:

> En els matrimonis mixtos, diguem-ho així, podem observar que quan la catalana és la dona, parla el català amb els fills i els fills amb ella,

però amb el marit no . . . De vegades el pare sembla un estranger, perquè cal canviar d'idioma per a adreçar-li la paraula.[31]

In mixed marriages, let's put it this way, we see that when the Catalan spouse is the wife, she speaks Catalan with the children and the children with her, though she does not speak it with her husband . . . Sometimes the father is like a foreigner, as the others must switch languages to address him.

Guillamon's portrait of a mixed marriage conveys relevant historical and demographic information. It symbolically reinforces the division in Barcelona's social imaginary during the long years of the Franco regime. It is a split between two separate worlds that the dictatorship further polarised.

The narrative strategy of structuring the tale of immigration around the conflicts that arise in a mixed marriage – which go on for decades and stem from a power imbalance between the two spouses, thus reproducing classic patriarchal patterns – essentially evokes similarities with Spanish cultural and linguistic domination during the long years of the Franco regime and beyond. Hence, a correlation is drawn between the dictatorship and the father's dominant masculinity on the one hand, and the subordination of Catalan culture and language and the mother's subordination, on the other.

The second issue to consider is that, as Xavier Pla suggests in his essay on autofiction,[32] the book aims to play the micropolitical function of reparation. Thus, as a form of individual reparation opportunistically linked with the emergence of feminism in Catalonia in recent years, Guillamon explicitly wants to give a well-deserved recognition to his mother that may also be read as a tribute to women in general. He explains that Maria Mota, having received her schooling in Spanish, as imposed by the Franco regime in its early years, decided to take her children to Voramar, 'una escola catalana' (*Barri*, p. 142) ('a Catalan school'), and bought the children books and records in Catalan, 'perquè érem nens catalans' (p. 143) ('because we were Catalan children'). She also worked to get them into private schools and the university.

Guillamon presents his mother as a woman who, despite having made constant sacrifices to please a domineering husband and suffered countless humiliations, gradually gains agency.[33] By embracing the duties of raising the children and family care,[34] she ultimately took on a fundamental role in terms of the children's identity, giving them access to Catalan language and culture under political, economic and social circumstances that were by no means favourable. Without this maternal legacy, Guillamon would not have been the Catalan writer he is today. For this reason, *El barri de la Plata* embodies a gesture of reparation for the memory of his mother, who, despite having suffered different forms of personal and systemic violence (both towards women and towards Catalan culture), fought so that her children would not experience the institutional prejudices against Catalan language that she had suffered, and so that they could live a dignified life as Catalans. In an essay on the memory of immigration in Catalonia, sociologist Salvador Cardús noted:

> the surprising capacity of the Catalan people for creating and maintaining their own particular culture and language despite the notable disadvantages arising from their lack of distinct political institutions from the beginning of the eighteenth century onwards.[35]

If not for the hidden nature of the household propagation of Catalan culture by women, and particularly the wives of mixed marriages like Maria Mota, Cardús would certainly not have used the adjective 'surprising'. By shedding light on their role in terms of both family care and Catalan linguistic and cultural propagation, *El barri de la Plata* constitutes a reparation and recognition of the historical importance of these women.

The third aspect that I wish to highlight is that, while Traverso laments that ego-histories often do not envision any future horizons,[36] Guillamon gestures through the reconstruction of the historical memory of Valencian immigration towards a model of integration for future newcomers.[37] Furthermore, in *El barri de la Plata* he tackles the two challenges that, as he states at the end of *La ciutat interrompuda* ('The Interrupted City', 2001), Catalan literature has to face: the composition of a new map of Barcelona that addresses the peripheries of the city, transforming them into spaces of identity and memory; and the documentation of the people's past, to bring history back to life and thus connect a world that has disappeared with the present, 'perquè el que vam ser no resti al marge del que som' ('so that what we were does not remain outside of what we are').[38] In this way, he defines the horizon of a society that positively values immigration. Indeed, *El barri* is a moral fable providing a historical reassessment of the benefits of immigration. The recognition of Catalonia's ethnically mixed culture aims to convey a sense of Catalan identity as the result of the sedimentary layers of multiple identities. Guillamon, who fully experienced the tensions between two worlds with no mutual recognition, embodies the achievement of his unambiguous recognition as a Catalan citizen. In view of the immigration flows from outside Spain, the life story of a son and grandson of immigrants who was born in a working-class neighbourhood of Barcelona, and who has not only achieved professional success but amassed extraordinary social and cultural capital, helps transform the imaginaries of Catalan society by presenting it as a community built largely by immigrants.

Finally, I wish to highlight that Guillamon has been considerably successful in his attempt to lend visibility to Valencian immigration and revive the feeling of identity among Valencians, a goal shared by demographer Kenneth Pitarch, as we saw at the beginning of this chapter. Beyond the media presence that Valencian immigration has gained in the wake of *El barri de la Plata* (newspaper articles, book reviews, television coverage), the creation of the literary route in Poblenou inspired by the book, led by Guillamon himself, attests to his great ability to connect with the public – a cultural operation that, to a certain extent, can be related to the dynamics of patrimonialisation and commodification that Traverso criticises.[39] Indeed, the ability of the author of ego-histories to connect with the public – which Traverso, Jablonka and Pla all underscore – is the subject matter of the sequel to *El barri de la Plata*, published under the title *El tren de la bruixa* ('The Witch's Train', 2018). This book is a sentimental, detailed chronicle of the launch events of *El barri de la Plata* in four places featured in this book: the Alt Millars county in Valencia, the Poblenou district (the Valencian public television went to both places to film the events for a documentary about immigration), the town of Arbúcies, and the bar Roure in Gràcia. The book describes the interest with which the people of these areas received *El barri de la Plata* (even two children of Maghreb origin from the Valencian town of Onda requested his autograph) and, above all, the emotions that the book elicited (one reader tells him that he has read the book three times and that it made him cry). Thanks to this success, the sequel provides new personal information on the Valencian immigrants who, according to the readers of the first book, had felt interpellated by Guillamon: by recounting the singular past of their ancestors to a spokesman, the family history is preserved for posterity thanks to writing. As a result, the local people of the places described in *El barri de la Plata* collectively contributed to the reconstruction of the microhistory of former ties of kinship, friendship and acquaintance between Valencians and Catalans. This symbiosis between the researcher and the object of study (Valencian immigrants and their descendants), it must be pointed out, further inflates the narcissistic historian. Guillamon, dedicated to narrating his own success as the saviour of collective memory, delights, like Narcissus, in self-contemplation and self-admiration.

Conclusion

In 2008, Josep-Anton Fernàndez pointed out the dearth of the subject of Spanish immigration in Catalan literature, suggesting that the relative lack of literary texts (in the second half of the twentieth century) depicting migrant experiences was indicative of a crisis of representation in Catalan culture. He claimed that the production of a body of works representing immigration '*en català i a partir d'un punt de vista identificat com a català*' ('in Catalan and from a point of view identified as Catalan') would be key to the 'reconeixement com a catalans, sense ambigüitats, dels immigrants d'origen espanyol i dels seus descendents' ('unamibiguous recognition as Catalans of migrants of Spanish origin and their descendants').[40]

Ten years later, *El barri de la Plata* contributed to fill the lack of representation observed by Fernàndez, dealing with a demographic contingent hitherto relegated to oblivion and placing it into a larger historical frame: indeed, the work reconstructs the memory of Valencian immigration *from a point of view identified as Catalan*. Guillamon does so by turning the neighbourhood of Poblenou in Barcelona into a place of memory that acknowledges and celebrates Catalan society's capacity for absorbing incoming population flows from the late nineteenth century to today – an integration that has not been free of tensions, as the text clearly states.

Using the analytic framework presented by Enzo Traverso in *Singular Pasts* and, to a lesser extent, Ivan Jablonka's argument in *History Is a Contemporary Literature*, I have argued that Guillamon formalises the representation of Valencian immigration as a literary ego-history, and he does so from a Catalan point of view. Through his participation in the subjective turn in historical writing, Guillamon not only contributes to the growing corpus of self-referential narrative in Catalan literature, but also complements the historical knowledge of one of Catalonia's most significant demographic phenomena, overlooked until recent years. By combining rhetorical and narrative strategies pertaining to the novel with scholarly tools, codes and research methodologies, Guillamon successfully reclaims the memory of a social and historical phenomenon that is deeply embedded in personal circumstances in a variety of ways. *El barri de la Plata* is one of the first literary portrayals, written from a filial perspective, of a mixed marriage in Catalan society. On the other hand, Guillamon's personal tribute to the figure of his mother can be interpreted as a homage to all those mothers who, within Catalan households, nurtured their families and safeguarded the Catalan language and culture in the face of institutional repression during the Franco dictatorship. Thus, he tackles the historical injustices endured by these women, marginalised and excluded from historical narratives. This gesture can be seen, following Xavier Pla, as a kind of micropolitics that is developed through an aesthetic proposal. Moreover, by making public his immigrant background and positing himself as a model of successful integration into Catalan society, Guillamon opens up a horizon of expectations for Catalans and immigrants alike, regardless of their origin, as equal members of a nation of immigrants. Embracing ego-history, Guillamon performs all these operations successfully through a remarkable ability to connect with the public and generate interest in the past among readers, but this success does not preclude the ambiguities and ambivalences that, according to Enzo Traverso, this genre entails.

Notes

1   Àlex Milian, 'Valencians a Catalunya: La invisible migració interior', *El Temps* (10 March 2015), www.eltemps.cat/article/4716/valencians-a-catalunya-la-invisible-migracio-interior.

2 Andreu Domingo and Kenneth Pitarch, 'La població valenciana a Catalunya al segle XXI: anàlisi demogràfica i espacial', *Treballs de la Societat Catalana de Geografia*, 79 (2015), 9. Unless otherwise stated, all translations from Catalan and Spanish are my own.
3 Kenneth Pitarch Calero, 'Anàlisi sociodemogràfica de la migració valenciana a Catalunya i altres destinacions' (unpublished PhD thesis, Universitat Autònoma de Barcelona, 2018), 7, *www.tdx.cat/handle/10803/663903#page=1*.
4 Pitarch, 'Anàlisi sociodemogràfica', 170. For the 1991 Spanish Sociodemographic Survey, see *https://datos.gob.es/en/catalogo/ea0010587-encuesta-sociodemografica-1991-microdatos1*.
5 For this reason, Guillamon defines *El barri de la Plata* as a post-industrial book. Julià Guillamon, '*L'atzar i les ombres*, novel·la total: L'atzar i les obres (II)', *La lectora* (20 December 2022), *https://lalectora.cat/2022/12/20/latzar-i-les-ombres-novella-total-latzar-i-les-obres-ii/*.
6 Enzo Traverso, *Passats singulars: El 'jo' en l'escriptura de la història*, trans. by Gustau Muñoz (Catarroja and Barcelona: Afers, 2021).
7 Traverso, *Passats singulars*, p. 24.
8 Pierre Nora (dir.), *Essais d'ego-histoire* (Paris: Gallimard, 1987).
9 Marianne Hirsch, *Family Frames: Photography, Narrative and Postmemory* (Cambridge MA and London: Harvard University Press, 1997).
10 Here we will not discuss Guillamon's role as interpreter of the urban palimpsest of Poblenou as presented by the narrative voice, which has been so valued by critics.
11 Pla examines the autofictional works by European authors such as Annie Ernaux, Emmanuel Carrère and Mircea Cărtărescu, and pays special attention to the production of Catalan authors: Baltasar Porcel, Francesc Serés, Sergi Pàmies and Toni Sala, among others. See Xavier Pla, *El soldat de Baltimore: Assaigs sobre literatura i realitat en temps d'autoficció* (Palma: Lleonard Muntaner, 2022).
12 Julià Guillamon, *El barri de la Plata* (Barcelona: L'Avenç, 2018), p. 13.
13 Guillamon's books, which often imitate the collage technique and are illustrated with photographs, are eclectic. His knowledge, stemming from his university training in Catalan language and literature, is interwoven with observations on cinema, photography, art, music and advertising. He often includes displays of written, oral and visual popular culture, as well as excerpts from interviews and other materials taken from historical archives, periodicals libraries and flea markets.
14 Francesc Candel, a Valencian immigrant, recalls that 'dir "murcià" era insultar' ('saying "Murcian" was insulting'). Francesc Candel, *Els altres catalans* (Barcelona: Edicions 62, 2008), p. 59.
15 Xavier Graset, 'Entrevista a Julià Guillamon, escriptor: Ens presenta el seu darrer llibre, *El Barri de la Plata*', *Més 324*, Canal 3/24, Televisió

de Catalunya (16 October 2018), *www.ccma.cat/tv3/alacarta/mes-324/ entrevista-a-julia-guillamon-escriptor-ens-presenta-el-seu-darrer-llibre-el-barri-de-la-plata/video/5792166/*.

16 The passion for bullfighting was a fundamental part of the father's identity: 'Els toros, potser el record del viatge a Sevilla; també, segur, l'ambient de la Barcelona franquista; i el contacte amb la gent que trobava a les feines; van fer que el meu pare comencés a fer-se l'andalús' (Guillamon, *El barri de la Plata*, p. 91) ('Bullfighting, maybe the memory of the trip to Seville; also, definitely, the atmosphere of Francoist Barcelona; and the contact with the people he met at work; they all spurred my father to begin to act Andalusian').

17 In this television interview, Guillamon states that the book begins with the reconstruction of various life stories of Valencian migrants, and 'es va focalitzant i es converteix en una novel·la' ('gradually focuses in, becoming a novel') that recounts 'el drama d'una família bilingüe . . . en una Barcelona dels anys 40 i 50, que està molt espanyolitzada' ('the drama of a bilingual family . . . in the Barcelona of the 1940s and 50s, which has become very Spanish'): the city of his parents. He further adds: 'el meu pare havia boxat, havia volgut ser torero, a casa escoltàvem rumbes a punta pala' ('my father had been a boxer and wanted to be a bullfighter. At home we listened to loads of *rumbas*'). Xavier Graset, 'Entrevista a Julià Guillamon, escriptor'.

18 Guillamon presents his parents' story as a literary metaphor, comparing the couple to popular culture and high culture. On the one hand, he makes reference to a fable: 'la meva mare era una rateta que escombrava l'escaleta, que pagava amb la vida la imprudència d'haver-se enamorat d'un gat' (*El barri*, p. 137) ('my mother was a little mouse who swept the stairs and who paid the ultimate price for the recklessness of having fallen in love with a cat'). On the other hand, he cites Mercè Rodoreda's *La plaça del Diamant*, comparing his father with Quimet and his mother with Natàlia (p. 94).

19 Traverso, *Passats singulars*, p. 19.
20 Traverso, *Passats singulars*, pp. 16–17.
21 Ivan Jablonka, *History Is a Contemporary Literature: Manifesto for the Social Sciences* (Ithaca NY and London: Cornell University Press, 2018).
22 Traverso, *Passats singulars*, p. 151.
23 Traverso, *Passats singulars*, p. 156.
24 Traverso, *Passats singulars*, pp. 148–9.
25 See Michel Winnock, *Jeanne et les siennes* (Paris: Seuil, 2003); Stéphane Audoin-Rouzeau, *Quelle histoire: Un récit de filiation* (Paris: École d'Hautes Études en Sciences Sociales, Gallimard and Seuil, 2013); and Carolyn Steedman, *Landscape for a Good Woman: A Story of Two Lives* (Londres: Virago, 1986).

26 Conversely, the Spanish edition, targeting an audience closer to bullfighting culture, displays a photograph of the staff of his father's bullfighting cape.
27 As a keen observer of literary events, Guillamon had witnessed the presentations of the following awards: the 2004 Columna Jove Award to Laila Karrouch for *De Nador a Vic* ('From Nador to Vic', 2004); the 2008 Ramon Llull Award to Najat El Hachmi for *L'últim patriarca* ('The Last Patriarch', 2008); the 2010 Prudenci Bertrana Award to Nadia Ghulam and Agnès Rotger for *El secret del meu turbant* ('The Secret of My Turban', 2010); the 2015 Sant Joan and Ciutat de Barcelona awards to El Hachmi for *La filla estrangera* ('The Foreign Daughter', 2015); the 2015 Gaudí Award for the Best Film in Catalan to film director Maria Ripoll for the adaptation of *Rastres de sàndal* ('Traces of Sandalwood', 2007) by Asha Miró and Anna Soler-Pont; and the 2017 Joan Fuster Award to Margarida Castellano Sanz for *Les altres catalanes: Memòria, identitat i autobiografia en la literatura d'immigració* ('The Other Catalan Women: Memory, Identity and Autobiography in Migrant Literature', 2018). In his own way, Guillamon, joins the ranks of this line of writing.
28 At home, Guillamon's father caused episodes of violence that the author recalls painfully, especially the first time that he saw his father drunk and when he hit his mother. The incident of gender violence led to a trial in court and resulted in the parents' separation. Thus, Julián Guillamón comes to embody the cliché of 'l'agressivitat i facúndia de l'immigrant' ('the aggressiveness and verbosity of an immigrant') that Maria Dasca identifies in the novel *Retorn al sol* ('Back to the Sun', 1936), by Josep M. Francès. Maria Dasca, 'La immigració com a fenomen en la literatura catalana', *Cercles: Revista d'Història Cultural*, 18 (2015), 68.
29 For instance, 'la postguerra va passar per sobre dels meus pares com un rodet uniformitzador: toros, *coplas* i pasodobles, toreros i *artistas*' (Guillamon, *El barri*, p. 88) ('The post-war period rolled over my parents like a standardising roller: bullfighting, Andalusian folk songs and *pasodobles*, bullfighters and performers').
30 Sigurður Gylfi Magnússon, 'The Singularization of History: Social History and Microhistory within the Postmodern State of Knowledge', *Journal of Social History*, 36/3 (2003), 701–35.
31 Candel, *Els altres catalans*, p. 97.
32 Pla, *El soldat de Baltimore*, p. 46–56.
33 Her agency, however, has an obliterated political dimension that cannot be intuited from the cover of the Castilian edition.
34 The presence of the mother and the appearance at the end of the book of Guillamon himself, looking after his wife Cris, essentially position the author as an example of Catalan narrative texts that pro-

mote the giving of care as a means of becoming involved with contemporary society. This is suggested by Xavier Pla, who associates *El barri de la Plata* with a similar literary trend in vogue in France. Xavier Pla, 'Reparar el món: La literatura catalana i el procés', *Revista de Catalunya*, 301 (2018), 5–11.
35 Salvador Cardús, 'The Memory of Immigration in Catalan Nationalism', *International Journal of Iberian Studies*, 18/1 (2005), 38.
36 Traverso, *Passats singulars*, p. 155.
37 Guillamon devotes several passages to the portrayal of cultural integration, which was never free of tensions. One such example is the start of Maria Mota's married life, when she is forced to live with five other immigrant relatives. Another is the sharing of chores by the paternal Valencian family and the maternal Catalan family at the Hostal d'Arbúcies, the inn run by the author's mother, where he describes the differences in the way Catalans and Valencians used to fry potatoes.
38 Julià Guillamon, *La ciutat interrompuda: De la contracultura a la Barcelona postolímpica* (Barcelona: La Magrana, 2001), p. 283.
39 Traverso, *Passats singulars*, p. 155.
40 Josep-Anton Fernàndez, *El malestar en la cultura catalana: La cultura de la normalització 1976–1999* (Barcelona: Empúries, 2008), p. 257 (emphasis in the original).

Chapter 6

'Catalunya termina aquí. Aquí comença Vietnam': Urbanism, Migration and Spatial Immunity in Jordi Puntí's *Els castellans*

William Viestenz

In 2019, the regional Catalan city of Manlleu held municipal elections that would determine, among other positions, the town's mayor. Within a kilometre of Can Garcia, a 1960s high rise constructed in l'Erm neighbourhood to house migrants from the south of Spain and that later became the primary residence for the city's north African community, one could find political advertisements from two candidates at opposite ends of the ideological spectrum. Along the Passeig de Sant Joan, which constitutes the western boundary hemming in l'Erm neighbourhood and is the primary entry point for travellers entering Manlleu from the north, an advertisement for Paco Zambrana, at the time member of the far-right Som Identitaris ('Identitarians') party, promised to place *manlleuencs* and *manlleuenques* first: 'Nosaltres t'escoltem, nosaltres ens preocupem per tu' ('We hear you, we care about you').[1] Though Zambrana later left the xenophobic Som Identitaris, he garnered over 6 per cent of the vote, gaining a seat as a *regidor* on the city council. At the Avinguda Puigmal, a street forming l'Erm's eastern boundary and half a kilometre to the north-east of Can Garcia, the Esquerra Republicana de Catalunya ('Republican Left of Catalonia') candidate and then mayor of the city, Àlex Garrido, urged potential voters to know that 'Comptem amb Tu!' ('We are counting on you!').[2] Garrido's party secured control of the *ajuntament* ('city council') and he was later re-elected as mayor, before resigning in scandal in 2020.

In Zambrana's message, it is clear that the *manlleuencs* and *manlleuenques* 'to be placed first' are not inclusive of the inhabitants of Can Garcia, whose presence is only acknowledged as the proximate source, given the location of the banner on the edge of l'Erm, of the threat that would preoccupy the Som Identitaris candidate on behalf of the community. Zambrana exhibits not only a xenophobic form of pastoral power, but also a textbook version of what Roberto Esposito calls a negative immunitary biopolitics. Esposito writes that in its founding moment, community is not forged around exclusive identity markers or immutable essences such as a shared language or common territorial origin. Instead, community forms around the reciprocal demand that each individual sacrifice what is proper to the collective, leading to an absolute openness to otherness without external boundaries. The demand that members of a community continually offer up their individual interests and be exposed to radical otherness, however, is eventually felt to be unbearable. To survive, political communities resort to immunitary devices, creating identity-making boundaries based on markers such as language, ethnicity and so on, to create and safeguard a sense of the proper. This boundary-setting movement expropriates the constitutive negativity of the community's founding to its outside, reframing the non-self as a threat to be protected against. As Esposito writes, 'to allow the community to withstand the entropic risk that threatens it . . . it must be sterilized of its own relational contents. It must be immunized from the *munus* that exposes it to contagion using that which, coming from within it, goes beyond it'.[3] Negation of the individual self, community's original relational content, is sterilised and exported beyond the collective and transformed into an annihilating threat. Nationalisms, to varying extents, negatively define what is proper against a constitutive outside that is represented as negation of the self. Far-right groups take this logic to an extreme level, and Som Identitaris and other *ultra* groups often centre immigration in the praxis of their negative biopolitics. As Mudde notes, 'Immigration proper has long been one of the core issues of almost every far-right group in Europe and North America'. In particular, 'the conspiracy theory of "The Great Replacement" is at the heart of much of the anti-immigration rhetoric of the populist radical right'.[4] Zambrana's campaign sign, through its geographical placement and acknowledgement of a threat worthy of collective concern, presents Som Identitaris as an agent of immunisation against a constitutive outside – l'Erm – that paradoxically is within the city limits of Manlleu.[5]

Jordi Puntí's *Els castellans* ('The Castilians', 2011), a recounting of the author's childhood in the north-eastern Catalan city of Manlleu in the 1970s that began as a series of articles in *L'Avenç* in 2007, presents episodic recollections that frequently feature l'Erm's beginnings from the hindsight made possible by the passage of several decades. This chapter will argue that *Els castellans* implicates the built environment, architectural aesthetics and Corbusian urbanism in the praxis of a negative biopolitics that was described above in relation to recent electoral politics. In the text, an immunitary paradigm overlays the spatiality of migration, both recalling and deconstructing earlier Catalan immigration discourses and intersecting with Esposito's immunological biopolitics, social systems theory, philosophies of dwelling in residential space and a logic of parasitism developed by Michel Serres to explain social relations.

In the United States, scholars in the twenty-first century began to dedicate ample attention to the phenomenon of redlining, the rise of the automobile and resulting suburbanisation and attitudes towards public housing in the production of inequality and racial segregation.[6] Architecture, infrastructure, housing and mid-century urbanism map society's biases and power differentials onto the neglected and unclaimed spaces of the late capitalist cityscape that, in addition to imperilling the fairness and vibrancy of the collective, also impacts collective responses to civilisational challenges such as climate change and pandemics. As David Harvey writes, the question of what kind of city a society creates is inseparable from 'what kind of social ties, relationship to nature, lifestyles, technologies, and aesthetic values are desired'.[7] In an immunitary sense, Harvey's list refers to the identity markers that differentiate the community from its negative non-self and urban design participates in producing and reifying immunological distinctions. Building aesthetics and development of the streetscape come to define a city's balance between openness and closure, producing social systems that in varying degrees engineer productive engagement between citizens, new and old, while allowing for expressions of difference to become visible and durable.

In Catalonia, the relationship between the built environment and migration highlighted by Puntí in *Els castellans* was already emphasised by Francesc Candel earlier in the twentieth century when he dedicated a substantial part of the second half of *Els altres catalans* ('The Other Catalans', 1964) to the living conditions of the Spanish post-war period from early Francoism to the *desarrollista* 1960s of Barcelonan migrants in the *barraques* ('shanties'), *estatges protegits* ('social housing') and the mass polygons of highrise towers constructed along the city's periphery. This process ultimately created, or rapidly inflated, neighbourhoods such as Cornellà de Llobregat, in the south-western part of the city, and condensed immigrant population within zones that tended to be distanced from centres of employment and lacking in basic services such as playgrounds and convenient public transit access.[8] Candel infamously declares that 'l'immigrant ha creat el suburbi' ('the immigrant created the suburb'); 'el suburbi ha estat el seu corralet, el lloc on ha estat acorralat' ('the suburb has been his corral, the place where he's been corralled').[9] Though with opposing directionalities and class compositions, the suburbs of both North America and Candel's Barcelona were created by prejudices that manifested in public policy that then intersected with the speculative impulses of private developers during moments of breakneck human migration. Candel's choice of third-person participle – *acorralat* – not only suggests that geographic segregation was not opted into by migrants, but as a conceptual metaphor also indicates a cityscape of graduated spatial ontologies, as the term conjures a more beastly, less than human condition to be kept at bay and out of sight. Urban policy, as a motor of (in)visibility, mirrored a general amnesia of the migrants' body in the cultural realm, a phenomenon that Salvador Cardús, writing in 2005, argued was then generally absent in Catalan discourses of collective identity, owing in part to a nationalism 'bereft of the mechanisms conferred upon independent states' acting 'in the absence of the usual instruments of symbolic domination'.[10] Further problematising the invisibility of the migrant in Catalan cultural production, Josep-Anton Fernàndez homes in on the double bind that the Pujolist discourse of voluntarism posed for incorporating newly arrived waves between 1945 to the late 1970s.[11] While emphasis on cultural roots and the essential nature of the Catalan language remained, the reduction of collective belonging to residency and work:

> [ha] buidat de contingut la identitat catalana perquè la redueixen a la residència, n'eliminen qualsevol referència a la llengua o a altres símbols, i pressuposen l'adhesió a aquesta definició alhora que s'emmascaren les condicions necessàries per aconseguir el reconeixement com a membre de la comunitat nacional.[12]

> [has] emptied the content of Catalan identity by reducing it to residency, eliminating any reference to language or other symbols, and presupposing adhesion to that definition while simultaneously masking the necessary conditions for acquiring recognition as a member of the national community.

As Candel first signals and Puntí later incorporates into *Els castellans*, the Pujolist emphasis on residency as an important precondition for *catalanitat* ('Catalanness') is undercut by the uneven and segregated spatial ontologies that followed intense waves of migration in the late Francoist period. Important to Candel's thesis of a desired-after adoption of Catalan identity on the part of the newly arrived groups primarily from the south of Spain, urbanism, or a complete lack thereof, is a critical structural force that produces 'societats a part' ('societies apart'):

> Jo crec que no formen un món a part, sinó que els obliguen a formar-lo. Tampoc no gaire intencionadament; més aviat és cosa de les actuals circumstàncies d'immigració en massa, el creixement a pegots de les ciutats i el desenvolupament urbanístic imprevist de com sigui i per on es pugui. I d'altres coses. Però el resultat és que formen grups a part. O se'ls obliga a formar-los.[13]

> I believe that they do not form a world apart, rather that they are forced to do it. And not at all intentionally; more than anything it concerns the present circumstances of mass migration, the blotchy growth of cities and the unplanned urban development of however and wherever. Amongst other things. But the result is that they form groups apart. Or they're obliged to form them.

One novelty of Puntí's text is the chronicling of how this phenomenon extended from the metropolis to the smaller and, often, industrial cities of Catalonia, such as Manlleu, Terrassa, Mataró and Sabadell. The segregationist function of architecture and urban design ties into Candel's description of the tense conflict that erupts in the encounter between Catalans and the new arrivals, which is an element of *Els altres catalans* that Najat el Hachmi argues is often subordinated to both his integrationist perspective and the mantra of Catalonia as a nation comprised of immigrants who shed outsider status through the voluntarist effort to live, work and speak the language of the welcoming land. El Hachmi also designates the focus on social fracture between migrants and established residents as an essential part of Candel's legacy, a cleavage that architecture, then as now, continues to foment.[14] In retrospect, the agonistic character of Candel's work easily manifests itself – the immigrants' arrival is termed an 'invasion' (Candel, *Els altres catalans*, p. 146) and second-generation children of migrants 'se senten conquistats per Catalunya' (p. 35) ('feel themselves conquered by Catalonia') – and the text sets the stage for classical questions about the Schmittian ties of friendship and enmity to the political as well as the objections to rationalist consensus made by Chantal Mouffe in which 'the question of power and antagonism' is placed at the centre of social practices, institutions and discourses.[15] Candel's *Els altres catalans* is clearly meant to be a reference point for *Els castellans*, and not only with respect to Puntí's goal of reframing the title in less politically correct terms.[16] Conflict, the built environment and the relationship between order and orientation neutralise the liminality of encounters with difference in the text and effectively immunise the potential presence of dialectical thresholds in which individual bodies engage with one another transformatively. Such engagement, depending on scale, speaks to municipal, regional and national context, both within Manlleu and Catalonia writ large.

Following from the agonistic ethos of Candel's work, *Els castellans* reveals how cities – like nation states in the Schmittian sense – are experienced in terms of boundaries that function as the pillars of 'strategic fictions' that provide an ontological basis for friendship and enmity.[17] Manlleu, today the second largest city in Osona county, changed rapidly between 1960 and 1975 due to migration, increasing its population nearly 60 per cent. By 1970, 25 per cent of the city was born outside of Catalonia, and in Can Garcia and Can Mateu, another residential development in l'Erm, 15 per cent of Manlleu's total population resided.[18] Puntí's autobiographical voice refers to his childhood conflicts with 'els castellans', often in an abandoned lot next to Can Garcia, as a 'ficció infantil' ('childhood fiction'), but it is not experienced as such by the children: 'vivíem en una ficció que ens semblava molt real. Una idea ens bullia al subconscient: "Ho fem perquè no ho hagin de fer els nostres pares"' ('we lived in a fiction that seemed very real to us. One particular idea bubbled up from the subconscious: "We do it so that our parents don't have to"').[19] On the one hand, Puntí provides a classic Marxian definition of an implanted false consciousness whose overall effect is one of class-based alienation, a dynamic Puntí lightly references later on in acknowledging that 'molts treballadors catalans se sentien més propers a l'amo que no als seus companys de feina arribats de fora' (*Els castellans*, p. 42) ('many Catalan workers felt closer to the boss than to their co-workers from other places of origin') in sharing a common distrust of the then-clandestine communist union *Comissions Obreres* (CCOO).[20] The staged enmity is amplified by the insistence from adults to flatten all newcomers into a homogenised group: 'com que ens havien inculcat des de petits, ens dominava aquesta lògica primària: tots els que no eren catalans, eren castellans' (*Els castellans*, p. 12) ('as had been drilled into us from an early age, one primary logic governed our thought: anyone who wasn't Catalan was Castilian'). 'Castilian' is a blanket term for Castilian-speakers of immigrant origin, not limited to those simply from the region of Castile. The verb 'inculcar', and its use in the text in relation to the patterns of social order emergent from cultural production, discourse and normative behaviour, encourages reference to Pierre Bourdieu's concept of *habitus* and its theorisation of how structural power is exercised.

In describing social acts of initiation, Bourdieu pinpoints 'the work of inculcation' as the mechanism by which arbitrary limits, foundational oppositions and dispositions towards taste are achieved.[21] And indeed, as Puntí later adds to his judgement of childhood as a fiction, 'els nens en edat infantil són per als pares exercicis de coherència, projeccions . . . de les il·lusions i expectatives que es van fer respecte del seu futur' (*Els castellans*, p. 125) ('children at an early age are for their parents exercises in coherence, projections . . . of the illusions and expectations that are made towards their futures'). Institutional inculcation communicates and legitimates boundaries and in doing so, 'sanctifies difference' and encourages subjective misrecognition of the arbitrariness at the core of social divisions and hierarchies.[22] As an ideological state apparatus, the family is one such institution. Power and order are written into the structure of social space, and this creates a mutually reinforcing engagement between the subject and the built environment. Habitus will affect the way constructed space is consumed, like the high-rise structure named Can Garcia bordering the *descampat* ('undeveloped lot') that anchors Puntí's narrative. As appendages to the undeveloped space where Puntí's *castellans* and *catalans* eye one another suspiciously, architecture and infrastructure both function as boundaries that sanctify difference and as blank slates for projecting the 'magical acts of institution' that allows a subject to 'become what [they] are'.[23] The ideologies inculcated into the minds of the ten-year-olds in the cultural and political realms are embodied by the subjective experience of the urban grid, which becomes both the stage and set pieces for subjects to play out the dramas that initiate them into the social order.[24]

Bourdieu's qualification of 'becoming what one is' as a magical act connects to the Freudian comparison of children's play to pre-modern understandings of the supernatural. In *Els castellans*, when native *manlleuenc* children go to war with Castilians, they do so 'perquè no ho hagin de fer els nostres pares' (Puntí, *Els castellans*, p. 13) ('so that our parents don't have to do it'), but unlike adults, they lack the full power to translate play acts to reality and must resort to magical hallucination for wish fulfilment. As Freud writes, in play children 'satisfy their wishes in a hallucinatory manner, that is, they create a satisfying situation by means of centrifugal excitation'.[25] Urbanism, hegemonic cultural objects like *Star Wars* and the migratory aftereffects of economic policy such as Franco's 1959 Stabilisation Plan and subsequent Social and Economic Development Plan, converge in Puntí's text with deeper cultural and linguistic differences to create the tension that motivates magical play-acts and predetermine the associations of contiguity attached to the major players in the drama. This point circles back to the function of strategic fictions at the heart of Esposito's notion of a negative biopolitics, where the inherent lack at the centre of *communitas* requires the production of a constitutive outside against which a given group defines (immunises) itself. This constitutive outside, like Freudian hallucinatory wish fulfilment, is a centrifugal phenomenon.

In *Els castellans*, culture and materiality thus intersect in a mutually reinforcing echo chamber in ways that are clear in the retrospective musings of an adult well into the twenty-first century, but appear naturalised and non-arbitrary through the immediate perspective of a ten-year-old already trained to see the world in the Manichaean paradigm dominant in the period, heavily established by *Star Wars*, the Barça-Madrid rivalry and the US-Soviet Cold War that had organised the late 1970s Western world into opposing geopolitical blocs. Puntí notes in the same chapter that the interim thirty years since his childhood saw the neighbourhood evolve in important ways. The streets are now paved and the *descampat* is the site of a newly constructed municipal market that was meant to draw in citizens from throughout Manlleu. The persistence of Can Garcia, however, up until its final removal in July 2021, continues to reify the spatial habitus of the neighbourhood, and though the boundary lines separating the high-rise from the rest of the city have been challenged, they persist in the thrownness of historical memory. Accumulation of capital is the only mode of departure that allows inhabitants of the neighbourhood to step beyond the segregating strictures of residential space, as the Castilians have now relocated to newly built satellite neighbourhoods, with their vacated apartments inhabited by North African migrants (*Els castellans*, p. 115). The intersection of capital accumulation with the ideology and praxis of assimilation reflects a shift that Teresa Vilarós situates beginning with the 1960s revival of Catalan nationalism. A remobilised Catalan nationalism was 'closely linked to modern capital development' and was 'responsible for or [was] at least one of the major contributing factors that serves to explain the truly successful story of upward mobility undergone by the '60s immigration populations'.[26]

Housing policy and residential development, however, limits the extent to which a 'new hegemonic Catalan market' emerging in the last decades of the century can eliminate all ideological traces of Vilarós's 'post-national *xarnego* subject' and the industrial, proletarian class consciousness that it symbolises.[27] In Manlleu, as documented by Puntí, the extent of integration by 1960s and twenty-first-century immigrants into the local and national social fabrics is an ongoing question, as both communities nevertheless still occupy fringe residential spaces, whether in l'Erm or in relatively new satellite communities. Furthermore, as Manel Ollé notes in a review of *Els castellans*, there exists a strong political tendency in certain sectors of Catalonia to 'eternitzar encara avui la condició hereditària d'immigrant (andalús, extremeny, gallec . . .) més enllà de la tercera i fins i tot la quarta generació, convertida en marca indeleble que assegura quotes de vot captiu' ('eternalise even today the hereditary condition of being an immigrant – Andalusian, Extremaduran, Galician, etc. – beyond the third and even the fourth generation, transformed into an indelible mark that assures shares of captive votes').[28] It is thus worth viewing with caution *Els castellans*' representation of l'Erm as a transitory space in which newly arrived groups undergo a process of acquiring the capital, residential stability and linguistic skills necessary for complete normalisation into the municipal and national communities. When Puntí writes that 'aquells castellans van trobar el seu espai i aquells moros van trobant el seu espai' (*Els castellans*, p. 117) ('Castilians found their space and North Africans are finding theirs'), the preterit verbal form insinuates a finality to the Castilians' integration into the city, while the gerund emphasises the North Africans' state of transition. In the former case, however, urban policy, residential development and market speculation still coincide to determine the city's assemblages of social ties, lifestyle modalities and aesthetic values.

Puntí's childhood avatar immanently experiences the aesthetics of Can Garcia and the other new developments in Manlleu's l'Erm neighbourhood as differentiating spaces that invoke immunitary classifications. In the opening chapter, which terms the *descampat* a 'camp de batalla' (p. 9) ('battlefield'), the brutalist, bare-concrete modernism of Can Garcia and *l'escola nacional* ('the national school') invoke an architectural sterility that is a metonym for the ontological othering of the migrants in the attitudes of the narrator and his companions. The framing photograph that announces the book's first chapter shows Can Garcia in the background from the 'camp de batalla', a conspicuous tower rising alone from the undeveloped margin of the city like a spacecraft dropped in from outer space. And indeed, the narrator comments that 'el descampat tenia les condicions ideals per aterrar-hi' (p. 17) ('the empty lot contained the ideal landing conditions for') a flying saucer redolent of the dimensions of the Millennium Falcon. Reference to *Star Wars* reflects the intrusion of the world economic market into Spain in the 1970s, implanting a culture that 'existed in tandem with national identity, and paradoxically encouraged the creation of cultural differences' in younger generations.[29] Indeed, the Millennium Falcon as avatar for the Can Garcia housing bloc amplifies, instead of minimising, identification with the nation and friction with the State. The narrator's description of l'Erm implies that urban planning decision-making primed the children to make such a connection. The Castilians' zone was delimited by:

> blocs de pisos d'una altura desproporcionada – com una anomalia urbana, una elefantiasi que hagués envaït el perfil encara rural de la vila –, unes escoles nacionals pintades d'un blanc nuclear d'una església moderna, podríem dir-ne *hippy* . . . l'altre cantó del no-barri – el nostre – el vertebrava un carrer principal, a mig urbanitzar. (p. 15)

> housing towers of a disproportionate height – like an urban anomaly, an elephantiasis that had invaded the still rural periphery of the town – national schools painted a nuclear white and a modern church, one could call it *hippy* . . . the other side of the non-neighbourhood – ours – was bordered by a major, half-asphalted road.

The 'nuclear white' of the schoolhouse reflects the double condition of its being a blank slate for the projection of infantile fictions of initiation as well as an agonistic symbol filtered through Cold War rhetoric that invites a friend-enemy distinction. Without seamless integration into the folds of the city, l'Erm also is described in immunitary terms, as if the development were the outsized reaction of the social body to a parasite – one of the primary causes of elephantiasis – that has breached its systemic defences on the rural outskirts of Manlleu. The parasitic re-emerges in a later chapter in which the children are warned of trichinosis from uncooked pork, which translates thereafter to an insult launched at the Castilians who are mystified at being compared to the microscopic roundworm (p. 55).

The presence of a half-asphalted street serving as a boundary line with the rest of Manlleu communicates the inclusively excluded nature of the neighbourhood; technically connected to the street grid and part of the community, but below standard, a sentiment strengthened by Puntí's use of the term 'no-barri' to describe a place only used to deposit refuse and detritus, which then becomes fodder for the children's play. The othering of the 'castellans' in the minds of the Catalan children owes primarily to their attachment to a space overdetermined by its architecture, namely the high-rise and school, which the undeveloped 'no-barri' seals off from the rest of Manlleu. Recalling Esposito, immunitary responses remedy the excessiveness of community, and in a situation in which locals and new arrivals are not easily distinguished, urban planning immunologically reasserts inner and outer distinctions through spatial segregation of the city. To demonstrate how statically the residential towers exercise this function, Puntí expounds on Can Garcia's continued concentration of migrants, only in the twenty-first-century newcomers from the north of Africa, Pakistan and others have substituted the Castilians, who have spread into other neighbourhoods of the city. Parés i Cuadras and Casas Deseures confirm Puntí's assessment, noting that 'en aquest àmbit s'hi dona una certa guetització del col·lectiu immigrant i que aquest es concentra de forma majoritària en aquells habitatges més deficients' ('in that area one finds a kind of ghettoisation of the immigrant collective which concentrates for the most part in the most deficient living spaces').[30]

The popularity of the residential tower as a form of public-housing assistance has roots in the writings of Le Corbusier and their influence on city planners in Europe and North America, most conspicuously on New York's city planning commissioner, Robert Moses, and moreover came to have an impact on Francoist responses to Spain's own housing crisis. In the 1930s, Le Corbusier developed a fascination with skyscrapers and designed city plans replete with sixty-storey towers purposed for office space with adjacent residential dwellings that were meant to not exceed seventeen storeys. These mass-residential developments were conceived as self-contained units set back from the streetscape, freestanding communities with sports, pools, schools and more that would cater to a spectrum of social classes.[31] High-rise dwellings were more spatially efficient and meant to create potential for more gardens and parkland. As Corbusian ideas infiltrated American, British and French urban planning in the subsequent decades, the original premise became deformed, with height, density of inhabitants, dwelling area, quality of elevators, poor construction materials and lack of amenities all contributing to making housing towers inconsistent with Le Corbusier's original vision.[32] Sub-standardly built high-rise housing, instead of catering to a mix of classes and prioritising the role of the built environment in community construction, became an option for rapidly solving residential shortages, which was certainly the case in Francoist Spain, and as Puntí stresses, not only in metropolitan centres such as Madrid and Barcelona.[33] As Bordetas writes, a feature of the disorganised and loosely regulated creation of neighbourhood polygons in Francoist Spain after the *apertura* was the prioritisation, 'tant en la promoció pública com en la privada, la quantitat, volum i ritme de construcció, sobre la qualitat, localització, serveis, tipologia d'habitatges i formes d'adquisició' ('in both the public and private spheres, the preference for quantity, volume and pace of construction, over quality, location, services, types of residences and forms of acquisition').[34]

The presence of an overgrown lot in *Els castellans*, immune from development and an inviting space for the detritus of the rest of Manlleu, is an expected consequence of a set-apart, monofunctional structure like Can Garcia. Jane Jacobs, writing in the late 1950s Greenwich Village that had become a target of Robert Moses's urban renewal, terms the deserted, abandoned or ignored spaces next to monofunctional developments (like a housing tower) 'border vacuums'. Jacobs writes that these emptied or undeveloped spaces are especially likely in zones without a mixture of uses and when other city elements near the monofunctional developments, such as expressways or even a college campus, function as a closed border. Border vacuums are the result of 'oversimplifying the use of the city at one place, on a large scale, they tend to simplify the use which people give to the adjoining territory too, and this simplification of use – meaning fewer users, with fewer different purposes and destinations at hand – feeds upon itself'.[35] L'Erm, a district constructed in the 1960s, was a speculative response to housing shortages tied to rapid migration to Manlleu from primarily Andalusia and Murcia. The 'oversimplification of use' described by Jacobs was tied to the overt land use there being tied only to real estate development. Initiatives such as the Projecte d'Intervenció Integral del Barri de l'Erm ('Project for an Integral Intervention on l'Erm District'), approved in 2004 by the Generalitat de Catalunya, ultimately set in motion the process that led to Can Garcia's removal and other attempts to more seamlessly integrate the neighbourhood into the rest of the city.[36]

As a memoir that oscillates between the 1970s and the 2010s, *Els castellans* makes explicit how urban policy and architecture contributed to the static residential segregation of Manlleu and questions the extent to which the border-vacuum *descampat* can be considered a threshold space in which social categories become fluid and capable of affecting quotidian life beyond its boundaries. Mueller writes that the memoir 'shows how the town's spatial layout mirrors a deep social rift', and the boys' attraction to overstepping boundaries opens up to interrogation 'assumptions about who does and does not belong in a given social space'.[37] Play, performance and the mutual gaze offer a pretext for interaction with the Castilian other, especially within shared spaces that belong to no one and require the blurring of lines that normally cleave Manlleu's social and political communities. The *descampat* is one such space where the children pass time 'negotiating borders through play', a zone that like the town's movie theatres Mueller terms 'liminal'.[38] Liminality, the anthropologist Victor Turner notes, is a phase tied to a rite of passage that temporarily displaces a subject from the familiar, only to return him or her to mundane life 'changed in some way'.[39] He further clarifies that play and experimentation are two crucial aspects of the liminal (Turner, *The Anthropology of Performance*, p. 25). Given the Bildungsroman-like quality of *Els castellans* and the predominance of play and experimentation in the dumping ground, it is logical to assert a liminal quality to the space as Puntí represents it.

At the same time, liminality also requires a domain in which a connection with an agent of transformation splits the self in two: into a subject to be seen objectively, on the one hand, and acted on as if it were another, on the other hand. This process, Turner adds, is distinct from simply 'doting upon or pining over the projected self (as Narcissus did over the face in the pool)' (Turner, *Anthropology*, p. 25). The narrator's cohort, acting out the dramas of their parents according to worldviews inculcated by ideological State apparatuses, never engage with their Castilian adversaries in a way that splits the self in an act of transformation that does violence to 'commonsense ways of classifying the world and society' (Turner, *Anthropology*, p. 25). In the immunitary biopolitics at work in the text, the children's tribalism coheres in response to a constitutive outside where the gaze functions as a centrifugal, negative projection of the self. As a border vacuum, the *descampat* threatens to deactivate efforts to revitalise and suture the fragmented urban fabric of the city, ensuring l'Erm's continued function as an antagonistic border with which to consolidate opposing identities.

The fragmented placement of Can Garcia calls to mind the historical precedent of using scattered, but substantial, accumulations of apartment units to hamper class consciousness in the name of solving a housing crisis. Adopting an immunological paradigm, Peter Sloterdijk writes that the post-Corbusian apartment block is an autogenous set of 'co-isolated' immunitary dwellings that, to be successful, must find a balance between the isolation of individuals and 'communitarian animation': 'an architecturally successful housing unit not only represents a portion of air that has been built around, but also a psycho-social immune system that can regulate its degree of insulation from the outside as required.'[40] Sloterdijk argues that post-war satellite towns in major North American and European cities feature a complete absence of communitarian animation entering into 'isolated immune units', with units understood here on a macro-level to refer to the developments as a whole and on a micro-scale to the consciousness of those individuals who occupy single dwellings. In such fragmented circumstances, workers spread throughout a region or nation cannot 'infer a common interest from the similarity of their situations' (Sloterdijk, *Foams*, p. 539), giving rise to 'the demand to convert the agglomeration of the self-enclosed hovels into a communicatively ventilated national workers' settlement . . . I would call them "solidarity foams" to express the fact that the oft-cited workers are, in systemic terms, neither a historical subject or a "mass" but rather an immunitary alliance' (Sloterdijk, *Foams*, p. 541). Sloterdijk's thought helps to unfold the complex immunitary dimensions of Puntí's description of Can Garcia as an elephantiasic reaction to a parasitical invasion. Since the units are isolated, the inhabitants there and the CCOO syndicalism they embrace are pathologised, and the infrastructure separating the neighbourhood from the community is perceived as a systemic frontier defence. Sloterdijk's conceptualisation of the apartment block would further add an autoimmunitary dimension to a reading of *Els castellans*. The Catalans in the text are immunised to *too great* of an extent from the inhabitants of Can Garcia, and as a result, no communitarian animation is able to penetrate the psychic ventilation of class consciousness and thus create what Sloterdijk refers to as an 'immunitary alliance' among Manlleu's working class.

This chapter has considered the immunitary dimensions of the spatiality of migration in *Els castellans*. In this analysis, the parasitic emerges as an important mode of the immunological, and a final dimension takes shape in the text's reflection on the changing social relations brought about by the globality of capital in the final decades of the twentieth century. In the wake of Franco's technocratic restructuring of the Spanish economy in the 1950s, Spain eventually participates in the revolution in space-time relations that David Harvey argues accelerates in the late 1960s and early 1970s as a 'spatial fix to capitalism's contradictions'.[41] This contradiction owes to a tension between spatial fixity and the mobility of multinational capital, with the latter always seeking out more profitable investment in an environment of intense competition between places, often thriving in ambits where former barriers have been lifted. The technocratic reformulation of Spanish economy, allowing the incursion of foreign investment to help fuel real estate speculation and instigating the mass movement of workers from the countryside to industrial areas, is one such floodgate that opens.[42] For Harvey, the end product of this process, one that resembles Puntí's description of Manlleu, is 'new territorial divisions of labor and concentrations of people and labor power, new resource extraction activities . . . the new geographical landscape which results is not evenly developed but strongly differentiated'.[43] Harvey's commentary allows for a nuanced reading of a chapter of *Els castellans* entitled 'Tornar al Vietnam' ('Return to Vietnam'), in which the children, influenced by films such as *The Deer Hunter* and *Apocalypse Now*, decide that Can Garcia enclosed 'un perill latent, una amenaça comparable a la del Viet-cong' (*Els castellans*, p. 65) ('latent danger, a threat comparable to the Viet-cong'). Referring to l'Erm as Vietnam leads to Puntí following the analogy to its conclusion: if the Castilians are the Viet-cong, then 'els catalans érem Estats Units – els senyors i alhora, per tant, els invasors' (p. 65) ('Catalans were the United States – the masters and at the same time, therefore, the invaders'). Puntí's division of the city according to Vietnam and the United States echoes Candel's work. In the preface, Candel discusses the genesis of *Els altres catalans*: an article in *La Jirafa* in which he describes a sign placed in the

Urbanism, Migration and Spatial Immunity in Els castellans 145

l'Hospitalet de Llobregat neighbourhood of la Torrassa that read 'Cataluña termina aquí. Aquí comienza Murcia' (Candel, *Els altres catalans*, p. 33) ('Catalonia ends here. Here begins Murcia'). In *Els castellans*, Puntí's framing is more complex in the sense that 'érem els senyors i alhora invasors' doubles as both a description of childhood play modelled agonistically on a Cold War-era conflict and, on a national level, references the *senyors* of the industrial bourgeoisie who reserve residential blocks for migrant labour power to arrive from poorer areas of the peninsula. These spaces are differentiated to the point of seeming a separate sovereign territorialisation altogether, as if they were expropriated from the Catalan commons. The deterritorialisation of certain municipal areas like l'Erm compresses space-time relations on the Iberian peninsula through a Deleuzian folding, as Catalonia's outside – Murcia, Andalusia and, today, the Global South – is not fixed but moves to the inside of the nation in an act of differentiation that paradoxically maintains a continuity; namely, the continuous attachment of the migrant community to its outsider status and external geographic place of origin.[44]

Importantly, the figurative deployment of the Vietnam-US conflict to conceptualise the arrival of Castilians in Puntí's memoir is not due to the war being contemporaneous with the book's events but is a result of the hegemony of the world market, mobilised and made fluid by the sovereignty of free-market capital. Vilarós puts forth that the late Francoist period witnesses the transformation of second-stage capital development, where labour, products and modes of production are territorialised, into a third one in which:

> old local industries [are] replaced by new global corporations [and] a new, spectrally deterritorialized nationalist space is suddenly made available . . . Nationalism is turned into a kind of virtual site, ready to be switched, traded, incorporated and reappropriated as a commodity.[45]

Els castellans documents the capitalistic transformation of local industry only indirectly, but is very explicit about how the hegemonic sites of cultural commodification – *Star Wars*, the Barça football club, *Apocalypse Now*, and so on – disrupt and dialectically inflect longstanding antagonisms. As Mueller argues, the Vietnam episode, where the Catalans are felt as invaders, reveals that the 'town's power dynamics are fluid and dependent upon context'.[46] While the fluidity of power is undoubtedly true, global capital floats throughout the text as an unexpected guest that destabilises and reframes the contexts in which the dynamics of ownership, senses of place and perceptions of the self play out. To the extent that this invasion of the world economic market thrives off and evolves the psychological inculcations already inscribed in the habitus of the social, it operates parasitically, and is the primary agent that allows the dynamics of power to be fluid.

What Vilarós refers to as the 'new corporate financial system'[47] is, in other words, merely the latest link on the chain of parasitical relations outlined in *Els castellans* and is foundational to the performance of social relations in the text. Serres theorises the parasitism of social relations as a chain that creates new forms of profit, dependency and coexistence through periodic disruption. In Manlleu, the industrial economy hosts migrants from the south who, in the 1960s, emigrate due to technocratic disruption of the regime's policies. But the hosting of these communities exists in a parasitical engagement with a bourgeois class who benefits from the surplus value of proletarian labour. Parasitism further mediates the representation of the newly formed communities, as Puntí's childhood narrator views l'Erm as an elephantiasic outgrowth of the city. Finally, global capital, whether in housing speculation, corporate substitution of local industry, or the dissemination of cultural objects, feeds off new and untapped markets. For Serres, each link in the chain is 'an interruption, a corruption, a rupture of information. Was the noise really a message? Wasn't it, rather, static, a parasite? A parasite who has the last word, who produces disorder and who generates a different order'.[48]

This chapter has argued that Puntí's *Els castellans* allows readers to perceive how different concepts of the immunological are inseparable from understanding the spatiality of migration, especially with respect to urban planning, during Francoism and in present-day Catalonia. Esposito's negative biopolitics, Sloterdijk's theorisation of the apartment bloc and immunitary alliances and Serres's concept of parasitism were shown to be particularly relevant to the processes of subjectivation experienced by a group of children on the brink of adolescence, being pushed along the paths towards 'becoming what they are'. As Can Garcia is demolished and vanished from the landscape, an open question concerns

Urbanism, Migration and Spatial Immunity in Els castellans 147

how to confront residential segregation while precluding that the histories and cultures tied to immigration do not fall prey to previous tendencies towards non-existence. In conclusion, the value of Puntí's text becomes clearly evident in this context, as does the Museu del Ter theatrical production centred on Can Garcia's residents titled *Novè 2a*, which debuted in 2021 after a delay caused by the COVID-19 pandemic. Together, these works contribute to creating a durable archival record of the populations that passed through l'Erm and respond to Salvador Cardús's exhortation to transform 'immigration into a "memory place" and fashion "a theory of country" that will allow for an accurate understanding of the past and present realities of the Catalan identity, beyond the limits of the formulas currently available to us'.[49] As described at the outset, one such formula is modelled on a negative biopolitics, with an immunitary dimension that manifests in both political rhetoric, as confirmed in recent electoral discourse, and in the built configuration of the urban landscape, which *Els castellans* crucially demonstrates.

Notes

1 Google Streetview, '272 Passeig de Sant Joan', *www.google.com/maps/place/Passeig+de+Sant+Joan,+272,+08560+Manlleu,+Barcelona,+Spain/@42.00 88586,2.2792581,3a,75y,176.63h,86.17t/data=!3m6!1e1!3m4!1sfiUN4li 4aixW-Lq5WJ00Bg!2e0!7i16384!8i8192!4m5!3m4!1s0x12a525a303ffdb 2d:0xf4593234487c0fc7!8m2!3d42.0082863!4d2.2799916.*
2 Google Streetview, '110 Avinguda Puigmal', *www.google.com/maps/@42.0092357,2.2832488,3a,75y,305.63h,75.33t/data=!3m6!1e1!3m4!1s1MygJJfdRgqZfrKyJ8veKg!2e0!7i16384!8i8192.*
3 Roberto Esposito, *Immunitas: The Protection and Negation of Life* (Cambridge: Polity, 2017), p. 13.
4 Cas Mudde, *The Far Right Today* (Cambridge: Polity, 2019), p. 32.
5 Som Identitaris' ideological platform is more explicit in evoking the Great Replacement theory: 'El capitalismo global amenaza las condiciones naturales de posibilidad de la civilización europea eliminando progresivamente la población que ha creado esta civilización a lo largo de los últimos 2.500 años' ('Global capitalism threatens the natural conditions of possibility for European civilisation, progressively eliminating the population that created this civilisation over the last 2,500 years'). Som identitaris, 'Manifest Ideològic (I)' (14 March 2017),

www.somidentitaris.cat/index.php/layout-1/layout-2/layout-3/layout-4/ style-2/style-4/style-6/columns--com-left-right/columns--left-com-right/ columns–right-left-com/columns–right-com-left/regions-1234/regions-1324/ regions-1423/regions-4123/root/layout/manifest-idiologic-1. Unless otherwise stated, all translations from Catalan and Spanish are my own.

6 For an overview of racial segregation in North American housing, see P. E. Moskowitz, *How to Kill a City* (New York: Bold Type Books, 2018), pp. 106–15; and Richard Rothstein, *The Color of Law* (New York: W. W. Norton, 2017), pp. 77–91.

7 David Harvey, 'The Right to the City', *New Left Review*, 53 (2008), *https://newleftreview.org/issues/ii53/articles/david-harvey-the-right-to-the-city*.

8 Martínez notes that 'Cornellà de Llobregat, per exemple, arribaria a principis dels anys setanta sense ni un parc públic' ('would enter the beginning of the 1970s without even a public park'): Francisco Martínez, 'Habitatge, habitatge social, especulació', in Josep Maria Solé i Sabaté (dir.), *El franquisme a Catalunya (1939–1977)*, vol. 2: *Catalunya dins l'Espanya de l'autarquia (1946–1958)* (Barcelona: Edicions 62, 2005), p. 157. Puntí references a similar neighbourhood on the other side of Barcelona in his most well-known novel, *Maletes perdudes*, published one year prior to *Els castellans* in 2010, as the main character Gabriel develops a habit of strolling through the Canyelles neighbourhood of Nou Barris as it is under construction in the 1970s; see Jordi Puntí *Maletes perdudes* (Barcelona: Empúries, 2010), pp. 366–7. Elsewhere, Castilian migrants to Barcelona and the south of France make prominent appearances in the novel.

9 Francesc Candel. *Els altres catalans* (Barcelona: Edicions 62, 2008), p. 206.

10 Salvador Cardús i Ros, 'The Memory of Immigration in Catalan Nationalism', *International Journal of Iberian Studies*, 18/1 (2005), 41.

11 Jordi Pujol, later the president of the Generalitat de Catalunya, wrote in a 1958 essay titled 'Per una doctrina d'integració' ('Towards a Doctrine of Integration') that 'la definició que ens agrada més es aquella que diu: català és tot home que viu i treballa a Catalunya, i, que amb el seu treball, amb el seu esforç, ajuda a fer Catalunya' ('the definition we most favour is the following: Catalan is any man who lives and works in Catalonia, and who helps to build Catalonia with his work and with his efforts'); cited in Andreu Domingo, *Catalunya al mirall de la immigració: Demografia i identitat nacional* (Barcelona: L'Avenç, 2014), p. 86. Pujol's approach to immigration throughout the years of *resistencialisme* remitted strongly to pre-dictatorship thought. While minimising the eugenics of Josep Antoni Vandellòs, Pujol shared with the author of *Catalunya, poble decadent* ('Catalonia, a Nation in Decline', 1935) a concern that unregulated migration posed a major

threat to the nation but as a phenomenon was necessary demographically. However, Pujol also echoed the early twentieth-century socialist Rafael Campalans in linking the migrants' social mobility to his vision for Catalan national identity (Domingo, *Catalunya al mirall de la immigració*, pp. 85–6). These genealogical roots provide context for the 'openly inclusive strategy' – with clear conditions – that defined the Generalitat's immigration policy in the 1980s and 1990s; see Kathryn Crameri, *National Identity and Cultural Policy, 1980–2003* (Cardiff: University of Wales Press, 2008), p. 184.

12 Josep-Anton Fernàndez, *El malestar en la cultura catalana: La cultura de la normalització 1976–1999* (Barcelona: Empúries, 2008), p. 282–3.

13 Candel, *Els altres catalans*, p. 292.

14 'Una de les sorpreses del llibre és que s'hi descobreixen paral·lelismes entre la immigració de llavors i la d'ara . . . No hi ha barraques, com llavors, però alguns "pisos patera" deixen en evidència uns problemes d'habitatge semblants' ('One of the book's surprises is the discovery of parallelisms between immigration then and now. Similar behaviours repeat themselves, similar disagreements are produced . . . Shacktowns may no longer exist, as before, but over-occupied apartments expose similar problems with housing'). Najat El Hachmi, 'Pròleg: L'home que apostava pel matís', in Francesc Candel, *Els altres catalans* (Barcelona: Edicions 62, 2008), p. 9.

15 Chantal Mouffe, *The Democratic Paradox* (London: Verso, 2009), p. 101. Setting the stage for Mouffe's work is Carl Schmitt's contention that 'the specific political distinction to which political actions and motives can be reduced is that between friend and enemy . . . the distinction of friend and enemy denotes the utmost degree of intensity of a union or separation, of an association or dissociation': Carl Schmitt, *The Concept of the Political*, (Chicago IL: University of Chicago Press, 2007), p. 26.

16 See Jordi Nopca, 'Jordi Puntí: M'indigna el que és políticament correcte', *Ara* (17 March 2011), https://llegim.ara.cat/actualitat/jordi-punti-mindigna-que-politicament-correcte_1_2996513.html.

17 Minca and Vaughan-Williams mobilise the term 'strategic fiction' in theorising the function of borders in Carl Schmitt's *Nomos of the Earth*. Because the State has no real ontological grounding, the border is 'the site where the [sovereign] "decision" . . . is enacted and where it shows perhaps its most visible face'. Claudio Minca and Nick Vaughan-Williams, 'Carl Schmitt and the Concept of the Border', *Geopolitics*, 17 (2012), 761.

18 Betlem Parés i Cuadras and Mariona Casas Deseures, 'L'experiència del barri de l'Erm de Manlleu', *Ausa*, 22/159 (2007), 60–1.

19 Jordi Puntí, *Els castellans* (Barcelona: L'Avenç, 2011), p. 13.

20 To add context to the suspicion described by Puntí, Dowling notes that in the late 1960s and early 1970s the shared repression of the mobilised working classes and those working for increased Catalan autonomy led to an 'immigrant understanding of Catalan discrimination': Andrew Dowling, 'Political Cultures, Ruptures, and Continuity in Catalonia under the Franco Regime', in Josep-Anton Fernàndez and Jaume Subirana (eds), *Funcions del passat en la cultura catalana contemporània* (Lleida: Punctum, 2015), p. 232. This, in turn, caused the Catalan national movement to reconfigure its pre-Francoist relationship with organised labour, including the CCOO that generally defended Catalan language and identity (pp. 230–2). Vilarós confirms this, arguing that 'the bridging of Catalan cultural and historical idiosyncrasy with Marxist ideology . . . proved to be most seductive for the immigrant populations; a link that enabled the Catalan Marxist left, mostly through unions such as *Comisiones Obreras*, to function both as a political and cultural model for many of the immigrants to Catalonia at the time': Teresa Vilarós, 'The Passing of the *Xarnego* Immigrant: Post-Nationalism and the Ideologies of Assimilation in Catalonia', *Arizona Journal of Hispanic Cultural Studies*, 7 (2003), 231.
21 Pierre Bourdieu, *Language and Symbolic Power* (Cambridge MA: Harvard University Press, 2003), p. 123.
22 Bourdieu, *Language and Symbolic Power*, p. 119.
23 Bourdieu, *Language and Symbolic Power*, p. 122.
24 Gabancho describes poignantly this phenomenon in her observation of Ciutat Vella in Barcelona: 'els immigrants acaben per dominar un tros de ciutat, una parcel·la en la qual se senten segurs . . . però continuen durant anys denegant-se el dret d'abastar la ciutat tota. És que no sabrien sortir del seu gueto virtual' ('immigrants end up mastering a small slice of the city, a parcel where they feel secure . . . but they continue for years denying themselves the right to step foot in the rest of the city. They don't know how to leave their virtual ghetto'). Patrícia Gabancho, *Sobre la immigració* (Barcelona: Columna, 2001), p. 29.
25 Sigmund Freud, *Totem and Taboo* (New York: W. W. Norton, 1950), p. 84.
26 Vilarós, 'The Passing of the *Xarnego* Immigrant', 236.
27 Vilarós, 'The Passing of the *Xarnego* Immigrant', 240.
28 Manel Ollé, 'Els de Can Garcia', *L'Avenç*, 367 (2011), 56.
29 Dowling, 'Political Cultures', p. 228.
30 Parés i Cuadras and Casas Deseures, 'L'experiència del barri de l'Erm', 62. There has been a substantial body of research on residential segregation in both Manlleu and Osona province writ large; see especially Rafa Madriarga, Joan Carles Martori and Ramon Oller, 'Renta salarial, desigualdad y segregación residencial en las

ciudades medianas de Cataluña', *Scripta Nova*, 24/640 (2020), 1–25, and specifically with respect to l'Erm, Betlem Parés i Cuadras, 'El Pla de Millora del Barri de l'Erm, una oportunitat per a la cohesió social', in *Osona: La cohesió social* (Manlleu: Fundació Antiga Caixa Manlleu, 2020), pp. 51–62. In general, the authors advocate social admixture, a point advanced also by Puntí: 'La solució és sempre la mateixa: evitar els tòpics i els llocs comuns, no caure en els prejudicis, i això només s'aconsegueix amb la barreja' ('The solution is always the same: avoid common topics and places, don't resort to prejudices, and that is only accomplished through intermixing'): Jordi Puig, 'Catalans i castellans ara fan front comú contra la nova migració', *El 9 nou* (26 March 2011), *https://el9nou.cat/osona-ripolles/ cultura-i-gent/catalans-i-castellans-ara-fan-front-comu-contra-la-nova-im migracio/*.
31 Alexi Ferster Marmot, 'The Legacy of Le Corbusier and High-Rise Housing, *Built Environment*, 7/2 (1981), 86–7.
32 Ferster Marmot, 'The Legacy of Le Corbusier', 92.
33 In Catalonia, housing shortages were one of the more pressing social issues in the post-war era, due to the destruction of war, scant access to materials such as iron and cement, and a lack of interest for speculators to invest in an impoverished country with an uncertain future (Martínez, 'Habitatge', p. 156). After the 1950s, the housing deficit remained, but housing speculation expanded rapidly. Aided by government support, after 1953 Barcelona prioritised the rapid construction of 'aglomeracions destinades a les classes populars . . . la construcció tornà a ser una inversió amb futur . . . Calien nous solars per bastir habitatges, o per construir-hi fàbriques i tallers' (Martínez, p. 157) ('agglomerations destined for popular classes . . . construction became again an investment with a future . . . New lots were needed to build residences, or to construct factories and workshops'). For more information on urban housing policy in smaller Catalan cities, see Ivan Bordetas, 'Habitatge i assentaments de la postguerra a l'estabilització', in Martí Marín (ed.), *Memòries del viatge 1940–1975* (Valls: Cossetània, 2009), p. 62.
34 Bordetas, 'Habitatge i assentaments', pp. 68–9.
35 Jane Jacobs, *The Death and Life of Great American Cities* (New York: Random House, 1992), p. 259.
36 Parés i Cuadras and Deseures, 'L'experiència', 64–5.
37 Stephanie Mueller, 'Jordi Puntí's *Els castellans*: Reshaping Catalan Narratives of Immigration and Integration', *Romance Quarterly*, 67/4 (2020), 215 and 219.
38 Mueller, 'Jordi Puntí's *Els castellans*', 220.
39 Victor Turner, *The Anthropology of Performance* (New York: PAJ Publications, 1988), p. 25.

40 Peter Sloterdijk, *Foams: Spheres III* (South Pasadena CA: Semiotext(e), 2016), p. 583.
41 David Harvey, *Justice, Nature, and the Geography of Difference* (Cambridge MA: Blackwell, 1996), p. 295.
42 Echoing Bordetas, Hamilton writes that in Francoist Spain, 'despite social scientists' urgent calls for "land use planning" (*ordenación del territorio*), unregulated development and land speculation gave rise to suburbs filled with tightly packed substandard apartment buildings, often erected without permits and in open violation of residential regulations, which were retroactively legalised by the enthusiastically pro-growth regime. These working-class slums suffered from a litany of problems, from leaky plumbing and collapsing roofs to unusable kitchens and foundations built without concrete': Sarah R. Hamilton, 'Environmental Change and Protest in Franco's Spain, 1939–1975', *Environmental History*, 22/2 (2017), 265. Casademon Falguera and Feu Gelis describe a similar phenomenon in 1960s Olot, where real estate speculation led to a habitual sight: 'grups de blocs en construcció, regleres de cases alineades, barris nous amb els carrers sense asfaltar' ('groups of housing towers under construction, straight rows of aligned houses, new neighbourhoods with dirt roads'): Xavier Casademont Falguera and Jordi Feu Gelis, 'La problemàtica de l'habitatge de la immigració andalusa a Olot durant el franquisme (1940–1975)', *Documents d'Anàlisi Geogràfica*, 63/1 (2017), 20.
43 Harvey, *Justice*, p. 295.
44 In his study of Leibniz's philosophy, Deleuze writes that the organic body, much like the body politic, is 'an interiority of space, and not yet of motion; also, an internalization of the outside, an invagination of the outside that could not occur all alone if no true interiorities did not exist *elsewhere*': Gilles Deleuze, *The Fold* (Minneapolis MN: University of Minnesota Press, 1988), p. 8. Transformation is thus a simultaneous movement of folding and unfolding in which the enveloping of an exteriority within a body is also a form of evolution for the organism.
45 Vilarós, 'The passing of the *xarnego* immigrant', 238.
46 Mueller, 'Jordi Puntí's *Els castellans*', 220.
47 Vilarós, 'The passing of the *xarnego* immigrant', 243.
48 Michel Serres, *The Parasite* (Minneapolis: University of Minnesota Press, 2007), p. 3.
49 Cardús i Ros, 'The Memory of Immigration', 43.

Part III
Disidentification, Dislocation and Mourning

Chapter 7

'Te deix, mare, un fill com a penyora': Disidentificatory Intertextuality in Najat El Hachmi's *La filla estrangera*

Natasha Tanna

Introduction

This chapter focuses on the role of literature, writing and intertextuality in navigating the experience of living within and between Catalan and Amazigh culture in Najat El Hachmi's 2015 novel, *La filla estrangera*. The protagonist, the 'filla estrangera' ('foreign daughter') of the title, navigates feelings of estrangement both from her biological Amazigh mother and from the world of Catalan letters.[1] I argue that what I describe as El Hachmi's disidentificatory intertextuality, drawing on Cuban American critic José Esteban Muñoz's 1999 theorisation of 'disidentification' in performance,[2] is a textual correlate for the navigation of her protagonist's (and her own) place as a perpetual 'filla estrangera' in Catalan society. In the novel, El Hachmi's literary practice involves citing and transforming now canonical but once marginalised Catalan works. A number of these intertexts depict erotic relationships between women (within and beyond the sexual realm, including mother/ daughter and romantic relationships) that we might consider as part of Adrienne Rich's 'lesbian continuum' (1980), a concept she coined to describe the radical political potential of homosocial bonds between women.[3]

El Hachmi's intertexts include Montserrat Roig's *Ramona, adéu* ('Goodbye, Ramona', 1972) and Mercè Rodoreda's *La plaça del Diamant* ('In Diamond Square', 1962). In this chapter, however, I focus on Maria-Mercè Marçal's poetry, especially *La germana, l'estrangera* ('Sister, Foreigner', 1985), a collection with which we see an affinity from the outset. The novel's title resonates with *La germana, l'estrangera*, which in turn echoes US writer and activist Audre Lorde's poem 'Sister Outsider' and the collection of essays by Lorde with the same name published in 1984, the year before Marçal's collection. I also consider El Hachmi's dialogue with Majorca-born writer Carme Riera's 'Te deix, amor, la mar com a penyora' ('I leave you, love, the sea as a token', 1975; henceforth, 'Te deix, amor'), to which the citation from *La filla estrangera* in the title of this essay refers. Via her protagonist, El Hachmi establishes a narrative of a permanent liminal status *vis-à-vis* the Catalan canon with which the protagonist and El Hachmi engage closely.[4] For the protagonist, the status of perpetual outsider and a sense of estrangement involve being intimately acquainted with the milieu from which she feels rejected and from which she subsequently distances herself, both in terms of Catalan society and her mother's Amazigh culture. Drawing on Sara Ahmed's theorisations of the figure of the stranger and 'stranger fetishism', as well as the final line of the final poem of *La germana, l'estrangera* – 'És perquè et sé estrangera que puc dir-te germana' ('it is because I know you a stranger that I can call you sister') – I argue that in El Hachmi's novel she plays with how a sense of 'foreignness' may be borne of intimacy, proximity and closeness.[5]

In what remains of the introduction, I offer a brief synopsis of the novel. I then move on to consider briefly some conceptualisations of the figure of the stranger in feminist and postcolonial theory and how these relate to the Catalan context. I explore the role of writing in confronting the dissociation that might result from traumatic experiences of racism and of forcing oneself to adhere to cultural expectations. In the latter part of this essay, I analyse references to and resonances with Marçal, Lorde and Riera in *La filla estrangera* and how these reflect El Hachmi's and the protagonist's navigation of the world.

La filla estrangera is the story of an unnamed protagonist who moved at a young age from the Rif region of Morocco to Vic, Catalonia, where she lives with her mother. They came to live with her father, but on arriving discovered that he had settled with a different family and they had to fend for themselves. In the novel, the protagonist recounts various experiences of racism that she endured in Catalonia. Aged eighteen, she is faced with a choice between following her single mother's desires for her to marry a cousin from Morocco or her own intellectual passions, borne partly of her voracious reading of Catalan literature. An excellent student, she defies the expectations of her teachers by opting not to go to university, instead starting to work as a cleaner in a monastery and taking on additional jobs to secure the funds required to secure a family relocation visa for her new husband. She gets pregnant with what she considers 'un fill incestuós' ('an incestuous child') due to her marriage to her cousin and subsequent pregnancy being the result of her love for her mother and of her desire to bring peace to her mother.[6] Her process of denying herself to fulfil her mother's wishes is also a period in which she rejects reading, as she believes that the critical thought and active imagination fostered by literature are unnecessary for the life she has chosen and, in fact, a threat to it. In any case, she had already doubted her place as a racialised woman in the male-dominated elite world of Catalan letters. After surviving a breakdown and disintegration of her sense of self, the protagonist runs away to Barcelona, leaving her son with her mother, and seeks to forget her mother entirely. However, the novel closes with the protagonist longing to stay in the presence of her mother's language when she hears a group of women speaking Tamazight on the bus. She resolves to explore her identity and relationship to her mother through a return to literature in writing both her story and that of her mother.

Some critics, such as Cristián Ricci in relation to El Hachmi, valorise highly sociological readings of literary works.[7] Others, such as Caragh Wells, are concerned by the tendency for critics analysing texts dealing with subjects often marginalised in literary canons or written by racialised writers to focus on sociopolitical readings of works at the expense of the 'aesthetic'; that is, of considerations of more literary or formal elements.[8] In interviews, El Hachmi has frequently lamented being classified as an 'immigrant' writer and when she won the Premi de les Lletres Catalans Ramon Llull for *L'últim patriarca* ('The Last Patriarch', 2008) much media coverage focused on her origins rather than the literary merit of her work.[9] Critics such as Rosi Song have also noted the overinterpretation of the fact that El Hachmi writes in Catalan as a 'choice', given that it was the language of her schooling and environment in Catalonia.[10] While I do consider issues relating to immigration in this chapter, I am interested primarily in how the sociopolitical context of the novel's creation relates to El Hachmi's engagement with other literary works and how she depicts the act of writing and the importance of literature for her protagonist. Language, writing and literature are thematised throughout the novel and El Hachmi's literary practice acts as a textual correlate for her sociopolitical experiences and concerns.

Soothing the Stranger: From Dissociation to Writing as Healing

When the protagonist of *La filla estrangera* starts wearing a headscarf, in line with her mother's and husband's wishes, she states 'caminant pel carrer em soc estranya a mi mateixa' (p. 179) ('walking down the street I feel like a stranger to myself'), a phrase that resonates with Bulgarian-French theorist Julia Kristeva's *Strangers to Ourselves* (1988). Kristeva universalises the sensation of not knowing oneself, centring on the world as a community of strangers. She calls for an attitude that is 'no longer that of welcoming the foreigner within a system that obliterates him but of promoting the togetherness of those foreigners that we all recognise ourselves to be'.[11] In a similarly persuasive vein, Martinican theorist Édouard Glissant writes of opacity and not fully knowing another as the only true basis for liberated community: 'Widespread consent to specific opacities is the most straightforward equivalent of nonbarbarism. We clamor for the right to opacity for everyone.'[12] For Glissant, then, opacity is the basis for ethical community and relationality. In his case the opacity is to the other, whereas for Kristeva it extends to opacity of the self for the self. While both stances are compelling, in their universalising utopianism they risk overlooking degrees of 'strangeness' and how being a particular sort of 'stranger' manifests in concrete realities such as that of Moroccans in Catalonia.

In contrast to the universalising thrust of these theorisations, Ahmed argues in *Strange Encounters* that some strangers are stranger than other strangers and calls for an attentiveness to hierarchies in different contexts, often relating to processes of racialisation.[13] However, importantly for my analysis here she notes that while the stranger is often rendered as distant and incompatible, the figure of the stranger is usually created through proximity. She describes this process as 'stranger fetishism' in which, paradoxically, the stranger is fashioned as already known, a process that comes about through encounter.[14] The Catalan and Spanish contexts provide an example of proximity and encounter creating the stranger. Alongside Ahmed, El Hachmi's *La filla estrangera*, Marçal's poetry and Muñoz's theory of disidentification bring a nuanced approach to the 'stranger debate' in postcolonial theory. Their bringing together of the known and unknown, the opaque and transparent, the close and distant allows the working through of desire and relationality amongst difference.

In Ahmed's comment that 'the stranger is produced through knowledge, rather than as a failure of knowledge',[15] there are resonances with Daniela Flesler's argument that anxiety about Moroccans among Spaniards of a Catholic background is the result of historical proximity:

> *Moriscos* constituted a problem because they were different – their Muslim lineage marked them as potential heretics and enemies – but, at the same time, because they were the same – as converted Christians, without their *Morisco* clothing, language, and customs, they could be transformed into 'real' Spaniards, they could 'pass'. They were simultaneously same and other, Spaniard and foreign . . . Moroccans turn into a 'problem', then, not because of their cultural difference, as many argue, but because, like the *Moriscos*, they are not different enough.[16]

Being 'simultaneously same and other' resonates with the notion of a 'foreign daughter'. Flesler goes on to emphasise the importance of Spanish history in contemporary reactions to Moroccan immigration, highlighting the slipperiness of the status of Moroccans. For example, she argues that the situation of Moroccans is different from that of Latin Americans:

> Unlike other Western European nations, Spain is not only experiencing the return of the colonized but also that of its medieval colonizers. While Latin Americans can be seen as the return of the colonized

and can be 'fixed' in this conceptual category, Moroccans not only embody the return of the colonized but also, especially, and more threateningly, the return of the colonizers or 'invaders' of Spain, and thus they cannot easily be 'fixed'.[17]

While other critics have argued against these 'particularising' explanations of racism towards Moroccans and Maghrebis in Spain,[18] Flesler seeks to understand how contemporary tensions between Moroccans/Maghrebis and Spaniards have historical roots. She generalises the Spanish position here, but it is also helpful for us to think about the particular sociohistorical context of Catalonia given where the novel is set.

Michelle Murray synthesises the long history of immigration to Catalonia, noting that in 2015 immigrants made up approximately 70 per cent of the Catalan population.[19] She summarises waves of immigration to Catalonia fuelled by industrialisation and the later so-called internal migration from elsewhere in Spain in the waves of the 1950s to the 1970s. For example, internal migration for construction work relating to the development of tourism on the Costa Brava is depicted in Josep Maria Forn's *La piel quemada* (1967). Murray posits that '[u]ntil recently, immigrants have been problematically instrumentalized in the service of nationalism; racism and Islamophobia, however, complicate the assimilation of African populations there'.[20] We might expect alliance and solidarity between Catalans and the Imazighen people given the parallels between the status of Tamazight as a minority language of a non-Arab people in an Arab Moroccan state and the situation of Catalan *vis-à-vis* Spanish in Spain. However, in *La filla estrangera* we observe the racism that the protagonist, her mother and 'Moroccans' (often actually Imazighen) experience in Catalonia. Indeed, the region has a distinct historical pride in resistance to the 'moors' given the early expulsion of occupation in the Marca Hispànica by Frankish forces in Catalonia. The region acted as a barrier between Al-Andalus and the Carolingian Empire and this history remains alive in contemporary parlance; for example, in ongoing references to Barcelona as 'Ciutat Comtal', a term that dates from this period. More recently, Catalan soldiers were conscripted to the colonial wars in northern Africa in the nineteenth century and early twentieth century, and others went as civilian volunteers.[21]

The novel describes various incidents of racism and Islamophobia in Catalonia. For example, we learn of the protagonist and her mother's struggle in securing housing, the protagonist's difficulty in getting a secure contract at work and Moroccan children being made to travel to attend school far away from home so that they are not all concentrated in a few schools, outnumbering the 'locals'. The novel also explores how racism is internalised by the protagonist through the depiction of her condescending and self-exoticising thoughts about her mother's culture. She questions whether pleasure can be expressed in her mother's language (El Hachmi, *La filla estrangera*, p. 37) and likens her sense of not knowing the places her mother and her mother's friends are talking about as 'una mica com aquestes dones que no llegeixen ni escriuen i encara menys poden fer-se imatges mentals d'una representació a escala de "la seva terra". Com deu ser pensar sense geografia?' (p. 37) ('a bit like these women who can't read or write and are even less capable of conjuring mental images of a scaled representation of "their lands". What must it be like to think without geography?'). Here, the protagonist ties an imaginative conceptual understanding of space to the written word in a manner that downplays the creativity, knowledge and engagement with space in oral cultures.

When she decides to distance herself from literature, the protagonist reflects that the elite world of letters is not her place anyway due to her family background:

> Vaig oblidant aquella mania de buscar refugi i emoció en paraules poc usuals, emprades només en lletra impresa o per aquells que formen part d'un món molt diferent del meu, el dels intel·lectuals, els savis, els literats, els gran mestres. Què en sé jo, de tot això, essent com sóc filla d'una analfabeta? (p. 118)

> I am forgetting my obsession with seeking refuge and excitement in unusual words, used only in printed text or by those who are part of a world very different to my own, the world of intellectuals, the wise, the well-read, the great masters. What do I know of all that, being as I am the daughter of an illiterate woman?

This is an ironic comment given that El Hachmi, the creator of this protagonist, shares her background and is a successful writer. As the protagonist loses literature, she loses herself, falling into what is described in the novel as a period akin to depression: 'Jo no ho sóc [feliç] perquè no sé ser sense llegir, encara, encara m'he d'avesar a deixar enrere les paraules . . . Com més lluny sigui de les paraules més podré assemblar-me a la meva mare' (p. 158) ('I am not happy because I still don't know how to exist without reading, I still have to get used to leaving behind words . . . The further I am from words, the more I'll be able to seem like my mother'). As both these quotations show, she is determined to force herself to learn how to be without words to better adapt to what she sees as her fate and because she doubts what she might contribute to the world of letters in any case. As she seeks desperately to contain her passion for the written word, she experiences numerous threats to her mission. For example, when she enters the former library building for a new job, the mere memory of words pose a visceral threat: 'les paraules amenacen de venir-me totes de cop a la memòria, amenacen de desbordar-me tota, d'esberlar-me del tot la línia vertical i fer que tota jo sigui per fora el que soc per dins' (p. 160) ('words threaten to flood my memory, they threaten to overflow from me, to tear the vertical line that runs down me and make my entire being on the outside the same as I am on the inside'). El Hachmi's protagonist fears being drowned and overwhelmed by words when she is seeking to deny them to herself.

As a consequence of both racism and the pressure to conform to her mother's desires and suppress parts of herself, the protagonist repeatedly describes what might be considered in psychotherapeutic terms as a dissociative experience of depersonalisation. Depersonalisation stems from a self-protective response to stress and trauma where a situation becomes so unbearable that one numbs oneself to survive it. In this way, one can have an experience happen to oneself with the sensation that one has not fully experienced it. There are many passages in the novel where the protagonist describes feeling separate to herself, viewing herself from outside. These experiences range from momentary feelings of shame to more traumatic incidents. An early example includes the scene at a course for women organised by the city council when the protagonist is asked publicly about what she is doing there by a woman who recognises her from the local newspaper, where she was featured as a 'model Moroccan' due to her high exam results. A friend of her mother replies on her behalf, saying that she is going to get married. The protagonist describes her experience of shame as follows: 'la situació se'm fa tan insostenible, tan irreal, que passo de sobte a veure'm des de fora, com si no fos jo la que estigués vivint un moment tan absurd' (p. 80) ('the situation seems so unsustainable to me, so unreal, that I suddenly shift to seeing myself from outside, as if it weren't me who was living such an absurd moment'). These feelings become intensified as the novel proceeds. For example, in a later scene when she lies passive as her husband penetrates her, in one of many scenes that could be considered representations of marital rape given the protagonist's total lack of participation – 'sembles de gel' (p. 150) ('you seem like ice'), comments her husband – the protagonist explains that 'jo ja era la que observava l'escena i no pas la que la patia' (p. 150) ('I was now the one observing the scene, not the one suffering it'). So, as a survival mechanism during her marriage, the protagonist increasingly experiences her life as if she were not fully living it. The sense of separation from the self in the protagonist's moments of trauma and shame starts to permeate the whole of her life. She explains how 'Tota jo, el meu cos, els meus actes, els meus pensaments, les meves passes pel carrer, tot em sembla que és d'algú altre.' (p. 187) ('My entire self, my body, my actions, my thoughts, my footsteps on the street, they all seem as if they belong to someone else'). The protagonist's experience of her disintegrating self proves unsustainable.

After giving birth to her son, El Hachmi's protagonist swings from denial of herself to rejection of her mother (and her husband). She leaves her son in her mother's care and flees Vic to go to Barcelona, carrying through the departure that she had attempted at the novel's opening. In Barcelona, at first, she seeks to avoid reminders of her mother's language and cooking, as if denying these realities will help her to erase her past and reclaim herself. However, in the final scene of the novel, when she hears a group of women speaking her mother's language on a bus, she longs for them not to disembark. We observe hints of the protagonist's desire for reconciliation with her mother as she considers her ability to write both of their stories, hers and her mother's, and therefore separate them from each other, to overcome the sense of fusion with her mother that she had experienced. The novel ends with lines that gesture towards both the text that we have in our hands and to El Hachmi's following novel, *Mare de llet i mel* ('Mother of milk and honey', 2018), which is the same story told from the perspective of the mother:

> Escriuria la història de la meva mare per recuperar-la, per recordar-la, per fer-li justícia i perquè tot el que em pensava que havia oblidat, tot el que tenia a veure amb ella, en realitat ho duia a dins sense saber on. Escriuria la seva història i així podria destriar-la de la meva. Escriuria la seva història i així podria ser jo sense ser per ella però també ser jo sense ser contra ella. (p. 213)

> I would write my mother's story to recuperate her, to remember her, to do her justice and because everything I thought I had forgotten, everything that had anything to do with her, I actually had inside me without knowing where. I would write her story and in that way be able to distinguish it from my own. I would write her story and in that way be able to be me without having to exist for her but also to be me without having to be against her.

The final lines therefore represent a reinforcement – 'escriuria' is repeated three times – of the importance of writing in the protagonist's healing process.[22] She sees words as a site of connection with herself, a place to reassert her own autonomy.

The protagonist's return to a connection with words resonates with a poem in Marçal's *La germana, l'estrangera* where she describes clinging onto words to keep her head above water, possibly in the context of motherhood or another erotic relationship:

> Aquest plaer sagnant
> vol estimbar-me.
> M'aferro amb força
> a les paraules
> que em permeten seguir
> dalt la maroma.[23]

> This bleeding pleasure
> seeks to topple me.
> I cling on tightly
> to words
> that allow me to keep
> my head above the water.

For Marçal, words are a response to a fear of losing oneself through a merging with another or becoming what the other wants. Similarly, in El Hachmi's novel, for the protagonist, writing is figured as a possible site of reconciliation with her mother and her Amazigh culture through differentiation; a bringing together to maintain distinction. Unlike Catherine Bourland Ross, who reads this rejection of the mother and abandoning of the child as definitive and final, I read the novel as affirming the possibility of reconciliation through the act of writing.[24]

We could see the ending of *La filla estrangera*, with the reference to the writing of both the mother's and the daughter's stories both to distinguish them and to permit a reconciliation as in line with this act of definition through writing as a broadening of the join, in Lorde's terms. In 'Man Child', Lorde writes that 'When we define ourselves, when I define myself, the place in which I am like you and the place in which I am not like you, I'm not excluding you from the joining – I'm broadening the joining'.[25] However, within this joining there are cracks – 'the place in which I am not like you'. In another collection, *Desglaç* ('Thaw', 1989), Marçal poetically defines desire as the 'dolor de ser i no ser tu' ('the pain of being and not being you'):

> Dolor de ser tan diferent de tu.
> Dolor d'una semblança sense termes . . .
> Dolor de ser i no ser tu: desig.[26]

> The pain of being so different to you
> The pain of a likeness without limits . . .
> The pain of being and not being you: desire.

This phrase poignantly captures the sense of being and not being, of identification and difference, indeed of disidentification at the heart of intimacy that may be, in Marçal's words, a 'plaer sagnant'. Also referring to the coexistence of similarity and difference, in the essay 'Eye to Eye' Lorde writes that 'I am who I am, doing what I came to do, acting upon you like a drug or a chisel to remind you of your me-ness, as I discover you in myself'.[27] It is in this productive disidentificatory space of 'being and not being', the ongoing work, the continuous chiselling of navigating closeness and separation, that El Hachmi's intertextual practice resides.

Through her many Catalan literary references El Hachmi seems to be inserting herself into a particular genealogy, engaging deeply with the Catalan literary tradition. However, the way in which such an abundance of references permeates the text could also be read as a playful enactment and conscious playing up to the image of the studious Moroccan girl who mastered Catalan. The celebration of the 'good immigrant' is depicted in the novel with the protagonist's appearance in the newspaper for her academic achievements and her being called on as a representative, an acceptable Moroccan, at a meeting in Vic that she assumes is to discuss Moroccans' problems, which she soon realises is a meeting to discuss *the* Moroccan problem. In part, she uses this disidentificatory strategy to highlight racism and Islamophobia in Catalan society in a 'civilised' format, using, as Lorde might put it, the master's tools to dismantle the master's house. We could see her engagement with her Catalan literary predecessors, her symbolic mothers, as continuing what Murray has described as her 'preoccupation with fractured genealogies' and her 'generative, genealogical rupture through a stunning panorama of symbols, specifically, allusions to fog, abysses, and broken family relations'.[28] She also uses this strategy to signal her rejection of patriarchal norms across cultures, but not as a simple 'Western' culture saves Moroccan girl from gendered oppression tale.

We see how the protagonist's facile distinction between the 'cultured' West and the limitations of her mother's oral language is complicated as the novel proceeds. El Hachmi has discussed how the oral traditions of her birthplace have influenced her writing.[29] The impact of oral culture is evident particularly in the style and structure of *L'últim patriarca*, as Josep-Anton Fernàndez has analysed.[30] The place of her healing does end up being the written word, but the ways she engages with the canon with which she is most familiar reveals her refusal to 'assimilate' in a way that would involve the 'forgetting' or denial of her mother's culture and her life experience, remaining instead, in Murray's terms in reference to El Hachmi, 'ambivalent about her positioning in Catalonia'.[31] Indeed, as Ricci notes, for El Hachmi, and other autors such as Laila Karrouch:

> their 'Catalanness' does not define itself through the antithesis of their 'Moroccanness' or 'Amazighness,' but rather, their identities

multiply themselves according to their class status, the male or female version of their testimony, and their place in the generational and immigration lines.[32]

For Núria Codina, El Hachmi's work involves both 'an emotional estrangement from Morocco and reconfiguring of a Catalan identity'.[33] Ultimately, then, the protagonist disidentifies both with Catalan and with her mother's Amazigh culture.

Earlier in the novel the protagonist describes listening to her mother and her mother's friends speaking Tamazight among themselves without intervening as a pleasant sensation akin to that of reading a book that you cannot change: 'Sí, m'agrada que parlin i escoltar-les sense implicar-me, com llegir un llibre que ja està escrit en què no pots intervenir per canviar-hi res.' (El Hachmi, *La filla*, p. 29) ('Yes, I like them talking and being able to listen to them without getting involved myself, like reading a book that's already written in which you can't intervene to change anything'). This is another ironic comment in the context of a novel in which the protagonist does effectively intervene and implicate herself in books that have already been written in Catalan, rewriting iconic lines and twisting well-known plots to accommodate the story of herself, her mother and their relationship. I turn to a couple of these intertextual engagements in the next part of this essay.

Disidentificatory Intertexts: Marçal's Poetry and Riera's 'Te deix, amor'

In *La filla estrangera*, Catalan cultural and literary references are invoked, but changed in the process, in a practice that I describe as 'disidentificatory intertextuality', drawing on Muñoz's theorisation of 'disidentification' in the US context. While Muñoz offers a useful lens through which to consider El Hachmi's practice, it is vital to note that in the case of El Hachmi and Catalonia, the culture with which she engages is itself minoritised. Writing of queer performers of colour in the United States, Muñoz analyses the survival strategies through which 'outsiders' negotiate more 'mainstream' cultural forms. Against the complete dismissal of something when we don't agree with part of it (e.g., the outright rejection of the mother in the novel), Muñoz argues for partial identifications, giving the example of a lesbian reader of Frantz Fanon who might reject the misogynist and homophobic elements of his work, and yet value and find use in his anti-colonial discourse. For Muñoz, these partial identifications result in a practice that 'resists an unproductive turn toward good dog/bad dog criticism and instead leads to an identification that is both mediated and immediate, a disidentification that enables politics'.[34] Muñoz goes on to expand on the concept with a term, 'the third mode', that recalls Homi Bhabha's highly influential concept of the 'third space' in postcolonial theory:

> Disidentification is the third mode of dealing with dominant ideology, one that neither opts to assimilate within such a structure nor strictly opposes it; rather, disidentification is a strategy that works on and against dominant ideology. Instead of buckling under the pressures of dominant ideology (identification, assimilation) or attempting to break free of its inescapable sphere (counteridentification, utopianism), this 'working on and against' is a strategy that tries to transform a cultural logic from within, always laboring to enact permanent structural change while at the same time valuing the importance of local or everyday struggles of resistance.[35]

For Muñoz, disidentification is a process of 'self-creation' and a practice with a 'worldmaking power'.[36] As such, for the protagonist, who has lost herself and feels excluded from the worlds she moves between, it comes to be a process of making a world for herself among these spheres and making a self that can move between these milieux without falling apart.

As mentioned above, disidentification is present in the title of the novel, *La filla estrangera* ('the foreign daughter'), which resonates with Marçal's *La germana, l'estrangera*, which in turn echoes Lorde's poem 'Sister Outsider' and collection of essays *Sister Outsider*. Whereas Marçal and Lorde's works focus on the horizontality of 'sisterhood', in El Hachmi a vertical hierarchy – in her relationship with her mother and with the Catalan canon – is brought to the fore. The key intertexts have numerous themes in common: negotiating inheritance, legacy and the importance of text, of writing, in this gesture. 'Te deix' consists entirely of a letter, *La filla* ends with the decision to write stories, Marçal's *La germana, l'estrangera* sees a turn to words to negotiate the delicate balance between fusion and continued autonomy in both mother/daughter and romantic relationships. Lorde's work emphasises the importance of writing for survival, as evident in her oft-quoted phrase 'poetry is not a luxury'.

In their engagements with Catalan literature of the late Franco period and transition to democracy, El Hachmi and the protagonist reference or cite the works of women who challenged the Catalan literary canon, especially through feminist writings or representations of same-sex desire between women. However, they alter these works in the process, in a gesture of rewriting. Marçal and Riera's work formulates a sense of horizontality in parent-child and other relationships in which a verticality of power and authority might be expected. In *La filla estrangera* the protagonist grapples with the imposition of cultural norms in a more vertical manner, be these from her mother's culture or in terms of assimilating to Catalan culture. In grappling with this reality, El Hachmi's process involves a sort of literalisation and reversal of the intertexts. Where Marçal writes of deciphering her daughter's 'llenguatge bàrbar' (*La germana, l'estrangera*, p. 51), El Hachmi seeks to decipher her mother's Berber language of Tamazight. In 'Te deix' the older teacher says to the younger student with whom she is briefly in a relationship that she would have liked to have been her mother and the younger one later leaves her a letter but also, metaphorically, invokes the continuation of their relationship through naming her daughter after her former lover. In *La filla estrangera* the daughter literally leaves her son to her mother, a son that she sees as effectively being born within an incestuous relationship with her mother. However, she, like the writer of the letter that makes up the story of 'Te deix', turns to writing to reconcile herself with her relationship with an older woman, in this case her literal mother.

In *La filla estrangera*, the protagonist refers repeatedly to the work of the 'poetessa'. Marçal is not mentioned by name in the text, testament to how iconic some of her lines now are in Catalonia. It is clear from the references to her work that she is the poet in question. The protagonist is introduced to Marçal's work by a friend with whom she has a deep intellectual relationship: 'El meu amor sense casa, el vers de la poetessa que ell tan admira, que em va presentar com a referent existencial perquè ella fou tres voltes rebel i jo cal suposar que en sigui quatre' (p. 95) ('My love without a home, the line by the poet whom he so admired, who he introduced me to as an existential reference because she was three times a rebel and I guess I was four times a rebel'). These lines are a reference to what are perhaps the most famous and oft-cited of Marçal's poems, the opening 'Divisa' ('Motto') from Marçal's first poetry collection *Cau de llunes* ('Den of Moons', 1977):

> A l'atzar agraeixo tres dons: haver nascut dona,
> de classe baixa i nació oprimida.[37]
>
> I am grateful to fate for three gifts: having been born a woman, working class and from an oppressed nation.

Marçal herself might later have added a fourth 'do' ('gift'), her desire for women. El Hachmi suggests that she has these characteristics too, with a fourth that she does not specify, presumably that of being a racialised woman, an immigrant. El Hachmi therefore draws attention to the racism she experiences that feeds her work, in addition to her sharing Marçal's gifts.

Another poem by Marçal that El Hachmi references directly in the quotation above is 'El meu amor sense casa' ('My love without a home'). In that poem Marçal evokes her love without a home: lesbian desire. In this and other works including her novel *La passió segons Renée Vivien* ('The passion according to Renée Vivien', 1994), she explores the lack of models of desire between women and how this simultaneously permits freedom for exploring new relational possibilities for living and loving, but also difficulties in terms of societal rejection and misunderstanding as well as disagreement about how to live; that is, whether to follow the path of more conventional relationships (e.g., through co-habiting) or to seek to live otherwise. Marçal's 'amor sense casa' is literalised in *La filla estrangera* when the protagonist and her mother are abandoned by the father and left 'sense casa, sense diners, sense res. Ben bé com el vers de la poetessa però de manera literal' (El Hachmi, *La filla*, p. 134) ('without a home, without money, without anything. Just like the words of the poet, but in a literal sense') and struggle to find a home due to racism and Islamophobia. Therefore, while influenced by writers such as Marçal, El Hachmi does not see her reality represented in their works. One element of this reality is the racism that she experiences in a country where, to take up the concept of home and shelter again, 'no ens ofereixen, a canvi de revoltar-nos contra les nostres famílies, un lloc alternatiu on arrecerar-nos' (p. 178) ('they don't offer us, in return for rebelling against our families, an alternative space where we can shelter'). Another reality is the difficulty of navigating her relationship with her mother as she grows up in a Catalan culture to which her mother has limited access. As such, El Hachmi brings different realities to bear on some iconic Catalan texts.

In *La filla estrangera* there is also a process of literalisation of part of the poem from which the title of Marçal's collection *La germana, l'estrangera* is taken:

> Com desxifrar el teu llenguatge bàrbar
> i violent que força els meus confins
> fins a la sang...
> ... jo inscrivia
> l'alfabet vegetal del teu missatge,
> poema viu que no urgia resposta...
> I malgrat tot t'anomeno victòria,
> heura marçal, germana, l'estrangera. (Marçal, *La germana*, p. 51)

> How to decipher your barbarous and
> violent language that forces my limits up to my blood...
> ... I inscribed the vegetal alphabet of your message,
> a living poem that didn't demand a response...
> despite everything I name you victory,
> Ivy of March/Heura Marçal [word play: Marçal's daughter is called Heura], sister, stranger.

For Marçal, the unrecognisable sounds that her child makes – her 'llenguatge bàrbar' – require deciphering. In El Hachmi's novel the language in question is literally a 'Berber language' and the process of deciphering is reversed. It is the daughter seeking to decipher her mother's Tamazight language, a language of the Imazighen, referred to by some with the dated and now widely considered derogatory term of 'Berber'. The term 'Berber' has its etymological routes in 'Barbarian', denoting a foreigner, an uncultured person, someone from the 'Barbary Coast' of north Africa. In Marçal's poem, the child's language is referred to as 'violent', emphasising the notion of threat to the self from the other tongue; the child changes the mother's identity, forcing her limits. There is a sense of estrangement from the child and yet the narrative voice insists on the daughter as sister connection, 'despite everything'. Indeed, the ivy plant is separate but attached to the structure that supports it, symbolic of a close bond between two separate entities. In contrast, in *La filla estrangera* the child initially tries to make her life easier by repressing her interest in written language, deciphering her mother's world and becoming more like her mother, even if this feels like a distortion and destruction of herself.

El Hachmi's description of her mother's language could be considered in the light of the simultaneous fragility and tenacity of Heura's 'alfabet vegetal' in Marçal's poem. The protagonist notes that there is no dictionary for Tamazight to other languages, repeatedly highlighting its oral rather than written existence: 'la seva llengua només vola per l'aire i només ha quedat fixada en la pell de les dones' (El Hachmi, *La filla*, p. 86) ('her language just flies through the air and just settles on women's skin'). She fears that this language that is 'del tot aliena al paper, que es transmet per l'aire sense deixar rastres de cap mena' (p. 31) ('totally alien to paper, that is transmitted through air without leaving any sort of trace') might be lost. Of course, in the very book that we have in our hands, which we could consider the text the protagonist refers to at the end of the novel, there is a trace of this language. However, as both Marçal and El Hachmi recognise, there are some sounds and sensations that escape the text. In the opening poem of *La germana, l'estrangera*, Marçal highlights the futility, the limitations of books and written language when faced with the fleshy existence of another human being:

> La carn, sense paraules,
> davant de mi i en mi.
>
> I jo que havia llegit tots el llibres. (Marçal, *La germana*, p. 43)
>
> Flesh, without words
> In front of me and within me.
>
> And I, who had read all the books.

The protagonist of *La filla estrangera* also points to the limits of the written word to capture her mother's tongue. She is fascinated by a sound that escapes being captured in text, a medium so valued and admired by the protagonist: 'A mi aquest so que no podria ser reproduït per l'escriptura, ni tan sols amb una transcripció fonètica, sempre m'ha fascinat' (El Hachmi, *La filla*, p. 106) ('That sound that couldn't be replicated in writing, not even through a phonetic transcription, has always fascinated me'). However, she also laments not being able to make that sound herself: 'I allà, palplantada davant del meu propi reflex, em sentia sobtadament forastera, incapaç de pertànyer al mateix grup que la mare encara que ho intentés i mires d'aprendre'n. Vet aquí com un espetec de la llengua et pot fer sentir desarrelada' (p. 107) ('There, stood in front of my own reflection, I suddenly felt like a foreigner, incapable of belonging to the same group as my mother even as I tried to, and even as I tried to learn how. See how a click of the tongue can make you feel unrooted'). Earlier she had described her sense of estrangement from her mother's language as a form of orphanhood: 'Em noto tot de sobte òrfena de paraules, expulsada de la llengua' (p. 37) ('I feel myself suddenly orphaned of words, expulsed from language'). The terms the protagonist uses to describe her relationship to Tamazight recalls Gloria Anzaldúa's description of chicanxs as 'deslenguados' ('tongueless people') who speak 'una lengua huérfana' ('an orphaned language or tongue').[38] Like Anzaldúa and Marçal, the protagonist ultimately turns to writing, despite an awareness of its insufficiency.

Marçal's reflections on separation and distance through communication and its impossibility seep into reflections on intimacy in the rest of the poems of the collection. In the seemingly paradoxical final poem of *La germana, l'estrangera*, she invokes sororal closeness as providing the conditions for the ability to distinguish oneself from an intimate other and the autonomy of being 'strangers' as enabling a healthy closeness without loss of the self:

És perquè et sé germana que puc dir-te estrangera.
Sense treva esbossada, sense treva abolida
aquesta guerra que m'uneix a tu
en un pacte de sang inestroncable.
És perquè et sé estrangera que puc dir-te germana. (Marçal, *La germana*, p. 132)

It is because I know you a sister that I can call you a stranger.
Without a sketched truce, without an abolished truce

this war unites me with you
in an unstemmable blood pact.
It is because I know you a stranger that I can call you sister.

Here, Marçal refers to there not being even a sketched or abolished truce in this war of intimacy; it will be ongoing. The negotiations of the relationship are always in progress, the balance between closeness and distance requires continuous attention and struggle.

In her novel, El Hachmi mentions idiomatic phrases that the mother uses to describe her love for her daughter. Like Marçal, she conjures the image of a blood bond: 'Em deia "fetge meu", que és com dir sang de la meva sang, però vol expresser un amor profund i inherent a la condició de mare. Però també em deia "pedrer meu", i era menys dramatic però igualment íntim, d'una vinculació irrompible' (El Hachmi, *La filla*, p. 146) ('She used to call me "liver of mine" that is like saying blood of my blood but is used to express a deep love inherent to being a mother. But she also used to call me "gizzard of mine" and it was less dramatic but equally intimate, said of an unbreakable bond'). The reference to blood conjures both a sense of closeness and of the possible violence of consumption of the daughter by the figure of the mother. The daughter as blood and organs, as something deeply within the self, inseparable, does not allow her development as an autonomous being. As mentioned above, the protagonist seeks to achieve a balance between closeness and separation from her mother through writing.

Aside from the direct references to Marçal and other resonances with her work, another key intertext of *La filla estrangera* is Riera's short story 'Te deix, amor, la mar com a penyora', published in a collection of the same name. This story consists of a letter written by a pregnant woman to her former teacher and lover who ended their relationship due to her position. In the letter the younger woman reflects on the time that they spent together and how, through writing, she sought to keep their relationship alive, despite their lack of contact. We do not know the teacher's name or gender until the very end of the text. The former lover's coming into being as Maria occurs at the moment of naming a hypothetical daughter in a gesture of desired inheritance and legacy of a love that could not be:

Pens que probablement no coneixeré la nina, perquè serà nina, n'estic segura, i no podré decidir, si no ho faig ara, el seu nom. Vull que li posin el teu, Maria, i vull, també, que llencin el meu cos a la mar, que no l'enterrin. Et prego que en aquell redós on l'aigua espià el nostre amor, llencin les meves despulles al fondal d'immensitat il·limitada. T'enyor, enyor la mar, la nostra. I te la deix, amor, com a penyora.[39]

I think that I probably won't meet the baby girl, because it'll be a girl, I'm sure, and I won't be able to decide her name, unless I do it now. I want them to give her your name, Maria, and I also want them to throw my body into the sea, rather than burying it. I beg you that in that very spot where the water spied on our love they should throw my remains into the depths of boundless immensity. I miss you, I miss the sea, our sea. And I leave it for you, love, as a token.

In *La filla estrangera*, El Hachmi uses the title of the short story, the words from the letter, in an address to her mother, altering them slightly. Once again this is a gesture of literalisation of part of the original text. Where in the original story the daughter is simply named after the lover, in *La filla estrangera*, the mother is literally left with the child. When Maria comments on another of the unnamed younger lover's relationships, the younger women replies, 'Parles com si fossis ma mare' ('You sound like my mother'), to which the older woman responds, 'T'assegur que m'hauria agradat ser-ho' (Riera, 'Te deix', p. 31) ('I can assure you I would've liked to have been [your mother]'. In El Hachmi, the relationship in question is literally a mother-daughter relationship. The replacement of the older lover for the mother in *La filla estrangera*, lends the mother-daughter relationship a hint of eroticism, as in Marçal's evocation in *La germana, l'estrangera*. Indeed, the protagonist's domestic life with her mother, especially cooking, was more erotic than her passive sexual encounters with her 'cousin-husband'.

El Hachmi's turn to Riera's text is a way of signalling her deep love for her mother, and also perhaps a way of horizontalising their relationship as they are both effectively parents of the child that she describes as 'el fruit del meu amor per la mare, un fill incestuós' (El Hachmi, *La filla*, p. 204) ('the fruit of my love for my mother, an incestuous child'), born in 'el meu casament per amor a la mare' (p. 193) ('my marriage of love for my mother'):

Te deix, mare, un fill com a penyora. No puc deixar-te la mar, que aquí a la nostra ciutat de la Plana no en tenim, si de cas et podria

> deixar el fred i la boira que se'ns arrapen als passos els nou mesos d'hivern i la xafogor insuportable dels tres mesos d'infern. Et deixo un fill, que et farà més companyia. (p. 199)
>
> I leave you, mother, a son as a token. I can't leave you the sea, because here in our city in the Plana [the Plain of Vic] we don't have a sea, but I could leave you the cold and the fog that cling to our footsteps during the nine months of winter and the stifling heat of the three months of hell. I leave you a son, who will be better company.

However, even in this moment of leaving an ambiguous gift of her child, the protagonist is faced with another moment of impeded communication as she cannot translate Riera's words to Tamazight: 'No sé com diria en la llengua de la meva mare la paraula *penyora*, no li trobo la correspondència, però li deixo aquest fill com a penyora' (p. 205) ('I don't know how to say "penyora" in my mother's language, I can't find a corresponding word, but I leave her this son as a token'). As she makes this ambivalent offering, it is the impossibility of communication with her mother that is emphasised.

Another commonality between *La filla estrangera* and 'Te deix' is the exploration of the fusion or lack of boundaries between two people. The narrator of the letter in 'Te deix' writes: 'Els meus ulls que eren els teus, car jo veia el món com tu el miraves . . . m'esforçava per endevinar i traduir les teves reaccions fent-les passar per meves, quasi inconscientment' (Riera, 'Te deix', p. 21) ('My eyes, which were yours, because I saw the world as you observed it . . . I tried to guess and translate your reactions, passing them off as my own, almost unconsciously'). This is reminiscent of the protagonist in *La filla estrangera* seeking to become her mother, before later going on to try to block even the memory of her out of her mind. Like El Hachmi's protagonist in her attempt to move on from her mother, the women in 'Te deix' ambivalently seek 'l'oblit' (p. 26) ('forgetting') of their relationship and Maria, the older woman, expresses a desire for time to 'esborrar-ho tot' (p. 27) ('erase it all'). However, also like El Hachmi's protagonist, for the younger woman reconciliation comes about not through forgetting but through writing. Text provides a space for reconciliation that has hitherto proven impossible in life:

I com que insistia a oblidar el teu nom i les teves senyes, vaig escriure a la mar amb la secreta intenció que les ones et donessin, ran del teu portal, noves meves . . . Certament vaig passar tota la nit amb tu. A estones la ploma sobre el paper escrivia amb tanta morositat, tan delicadament que era com si t'acaronés en silenci. (p. 32)

And given that I was insisting on forgetting your name and features, I wrote to the sea with the secret intention that the waves would give you, in the vicinity of your door, news of me . . . I definitely spent the whole night with you. Sometimes my pen on paper moved so slowly, so delicately that it was as if I were caressing you in silence.

Writing is a way of conjuring the presence of the other, but in silence, in solitude. In 'Te deix' as in *La filla estrangera* the endings are ambiguous: we do not know if the protagonist of *La filla estrangera* sees her mother again; we do not know if the writer of the letter in 'Te deix' survives childbirth. In 'Te deix' the writer imagines her former lover reading her letter and of them effectively being together again as she reads through many past letters. In *La filla* the writing of the texts described by the protagonist at the end of the novel are part of the protagonist's process, but it seems highly unlikely that the illiterate mother will learn to read Catalan. Indeed, in both cases it is unclear whether the recipients – the mother, the lover – even receive the texts in question. Nonetheless, the writing of them clearly provides both protagonists with a sense of peace and reconciliation with a painful and difficult past.

Conclusion

In this chapter I have explored the importance of writing in El Hachmi and the protagonist of *La filla estrangera*'s processes of navigating their migrant identities. They reflect on their positions in Catalan society through engaging with the literary establishment, albeit with a focus on works that themselves challenge a predominantly male and heteronormative canon before coming to be accepted within that canon themselves. As part of this process of navigating their autonomy through literature, both El Hachmi and the protagonist see themselves partially reflected in the writers and characters of their predecessors, but with some important differences relating to racialisation and migration to which they gesture through disidentificatory intertextuality. Their engagement with some iconic works and lines involves processes of literalisation to signal the difference in their situations, and the reversal of certain power dynamics and hierarchies, as shown in the examples of Marçal and Riera.

While the orality of her mother's tongue cannot be represented fully in text, El Hachmi does register its impact on her life in her works in this lasting record. The protagonist passes through a process of internalised racism, self-exoticisation and problematic comments that seem to underestimate the knowledge contained in oral cultures. While at the end of the novel she turns to text to write her story and that of her mother, it is without a sense of superiority, and rather with an awareness of the power and limitation of text. Perhaps a further rewriting of the line from Riera is apt: 'Te deix, mare, els meus llibres com a penyora' ('I leave you, mother, my books as a token'). Her mother may well never read or understand her books, but their love and connection will be preserved through the maintenance of their difference, as well as their undeniable connection and similarities. After all, as Marçal affirms, '[é]s perquè et sé germana que puc dir-te estrangera' (Marçal, *La germana*, p. 132) ('it is because I know you as a sister that I can call you stranger'). For El Hachmi's protagonist, a sense of autonomy and difference are achieved and reinforced through writing that protects a space of love and desire that had previously been endangered through an unbounded sense of fusion and negation of the self.

Notes

1 Najat El Hachmi, *La filla estrangera* (Barcelona: Edicions 62, 2015).
2 José Esteban Muñoz, *Disidentifications: Queers of Color and the Performance of Politics* (Minneapolis MN: University of Minnesota Press, 1999).
3 Adrienne Rich, 'Compulsory Heterosexuality and Lesbian Existence', *Signs: Journal of Women in Culture and Society*, 5/4 (1980), 648.
4 On El Hachmi's 'autobiographical fiction', see Cristián Ricci, 'The Reshaping of Postcolonial Iberia: Moroccan and Amazigh Literatures in the Peninsula', *Hispanófila*, 180 (2017), 32. Miquel Pomar Amer describes El Hachmi's use of the slippage between herself and her protagonists as a deliberate play with 'dominant culture's voyeurism';

see 'Voices Emerging from the Border: A Reading of the Autobiographies by Najat El Hachmi and Saïd El Kadaoui as Political Interventions', *Planeta Literatur: Journal of Global Literary Studies*, 1 (2014), 43.
5   Sara Ahmed, *Strange Encounters: Embodied Others in Post-Coloniality* (New York: Routledge, 2000), p. 6. Maria-Mercè Marçal, *La germana, l'estrangera (1981–1984)* (Barcelona: Edicions 62, 1995), p. 132.
6   Najat El Hachmi, *La filla estrangera* (Barcelona: Edicions 62, 2015), p. 204. Unless otherwise stated, translations from Catalan and Spanish are my own.
7   Ricci, 'The Reshaping of Postcolonial Iberia', 21–40.
8   Caragh Wells, 'The Freedom of the Aesthetic: Montserrat Roig's Use of the City in *Ramona, adéu*', *Catalan Review*, 21/1 (2007), 87–99.
9   Núria Codina, 'The Work of Najat El Hachmi in the Context of Spanish-Moroccan Literature', *Research in African Literatures*, 48/3 (2017), 119.
10 H. Rosi Song, 'Narrating Identity in Najat El Hachmi's *L'últim patriarca*', in Lucia Aiello, Joy Charnley and Mariangela Palladino (eds), *Displaced Women: Multilingual Narratives of Migration in Europe* (Newcastle: Cambridge Scholars Publishing, 2014), p. 49.
11 Julia Kristeva, *Strangers to Ourselves*, trans. by Leon S. Roudiez (New York: Columbia University Press, 1991), p. 3.
12 Édouard Glissant, *Poetics of Relation*, trans. by Betsy Wing (Ann Arbor MI: University of Michigan Press, 1997), p. 4.
13 Ahmed, *Strange Encounters*, pp. 3–4.
14 Ahmed, *Strange Encounters*, p. 6.
15 Ahmed, *Strange Encounters*, p. 16.
16 Daniela Flesler, *The Return of the Moor: Spanish Responses to Contemporary Moroccan Immigration* (West Lafayette IN: Purdue University Press, 2008), pp. 8–9.
17 Flesler, *The Return of the Moor*, p. 9.
18 See, for example, Carlos Cañete and Gonzalo Fernández Parrilla, 'Spanish-Maghribi (Moroccan) Relations Beyond Exceptionalism: A Postcolonial Perspective', *Journal of North Africa Studies*, 24/1 (2019), 111–33.
19 N. Michelle Murray, 'Migration and Genealogies of Rupture in the Work of Najat El Hachmi', *Research in African Literatures*, 48/3 (2017), 19.
20 Murray, 'Migration and Genealogies of Rupture', 19.
21 See Alfonso Iglesias Amorín, 'Sub-state Nationalisms in Spain during the Moroccan War and the Rif War (1909–1927)', *Studies on National Movements*, 8 (2021), 1–25; and Pedro Panera Martínez, '"Endavant, catalans!": Voluntarios de Cataluña para la guerra de África (1859–1860)', *Revista Digital Guerra Colonial*, 1 (2017), 89–107.

22 Ricci refers to writing as a 'therapeutic process' for many of El Hachmi's characters; see 'The Reshaping of Postcolonial Iberia', 32.
23 Marçal, *La germana, l'estrangera*, p. 56.
24 Catherine Bourland Ross, 'Left Behind: Cultural Assimilation and the Mother/Daughter Relationship in Najat El Hachmi's *La hija extranjera* (2015)', *Hispanófila*, 183 (2018), 363.
25 Cited by Nancy Bereano, 'Introduction' to *Sister Outsider*, in Audre Lorde, *Zami; Sister Outsider; Undersong* (New York: Quality Paperback Book Club, 1993), p. 10.
26 Maria-Mercè Marçal, *Llengua abolida: Poesia completa 1973–1998* (Barcelona: Edicions 62, 2017), p. 434.
27 Lorde, *Sister Outsider*, in *Zami; Sister Outsider; Undersong*, p. 147.
28 Murray, 'Migration and Genealogies of Rupture', 19.
29 Adolfo Campoy-Cubillo, *Memories of the Maghreb: Transnational Identities in Spanish Cultural Production* (London and New York: Palgrave Macmillan, 2012), pp. 138–9.
30 Josep-Anton Fernàndez, 'Dislocated Temporalities: Immigration, Sexuality, and Violence in Najat El Hachmi's *L'últim patriarca*', in Teresa Iribarren, Roger Canadell and Josep-Anton Fernàndez (eds), *Narratives of Violence* (Venice: Edizioni Ca' Foscari, 2021), pp. 121–42.
31 Murray, 'Migration and Genealogies of Rupture', 18.
32 Ricci, 'The Reshaping of Postcolonial Iberia', 32.
33 Codina, 'The Work of Najat El Hachmi', 116.
34 Muñoz, *Disidentifications*, p. 9.
35 Muñoz, *Disidentifications*, p. 11.
36 Muñoz, *Disidentifications*, p. 4 and p. ix.
37 Marçal, *Llengua abolida*, p. 19.
38 Numerous critics have read the work of El Hachmi through Anzaldúa's notion of borderland, hybrid writing, emblematic as it is of a straddling of cultures, either to emphasise similarities (such as Ricci, 33) or differences (such as Murray, 27, who says, 'El Hachmi's borderlands are less tangible') between the borderlands in question: the US-Mexico border and the Spanish/Catalan-Moroccan/Maghrebi situation.
39 Carme Riera, *Te deix, amor, la mar com a penyora* (Barcelona: Columna Jove, 2005 [1975]), p. 33.

Chapter 8
Limits and Borders in *No*, by Saïd El Kadaoui

Roger Canadell Rusiñol

Throughout history, concepts such as 'limit' and 'border' have often been tied to processes of geographical separation and national or cultural differentiation, while also being associated with realities linked to exile or migration. This has imbued them with meaning and connotative power that literary texts have used to offer complex works giving pause for thought on the divided condition of the modern writer, the trauma of migration and exile and the impossibility of putting into words the ultimate consequences of these phenomena in terms of identity building.

The aim of this chapter is not to explore the theoretical depths of so-called borderlands studies, but rather to analyse how Saïd El Kadaoui Moussaoui – a Moroccan-born Catalan writer, psychologist and psychoanalyst and well-known lecturer on identity building in immigration contexts – incorporates explicit theoretical reflection on otherness, difference and borders into his work, to the point of constructing a metaliterary reflection in his novel *No*. That being said, we cannot ignore the fact that this reading of *No* echoes the words of Gloria Anzaldúa in the preface to *Borderlands/ La Frontera*:

> the Borderlands are physically present wherever two or more cultures edge each other, where people of different races occupy the same territory, where under, lower, middle, and upper classes touch, where the space between two individuals shrink with intimacy.[1]

The central character in *No* migrates from Morocco to Catalonia, and his experience of this process – to a large extent an autofictional account of the personal, geographical and intellectual journey of the novel's author – reflects some of the consequences of exile, understood according to one of the meanings that Robert Spencer[2] drew from Edward Said's *Reflections on Exile*: 'Exile . . . is a means not an end; it is above all a way of thinking. Exile involves a willingness to step outside the province of ideological preconceptions, sectarian loyalties, and insentient theoretical and philosophical systems.'[3] In this sense, El Kadaoui's work stems from a radical desire to shun well-meaning clichés about migration and to use literature to tell a story of transgression, which serves as the gateway to the new identity longed for and sought after by the protagonist. Paradoxically, as an epigraph or headline to this study, one might use the sentence featured on the back cover of *No*: 'És en el fet de decebre, de sorprendre, de transgredir i de subvertir on es troba la llavor d'aquest nou ésser que anhelem' ('It is by disappointing, surprising, transgressing and subverting that we find the seed of this new being we long for').[4] Thus, to fulfil the quasi-messianic desire of this 'new man', who is not yet complete, a seed will have to be sought, and to find it the author notes that it will be necessary to disappoint, surprise, transgress and subvert; an attitude that *No*'s protagonist explores and experiences in a number of situations in which these four verbs turn in on himself and out towards his environment: he disappoints and surprises himself and others while transgressing and subverting his own limits and those of the society in which he lives. His exile, therefore, becomes a way of thinking and living through which the author shows, in an uncomfortable and pointed way, the possible place and meaning of a dislocated identity.

No is a piece of narrative fiction composed of writing fragments, reflections and comments that the main character, an unnamed Moroccan-born, middle-class, forty-year-old Catalan man, addresses to his friend, who was also a migrant in Catalonia for many years before returning to live in Morocco when he became a father. The protagonist, upset and saddened by his friend's departure, feels the need to write down his thoughts and reflections on identity, family relationships, his sexuality, friends, literature, the personal and social disengagement that he is experiencing, and so on. As in so many other literary works in which the clichéd return to one's homeland, country of birth or parents' place of origin is the starting point of the narrative, *No*'s central character, whose name we do not know, feels the need to write down his reflections after the return to Morocco, seven years earlier, of his friend, 'Maati Kaabal, psiquiatre cap de servei d'un centre de salut mental de Girona' (El Kadaoui, *No*, p. 105) ('Maati Kaabal, head psychiatrist at a mental health centre in Girona'), who comes from a well-to-do family. In the process of writing, the narrator searches for a place (not necessarily a physical one) where he can live without torment, seeks meaning in his identity, and most importantly, endeavours to discover his homeland of Morocco, which for him has become a 'fiction', 'a vague place', a 'construction':

> Vas decidir tornar, i allà t'esperava bona part de la família, les teves llengües, alguns dels amics de la infància i una ciutat dinàmica i atractiva com és Casablanca. Trepitges terreny ferm. Has viscut una aventura intricada i complexa que de ben segur t'haurà eixamplat la perspectiva vital. Després de néixer el teu fill, els temors i les inseguretats van augmentar i vas començar a preguntar-te què seria el millor per a ell . . . Vas optar per estalviar-li la feridora experiència del racisme i te l'has emportat. Allà ha nascut el teu segon fill, i tots dos estan al costat dels avis i alguns dels oncles i cosins. Estudiaran el que voldran a les millors escoles i, si per atzar els ve de gust l'aventura europea, podran venir amb els seus visats d'estudiants. Amb tu he après que el Marroc també és un país normal.
> El meu cas és diferent. El meu Marroc és una ficció. Una construcció. Un lloc nebulós. En tot cas, és un país que cal descobrir, i és justament aquesta la tasca que ara m'ocupa. (*No*, pp. 29–30)

You chose to go back, and there you were met by a good part of your family, languages, some of your childhood friends and the bustling and attractive city of Casablanca. You are on solid ground. You have been on an intricate and complex adventure that is sure to have broadened your outlook on life. After the birth of your son, your fears and insecurities heightened and you began to wonder what would be best for him . . . You chose to spare him the painful experience of racism and you took him away. Your second child was born there, and both are with their grandparents and some of their uncles and cousins. They will study whatever they want in the best schools and, if by chance they crave a European adventure, they will be able to come on their student visas. From you I have learned that Morocco is a normal country too.

My case is different. My Morocco is a fiction. A construction. A vague place. In any case, it is a country to be discovered, and that is precisely the task that occupies me now.

There are obvious parallels between the above and the process that Sultana – the heroine of Malika Mokeddem's *L'interdite* (1993) – undergoes when she rediscovers the country of her birth. In this novel, Sultana, a doctor living in France, returns to Algeria, where she critically reconstructs her relationship, somewhere between love and hate, with a culture and world that she thought she had left behind. Mokeddem, in fact, is the subject of the doctoral thesis written by Maite, the partner of *No*'s main character, who is said on several occasions to know more about Morocco and its intellectuals than the narrator himself.

The deluge of seemingly unconnected thoughts and confessions within the book form a discourse that becomes, in essence, a triple dialogue. First, *No* is a dialogue between the protagonist and the constant conflict that he experiences in his relationship with his environment, with the other; second, it is a dialogue between the book itself and El Kadaoui's previous works; and third, it is also very evidently a dialogue between the narrator and intellectuals, mostly from Arab countries or of the Muslim religion.

If we look first at the internal conflicts experienced by the central character, we notice that most of them come from dialogue and questions – asked by himself or the people around him – about the life decisions he has made at critical moments or in traumatic situations. It should not be forgotten that *No*'s author, as well as being a writer, is a psychologist and psychoanalyst, which is why it is unsurprising that the idea of conflict linked to the concept of trauma appears recurrently throughout the novel. Thus, the protagonist of *No* is a man who, at the age of forty, realises that he does not want to be a father, does not want to have a stable partner, does not want to get married, does not want to uncritically conform to the traditions that his family tries to impose on him, does not want to embrace a European identity that is also uncritical, does not want to hear about immigrant associations or Moroccan cultural centres, cannot stand how the Catalans view migration with an air of benevolent but accommodating superiority, and does not believe in categories that exclude or divide between cultures that are local or have recently arrived, between natives and foreigners. In short, he is someone who has not found his place in life amid a complex social, cultural, work and family reality; he does not feel fulfilled; he cannot give up his unbridled sexuality; he cannot help feeling a vast emptiness after every little pleasure; and, of course, he does not want to go back to Morocco like his friend. He does not feel torn between two cultures and does not want to have a 'hybrid' identity. He simply wants to be himself and to live fully in his singularity.

The identity building of the protagonist and narrator in *No* constantly revolves around the series of negations mentioned in the previous paragraph, giving the juxtaposed texts written and addressed to his absent friend a common thread that organises the novel literarily. These negations stem from dialogue and constant questioning about his own life and the experiences of the people close to him, as a literature professor who conducts 'un seminari dedicat a Edward Said i un altre que he batejat amb l'altisonant nom de "Literatura de l'altre"' ('a seminar dedicated to Edward Said and another that I have given the bombastic name of "Literature of the Other"') and who is becoming 'un especialista en això de les identitats perifèriques' ('a specialist in this matter of peripheral identities') to the point of 'rebre invitacions per anar a congressos per tot l'Estat i part de l'estranger!' (pp. 16–17) ('receiving invitations to attend conferences all over Spain and part of the world!').

The novel deals with many conflicts that derive from this dialogue about life. The perpetual crisis suffered by the protagonist due to his 'desmesurat desig pels cossos femenins' (p. 19) ('inordinate desire for female bodies') is one of them, lasting from cover to cover. He also constantly questions his emotional relationship with Maite – 'puc retenir-la sense donar-li res del que em demana? Posem que ella accedeix a renunciar a una relació marital i als fills. Seria moralment acceptable?' (p. 64) ('can I hold on to her without giving her anything she asks for? Let's say she agrees to do without marriage or children. Would that be morally acceptable?'). His outlook is conditioned by the remorse of infidelity and by the postcoital existential void that brings to mind the classic and Freudian dictum 'Omne animal post coitum triste':[5] 'Ahir va succeir i avui em vull morir' (El Kadaoui, *No*, p. 183) ('Yesterday it happened and today I want to die'); 'Ha estat excel·lent. Però aquí em tens ara. Trist, absort, culpós i sentint-me com un ésser fastigosament insensible i irrespectuós' (p. 185) ('It was wonderful. But here I am now. Sad, consumed, guilty and feeling like a disgustingly insensitive and disrespectful creature'). Beyond the constant reference to his sexuality-driven inner turmoil, there are other crises that challenge the protagonist's conscience throughout the novel like a steady drip. The main one is brought about by the return of his psychiatrist friend to Morocco and, in turn, by the discovery of the answers that he has been giving (himself) since he began writing his reflections. From the outset, the decision reveals a confrontation with a previously falsified reality and the void left by his friend's absence:

> Una part de la càrrega emotiva que ha suposat la teva partida és la confrontació amb la realitat. Aquest altre que falsejava la realitat ara s'ha esvaït. El seu espai l'ha ocupat un buc, un abisme d'angoixa i la certesa que tu vius al Marroc i jo no. (p. 19)

> Part of the emotional toll of your departure is the confrontation with reality. That other someone who falsified reality has now vanished. His space has been taken by a void, an abyss of anguish and the certainty that you live in Morocco and I don't.

Despite his theoretical knowledge of the 'literatura de l'altre' ('literature of the other'), he does not appreciate the social divide suffered by many of the people around him until he remembers and writes down the experience that he and his friend Maati had, triggering the latter's decision to return to his home country. After doing some work in Badia del Vallès, a town on the outskirts of Barcelona populated mainly by Spanish migrants from the 1960s and by migrants from all over the world since the 1990s, the protagonist becomes aware of the pain caused by the gaze of others: 'El que et va humiliar va ser que aquella gent que et demanava ajuda et posava a tu en aquell mateix sac. La *vostra* cultura. Mai no has pogut pair que a tu se't pogués mirar com el marroquí tipus segons l'imaginari europeu' (p. 44) ('What humiliated you was that those people asking you for help put you in the same basket. *Your* culture. You have never been able to stomach the fact that you could be seen as the typical Moroccan according to the European imaginary'). It is no coincidence that El Kadaoui uses the impact caused by someone else's way of viewing his identity as the motif that drives the whole conflict and, in turn, the novel itself. For immigrants, the gaze of the other as a shaper of one's identity is an even more determining factor in the construction of one's own life story, insofar as the distances between here and there, or between the self and the other, gain significance. In other words, at the origin of *No* there is the experience of the border, of the limit behind which the characters place themselves or are placed and which, consequently, triggers a crisis. This is because, as Claudio Magris says, the border is ambiguous and can serve both as a bridge to meet the other and as a barrier to turn him away.[6] Despite everything, the negativity and disengagement embodied by the main character bring together his own experience and that of his friends and family in a reflection that becomes literature. Indeed, as Magris also says, 'la literatura, entre otras cosas, es también un viaje en busca de la refutación de ese mito del otro lado, para comprender que cada uno se encuentra ora de este lado ora del otro' (p. 56) ('literature, among other things, is also a journey to refute the myth of the other side, in order to understand that everyone is on this side at times and on the other side at other times').

In the novel, the figure of the other is thus the realisation of a border, which becomes both a divider and a mirror. For this reason, conflict is present in every chapter in which the narrator explains the opinions that he hears, which are motivated by the border or the limit established by the positioning of the other. For example, on a trip to Marrakech, his friend Anna asks him, 'Com podeu sortir d'un món i entrar en un altre amb tanta facilitat?' ('How can you leave one world and enter another so easily?'), a question that in turn prompts his 'canvi de mirada cap a l'Anna ... depenent del costat de la frontera on ens trobem' (El Kadaoui, *No*, p. 69) ('change of perspective towards Anna ... depending on which side of the border we are on'). Moreover, despite not wanting to take a simplistic position on anything to do with identity, he does not hold back his scathing criticism of both the toxicity of the capitalist Western world and the simple nature of the Moroccan culture adopted by many migrants and, of course, by his family: 'm'adono que soc un europeu de classe mitjana indecent, d'una banda, i membre d'una tribu primària de l'altra, intoxicat per un pensament màgic i infantil' (p. 161) ('I realise that I am an indecent middle-class European on the one hand, and a member of a primitive tribe on the other, intoxicated by magical and infantile thinking').

And yet, the other is also his own father and mother, from whom he feels separated by a border across which both emotional kinship and fierce criticism circulate:

> Al·là mai no m'ha escoltat. Durant un temps li vaig pregar que la mare s'aprimés i que es vestís amb gust. Lluny de concedir-me el desig, li va inflar el ventre, li va engrandir l'enorme cul que ja tenia i li va imposar tornar a enfundar-se el mocador al cap. Aquest va ser el meu regal dels catorze anys . . . Els pares cultes i rics poden castrar. Pretenen que no els superis, em vas dir una vegada. I els pares analfabets i pobres són pitjor, et dic jo. Et diuen que desitgen que els superis, que siguis millor que ells, i fan tot el possible perquè no ho aconsegueixis. Vestida d'aquella manera, presentar-se a l'institut amb aquella pinta, em va deprimir de tal manera que gairebé vaig abandonar els estudis. (p. 139–40)

> Allah has never listened to me. For a while I begged him to make my mother lose weight and dress nicely. Far from granting my wish, he swelled her belly, enlarged her already huge backside and made her wear a headscarf again. This was the present I got when I turned fourteen . . . Educated and rich parents can castrate. They don't want you to rise above them, you once told me. And illiterate and poor parents are worse, I tell you. They say they want you to rise above them, to be better than they are, and they do everything they can to stop you from succeeding. Dressed like that, showing up at school looking like that, depressed me so much that I almost dropped out of school.

Symbolically killing his father and mother with this harsh confession, shortly before receiving the news that he too will be a father, is the only way for the protagonist to unveil what is hidden. Paradoxically, the place in the novel where this need to reveal the truth most clearly appears is in the narration of a dream in which he is unable to save his father. His father asks him for help in the midst of a raging sea, but the son scolds him, saying 'no hauries d'haver marxat' ('you shouldn't have left'). It is this dream that provides insight into the various reasons why the protagonist believes it would have been better not to move and thus avoid his life's conflicts:

> Per tot això, pare, ofega't al teu mar i deixa'm marxar!
> Un parricidi freudià per poder existir. No em negaràs que aquí tinc un material extraordinari. (p. 159)
>
> For all this, Dad, drown in your sea and let me go!
> A Freudian parricide to be able to exist. You can't deny that I have some extraordinary material here.

However, the protagonist's main dialogue with the *other* is with the psychiatrist friend to whom he is writing, who acts as a counterpart for him in his existential quest, and his psychoanalyst, to whom he periodically explains his conflicts and obsessions. In this periodic recounting of personal experiences, the protagonist is not the only one who expresses desires and fears conditioned by the fact of being a migrant. Rather, the other becomes the one on whom he projects himself and whom he makes shoulder the burden of representing his own desires. As Iain Chambers says, 'We seek to return to the beginnings, no longer our own, but that of an "other" who is requested to carry the burden of representing our desire'.[7]

The bond with his friend, rather than a salve for his conscience and intellect, becomes a new wound opened by the discomfort of his decision to leave. The protagonist realises this and writes to Maati that '[n]o portaves bé haver de respondre amb els teus actes i opinions per tot un país, per tota una religió' (El Kadaoui, *No*, p. 166) ('you didn't cope well with having to answer with your actions and opinions for a whole country, for a whole religion') and that he had once told him that he wanted to look 'en el costat lluminós. Ser marroquí sense necessitat de ser-ne conscient' (p. 166) ('on the bright side. Being Moroccan without having to think about it'). However, whereas the psychiatrist friend can leave because he believes he lives in a country that is not his, the narrator does not have 'un país al qual retornar com tu. I, alhora, tampoc pertanyo –i et diré més, no vull pertànyer del tot– a aquest' (pp. 168–9) ('a country to go back to like you. And at the same time, I don't belong – nor do I want to belong entirely, I'd add – to this one either').

At this point, El Kadaoui puts the protagonist of his novel in the most complicated place of all: as an inhabitant of the non-place. As Jean-Luc Nancy writes, the clichéd conception of exile as a passage between departure and return has radically changed its meaning in Western modernity and now 'parece ser en muchos aspectos la experiencia de un exilio definitivo y sin retorno' ('seems to be in many respects the experience of a definitive exile without return').[8] The protagonist does not belong anywhere and does not want to be from anywhere. He is not in exile, nor does he consider himself a migrant, but his life experience is, in itself, an experience of exile. His struggle to form lasting bonds, especially with women, his constant out-of-place feeling and the fact that he cannot find a context in which the other is seen for what he is and not for the group he belongs to are consequences of this exile that is constitutive of modern existence, which is none other than 'un exilio fundamental: un "estar fuera de", un "haber salido de"' ('a fundamental exile: a "being out of", a "having left"') like 'el que parte, no hacia un lugar determinado, sino el que parte absolutamente' ('one who leaves, not for a particular place, but one who leaves absolutely') for an 'existencia exiliada' ('exiled existence').[9] This is why he feels such deep discomfort both when asked as a Moroccan to answer questions about djellabas, headscarves and beards, and when he is compelled to say as a Catalan that 'el submón àrab a Europa no té interès. És una bombolla de misèria material i intel·lectual' (El Kadaoui, *No*, p. 147) ('the Arab underworld in Europe is of no interest. It is a bubble of material and intellectual misery').

The second of the dialogues making up the discourse underpinning *No* is the dialogue that this novel engages in, either explicitly or covertly, with two of El Kadaoui's earlier works: *Límites y fronteras* ('Limits and Borders', 2008) and *Cartes al meu fill: Un català de soca-rel, gairebé* ('Letters to My Son: A Catalan Born and Bred, Almost', 2011).[10] While it is true that a long, in-depth study of *No* could dwell on very interesting aspects, such as its narrative structure or point of view, or its thematic complexity (which can be analysed comparatively with other works that deal with the reality of being a migrant), I will limit myself to discussing the interpretative richness provided by a thorough reading of these three works, in which autofiction appears repeatedly and significantly. As one can surmise, the title of this chapter is borrowed from the first of these other books.

The main character in *Límites y fronteras* is a Moroccan immigrant living in Catalonia who suffers a psychotic episode and is admitted to a psychiatric clinic to recover. The novel's entire plot and the events that take place in it come from a reflection that teeters between sanity and madness. The period of institutionalisation is for Ismaïl a time to reflect on his condition as a foreigner, his identity, his sense of belonging, his dreams. Meanwhile, *Cartes al meu fill*, like *No*, is a book structured around a fragmented discourse that is organised in the form of an epistolary. The letters in this case are written by the author himself to his son, Elies El Kadaoui Serrats, just as in *Jo també soc catalana* ('I Am also Catalan'), Najat El Hachmi describes 'una trajectòria vital amb relació al fet migratori però que alhora vol reflectir les idees macerades a partir d'aquesta trajectòria' ('a life's journey about being a migrant, but which at the same time aims to reflect the ideas macerated from this journey'),[11] which is also built around questions asked by her son. In *Cartes al meu fill*, El Kadaoui assumes the role of narrator, saying that:

> sentia el deure de preparar-te el terreny. Si jo patia quan notava que se'm tractava permanentment com un foraster, com no ho havies de fer tu que, a diferència meva, tens una mare amb noms i cognoms ben ancorats en aquest meravellós tros de terra . . . He escrit aquest llibre per preparar-te un lloc més confortable.[12]

> I felt it my duty to prepare the way for you. If I suffered when I felt I was constantly treated as an outsider, how could you not? You who, unlike me, have a mother with names and surnames firmly anchored in this wonderful slice of land . . . I have written this book to prepare a more comfortable place for you.

In all three of El Kadaoui's works, the immigrant is shown as someone who has had to cross a border, but who also finds himself facing new limitations imposed by other types of border from his new place in life, that is, the non-place mentioned before: the border between madness and sanity, the border caused by fatherhood, or the border self-imposed by the main character in *No* due to his age. And it is neither gratuitous nor coincidental that the migrant, the madman, the displaced and the disengaged should appear because, as Simona Škrabec says: 'La literatura sobreviu només si tracta les qüestions decisives i ajuda a comprendre la realitat . . . [Aquesta és] la raó principal de conservar la posició perifèrica, perquè només des dels marges podem conservar la capacitat del discerniment crític'[13] ('Literature survives only if it deals with the decisive questions and improves our understanding of reality . . . [This is] the main reason for maintaining a peripheral position, because it is only from the fringes that we can retain the capacity for critical judgement'). Everything seems to indicate that El Kadaoui, by creating characters who traverse the marginal non-place where life has led them – like Ismaïl – or where they themselves have decided to live – like the protagonist in *No* – directs his work towards the space of judgement mentioned by Škrabec and prompts the reader's critical reflection. However, the desire to construct a literary discourse on life, when the characters and the author himself are crossing the swampy terrain of a dislocated identity, comes up against another difficulty: the need to acquire a language and craft a narrative in order to articulate the experience.

To subvert matters, transgress what is established and ultimately pacify his existence and the trauma, doubt and shock caused by his friend's return to Morocco, the central character in *No* takes the path of writing. He writes and reads like Ismaïl in *Límites y fronteras*, for whom writing, followed by a restorative trip to Morocco, is therapy, healing and a return to sanity. Guided by his therapist, Ismaïl writes to put his own existence down in words.

The father in *Cartes al meu fill*, Saïd El Kadaoui himself, says:

> La ficció, la literatura, sovint ens dóna una visió molt més àmplia i completa de la majoria dels aspectes de la vida. Ens permet endinsar-nos en l'intricat món dels sentiments i de les relacions humanes i aprofundir en la indefugible relació de l'individu amb el temps.[14]

> Fiction, or literature, often gives us a much broader and more rounded perspective on most aspects of life. It allows us to enter the intricate world of feelings and human relations and explore the inescapable relationship between the individual and time.

The protagonist in *No*, seven years after the crisis triggered by his friend's departure, becomes aware of the need to write a book:

> La teva partida m'ha deixat amb un llibre dins.
> Honestament, tot esdeveniment transcendental de la meva vida em deixa amb un llibre dins, el darrer dels quals i, per tant, el que

més hores de la meva no-escriptura m'ocupa actualment té a veure amb tu, amb la teva partida. Soc un escriptor sense obra. Ja veus que m'he adjudicat l'honorable títol d'escriptor encara que no hagi escrit res. Ho has d'entendre, escriure esgota. (El Kadaoui, *No*, p. 12)

Your departure has left me with a book inside.

Honestly, every transcendental event in my life leaves me with a book inside, the latest of which, and therefore the one that occupies most of my non-writing hours at the moment, is about you, about your departure. I am a writer without writings. You see, I have awarded myself the honourable title of writer even though I have written nothing. You must understand; writing is exhausting.

He is thus a non-writer with non-writings. But the text itself, born from the stories addressed to his friend, can be conceived as the building process of this 'llibre que porto dins' ('book I have inside me').

As Joep Leersen and Manfred Beller say:

As a category of cultural analysis, representation has become the preferred term to designate the ways in which texts (and other media) provide images of the world . . . Indeed, representations bring the world into being, as an object of knowledge and a source of meaning.[15]

What happens to the character in *No* is precisely that: he is a person in search of the complex meaning of life, of the seed that will bring forth a 'new being'. Taking his experience to the realm of representation – that is, of the symbolic, of the literary – is what helps him to move forward.

In fact, in the three books by El Kadaoui, the main characters struggle against the idea of migration-driven exile, taken in a broad sense. This is why they feel the need to write, to take refuge in words and, in so doing, feel that they are non-excluded participants in a reality they are trying to understand. When they write, they seek, through language, to have a place. To cite Heidegger,[16] making language 'the house of being' is what the protagonist of *No* is after, at one point stating that 'la meva pàtria ha de ser la ficció' (El Kadaoui, *No*, p. 109) ('fiction must be my homeland').

One of the most literary forms of representation is metaphor. Salvador Cardús, discussing the representations of immigration in Catalonia and the experience of immigrants, has stressed the need to change the metaphors that we use in this regard and adopt new ones. He proposes, first, abandoning the image of the 'root' to refer to a place of origin, to a past, to origins with which we must identify as a people, to instead emphasise forward thinking and the idea of the 'seed'.[17] Second, he advocates replacing the metaphor of 'integration' with that of 'grafting': 'imaginar els catalans com a antics immigrants i la catalanitat com a l'àmbit de la dissolució d'aquesta condició a través d'un procés reeixit d'empeltament' ('to imagine Catalans as former immigrants and Catalanness as the dissolution of this condition through a successful grafting process').[18] And third, he argues for a necessary rethinking of the term 'identity', to represent it using the new metaphor of the 'skin': 'la identitat funciona com una pell que estalvia la descripció . . . oculta més que no ensenya als altres. I és gràcies a aquestes ocultacions que es pot establir tota mena de relacions personals complexes' ('identity functions as a skin that is sparing of description . . . it conceals more than it shows to others. And it is thanks to these concealments that all kinds of complex personal relationships can be established').[19]

Much like what Cardús proposes, the protagonists in El Kadaoui's three books struggle so that they do not have to live a life torn between distant roots and a present that they want to be fruitful (the 'new man' mentioned above), so that they do not have to constantly prove their integration, and so that they do not have to define or explain themselves according to the clichés expected by their host society. Because, as Pilar Arnau says: 'Dans les textes d'El Hachmi, Karrouch et El Kadaoui Moussaoui . . . [ils] sont les sujets migrants, des identités transfrontalières qui sont en tension perpétuelle et qui doivent négocier chaque jour leur place dans le monde'[20] ('In the texts by El Hachmi, Karrouch and El Kadaoui Moussaoui . . . [they] are the migrant subjects, cross-border identities that are in perpetual tension and have to negotiate their place in the world every day'). This negotiation is present in *No* as a reflection directed at the protagonist's friend who has returned to Morocco, but it also appears in El Kadaoui's two previous works. In fact, this constant search for the 'marroquí criat a Europa i que no pateix desajustos atàvics' (El Kadaoui, *No*, p. 190) ('European-raised Moroccan who does not suffer atavistic maladjustments') takes shape in the book by means of cross reference, in a more than obvious dialogue with *Cartes al meu fill*. The protagonist, while preparing for his seminars on the other, goes to Madrid to meet Farid (a fictitious version of Said El Kadaoui), the author of a book with a near-identical title to the Catalan-Moroccan writer's.

> En Farid acaba de publicar un llibre que, tot i no ser totalment del meu grat, m'interessa. Potser l'ham, i ho entendràs de seguida, sigui Hanif Kureishi. *Cartes al meu fill. Un madrileny de soca-rel, gairebé.*
> 'Em dic Karim Hamid i soc anglès de soca-arrel, gairebé.' Així arrenca la primera novel·la de Kureishi, *El buda dels suburbis.* Te'n recordes?
> En Farid és un entusiasta admirador de Kureishi. (p. 190)

> Farid has just published a book that, despite not being entirely to my liking, interests me. Perhaps the lure, and you will get it immediately, is Hanif Kureishi. *Letters to My Son: A Madrilenian Born and Bred, Almost.*
> 'My name is Karim Amir, and I am an Englishman born and bred, almost.' This is how Kureishi's first novel, *The Buddha of Suburbia*, starts. Remember?
> Farid is an enthusiastic admirer of Kureishi.

It seems evident that these cross references and the dialogue between El Kadaoui's various novels comprise a literary device that, in addition to presenting a continuum of themes and thought, reinforces the idea of autofiction mentioned above. Thus, the passage connects Kureishi's famous novel to El Kadaoui's book *Cartes al meu fill: Un català de soca-rel, gairebé* and that of a supposed Madrilenian who also ponders his and his son's identity in a book with practically the same title as the one by the author of *No.* However, El Kadaoui does not clarify whether the parallelism between the two books is an ironic way of pointing out the distinct identities of Catalans and Madrilenians, or whether he overlooks, with simplifying consequences, the cultural border between the two realities socially, linguistically and in terms of identity. Regardless, what is clear is that by fictionalising his own experience in a more or less transparent way, the author once again demonstrates his ground-breaking will to transgress through a story in which the self is central to understanding the proposed reflection. As Fizia Hayette Mokhtari says: 'Dans les récits de vie, les auteurs racontent leur existence: dans les sociétés arabo-musulmanes, cela est encore mal vu; car un musulman ne parle jamais de lui, ne dit pas "je" avec la même facilité que dans la littérature occidentale'[21] ('In life stories, authors recount their lives: in Arab-Muslim societies, this is still frowned upon, for a Muslim never talks about himself, does not say "I" with the same ease as in Western literature').

El Kadaoui, for his part, again crosses the boundary into rule breaking under the justification that 'la descendència desperta en els autors l'obligació moral de deixar-los a través de l'escriptura un llegat identitari' ('offspring awaken in authors the moral obligation to leave them a legacy of identity through writing').[22]

Finally, the third dialogue in *No* is with the works of north African thinkers and writers. As already mentioned, the protagonist is a literature teacher at a secondary school and also lectures at the University of Barcelona, leading a seminar on Edward Said and another on the literature of the other. Moreover, when speaking about his girlfriend, Maite – his beloved, to whom he is constantly unfaithful but whom he loves madly and who occasionally fills his existential void – he says:

> Coneix el Magrib millor que jo. I, el més important, no el coneix solament a través de la mirada – viatjar avui dia amaga molt més del que ensenya –, l'ha llegit. Coneix Malika Mokeddem, Fàtima Mernissi, Abdellatif Laâbi, Boualem Sansal; ha llegit tota l'obra de pensadors com Al Jabri i Mohamed Arkoun, d'escriptors com Choukri i Chraïbi. Ha dedicat tota una tesi a la literatura magribina contemporània. Ha publicat assajos sobre escriptores magribines, sobre la literatura magribina de l'exili i l'emigració. Tot aquest coneixement me l'ha brindat amb gran generositat. Puc parlar-hi sabent que és algú que ha creuat la frontera, que pot entendre la meva complexitat i el millor i més important: lluny de considerar-se una experta, manté la curiositat de l'aprenent i a cada moment descobreix textos i autors nous. (El Kadaoui, *No*, p. 77)

> She knows the Maghreb better than I do. And most importantly, she knows it through more than sight alone – travelling nowadays hides much more than it teaches; she has read it. She knows Malika Mokeddem, Fàtima Mernissi, Abdellatif Laâbi, Boualem Sansal; she

has read all the work of thinkers like Al Jabri and Mohamed Arkoun, of writers like Choukri and Chraïbi. She has devoted an entire thesis to contemporary Maghrebi literature. She has published essays on Maghrebi women writers, on the Maghrebi literature of exile and emigration. She has given me all this knowledge so generously. I can talk to her knowing that she is someone who has crossed the border, who can understand my complexity, and the best and most important part: far from considering herself an expert, she still has the curiosity of a learner and discovers new texts and authors all the time.

Her letter of presentation is, thus, her knowledge of the Maghreb and its thinkers and writers. The whole book is full of more or less direct references to the above-mentioned authors and others. It is also noteworthy that the protagonist's relationship with Maite, which serves as a plot thread, began after the two characters attended a lecture by the thinker Mohamed Arkoun at the Institut du monde arabe in Paris, titled 'Sociology of the Failure of Modernity in Islam'. Evoking this lecture, besides placing the start of their relationship in a very specific ideological setting, is another example of fictionalised reality, considering that a lecture of the same name was actually given by Arkoun, not in Paris but in Cairo, in 2007.

The knowledge of both characters can also be interpreted as an expression of the author's desires and intellectual tendencies. In that lecture, Arkoun spoke in favour of the rationalist tradition of the Islamic world – Averroes, for example – and a contextualised and updated reading of the Qur'an, among other things, which resonates with the thinking of both the author and the two characters in *No*. In the literary fiction, Maite possesses excellent knowledge of the most important writers and thinkers of the Arab world, many of them based in Europe: 'La Maite està escrivint un assaig sobre el paper de l'insomni en l'obra de Malika Mokeddem' (p. 15) ('Maite is writing an essay on the role of insomnia in the work of Malika Mokeddem'). For his part, the protagonist also demonstrates an extensive knowledge of both Arabic literature and other traditions. This knowledge leads him to reflect on his own identity: 'Hanif Kureishi deia que durant la infància l'avergonyia la seva condició de pakistanès per considerar-la una mena de maledicció de la qual calia alliberar-se. Per descomptat, jo detestava la meva condició de marroquí pel mateix motiu' (p. 30) ('Hanif

Kureishi said that during his childhood he was ashamed of being Pakistani, considering it a kind of curse from which he had to free himself. Of course, I hated being Moroccan for the same reason'). This knowledge simultaneously draws attention to the idea of impurity or difference: 'Philip Roth, per la seva banda, em feia la mateixa pregunta que una vegada li havia formulat a Primo Levi: ¿segueixes sent una impuresa, "un gra de sal o mostassa", o ja has perdut aquella sensació de ser diferent?' (p. 68) ('Philip Roth, for his part, asked me the same question he had once asked Primo Levi: are you still an impurity, "a grain of salt or mustard", or have you now lost that sense of being different?').

In fact, another important knowledge – that of the psychiatrist friend – also appears in the context of an academic conference, in this case titled 'Story, Memory and Identity: Approaches to Literature from the Perspective of Psychoanalysis'. Although I am not aware of any conference with this title ever taking place, the anecdote gives clues as to how to approach the reading of *No* and once again takes us closer to the biographical reality of the author, a psychologist and psychoanalyst himself. At the same event, Maite also presents a paper on Malika Mokeddem:

> La seva ponència sobre *Els homes que caminen (Les hommes qui marchent)* em va causar una profunda impressió i va acréixer l'afecció que li tenia. Desitjant-la a ella, desitjava també conèixer Malika Mokeddem, el seu insomni, el seu món marcat per fronteres dispars. (pp. 104–5)

> Her talk on *The Walking Men (Les hommes qui marchent)* made a deep impression on me and deepened my affection for her. Desiring her, I also desired to know Malika Mokeddem, her insomnia, her world marked by disparate borders.

In the seminar on the literature of the other, the protagonist talks about the thinker and writer Mohamed Al Jabri, the historian Abdellah Laroui and Driss Chraïbi, whose book *The Simple Past* shakes up Arab thought and Maghrebi traditionalism by presenting tradition as something historical and not as absolute truth, thus defending Arab rationalist thought.

This list of intellectuals, writers and other such figures is rounded out by several names that are most likely of new literary construction, a mix of fiction and reality. For instance, there is mention of a supposed Algerian writer named Salim Yassin and a Professor Mehdi el Fitahi. Amid the constant dialogue with North African thinkers and writers – some real and some made up – the name of the friend who returned to Morocco, Maati Kaabal, is a nod at the attentive reader, since it is almost identical to that of Maati Kabbal, an essayist and writer specialising in Moroccan literature.

All these references to writers, thinkers and teachers could be, up to this point, resources drawn from reality and integrated into the narrative fiction, but El Kadaoui seems to want to construct a network of connections and, at the same time, of evident separations between his thoughts, his ideas and his readings, and the ideas, texts and thoughts of the protagonist of *No*, who, like him, is a well-educated, middle-class, Moroccan-born immigrant, an expert in literature and psychoanalysis and someone interested in talking about the fact that he does not feel like he fits in because he is an immigrant.

Having analysed the rationale as to why *No* can be interpreted as a triple dialogue – with the self; between *No* and the author's two previous books; and between the characters, the author and the readers, and intellectuals from Arab countries, most of them living in Europe – it is possible to say that the book in question is not autobiographical, but neither is it entirely fictional or a diary. Philippe Lejeune says that '[l]'autobiografia viu sota l'encís de la ficció, el diari queda imantat per la veritat'('[the] autobiography lives under the spell of fiction, the diary is magnetised by the truth'),[23] and perhaps that is why, in the case of *No*, we could speak of a book of autofiction. Lejeune is not fond of this term because he, an expert in autobiography and diary writing, is interested in demonstrating that one can make art out of the truth. Perhaps, however, what he does not realise is that when dealing with certain themes related to disengagement, dislocation, crisis or rupture, be it personal, identity-related or otherwise, the mixture of reality and fiction allows literature to become a possible space for mediation.

Ultimately, genre also becomes a limit, a border that must be subverted. Mercè Picornell, in her book *Discursos testimonials en la literatura catalana recent* ('Testimonial Discourses in Recent Catalan Literature'), when speaking of genre in relation to testimonial literature, says:

> Cada gènere té així la seva història que és, en certa manera, la de la difícil definició de les seves fronteres tant pel que fa al deure que té

amb els gèneres que l'han precedit com pel que fa als límits que comparteix amb els que li són contemporanis. Aquests límits són inestables, varien en eixamplar o reduir el seu abast . . . Sigui com sigui, tot plegat ens fa pensar que els límits genèrics no són en cap cas impermeables, permeten el contagi i tendeixen al mestissatge de formes.[24]

Every genre thus has its history, which in some way is that of its hard-to-define borders, with respect to both its duty towards the genres that came before it and the limits it shares with its contemporaries. These limits are unstable, varying as they widen or narrow their extent . . . Be that as it may, all this leads us to think that the limits of genre are by no means impermeable; they allow for contagion and tend towards the crossbreeding of forms.

Or as Margalida Pons says in the prologue to the same book: 'La literatura testimonial se situa en un espai ambigu que exclou, i alhora invoca, la ficcionalitat' ('Testimonial literature is situated in an ambiguous space that both excludes and invokes fictionality').[25]

What is common to all the manifestations of personal conflict experienced by the narrator is that they always ultimately prompt metaliterary reflection. That 'llibre que [el protagonista] porta dins' (El Kadaoui, *No*, p. 12) ('book [the protagonist] has inside'), the 'llibre que no surt' (p. 15) ('book that won't come out'), that 'llibre que he intentat escriure mil vegades i que ha fracassat' (p. 38) ('book I have tried to write a thousand times and failed') becomes in the protagonist's mind 'l'espai de les possibilitats infactibles' (p. 39) ('the space of infeasible possibilities'). He constantly says that he is failing as a writer (p. 40) and that his longing is to 'matar la família . . . matar les lleialtats de grup i fer-ho a través de l'escriptura' (p. 42) ('kill the family . . . kill group loyalties and do it through writing'), but he cannot because, although life bestows him with material for the book, he cannot write it due to the 'rebel·lió, la crítica, la pena barrejada amb el profund amor' (p. 55) ('rebellion, criticism, sorrow mixed with profound love') that he professes for his parents.

He says that the failed lives of the immigrants he sees around him 'només se'm fan suportables portant-les a la ficció' ('are only made bearable to me by bringing them into fiction') and that he would like to write a book about 'fracàs migratori' (p. 84) ('migratory failure'). And finally, when he wonders whether a possible return to Morocco would be a failure, he says, 'em dec un llibre, una novel·la on relatar aquest retorn. Ja que no puc decidir-me en la vida real, fer-ho en la ficció' (pp. 108–9) ('I owe myself a book, a novel in which to recount this return. Since I cannot decide in real life, I will do so in fiction').

Creation itself, therefore, or impossible writing, becomes a motif of metaliterary reflection throughout the book, and ultimately another limit and border that the narrator manages to overcome in order to explain his condition, his convictions and his contradiction. And the protagonist of *No* only manages to overcome this limit thanks to the feeling of disengagement caused by his friend leaving for Morocco:

> Al llarg d'aquest any he estat escrivint fragments d'una vida que, d'alguna manera tenen a veure amb tu . . . Avui és la primera vegada que repasso tota aquesta conjunció de fragments que he escrit pensant en tu, i la primera impressió és que les grans peces del meu trencaclosques totes hi són presents: el sexe, la meva identitat marroquina, la meva identitat europea, els amics, la família, l'escriptura, la literatura, la docència, la Maite, i ara el meu fill. No sé si encaixen. Sí que sé, en canvi, que n'emana una història. Potser no una història completa. (p. 198)

> Over this year I have been writing fragments of a life that, in some way, have to do with you . . . Today is the first time I have reviewed this whole conjunction of fragments that I have written thinking of you, and my first impression is that the big pieces of my puzzle are all present: sex, my Moroccan identity, my European identity, friends, family, writing, literature, teaching, Maite, and now my son. I don't know if they fit together. I do know, however, that there is a story in them. Perhaps not a complete story.

But the fitting together of the pieces offered to us in *No* is perhaps not even necessary. Because real lives are all jumbled, whether a little or a lot, and to neatly arrange them would simply be an illusion perhaps unsuitable for the kind of literature that Saïd El Kadaoui is after.

Notes

1. Gloria Anzaldúa, *Borderlands/La Frontera: The New Mestiza* (San Francisco CA: Spinsters/Aunt Lute, 1987), p. vii.
2. Robert Spencer, 'Contented Homeland Peace: The Motif of Exile in the Work of Edward W. Said', in Adel Iskandar and Hakem Rustom (eds), *Edward Said: A Legacy of Emancipation and Representation* (Berkeley CA, Los Angeles CA and London: University of California Press, 2010), p. 389.
3. Edward Said, 'The Politics of Knowledge', in *Reflections on Exile and Other Literary and Cultural Essays* (London: Granta, 2000), p. 385.
4. Saïd El Kadaoui, *No* (Barcelona: Catedral, 2016), p. 117. Unless otherwise stated, translations from Catalan, Spanish and French are my own.
5. Enrique Montero Cartelle, 'Omne animal post coitum triste: De Aristóteles a S. Freud', *Revista de Estudios Latinos*, 1 (2001), 107–19.
6. Claudio Magris, 'Desde el otro lado: Consideraciones fronterizas', *Utopía y desencanto: Historias, esperanzas e ilusiones de la modernidad* (Barcelona: Anagrama, 2001), p. 56.
7. Iain Chambers, *Migrancy, Culture, Identity* (London: Routledge, 1994), p. 72.
8. Jean-Luc Nancy, 'La existencia exiliada', *Archipiélago: Cuadernos de crítica de la cultura*, 26–7 (1996), 35.
9. Nancy, 'La existencia exiliada', 35.
10. Saïd El Kadaoui, *Límites y fronteras* (Lleida: Milenio, 2008); *Cartes al meu fill: Un català de soca-rel, gairebé* (Barcelona: Ara Llibres, 2011).
11. Najat El Hachmi, *Jo també soc catalana* (Barcelona: Columna, 2004), p. 13.
12. El Kadaoui, *Cartes al meu fill*, pp. 15–17.
13. Simona Škrabec, 'El repte d'acceptar la diferència', in Gabriella Gavagnin and Víctor Martínez-Gil (eds), *Entre literatures: Hegemonia i perifèries en els processos de mediació literària* (Lleida: Punctum, 2011), p. 57.
14. El Kadaoui, *Cartes al meu fill*, p. 15.
15. Joep Leersen and Manfred Beller, *Imagology: The Cultural Construction and Literary Representation of National Characters: A Critical Survey* (Amsterdam and New York: Rodopi, 2007), p. 413.
16. Martin Heidegger, *Carta sobre el humanismo* (Madrid: Alianza, 2009), p. 11.
17. Salvador Cardús i Ros, *Tres metàfores per pensar un país amb futur: Discurs de recepció de Salvador Cardús i Ros com a membre numerari de la Secció de Filosofia i Ciències Socials, llegit el dia 12 de novembre de 2009* (Barcelona: Institut d'Estudis Catalans, 2009), pp. 8–12.
18. Cardús, *Tres metàfores*, p. 14.

19 Cardús, *Tres metàfores*, p. 19
20 Pilar Arnau, 'L'hybridité identitaire dans une littérature émergente: l'écriture du "moi" hybride dans l'oeuvre autobiographique des écrivains catalans d'origine maghrébine', *Babel: Littératures plurielles*, 33 (2016), 251.
21 Fizia Hayette Mokhtari, 'Autobiographie et transgression générique dans *Les homes qui marchent, La Transe des insoumis* et *Mes hommes*, de Malika Mokeddem', *Lublin Studies in Modern Languages and Literature*, 40/2 (2016), 83.
22 Isabel Marcillas-Piquer, 'Veus de frontera: *Els altres catalans* d'ara', *Caplletra*, 65 (2018), 189.
23 Philippe Lejeune, 'El diari com a antificció', in Joan Borja, Joaquim Espinós, Anna Esteve i M. Àngels Francés (eds), *Diaris i dietaris* (Alicante and Valencia: Denes, 2007), p. 13.
24 Mercè Picornell, *Discursos testimonials en la literatura catalana recent* (Barcelona: Publicacions de l'Abadia de Montserrat, 2002), pp. 22–3.
25 Margalida Pons, 'El discurs testimonial: memòria compromesa, pràctica lectora, creació crítica', preface to Mercè Picornell, *Discursos testimonials en la literatura catalana recent* (Barcelona: Publicacions de l'Abadia de Montserrat, 2002), p. 6.

Chapter 9
Mourning, Trauma and Ambivalence in the Catalan Literature of the Argentine Diaspora: Silvana Vogt's *La mecànica de l'aigua*

Josep-Anton Fernàndez

Compared to other migrant experiences in Catalonia, the case of the Argentine diaspora is singular because, generally speaking, it has been caused not by a desire to seek opportunities in a new land, but by deeply traumatic events, be it a military dictatorship or a devastating financial crisis.[1] These migrations were built on a long-standing history of transatlantic exchanges, whereby thousands of people from the Catalan-speaking territories settled in Argentina in the nineteenth century and early twentieth century, later followed by the republican exile of 1939. In the mid-1970s, a population flow began in the opposite direction, when large numbers of Argentine political exiles sought refuge in Catalonia, escaping from a murderous military dictatorship. A sizeable Argentine community was then established, especially in large cities such as Barcelona, giving rise to important cultural, economic and intellectual exchanges.[2] Two decades later, following the financial crisis of the *corralito* in 2001 that led to the collapse of the country's economy, another important wave of migration from Argentina to Catalonia occurred, now motivated by economic reasons.

Scholars have stressed the specificity of this latter migratory process. Susana Schmidt underscores the 'carácter económico de la migración' ('economic nature of the migration'), which would not have taken place without the country's financial collapse, and so this second wave 'lleva la impronta de la debacle' ('carries the mark of the debâcle').[3] According to Schmidt, the consequences of the crisis (unemployment, crime, street violence, blocking of bank accounts, deterioration of public services, etc.) impacted heavily on public perceptions of the political system leading to 'desencanto democrático' ('democratic disenchantment') and 'pesimismo social' ('social pessimism').[4] A further element that favoured migration to Spain was that many Argentine descendants of Italian and Spanish immigrants were eligible for an EU passport.

Although Barcelona has for years been a distinct destination for expatriate Argentine authors, Catalan literature has been slow to incorporate the experience of Argentine exile and migration into its symbolic landscape. However, there is a small but significant contingent of Argentine women authors who have chosen Catalan as their main language for literary expression, such as Patrícia Gabancho, or who alternate between Catalan and Spanish, such as Flavia Company and Victoria Szpunberg. Silvana Vogt (Morteros, 1969) joined their ranks with her novel *La mecànica de l'aigua* ('The mechanics of water', 2016), which offers a deeply moving account, to some degree autobiographical, of this more recent migratory process. The novel presents the story of Vera, a philosophy graduate and journalist from Buenos Aires who, in the midst of economic, social and personal chaos, decides to leave a country that she despises in order to start a new life in Barcelona. The narrative starts just before Argentina's default on its national debt and the subsequent confiscation by the government of all bank accounts, leading to economic collapse, political crisis and social unrest. Trapped in an unhappy relationship with a married man, jaded by the cynicism of the corrupt politician who sponsors the community radio station where she works, and frustrated by the closure of her favourite cinemas and the unavailability of the books by her most admired author, Vera is devastated by the death of her friend Fierita, one of the volunteers at the station. This loss prompts Vera to demand more funding from the local councillor, who gives her 5,000 dollars in cash to further the radio station project, in exchange for not revealing his corrupt dealings and supporting his political campaign. Shortly afterwards, however, the country defaults, and in the face of increasing social unrest Vera decides to use the money to migrate to Barcelona with her dog Kantiano. In Barcelona she will meet Nil, an aspiring novelist fascinated by Julio Cortázar and Buenos Aires, and Eliseu Mussol, a publisher whose life has been marked by traumatic losses that he is still struggling to mourn. Little by little, Vera will be able to build a new life in Catalonia: after getting some precarious employment, she will start writing for the press and acting as a reader for Eliseu Mussol, subsequently legalising her status as a migrant in Spain. Vera will develop an intense friendship with Eliseu that will help both of them come to terms with their losses, only to meet a tragic ending.

La mecànica de l'aigua achieved considerable success among readers and critics alike. The novel's critical reception focused mostly on the autobiographical elements in the narrative, and valued its structure and the author's command of narrative technique.[5] Mireia Ferrando remarked that the novel 'ens permet accedir a una mirada externa a la nostra cultura' ('grants us access to an external perspective on our culture'), J. A. Masoliver Ródenas stressed the text's 'densitat emocional' ('emotional density') and its avoidance of clichés in its portrayal of Argentina, while Vicenç Pagès Jordà noted that Vera's journey departs from the most common patterns of the *corralito* migration: 'El detonant del viatge és més literari que econòmic, igual com són literàries les relacions que Vera estableix a Barcelona, les paraules que pronuncia i les feines que realitza' ('The trigger for her journey is literary rather than economic, as are the relationships Vera establishes in Barcelona, the words she utters and the work she does').[6]

The critics' emphasis on the novel's formal elements and the mediation of literature to articulate the affective dimension of migration is relevant for my analysis. Indeed, *La mecànica de l'aigua* inscribes the narrative of immigration within the frame of the work of mourning. Immigration is a traumatic experience of loss (of a familiar landscape, relationships, cultural references, language, customs and so on) that deeply affects identification processes, both subjective and social, on the part of the migrant, but also transforming the society that receives them. Vogt's novel features some elements that make it eminently interesting for an analysis of the vicissitudes of mourning in this context: a traumatic scene that causes the loss of the protagonist's country, an original transgression that leads to deep ambivalence with regard to the lost country and the prominence of repetition. The present chapter offers an analysis of these elements from a psychoanalytic point of view, by reference to Freud, Darian Leader, Laurie Laufer and other authors. In particular, I show how Vogt's novel highlights the importance of the social dimension of mourning in terms of the symbolisation of loss, and how it articulates the work of mourning by means of what Leader calls a 'dialogue of mournings'. This is particularly relevant, as the protagonist's trajectory evolves in parallel with Eliseu Mussol's work of mourning. I also explore the ways in which the text works through ambivalence to constitute the object as effectively lost, in order to register an empty space that allows for a new subjective narrative to be created.

However, what is precisely the object the protagonist loses? It might be difficult to characterise the psychic process in this text as migratory mourning, given the disdain that Vera expresses for her country and how she presents herself as fully disidentified from Argentina. Furthermore, the narrator of *La mecànica* significantly makes no reference to the family that Vera has left behind, to other relationships besides her dead friend and her estranged lover, or to the historical background of population exchanges between Argentina and Spain, especially in the mid-1970s. It is almost as though history, both personal and collective, had been deleted to create a blank slate for a new beginning. This contrasts with the effects of the transgressive acts and the attachment to identities, which are presented as indelible marks that cannot be removed. As I will argue, ambivalence in this novel pivots on the tension between the blank slate of a new beginning and these indelible marks, and is organised around a series of oppositions that, as though present on both sides of a Möbius strip, have contradictory effects. This tension – corresponding to a more fundamental conflict between repetition and a desire for the new – reveals the importance of ambivalence in the experience of mourning and plays a crucial role in the dialectic of identification and disidentification that the protagonist of *La mecànica* undergoes through the experience of migration.

Mourning and Migration

Immigration is a painful experience: the migrant loses his or her familiar landscape, social environment and status, and must face the difficulties of adjusting to sociopolitical and cultural differences, to a new linguistic context and to racism and discrimination. Scholars have approached this experience in a variety of ways. For instance, Madelaine Hron, writing on literary texts, focuses on immigrant pain as a specific psychological phenomenon in order to explore the ways in which it may be expressed, but she does not analyse specifically the role played by mourning in the migrant experience.[7] Object-relations psychoanalysis has also devoted a great deal of attention to immigration. Salman Akhtar's work has been particularly influential thanks to his definition of 'immigrant nostalgia': the immigrant is often unable properly to settle in his or her new country, and this is explained in terms of a 'fantasy of a lost paradise' expressing 'a position whereby primary objects are neither given up through the work of mourning nor assimilated into the ego through identification', with the result of 'a temporal fracture of the psyche'.[8] However, authors such as Ghislaine Boulanger have critiqued this approach for its conflation of 'mother and country' and a developmental emphasis that favours a process of assimilation now seen as 'neither achievable nor desirable', as it would entail 'the cost of dissociation'.[9] Instead, Boulanger favours a 'less confined' psychoanalytic framework that 'privileges multiplicity' and 'facilitates the exploration of subtle shifts in identity, the longing to belong and the sometimes contradictory longing for recognition of a self that had to remain hidden'.[10] Writing from a similar perspective, Ricardo C. Ainslie focuses on the 'psychic dislocation' that immigration entails, resulting in the 'fragmentation of one's sense of community'.[11] The 'clustering in immigrant communities', he says, facilitates the reconstruction of 'usable spaces' of community that constitute a 'transitional space' in Winnicott's sense of the term.[12]

However, *La mecànica de l'aigua* resists all these approaches because its protagonist neither suffers from nostalgia for a country she decidedly rejects, nor seeks a sense of community with fellow countrymen whom she despises. Yet mourning is at the forefront of this text, and to account for this novel's specificities, we must consider the social dimension of mourning, the effects of traumatic loss and how mourning sets into play unconscious desire, memory and the temporality of the subject. Therefore, I propose to return to Freud's ideas on mourning and then revise two recent theoretical elaborations of the issue. In his 1917 essay 'Mourning and Melancholia', Freud discusses the process that we undergo when we experience a loss. Mourning, he says, is 'commonly the reaction to the loss of a beloved person or an abstraction taking the place of the person, such as fatherland, freedom, an ideal and so on'.[13] By contrast, melancholia or pathological mourning, while exhibiting the same traits, also features 'a reduction in the sense of self, expressed in self-recrimination' (Freud, 'Mourning', p. 203). In his account of the 'work of mourning', Freud argues that 'reality-testing has revealed that the beloved object no longer exists, and demands that the libido as a whole sever its bonds with the object', but this is opposed by a contrary tendency, as 'people are reluctant to abandon a libido position, even if a substitute is already beckoning' (p. 204). Thus, in this process the ego will confront the representations of the lost object: 'Each individual memory and expectation in which the libido was connected to the object is adjusted and hyper-invested, leading to a detachment from the libido' (p. 205). In melancholia or pathological mourning, this process cannot be completed because the subject identifies with a lost object tainted by 'the ambivalence of love relationships' (p. 210), and so the recriminations against the lost object are mercilessly directed against the ego.

Nevertheless, ambivalence is present in every affective relationship between human subjects.[14] Freud later developed his concept of the ego on the basis of the identification mechanisms that he described in melancholia.[15] Thus we identify with the objects that we love and lose, and as Diana Fuss points out, 'Freud suggests that the subject in mourning simply converts the lost love object into an identification, in effect becoming the object that it can no longer have'.[16] So in mourning we work through the loss of a loved person, but we also mourn the part of ourselves that we lost in the other person. In other words, Freud's statement that the mourner 'knows *who* it is, but not *what* it is about that person that he has lost' ('Mourning', p. 205; emphasis in the original) does not just apply to the melancholic. In this respect, mourning entails an enigmatic dimension, and through the identifications it facilitates the subject becomes 'a veritable cemetery of lost, abandoned, and discarded objects'.[17]

Whereas Freud presents the work of mourning as an individual endeavour, recent psychoanalytic approaches emphasise its social dimension. Darian Leader stresses in his book *The New Black* the subjective need for representations in order to undergo bereavement. The ego, he says, 'is built up not simply through our experience of loss, but through the *registration* of loss . . . A separation . . . only becomes a loss when it is registered'.[18] This act of registration, essential to symbolise loss, requires the participation of the other, of a third party that authenticates the experience of loss (Leader, pp. 58–9). In other words, mourning has a crucial public, social dimension that according to Leader is manifested in two ways: in a 'dialogue of mournings' (p. 76), that is, an 'unconscious transaction between mourners' that mediates the relation of each one to their own loss (pp. 90–1), and in the artificiality required for the inscription of loss 'in a symbolic space', making it possible to frame the representations of the lost object as representations, such as it happens with commemorations and monuments (pp. 103–5).

For her part, French analyst Laurie Laufer, in her book *L'énigme du deuil*, presents mourning as 'une énigme de l'inconscient'[19] ('an enigma of the unconscious') that sets into play and questions the subject's desire, its temporality and its relation to the lost object: the mourner has not simply lost the object, she has lost 'l'histoire et le temps de l'objet, c'est-à-dire un temps et une histoire l'identifiant' (Laufer, p. 17) ('the history and the time of the object, that is, a time and a history that identified her'). Thus, what can be traced in mourning is 'la position de désir du survivant pour le mort' (p. 22) ('the survivor's position of desire *vis-à-vis* the deceased'). The experience of mourning consists in confronting the enigma of the desire of the Other by means of the reconstruction of the image of the lost object through its representation and inscription into what Laufer terms 'un lieu psychique de sépulture' (p. 23) ('a psychic place of burial'). For Laufer, the analysis of mourning requires considering the effects of the traumatic event of loss, which give rise to a shattering discontinuity and a psychic 'hémorragie' (p. 30) ('haemorrhage'), profoundly altering the subject's memory and temporality. On the other hand, like Leader, she emphasises the social dimension of mourning, not only because it facilitates public rituals and the symbolisation of loss, but also because it situates mourning within the symbolic exchange of gifts described by Marcel Mauss (pp. 44–50).

Later in this chapter I will discuss the relevance of the social dimension of mourning in *La mecànica*. However, I will start my discussion by examining the effects of traumatic loss and their context in the narrative. According to Laufer, the traumatic event of loss upsets the temporality of the subject, which becomes a frozen, fixed time, 'un pur instant qui excède le temps . . . un "toujours-présent"' ('a pure instant that exceeds time, an "always-present"') that keeps the psychic haemorrhage open (p. 30). Immersed in this abyssal present, the mourner must revive her fossilised memory and make her desire flow once again. It is therefore highly relevant that Vogt's novel is narrated in the present tense and inscribes the scene of writing into the text: the narrative voice repeats in an insistent *staccato* the words 'La veig. Puc veure-la' ('I see her. I can see her'), with which four of the novel's ten chapters begin.[20] This scene of writing is superimposed on the events of the past, as though time had stopped in an eternal present. At play here is also a dissociation between narrative voice and character: the first-person narrator that witnesses Vera's past not only reminisces but also constructs Vera's image. Moreover, the verb 'poder' in 'Puc veure-la' suggests that an obstacle has been overcome – significantly, *La mecànica* is structured in four sections Vogt calls 'esculls', a word that could be translated variously as 'skerries', 'obstacles' or 'stumbling blocks'. The first 'escull', consisting of two chapters, sets the scene for the plot. In the first chapter we witness the double traumatic event that motivates Vera's migration: the death of Fierita and the *corralito*.

The former is particularly painful. Fierita is a drug-addict who volunteers at the community radio station that Vera runs; they have developed a particularly strong bond, but Vera is unable to save him. Fierita's gruesome death – he injected some of the glue that he used to inhale (Vogt, *Mecànica*, p. 15) – severely impacts on Vera's life, leaving her with a 'buit a la cintura' (p. 18) ('a hole in her waist'), roaming Buenos Aires absent and numb, '[s]ense mirar ningú. Sense esperar res de ningú. Sense sentir res per ningú' (p. 19) ('Looking at nobody. Expecting nothing from nobody. Feeling nothing for nobody'). However, the latter event, the *corralito*, upsets the life of the entire Argentine society. It is described as an event with a life of its own, acting out of its own will:

> L'inici de la fi arriba per sorpresa a la vida privada de la Vera i a la vida conjunta del país. I la seva astúcia és directament proporcional al caos que provoca, al naufragi que origina, com si fos un bloc de

gel surant al bell mig de l'oceà, calculant en quin lloc del vaixell ha d'impactar per trencar la línia de flotació. (p. 20)

The beginning of the end comes by surprise into Vera's private life and into the country's common life. And its craftiness is directly proportional to the chaos it provokes, the wreck it causes, like a block of ice floating in the middle of the ocean, calculating where on the ship it needs to hit to break the waterline.

The *corralito* disrupts social life because it brings the circuit of economic exchange and the flow of capital to a complete halt, destroying the possibility of making plans for the immediate future. Thus, social time is out of joint, but so is psychic temporality. The traumatic event has suspended time, and it itself becomes suspended in time – in the frozen present of trauma. As Laufer argues, trauma fossilises the subject's flow of desire and fixes it into a state of trance: the pain brought about by the trauma does not cease because it is set into 'un temps de transe, un état intermédiaire, mélancolique et silencieux qui hypnotise la vie psychique du sujet' (Laufer, p. 30) ('a time of trance, an intermediate, melancholic and silent state that hypnotises the psychic life of the subject'). Indeed, the *corralito* leaves the entire society in a state of shock: people are trapped in an unending 'malson' ('nightmare'), walking about the city 'com un ramat de sonàmbuls' ('like a herd of sleepwalkers') (*Mecànica*, p. 20), yet the *corralito* also produces an effect of national catharsis, a communion 'tan perfecta, tan efímera' (p. 20) ('so perfect, so ephemeral') that eventually leads to a social revolt (p. 24). By contrast, Vera falls into a state of psychic numbness, fully absorbed 'dins del seu univers màgic, on només hi ha lloc per a dos habitants: el Kantiano i ella. Absent del món real, en ruïnes' (pp. 25–6) ('into her own magical universe, with room for only two dwellers: Kantiano and herself. Absent from the ruins of the real world').

Unable to find refuge in the world of literary fiction, Vera begins an unending mourning marked by two distinct elements. First, a failed attempt to symbolise her loss, which becomes instead a bodily inscription of pain that literalises the paralysis of time: after Fierita's death, she decides to get a tattoo of the figure '365', the number of pages of her favourite book. As the tattoo artist repeatedly pierces her skin, Vera is 'sorda, indiferent a les paraules de l'altre' (''deaf, indifferent to the words of the other') and 'es concentra en el dolor. Amb cada fiblada, un record. Amb cada laceració, un oblit' ('she concentrates on her pain. Each sting brings her a memory. Each laceration makes her forget') (p. 29). The tattoo artist asks if she wants anything, and she replies: 'Un cactus . . . Vull menjar-me'l i clavar-me les espines a les vísceres per recordar el dolor cada vegada que se m'acudeixi oblidar els traïdors' (pp. 29–30) ('A cactus. I want to eat it and thrust its spines into my entrails so I can remember the pain every time I happen to forget the traitors'). Vera's tattoo signifies 'une suspension du temps psychique . . . une saturation du temps dans le corps pulsionnel' ('a suspension of psychic time, a saturation of time in the body of the drives') that amounts to 'une jouissance douloureuse de l'événement' ('a painful *jouissance* of the event') (Laufer, p. 32). This suspension of time – and of the flow of desire – is also suggested by the compass Fierita had given Vera as a present, which she treasures as a fetish and whose needle is fixed on the south (*Mecànica*, p. 21). Moreover, Vera's grief is haunted by the horror of the materiality of death. She visits Fierita's grave to pay her respects, but her parting ritual is disrupted by 'l'horror': her dog Kantiano, who had been digging between two gravestones, emerges 'amb un fèmur humà entre les dents, se la mira amb orgull caní, assegut al costat d'una calavera' (p. 33) ('holding a human femur between his teeth, stares at her with canine pride, sitting next to a skull'). Vera's attempt at symbolisation is thwarted by a sudden irruption of the real.

The second element in Vera's unending mourning is an act of transgression. As already mentioned, after Fierita's death Vera confronts a corrupt local councillor to demand more funding for her radio station, and she is given 5,000 dollars in cash, in exchange for supporting the councillor's political campaign (pp. 16–8). Later, when the government declares the country's default and decrees the confiscation of all bank accounts, Vera hides the money inside a pot of rice in the kitchen (p. 20). But at the end of the first chapter, in the midst of a deepening social chaos, when her lover lets her know that the radio station is being closed down, she makes 'una decisió' ('a decision'): she takes the money and leaves Buenos Aires for Barcelona. Thanks to this decision, Vera 'ressuscita' (p. 40) ('resuscitates'). But this act of transgression that allows her to survive will also fill her with guilt and a sense of debt.

A Dialogue of Mournings

La mecànica establishes a parallelism between the death of a loved person and migration, as though finding representations that would help to register the latter necessitated the literality of the former. I would suggest that, in order to make sense of this parallel, we need to consider the ambivalence that taints the protagonist's relationship with Argentina: she loves its literature and its capital, Buenos Aires, but despises the corruption and populism of its politics, the irrationality of its society, the unreliability of her fellow citizens. How can a despised country be mourned? What does one lose when leaving a country that disappoints and does not provide? It is almost as if Vera could not mourn Argentina and the separation from her country were a loss that had been negated, hidden, repressed or simply left unrepresented – like Vera's past, which is not portrayed in the novel. Vera's mourning will be performed by reference to Eliseu Mussol, a character with a strong attachment to his own country, Catalonia, but also with a past that tortures him, for he is unable to mourn his losses.

Eliseu is an editor in his early fifties, the head of Catalonia's most prestigious publishing house. Strict, obsessive and meticulous, at times scathing, he was able to overcome his humble social origins in the countryside thanks to the support of Hilari, his schoolteacher and mentor, who encouraged him to further his education. Eliseu is haunted by the memory of the transgression that he committed in order to break his parents' opposition to his getting an education: he burned down the barn that housed the three pigs that ensured the family's subsistence. Eliseu's life is scarred by a series of painful deaths, beginning with that of Virgili, a poet, Hilari's son and Eliseu's best friend, who was struck by lightning – an event for which Eliseu feels guilty. At the end of the second chapter we find him devastated by the passing of Hilari; later, in chapter four, we witness his difficulties in mourning Hilari, and we find out that after the accident that killed his ex-wife Lila and their son Hug, he has been unable to form new attachments. Eliseu's unending mourning thus becomes an echo of Vera's, establishing what Darian Leader calls a 'dialogue of mournings'. As Leader argues, 'finding a representation that echoes' a person's experience of loss 'can initiate a mourning process' (Leader, p. 79). In a dialogue of mournings, '[t]he relation of the mourner to their loss is mediated through the relation of another mourner to their own loss. In this way . . . lack becomes an object' (pp. 90–1). This 'unconscious transaction between mourners' (p. 91) is introduced in Silvana Vogt's novel as a fortuitous encounter between the two main characters, almost as a matter of destiny: after Eliseu attends Hilari's cremation, he watches an aeroplane – presumably where Vera travels – make its descent into Barcelona's airport (*Mecànica*, p. 53). The juxtaposition of scenes and motifs and the structure of the novel itself – where the first four chapters focalise alternately on Vera and Eliseu – reinforce this effect.

The dialogue of mournings in *La mecànica* is significant because it articulates a double dialectic as a means of working through the ambivalence at the root of the characters' definition. There is, first, a dialectic between identification and disidentification, manifested in a conflict between experiencing the past as an indelible mark and rejecting or letting go of the past to create a blank slate; and second, a dialectic between guilt and debt, and transgression. The latter set of terms is important because the existence of a debt seems to be at the heart of the characters' ambivalence. What has Vera lost? She has not only lost her friend, but also a country that she despises. And yet, what has she lost *in them*? What part of herself has she lost in the death of Fierita and in leaving Argentina? One possible answer would be the sense of direction that the lost other helped Vera define, symbolised in the compass that Fierita gave her as a present. This is echoed in Eliseu's story: in Hilari he lost 'l'amic, el mentor, el conseller, l'agulla de la brúixola que indicava el punt cardinal correcte' (p. 52) ('the friend, the mentor, the adviser, the needle of the compass that indicated the right cardinal point'). Yet the quality of this sense of moral direction is somehow questioned by the fixity of Fierita's compass, always pointing south, and by the effects of Hilari's guidance, which had led to an act of destruction. The idea of fixity is also present in the transgressive act Vera performs: the possibility of her escaping a position of subjective and economic stagnation depended on her theft. Vera's survival requires a decision and an act, but this act in turn becomes a burden and a stumbling block, because the ambivalence at the root of her decision will be internalised through identification with the belief that all Argentinians are thieves. Again, this is echoed in Eliseu's narrative: the act that breaks the chain of repetition – satisfying the demands of tradition in order to follow his parents' way of life – and ensures his personal autonomy is also what chains him to a subjective debt and puts him in front of 'un abisme' (p. 50) ('an abyss').

Ambivalence may create a sense of debt in the mourner. As Leader argues: 'A problem . . . occurs when a pervasive feeling of loyalty to the dead prevents any expression of ties to the living', giving rise to a powerful feeling of guilt. 'Our unconscious hatred is reversed into an overpowering sense of owing something to the dead . . . Loyalty always implies a certain sense of debt' (Leader, pp. 124–5). This point suggests that the social dimension of mourning is implicit in the idea of debt. Laufer claims that losing the other involves losing a part of oneself that the other has taken away with them, and it is this part of oneself that is mourned. The loss of a piece of oneself is a 'sacrifice signifiant la trace d'appartenance' ('sacrifice signifying the trace of belonging'), turning mourning into 'un circuit d'échange' ('a circuit of exchange') in which 'le mort laisse quelque chose au vivant' ('the deceased leaves something to the living'); not knowing *what* has been lost in the departed object is what causes a sense of debt: 'selon les règles de l'échange, l'endeuillé a une dette envers le mort' ('according to the rules of the exchange, the bereaved has a debt towards the deceased') (Laufer, pp. 44–5).

For Laufer, mourning is a part of the circuit of exchange of gifts that Marcel Mauss described in the potlatch. The ritual of sacrifice and destruction in the potlatch sets in motion a circuit of giving, receiving and returning that eroticises the exchange and 'permet de sauvegarder la stabilité de la société' (p. 47) ('helps to safeguard the stability of society'). The excessive expenditure characteristic of the potlatch allows the giver to maintain their *persona*, that is, their prestige and social standing. However, the potlatch is also, according to Laufer, a paradigm for understanding subjectivity in relation to loss:

> La subjectivité se déploie là où quelque chose du sujet tombe, se défait, quelque chose d'appartenance imaginaire. Comme si la position de subjectivation ne pouvait se concevoir sans coupure et sans perte . . . [L]a subjectivation serait une subjectivité sans sujet, une subjectivité qui ne pourrait se concevoir que dans l'écart avec soi-même, que dans la division du sujet. On n'accéderait à soi-même que dans l'expérience de la perte. (p. 46)

Mourning, Trauma and Ambivalence of the Argentine Diaspora 217

> Subjectivity unfolds where something of the subject falls, comes undone, something of the order of imaginary belonging. As if the position of subjectivation could not be conceived without a cut and without loss . . . [S]ubjectivation would then be a subjectivity without a subject, a subjectivity that could only be conceived in the separation from oneself, in the division of the subject. One would only have access to oneself in the experience of loss.

Mourning is therefore at the basis of the construction of the subject in relation to a social bond founded on the experience of loss. Hence the importance of collective rituals regarding the dead. At a subjective level, failure to participate in the symbolic exchange with the lost object leads to an unending mourning: 'Le deuil infini serait l'impossibilité imaginaire à pouvoir rendre ce que l'autre a donné, c'est-à-dire à érotiser le circuit de potlatch, en y laissant un "morceau de soi"' (p. 51) ('An unending mourning would be the result of the imaginary impossibility of being able to give back what the other has bestowed, that is to say, the impossibility of eroticising the potlatch circuit, by relinquishing a "piece of oneself"').

The sacrificial expenditure involved in mourning, requiring that a piece of oneself be given up, will only occur at the end of *La mecànica*. In the meantime, Vera's transgression, the theft of 5,000 dollars, becomes at once a secret and a debt, with a paradoxical effect: it is what helps her survive and build a new life for herself, but the debt will attach to her sense of self in the form of an identification. This leads us to the second dialectic brought about by the dialogue of mournings in Vogt's novel, between past and future, old and new, fixity and movement. Vera's arrival in Barcelona is for her a liberating experience: 'L'urbs, àrida de records, de costums, de rutines i d'ecos, la fascina. És una pàgina en blanc. L'indret on es torna, per fi, invisible' (*Mecànica*, p. 57) ('The city, barren of memories, habits, routines and resonances, fascinates her. It's a blank page. The place where she can finally become invisible'). The city affords Vera a blank slate for a fresh start, the opportunity to compose 'la versió senzilla, neta i directa del relat de la vida' (p. 62) ('the simple, clean and direct version of her life's narrative'). She will subsequently busy herself rebuilding her life, trying to legalise her situation in Spain as a migrant and finding work; but this is not the same as the work of mourning.

Rather, Vera keeps pursuing her attempt at disidentification from Argentina, already implicit in the first chapter; for example, when the narrator describes the flag waving outside a public building as 'un drap blanc-i-blau' (p. 16) ('a white and blue rag'). Her rejection of Argentina becomes explicit when her new friend Nil asks her why she left the country:

> No soc una emigrant econòmica. El problema va ser que l'única cosa que em feia bé al mig de tanta irracionalitat, els llibres del meu escriptor favorit, també van desaparèixer rere les tanques del corralito. Llavors em vaig adonar que no estimava el meu país, perquè ningú pot estimar allò que sempre li fa mal . . . No sento orgull de ser argentina. I no crec que mai pugui arribar a sentir-me'n. Si més no, de la manera que cal per justificar el modus operandi nacional. (p. 63)

> I am not an economic emigrant. The problem was that the only thing that made me feel good in the middle of so much irrationality, the books of my favourite writer, also disappeared behind the barriers of the *corralito*. Then I realised that I didn't love my country, because no one can love what always hurts them . . . I don't feel proud to be Argentine. And I don't think I'll ever be able to. At the very least, in the way that is needed to justify the national modus operandi.

Vera's rationalisations, the denial of her migrant status and her indifference to a national attachment ultimately conceal the impossibility of her fully rejecting her country: not knowing what she has lost in leaving Argentina, her debt becomes an indelible mark inscribed in her body as an identification based on ambivalence. When Nil invites her to write an op-ed column on Argentina, the proposal causes in her '[u]n terratrèmol que desperta un volcà que escup lava' (p. 72) ('an earthquake that wakes up a volcano that spews lava'). As she stands in the shower, the lava of this subjective volcano 'desglaça les llàgrimes' (p. 72) ('melts the tears') of her frozen memory: she cries while remembering the traumatic events that led to her departure and her decision to steal the money, 'que li pesarà tota la vida' (p. 73) ('that will weigh on her for the rest of her life'). Despite her best intentions to return the money, 'res no esborrarà de la seva consciència la taca que la converteix en una argentina arquetípica més: una lladre amb justificació. Una traïdora amb excusa. Una corrupta eventual' (p. 73) ('nothing will erase from her conscience the stain that turns her into yet another stereotypical Argentine: a thief with a justification. A traitor with an excuse. Eventually a crook'). However, 'com que [the theft] està fet i no hi ha marxa enrere' (p. 73) ('since the theft is done and there is no turning back'), her life in Barcelona must succeed. The pressing need for survival is thus an obstacle for carrying out the work of mourning.

Once again, this tension is echoed in the dialogue of mournings. Shortly after this scene, we see Eliseu having a shower, trying to remove from his body 'la pudor dels porcs enganxada a la pell' ('the stench of the pigs, clinging to his skin') that has become 'indeleble, gairebé sòlida' ('indelible, almost solid') (p. 75). Eliseu's ambivalence about his origin has turned into an indelible mark that cannot be given up and that prevents him from detaching himself from the dead. Later, he goes on a hike in the same mountain where Virgili died, in order to scatter Hilari's ashes. Eliseu opens the urn and takes some of the ash in his fingers: 'Li costa acceptar que aquella pols grisa siguin els ossos, les vísceres, la pell, els ulls, els dits, les ungles, les venes, els llavis, les dents, el cos i el cervell de l'Hilari' (p. 80) ('He finds it hard to accept that that grey dust is Hilari's bones, viscera, skin, eyes, fingers, nails, veins, lips, teeth, body and brain'). He brings the ash to his nose, but 'no ensuma res' (p. 80) ('he cannot smell anything'). The overpowering, imaginary stench of the burned pigs attached to his skin results in a lack of sense of smell that prevents Eliseu from bestowing a quantum of libido on the representation of his lost object. Unable to perform his ritual, he returns the ashes home. Hiking back, '[t]ravessa el purgatori amb la companyia de tres espectres: l'Hilari, el Virgili, la Lila' (p. 83) ('he crosses purgatory in the company of three ghosts: Hilari, Virgili, Lila'), and the continued presence of these spectres makes him unable to form new affective attachments with the living: his pain is 'com un escut que el protegeix dels vius' (p. 94) ('like a shield that protects him from the living').

At the end of this chapter, Vogt poignantly conveys the sense of frozen temporality and congealed desire of an unending mourning. Eliseu takes an hourglass from his bookshelves, empties it, cleans it, fills it with Hilari's ashes, and turns it over: 'Amb la mirada fixa a la pols grisa que cau formant una petita muntanya a la base, l'Eliseu va marcant els segons picant amb els artells de la mà la fusta freda de l'escriptori, fins que una engruna, gruixuda, s'encalla al coll i atura el pas' ('With his gaze fixed on the grey dust that falls forming a small mountain at the base, Eliseu marks the seconds by tapping his knuckles on the cold wood of the desk, until a thick grain gets stuck on the neck and stops the flow'), and then he says, '"Temps mort"' ('time-out'; 'dead time') (p. 95). The flow of subjective time has frozen in a kind of limbo that also interrupts the circulation of desire. Yet throughout this chapter Eliseu revisits and confronts the painful memories of loss. In the case of Vera, the effect of the debt persists in the abuse that she receives from fellow Argentines living in Catalonia when her first column is published (pp. 99, 105), and is also apparent in her anxiety as an illegal immigrant (p. 123). Just as Argentina defaults on its debt, Vera is unable to return hers, and just as she despises traitors and liars, she is dubbed as one by her fellow Argentine expatriates.

Symbolising Loss

The second half of *La mecànica* – the third and fourth 'esculls' and the 'Rompent' ('breakwater') that closes the novel – focuses on the developing friendship between Vera and Eliseu. They meet thanks to the mediation of Nil, whose novel has been accepted for publication by Eliseu. Having established a close connection through their common love of literature, Vera finds in the publisher a mentor who offers her work as a reader and later employs her as a private librarian, thereby helping her to become a legal immigrant. Their bond is deep and healing: it will help Eliseu conclude the mourning for his losses, and Vera will begin to miss Argentina while feeling part of Catalan society. In the fourth 'escull' we witness how Eliseu confronts, with Vera's constant support, the cancer that will lead to his passing – and we also encounter a final, unexpected twist, the death of Vera's dog Kantiano.

If the dialogue of mournings had hitherto been presented by the third-person narrator as a series of coincidences and juxtapositions, now it turns into an actual conversation. However, this dialogue of mournings is narratively constructed *après-coup*, and the juxtapositions Silvana Vogt introduces in the first half of the novel reinforce the impression that the transaction between mourners is actually an unconscious one. Both this fact and the aforementioned final twist are indications of Vogt's careful attention to form that several critics have underscored. For instance, Mireia Ferrando stresses '[e]l treball intens a què [Vogt] sotmet el text' ('the intense work to which [Vogt] subjects the text') in order to produce 'una prosa punyent i continguda' ('poignant and restrained prose'), and values her 'domini de les tècniques de construcció literària' ('mastery of the techniques of literary construction').[21] For his part, J. A. Masoliver mentions the alternation between long paragraphs 'amb altres que es limiten a una sola frase, breu i impactant' ('and others that are limited to a single sentence, short and striking'), a device that vividly conveys 'la densitat emocional, un dels aspectes més poderosos del llibre' ('emotional density, one of the most powerful aspects of the book').[22] By contrast, Albert Forns criticised Vogt for the 'diàlegs afectats' ('affected dialogues') and the 'frases de tango' ('tango lines') that pepper the narrative.[23]

All these critical comments, positive or negative, emphasise the text's quality of being a literary artefact, the product of literary artifice, that the novel amplifies rather than conceals. This is relevant because it denotes one of the processes that Darian Leader identifies in the work of mourning: the introduction of a symbolic, artificial space. Mourning, he argues, involves 'the idea of an exhaustion of representations' (Leader, p. 101): the mourner confronts the memories and objects that remind her of the deceased, and eventually the pain associated with these memories gives way to the judgement that the object has been lost. Here is of special importance 'the register of artificiality' that permits to symbolise the loss (p. 103). All the representations of the lost object, says Leader, must be subject to a transformation: 'the representations must be framed: they must be represented *as representations*' (p. 103; emphasis in the original). Through the intervention of language, the register of artificiality in the work of mourning enables loss to be 'inscribed in a symbolic space' (p. 105), thus launching an impossible but necessary task: to symbolise the unrepresentable, tracing the contours of the 'hole in the real' that loss has left.

One of the formal devices whereby *La mecànica* creates this 'register of artificiality' is the use of repetitions, beginning with that of the words 'La veig. Puc veure-la' ('I see her. I can see her'). This is unsurprising, given the close relationship repetition holds with trauma and separation and with the operation of *jouissance* and the death drive.[24] It is also linked to the process of working through in psychoanalysis, in which the subject goes over the material again and again,[25] and also to the functioning of memory and its cultural coding in tradition. Indeed, the repetition at the core of tradition appears in *La mecànica* as a source and a manifestation of ambivalence. In the second chapter, Eliseu and Hilari are in their home village, taking part in an Easter procession, '[f]idels a les arrels, a les tradicions, a les formes d'actuar que es transmeten de generació en generació' (*Mecànica*, p. 48) ('loyal to their roots, to traditions and to the ways of doing things transmitted from generation to generation'). Even though returning to the village is a painful experience for both, they abide by the cultural imperative to respect tradition:

> El país i la cultura així ho manen.
> Els morts i les tradicions així ho exigeixen.
>   No respectar els costums, deixar de participar-hi, no perpetuar el ritual, els suposaria obrir una porta prohibida i els obligaria a enfrontar-se a una veritat impossible d'assumir: es pot viure d'esquena al passat si el passat fa tant de mal. (p. 49)

> The nation and its culture dictate it.
> The dead and tradition demand it.
>   Not respecting customs, ceasing to participate in them, not perpetuating the ritual would open a forbidden door; they would be forced to face an unbearable truth: it is possible to live with one's back to the past if the past hurts so much.

There is therefore an imperative to repeat in order to preserve, and it is precisely this cultural imperative that engenders ambivalence in the characters. Immediately after this scene, Eliseu remembers his destruction of the pig shed, and is overcome with guilt (p. 50). Yet the gift of tradition may also afford the recipient a new lease on life: later, Eliseu gives Vera a selection of the main works of Catalan literature, and this gift amounts to her 'partida de naixement' (p. 118) ('birth certificate'). Thus, our relationship with tradition and its transmission partakes of the dialectic of memory at work in mourning; in Laufer's words: 'Comment conserver et modifier à la fois, telle est la question dialectique de la mémoire: accéder à la mémoire et modifier son matériau' (Laufer, p. 104) ('How to preserve and modify at the same time, such is the dialectical question of memory: accessing memory and modifying its material'). This dialectic of conservation and change is built on memory as a site of subjective conflict: 'L'endeuillé veut conserver quelque chose de l'objet disparu et, en un même mouvement, accéder à sa propre mémoire modifie l'objet disparu' (p. 104) ('The mourner wants to keep something of the lost object and, in the same movement, accessing her own memory modifies the lost object'). The movement of preservation and change is what causes the subject pain, but also what sets her desire back in motion (p. 108).

In the novel, the unconscious movement of memory is beautifully evoked by the metaphor that lends the novel its title. It refers to a passage in the first chapter in which Vera, still in Buenos Aires, contemplates the Río de la Plata:

> es queda hipnotitzada amb les onades que colpegen amb força contra el ciment, com si el riu no estigués d'acord amb la manera com l'han empresonat i volgués alliberar-se a força d'insistir.
> Colpeja, rebota i torna.
> Colpeja, rebota i torna.
> Taxatiu.
> Incontestable. (*Mecànica*, p. 34)

> She is mesmerised by the waves that hit hard against the concrete, as if the river did not agree with the way it was imprisoned and wanted to free itself by force of insistence.
> It hits, bounces and returns.
> It hits, bounces and returns.
> Unequivocal.
> Irrefutable.

This kind of repetitive movement is also present in Eliseu's practice of inserting his *ex libris* in pages three, 103 and 203 of all his books. He does so '[p]er no oblidar la pudor que feia la infantesa . . . Per tenir present, cada cop que obro un llibre, d'on vinc. I qui soc' (p. 132) ('in order not to forget the stench of my childhood. To keep in mind, every time I open a book, where I come from. And who I am'). The remembrance of Eliseu's origin and identity is thus bound to the three deaths he mourns (Virgili, Hilari, Lila), and the repetition of the *ex libris* is 'el motor que tira endavant el desig d'un futur diferent' (p. 132) ('the engine that drives forward the desire for a different future'). Indeed, as Laufer puts it, repetition allows the subject to 's'inscrire dans une histoire' ('inscribe herself in a narrative'), it is a means of symbolising trauma and facilitates 'récréer du mouvement psychique, un accès à la parole' ('to restore psychic movement and the access to speech') (Laufer, p. 109).

The symbolisation of loss ultimately depends on and must result in the construction of a subjective narrative. Vogt thematises in a variety of ways the prominence of language and narration in the mourning process of the two protagonists. For example, Eliseu's proud transmission of 'la seva versió de la història del país' ('his own version of Catalonia's history') makes Vera feel 'enveja per algú que pot estimar amb tanta convicció un tros de terra' ('envious of someone who is able to love a piece of land with such conviction') (*Mecànica*, p. 103). Vera also discovers the liberating potential of narrative: when Nil asks her the dreaded question of how she obtained the money to travel to Barcelona, given that banks were closed at the time, she realises that '[e]lla és el relat' (p. 121) ('she herself is the narrative'), and therefore can fashion at will the story she tells. Above all, Vera's speech, her desire to tell her own story, helps Eliseu unblock his own desire. In his eyes, Vera's voice engages her whole body: 'la veu li brolla pels ulls, per la pell, per les mans' (p. 126) ('her voice flows through her eyes, her skin, her hands'); this awakens in Eliseu a desire for the new, a fresh approach to the enigma of the other: 'Només li interessa estar amb algú nou, que funciona amb un codi diferent, amb un manual d'instruccions d'ús desconegut' (p. 127) ('He's only interested in being with someone new, someone running on a different code, with an unfamiliar instruction manual'). Ultimately, opening oneself to the enigma of the other involves accepting the paradox of embracing the social bond that language makes possible, while taking on the foreignness of language to human beings: according to Vera, God was a foreigner who created the adjectives 'per a nosaltres [els estrangers]. Per assegurar-nos que ens entenen ... Per si de cas algú entengués "amor" quan estàs dient "ha mort"' (p. 152) ('for us foreigners. To make sure others understand us ... In case someone understood "love" [amor] when you said "he died" [ha mort]').

Like in this quotation, love and death are intimately linked in the final pages of *La mecànica*, and also in the process of mourning.

Darian Leader reminds us that, for Freud, the work of mourning involves a declaration on the part of the subject that the lost object is dead; this declaration amounts symbolically to killing the dead, opening the way for mourning to take place (Leader, p. 114), and eventually leading to the acceptance of ambivalence (p. 121). However, such declaration is not sufficient because the mourner must still resolve the question of *what* she has lost in the deceased.[26] Following Lacan, Leader argues that mourning requires constituting the object as effectively lost, that is, 'having registered psychically an empty space' that must be internalised: 'Constituting an object means separating the images of those things that matter to us from the place they occupy' (p. 131), in order to facilitate 'a recognition of the fundamental alterity' of the lost object, showing that beyond the familiar image (of ourselves, of the object) lies 'the presence of something else, unrepresentable, opaque, a hole in our psychical world' (p. 132). This unrepresentable hole is what Lacan terms *objet petit a*, the enigmatic cause of desire, and it reveals that 'at an unconscious level, that part of the one we love *was always lost*, even when they were with us' (p. 133; emphasis in the original). However, since love is narcissistically structured, the problem of mourning is how to restore the links to the object as lost, while relinquishing the image of who we were for them.[27] For this reason, mourning demands 'a certain sacrifice, a sacrifice of our own links to the image . . . Mourning must mark out the place of a symbolic sacrifice, so that other objects can go into the place of the lost loved one' (pp. 135–6).

At the end of *La mecànica*, we witness Vera's double sacrifice. Eliseu develops a very aggressive cancer, and Vera will look after him while both the illness and the administrative process of her legal status progresses. Eventually Eliseu will endure excruciating pain and lose most of his mental faculties, but meanwhile he conveys to Vera some messages that become 'ecos' ('echoes') in her mind: 'Els consells. "No parlis malament del teu país, Vera; la gent no confiarà en tu si no respectes les arrels." . . . Les respostes exactes. "Recordar serveix per escriure, Vera." . . . Els clams. "Tu saps on és la morfina."' (*Mecànica*, p. 178) ('The advice. "Don't speak badly of your country, Vera; people won't trust you if you don't respect your roots." . . . The exact answers. "Remembering is useful for writing, Vera." . . . The pleas. "You know where the morphine is."') In the last few pages of the novel, Vera arrives in Eliseu's house, only to find a stunned nurse and an agitated Eliseu just returned from a stroll with Vera's dog Kantiano, who has been run over by a car and now lies dead in his lap (p. 180). Shortly thereafter, a devastated, numb Vera carries out Eliseu's request and administers him a lethal dose of morphine to ease him into a painless, dignified death (pp. 183–4). Eliseu's death involves her own, 'metafòrica però igual de contundent i irreversible' (p. 184) ('metaphorical, but just as blunt and irreversible'): something inside her has been declared irretrievably lost. We are witnesses to Vera's double sacrifice: to mourn her lost country, she has had to relinquish both the person who has helped unfreeze her subjectivity and the only thing that she brought with her from Argentina, Kantiano.

The last lines of *La mecànica de l'aigua*, which I quote at length, convey beautifully and poignantly this sense of detachment and bring together the main motifs of the book:

> Li tanca les parpelles i, després, es fica carn endins. En una mena d'exili interior. Fins a desaparèixer.
> Per sempre.
> Els ulls enganxats al clatell. L'ànima girada cap enrere.
> Contra natura.
> Però jo la veig.
> Encara puc veure-la.
> Perquè la memòria, com l'aigua, colpeja, rebota i torna amb la seva mecànica implacable.
> Tossuda com l'Eliseu.
> Constant com la impossibilitat d'una brúixola que sempre assenyala el sud.
> Forta com la compassió.
> I la ràbia.
> Imprescindible, com la distància entre la primera i la tercera persona a l'hora d'escriure aquesta història.
> Colpeja, rebota i torna.
> Colpeja, rebota i torna.
> Com l'ona expansiva de les paraules.
> Em veig.
> Colpeja, rebota i torna.
> Puc veure'm.
> Colpeja, rebota i torna fins que trenca la pedra.
> I llisca . . . (pp. 184–5)

She closes his eyelids and then withdraws into her own flesh. In a kind of inner exile. Until she disappears.
Forever.
Her eyes are glued to the back of her head. Her soul is turned backwards.
Against nature.
But I see her.
I can still see her.
Because like water, memory hits, bounces and returns with its relentless mechanics.
Stubborn like Eliseu.
Constant like an impossible compass that always points south.
Strong as compassion.
And anger.
Indispensable, like the distance between the first and third person when writing this story.
It hits, bounces and returns.
It hits, bounces and returns.
Like the shockwave of words.
I see myself.
It hits, bounces and returns.
I can see myself.
It hits, bounces and returns until it breaks the stone.
And glides . . .

Vera appears to us deep into her mourning, withdrawn into herself in exactly the same way that Eliseu had been presented earlier in the narrative. What is most remarkable about this ending, however, is the inscription of the scene of writing and the dissociation of the narrative voice, both of which denote an act of witnessing. Indeed, as Laufer points out:

> Le deuil est un événement qui, pour s'inscrire dans l'histoire du sujet, doit devenir un témoignage . . . La division entre le sujet de l'énoncé et le sujet de l'énonciation permet l'irruption d'une parole autre . . . La parole du deuil vient renforcer par la parole divisée la séparation du sujet qui parle, séparation d'avec le mort autant que séparation d'avec soi-même. La parole du deuil . . . est une parole qui déchire le moi de l'idée de sa 'force' ou de sa maturation . . . Parler déchire. (Laufer, pp. 197–8)

Mourning is an event that in order to be inscribed into the subject's history must become a testimony. The split between the subject of the statement and the subject of the enunciation allows the irruption of a new, different speech. Through this split the speech of mourning reinforces the separation of the speaking subject, both from the deceased and from itself. The speech of mourning tears the ego away from the idea of its 'strength' or its maturation. Speaking has a tearing effect.

Through her sophisticated textual symbolisation of loss, Vera undergoes mourning as an 'expérience de l'exil intérieur' (Laufer, p. 199) ('experience of inner exile') that has torn her from herself, and in the act of witnessing she has created the psychic place of burial necessary to symbolise absence and open up a space for the new. It is in this sense that the 'relentless mechanics' of water resembles the work of memory: not only in the patience and persistence of the mourner, as she confronts and exhausts the representations of the lost object, but also in the insistent movement of the drives, that finally win the day and allow both body and writing to be flooded with desire.

In this chapter I have shown how in *La mecànica de l'aigua* Silvana Vogt offers an alternative view of migratory mourning based not on nostalgia but on the acknowledgement of negativity, ambivalence and the traumatic dimension of immigration. I have traced the ways in which Vogt highlights the importance of the social dimension of mourning, manifested in a 'dialogue of mournings' that is crucial for the symbolisation of loss, and how this symbolic work relies on certain stylistic devices that make mourning a creative process that allows for the production of new narratives of identity. I have further argued that the registration of the empty space of loss resulting from this work requires engagement with ambivalence, which in this novel pivots on the tension between the idea of a blank slate that makes new beginnings possible and the effects of fixed attachments and identifications.

Vogt's novel thus facilitates a conception of subjectivity based on emptiness, absence, separation and loss, whereby mourning transforms not only the identity of the migrant but also the reception society, through the rejection of fixed identifications. These identifications are obviously related to the idea of cultural roots: we have seen how Vera rejects her national roots, whereas Hilari honours his from a position of strong ambivalence. As Salvador Cardús has argued, the trope of the roots plays an important role in Catalan cultural discourses, as a defence against the risk of dissolution of the national identity; the epitome of this position is the well-known verse by Raimon, the songwriter *par excellence* of anti-Franco resistance: 'Qui perd els orígens, perd identitat' ('He who loses his origins, loses his identity'). However, this idea is false, because identity is always contingent and, as Cardús claims, it may only survive and last if origins are subject to constant revision.[28] This claim posits a subjectivity that can only be conceived in the separation from oneself, in the experience of loss; emptiness is what allows for the circulation of desire and the creation of the new. Thus, mourning makes it possible to forge new identifications, and so perhaps we could rewrite Raimon's verse in a different way: 'She who loses her origins will gain an identity if she performs the work of mourning.'

Texts like *La mecànica de l'aigua*, in their presentation of immigration as a transformative experience that engages with negativity, ambivalence and loss, may facilitate a dialogue of mournings in Catalan culture: migrants work through the loss of country with which they may maintain an ambivalent relationship, and this echoes a process in which Catalan culture must mourn the loss of its own attachment to the idea of an identity centred on a full, substantive origin. If this is the case, then the promise of a new beginning arising from loss suggests that our analyses of Catalan identity must take into account the place and the role of mourning in its discursive constitution in order to define an idea of a Catalan identity that is decentred and constituted around an empty origin – and to deploy the social, cultural and political potential of this idea.

Notes

1 Research for this chapter was conducted under the project 'La poesia catalana contemporània des de la perspectiva dels estudis afectius: teories, implicacions de gènere i aplicacions a pràctiques textuals i performatives', funded by the Spanish Ministry for Science and Innovation (PID2019–105083GB–I00).
2 On the history of population exchanges between Argentina and Spain and their literary and audiovisual representations, see, for example, Ignacio Dionisio Arellano-Torres, 'El fracaso del diálogo migratorio transatlántico en *Vientos de agua*', *Catedral Tomada: Revista de*

Crítica Literaria Latinoamericana, 5/9 (2017), 424–40; Jorge Ginieniewicz, 'The Weight of Social Assets: Argentinian Migrants in Spain', *European Review of Latin American and Caribbean Studies*, 92 (2011), 23–38; Graciela Wamba Graviña, 'Emigración e identidad cultural en la reciente narrativa argentina', *Puertas abiertas*, 6 (2010); and Luis Roniger, 'Changing Cultural Landscapes under the Impact of Exile, Diasporas and Return Migration', *Araucaria*, 20/40 (2018), 185–208.

3   Susana Schmidt, 'Migraciones y exilios en la historia reciente de Argentina: Una interpretación a la luz de la teoría de espacios transnacionales', *Studia Historica: Historia contemporánea*, 28 (2010), 164. Unless otherwise stated, all translations from Catalan, Spanish and French are my own.

4   Schmidt, 'Migraciones y exilios', 165.

5   See, for example, Albert Forns, 'Fitxatge al mercat argentí', *Ara* (15 October 2016), 48; and Eva Piquer, 'Qui m'ha robat el mes d'abril?', *Ara* (10 September 2016), 45.

6   Mireia Ferrando, 'L'estrena literària de Silvana Vogt', *Caràcters*, 77 (2016), 8; Juan A. Masoliver Ródenas, 'Els abismes del cor', *La Vanguardia*, supplement *Cultura/s* (17 September 2016), 7; Vicenç Pagès Jordà, 'Una mirada convincent', *El Periódico de Catalunya* (28 September 2016), 59.

7   Madelaine Hron, *Translating Pain: Immigrant Suffering in Literature and Culture* (Toronto, Buffalo NY and London: University of Toronto Press, 2009).

8   Salman Akhtar, 'The Immigrant, the Exile, and the Experience of Nostalgia', *Journal of Applied Psychoanalytic Studies*, 1/2 (1999), 125–6. See also Salman Akhtar, 'A Third Individuation: Immigration, Identity, and the Psychoanalytic Process', *Journal of the American Psychoanalytic Association*, 43/4 (1995), 1051–84.

9   Ghislaine Boulanger, 'Seeing Double, Being Double: Longing, Belonging, Recognition, and Evasion in Psychodynamic Work with Immigrants', *The American Journal of Psychoanalysis*, 75 (2015), 289.

10 Boulanger, 'Seeing Double', 289.

11 Ricardo C. Ainslie, 'Immigration, Psychic Dislocation, and the Re-creation of Community', *Psychoanalytic Review*, 104/6 (2017), 700.

12 Ainslie, 'Immigration', 704.

13 Sigmund Freud, 'Mourning and Melancholia', in *On Murder, Mourning and Melancholia* (London: Penguin, 2005), p. 203.

14 As Vargas Castro claims, 'Todo objeto digno de duelo no solo es un objeto de amor y de odio, sino que es un objeto que se ha asesinado antes de su muerte' ('Every object worth of mourning is not only an object of love and hatred, but also one that has been murdered before its death'). David Andrés Vargas Castro, 'El odio en la clínica del duelo', *Desde el jardín de Freud*, 19 (2019), 165.

15 See Sigmund Freud, 'The Ego and the Id', in *Beyond the Pleasure Principle and Other Writings* (London: Penguin, 2003), pp. 103–49.
16 Diana Fuss, *Identification Papers* (New York and London: Routledge, 1995), p. 37.
17 Fuss, *Identification Papers*, p. 38.
18 Darian Leader, *The New Black: Mourning, Melancholia and Depression* (London: Hamish Hamilton, 2008), pp. 56–7.
19 Laurie Laufer, *L'énigme du deuil* (Paris: Presses Universitaires de France, 2006), p. 14.
20 Silvana Vogt, *La mecànica de l'aigua* (Barcelona: Edicions de 1984, 2016), pp. 13, 18, 57, 161, 183.
21 Ferrando, 'L'estrena literària de Silvana Vogt', 8.
22 Masoliver Ródenas, 'Els abismes del cor', 7.
23 Forns, 'Fitxatge al mercat argentí', 48.
24 See Sigmund Freud, 'Beyond the Pleasure Principle', in *Beyond the Pleasure Principle and Other Writings* (London: Penguin, 2003), pp. 50–5 (on trauma, separation and repetition in the *Fort/Da*), pp. 56–62 (on the compulsion to repeat) and pp. 91–5 (on sexuality and the death drive).
25 Sigmund Freud, 'Remembering, Repeating, and Working Through', in *Beyond the Pleasure Principle and Other Writings* (London: Penguin, 2003), pp. 31–42.
26 As Jacques Lacan puts it in his seminar on anxiety: 'We mourn but for he or she of whom we can say *I was his lack*. We mourn people that we have treated either well or badly, but with respect to whom we don't know that we fulfilled the function of being in the place of their lack. What we give in love is essentially what we haven't got and when this *not having* comes back at us there is most certainly regression and at the same time a revelation of the way in which we left him wanting, so as to represent this lack. But here, given the irreducible character of the misrecognition of this lack, this misrecognition simply switches round, namely, we believe we can translate our function of being his lack into us having left him wanting – even though it was in this respect that we were precious and indispensable for him.' Jacques Lacan, *Anxiety: The Seminar of Jacques Lacan: Book X*, trans. by A. R. Price (Cambridge: Polity, 2014), p. 141 (emphasis in the original).

For an excellent explanation of Lacan's point, see Richard Boothby, 'The Lost Cause of Mourning', *Continental Philosophy Review*, 46 (2013), 209–21. Boothby clarifies the relation between love in mourning in Lacan: 'What mourning most sorely misses is precisely the lack in the other, not what was there but rather what was not. The decisive thing that I find in the other, the point at which love binds me most profoundly to the other, is the moment of non-being, the empty, absent, missing encounter that was already there in the other before death ... Death wounds love most profoundly by closing the open space of lack' (213). Thus, love can be said to revolve 'around an empty center' (214). Boothby adds: 'What is crucial for the experience of the mourning subject is not related simply to the lack in the other, to the fact that this lack is now painfully lacking, so much as it is to the way in which the lover has offered her- or himself in identification with that lack ... The death of the other triggers a catastrophic collapse in this long-established project of putting oneself at the place of the other's lack' (215).

27 As Analía Batista argues, mourning requires a symbolic and an imaginary work in the face of the hole in the real caused by loss: 'El trabajo [simbólico] operado por el duelo, su operación, es hacer de la ausencia una falta, y de la falta, inexistencia; es hacer de un agujero, una causa ... El duelo por el objeto es equivalente a la caída de las identificaciones imaginarias' ('The [symbolic] work of mourning, its operation, is to turn absence into lack, and lack into inexistence; it is to turn a hole into a cause ... Mourning the object is equivalent to the collapse of imaginary identifications'). Analía Batista, 'El problema del duelo', *Desde el jardín de Freud*, 11 (2011), 27.

28 Salvador Cardús i Ros, *Tres metàfores per pensar un país amb futur: Discurs de recepció de Salvador Cardús i Ros com a membre numerari de la Secció de Filosofia i Ciències Socials, llegit el dia 12 de novembre de 2009* (Barcelona: Institut d'Estudis Catalans, 2009), p. 11.

Bibliography

Afinoguénova, Eugenia, and Jaume Martí-Olivella, 'Introduction: A Nation under Tourist's Eyes: Tourism and Identity Discourses in Spain', in Eugenia Afinoguénova and Jaume Martí-Olivella (eds), *Spain Is (Still) Different: Tourism and Discourse in Spanish Identity* (Lanham MD: Lexington Books, 2008), pp. xi–xxxviii.

Ahmed, Sara, *Strange Encounters: Embodied Others in Post-Coloniality* (New York: Routledge, 2000).

Ainslie, Ricardo C., 'Immigration, Psychic Dislocation, and the Re-creation of Community', *Psychoanalytic Review*, 104/6 (2017), 695–706.

Akhtar, Salman, 'A Third Individuation: Immigration, Identity, and the Psychoanalytic Process', *Journal of the American Psychoanalytic Association*, 43/4 (1995), 1051–84.

— 'The Immigrant, the Exile, and the Experience of Nostalgia', *Journal of Applied Psychoanalytic Studies*, 1/2 (1999), 123–30.

Alexandre, Víctor, *Nosaltres, els catalans* (Barcelona: Pòrtic, 2008).

Alomar, Antoni I., *La llengua catalana a les Balears en el segle XX* (Palma: Documenta Balear, 2002).

Amat, Jordi, 'Nota a l'edició: *Els altres catalans* a censura', in Francesc Candel, *Els altres catalans* (Barcelona: Edicions 62, 2008), pp. 16–25.

Amorín, Alfonso Iglesias, 'Sub-state Nationalisms in Spain during the Moroccan War and the Rif War (1909–1927)', *Studies on National Movements*, 8 (2021), 1–25.

Anonymous, 'Para preservar la raza catalana', *La Vanguardia* (3 May 1934), 8.

Anzaldúa, Gloria, *Borderlands/La Frontera: The New Mestiza* (San Francisco CA: Aunt Lute Books, 2012 [1987]).

Aragay, Ignasi, 'Sentís reviu el Transmiserià', *Avui* (18 October 1994), B1.

Arellano-Torres, Ignacio Dionisio, 'El fracaso del diálogo migratorio transatlántico en *Vientos de agua*', *Catedral Tomada: Revista de Crítica Literaria Latinoamericana*, 5/9 (2017), 424–40.

Arnau, Pilar, *Narrativa i turisme a Mallorca* (Palma: Documenta Balear, 1999).

— 'L'hybridité identitaire dans une littérature émergente: l'écriture du "moi" hybride dans l'œuvre autobiographique des écrivains catalans d'origine maghrébine', *Babel: Littératures plurielles*, 33 (2016), 247–59.

Aroca Mohedano, Manuela, *Sindicatos y turismo de masas en las Baleares: Del Franquismo a la democracia* (Palma: Documenta Balear, 2018).

Asensi, Manuel, 'La subalternidad borrosa: Un poco más de debate en torno a los subalternos', in Gayatri Chakravorty Spivak, *¿Pueden hablar los subalternos?* (Barcelona: Macba, 2009), pp. 9–40.

Audoin-Rouzeau, Stéphane, *Quelle histoire: Un récit de filiation* (Paris: École d'Hautes Études en Sciences Sociales, Gallimard and Seuil, 2013).

Bal, Mieke, *Double Exposures: The Subject of Cultural Analysis* (London and New York: Routledge, 1996).

Ballbona, Anna, 'Francesc Serés: "Tens possibilitat de literatura quan hi ha un desplaçament"', *El Temps* (16 December 2014), 64–5.

Barceló, Bartomeu, 'Història del turisme a Mallorca', *Treballs de la Societat Catalana de Geografia*, 15/50 (2000), 31–55.

Batista, Analía, 'El problema del duelo', *Desde el jardín de Freud*, 11 (2011), 17–30.

Benjamin, Walter, 'Theses on the Philosophy of History', *Illuminations* (New York: Schocken, 1968), pp. 253–64.

— 'The Storyteller', *Illuminations* (New York: Schocken, 1968), pp. 83–109.

Bereano, Nancy, 'Introduction' to *Sister Outsider*, in Audre Lorde, *Zami; Sister Outsider; Undersong* (New York: Quality Paperback Book Club, 1993), pp. 7–12.

Bhabha, Homi, *The Location of Culture* (London and New York: Routledge, 2004 [1994]).

Boothby, Richard, 'The Lost Cause of Mourning', *Continental Philosophy Review*, 46 (2013), 209–21.

Bordetas, Ivan, 'Habitatge i assentaments de la postguerra a l'estabilització', in Martí Marín (ed.), *Memòries del viatge 1940–1975* (Valls: Cossetània, 2009), pp. 51–69.

Boulanger, Ghislaine, 'Seeing Double, Being Double: Longing, Belonging, Recognition, and Evasion in Psychodynamic Work with Immigrants', *The American Journal of Psychoanalysis*, 75 (2015), 287–303.

Bourdieu, Pierre, *Language and Symbolic Power* (Cambridge MA: Harvard University Press, 2003).

Bourland Ross, Catherine, 'Left Behind: Cultural Assimilation and the Mother/Daughter Relationship in Najat El Hachmi's *La hija extranjera* (2015)', *Hispanófila*, 183 (2018), 351–65.

Braidotti, Rosi, *Metamorphoses: Towards a Materialist Theory of Becoming* (Cambridge: Polity, 2002).

Bromley, Roger, 'A Bricolage of Identifications: Storying Postmigrant Belonging', *Journal of Aesthetics and Culture*, 9/2 (2017), 36–44.

Cabot, Just, 'El problema de la immigració', *Mirador* (26 January 1933), 3.

Cabré, Anna, *El sistema català de reproducció* (Barcelona: Proa, 1999).

Cabrera, Lluís, Pedro Morón, Marta Riera et al., *Els altres andalusos: La qüestió nacional de Catalunya* (Barcelona: L'Esfera dels Llibres, 2005).
Campoy-Cubillo, Adolfo, *Memories of the Maghreb: Transnational Identities in Spanish Cultural Production* (London and New York: Palgrave Macmillan, 2012).
Candel, Francisco, *Donde la ciudad cambia su nombre* (Barcelona: Janés, 1957).
— *¡Dios, la que se armó!* (Barcelona: Ediciones Marte, 1964).
— 'El amazacotamiento', *CAU*, 60 (1965), 5–8.
— *Han matado a un hombre, han roto un paisaje* (Barcelona: Ediciones GP, 1967).
— *Barrio* (Barcelona: Ediciones Marte, 1977).
— *Los otros catalanes veinte años después* (Barcelona: Plaza y Janés, 1985).
Candel, Francesc, *Els altres catalans* (Barcelona: Edicions 62, 1964).
— 'Barraques de la riera Comtal: Uns veïns als quals ningú no fa cas', *Serra d'Or*, 7/5 (May 1965), 71–3.
— *Els altres catalans vint anys després* (Barcelona: Edicions 62, 1985).
— *Els altres catalans: Edició no censurada* (Barcelona: Edicions 62, 2008 [1964]).
Cañete, Carlos, and Gonzalo Fernández Parrilla, 'Spanish-Maghribi (Moroccan) Relations Beyond Exceptionalism: A Postcolonial Perspective', *Journal of North Africa Studies*, 24/1 (2019), 111–33.
Cardús i Ros, Salvador, 'The Memory of Immigration in Catalan Nationalism', *International Journal of Iberian Studies*, 18/1 (2005), 37–44.
— *Tres metàfores per pensar un país amb futur: Discurs de recepció de Salvador Cardús i Ros com a membre numerari de la Secció de Filosofia i Ciències Socials, llegit el dia 12 de novembre de 2009* (Barcelona: Institut d'Estudis Catalans, 2009).
Carranza Castelo, Ernest, '¿Integración o desintegración?: El cuestionamiento de Cataluña como tierra de acogida en textos de ficción y no ficción de Najat El Hachmi', *Journal of Catalan Studies*, 1/20 (2017).
Casademont Falguera, Xavier and Jordi Feu Gelis, 'La problemàtica de l'habitatge de la immigració andalusa a Olot durant el franquisme (1940–1975)', *Documents d'Anàlisi Geogràfica*, 63/1 (2017), 7–28.
Castellano, Margarida, 'La construcció del subjecte autobiogràfic femení en la literatura catalana de la immigració' (unpublished PhD thesis, Universitat de València, 2013).
— *Les altres catalanes: Memòria, identitat i autobiografia en la literatura d'immigració* (Valencia: Tres i Quatre, 2018).
Chambers, Iain, *Migrancy, Culture, Identity* (London: Routledge, 1994).
Clua i Fainé, Montserrat, 'Catalanes, inmigrantes y charnegos: "raza", "cultura" y mezcla en el discurso nacionalista catalán', *Revista de Antropología Social*, 20 (2011), 55–75.

Codina, Núria, 'The Work of Najat El Hachmi in the Context of Spanish-Moroccan Literature', *Research in African Literatures*, 48/3 (2017), 116–30.
Colom Cañellas, Antoni, 'Pròleg', in Toni Morlà, *Memòries d'un brusquer: Diccionari dels anys 60 i 70* (Palma: Clayton's Book, 2001).
Colom-Montero, Guillem, 'Mass Tourism as Cultural Trauma: An Analysis of the Majorcan Comics *Els darrers dies de l'Imperi Mallorquí* (2014) and *Un infern a Mallorca (La decadència de l'Imperi Mallorquí)* (2018)', *Studies in Comics*, 10/1 (2019), 49–71.
Conversi, Daniele, *The Basques and the Catalans: Alternative Routes to Nationalist Mobilisation* (London: C. Hurst, 1997).
Coronil, Fernando, 'Listening to the Subaltern: The Poetics of Neocolonial States', *Poetics Today*, 15/4 (1994), 643–58.
Crameri, Kathryn, *Catalonia: National Identity and Cultural Policy, 1980–2003* (Cardiff: University of Wales Press, 2008).
Cruells, Manuel, *Els no catalans i nosaltres* (Barcelona: Edicions d'Aportació Catalana, 1965).
Crumbaugh, Justin, *Destination Dictatorship: The Spectacle of Spain's Tourist Boom and the Reinvention of Difference* (Albany NY: State University of New York, 2009).
Darici, Katiuscia, 'Literatura transnacional en Cataluña: *La filla estrangera* de Najat El Hachmi', *Diablotexto Digital*, 2 (2017), 106–34.
Dasca, Maria, 'La immigració com a fenomen en la literatura catalana', *Cercles: Revista d'Història Cultural*, 18 (2015), 61–78.
— 'Confused Otherness: A Reading of the *L'atzar i les ombres* (1997–2005) trilogy by Julià de Jòdar', in Xabier Payá and Laura Sáez (eds), *National Identities at the Crossroads: Literature, Stage and Visual Media in the Iberian Peninsula* (London: Francis Boutle, 2018), pp. 55–67.
Deleuze, Gilles, *The Fold* (Minneapolis MN: University of Minnesota Press, 1988).
Delgado, Manuel, 'El mite de la multiculturalitat: De la "diversitat" cultural a la desigualtat social', *Revista Catalana de Seguretat Pública*, 2 (1998), 55–72.
— *Memoria y lugar: El espacio público como crisis de significado* (Valencia: Ediciones Generales de la Construcción, 2001).
Derrida, Jacques, *La hospitalidad* (Buenos Aires: Ediciones de la Flor, 2000).
Domingo, Andreu, '"Català és . . .": El discurs sobre immigració i identitat nacional durant el franquisme: Francesc Candel i Jordi Pujol', *Treballs de la Societat Catalana de Geografia*, 75 (2013), 9–32.
— *Catalunya al mirall de la immigració: Demografia i identitat nacional* (Barcelona: L'Avenç, 2014).
— 'L'empremta de Candel', *Ara* (16 March 2014), 6–7.
— 'La literatura sobre la immigració al segle XXI', *L'Avenç*, 408 (2015), 28–34.

Domingo, Andreu, and Kenneth Pitarch, 'La població valenciana a Catalunya al segle XXI: anàlisi demogràfica i espacial', *Treballs de la Societat Catalana de Geografia*, 79 (2015), 9–37.
Dowling, Andrew, 'Political Cultures, Ruptures, and Continuity in Catalonia under the Franco Regime', in Josep-Anton Fernàndez and Jaume Subirana (eds), *Funcions del passat en la cultura catalana contemporània: Institucionalització, representacions i identitat* (Lleida: Punctum, 2015), pp. 221–41.
Duane, Lucas, 'Castilian Takes Backstage in the Balearic Islands: The Activation of Castilian Standardization Recursions in Facebook', *Journal of Linguistic Anthropology*, 27/1 (2017), 71–91.
El Hachmi, Najat, *Jo també soc catalana* (Barcelona: Columna, 2004).
— 'Pròleg: L'home que apostava pel matís', in Francesc Candel, *Els altres catalans* (Barcelona: Edicions 62, 2008), pp. 7–11.
— *La filla estrangera* (Barcelona: Edicions 62, 2015).
El Kadaoui, Saïd, *Límites y fronteras* (Lleida: Milenio, 2008).
— *Cartes al meu fill: Un català de soca-rel, gairebé* (Barcelona: Ara Llibres, 2011).
— *No* (Barcelona: Catedral, 2016).
Esposito, Roberto, *Immunitas: The Protection and Negation of Life* (Cambridge: Polity, 2017).
Fabian, Johannes, *Time and the Other: How Anthropology Makes its Object* (New York: Columbia University Press, 2002 [1983]).
Fernàndez, Josep-Anton, 'Thou Shalt Not Covet Thy Roots: Immigration and the Body in Novels by Roig, Barbal, and Jaén', *Romance Quarterly*, 53/3 (2006), 223–35.
— *El malestar en la cultura catalana: La cultura de la normalització 1976–1999* (Barcelona: Empúries, 2008).
— 'Impossible Sutures: Loss, Mourning, and the Uses of Catalonia's Past in TV3's *La Mari*', in Xabier Payá and Laura Sáez (eds), *National Identities at the Crossroads: Literature, Stage and Visual Media in the Iberian Peninsula* (London: Francis Boutle, 2018), pp. 132–55.
— '"Virilitat del país": Gender, Immigration, and Power in Jaume Vicens Vives's *Notícia de Catalunya*', *Hispanic Research Journal*, 21/2 (2020), 143–58.
— 'Dislocated Temporalities: Immigration, Sexuality, and Violence in Najat El Hachmi's *L'últim patriarca*', in Teresa Iribarren, Roger Canadell and Josep-Anton Fernàndez (eds), *Narratives of Violence* (Venice: Edizioni Ca' Foscari, 2021), pp. 109–20.
Ferrando, Mireia, 'L'estrena literària de Silvana Vogt', *Caràcters*, 77 (2016), 8.
Ferster Marmot, Alexi, 'The Legacy of Le Corbusier and High-Rise Housing', *Built Environment*, 7/2 (1981), 82–95.
Flesler, Daniela, *The Return of the Moor: Spanish Responses to Contemporary Moroccan Immigration* (West Lafayette IN: Purdue University Press, 2008).

Folkart, Jessica A., 'Scoring the National Hym(e)n: Sexuality, Immigration, and Identity in Najat El Hachmi's *L'últim patriarca*', *Hispanic Review*, 81/3 (2013), 353–76.
'Foraster', in *Diccionari Català-Valencià-Balear*, Antoni Maria Alcover, Francesc de Borja Moll, Manuel Sanchis i Guarner and Aina Moll (Barcelona: Institut d'Estudis Catalans), https://dcvb.iec.cat/.
de Forestier, Guy, *Queridos mallorquines: Claves del trato personal en la isla de Mallorca* (Palma: La Foradada, 1995).
Forns, Albert, 'Fitxatge al mercat argentí', *Ara* (15 October 2016), 48.
Foucault, Michel, 'Des espaces autres', *Architecture, Mouvement, Continuité*, 5 (1984), 46–9.
— *The Order of Things: An Archaeology of the Human Sciences* (New York: Vintage, 1994).
Freud, Sigmund, *Totem and Taboo* (New York: W. W. Norton, 1950).
— 'Beyond the Pleasure Principle', in *Beyond the Pleasure Principle and Other Writings* (London: Penguin, 2003), pp. 42–102.
— 'Remembering, Repeating, and Working Through', in *Beyond the Pleasure Principle and Other Writings* (London: Penguin, 2003), pp. 31–42.
— 'The Ego and the Id', in *Beyond the Pleasure Principle and Other Writings* (London: Penguin, 2003), pp. 103–49.
— 'Mourning and Melancholia', in *On Murder, Mourning and Melancholia* (London: Penguin, 2005), pp. 201–18.
Frontera, Guillem, 'Mallorquins, forasters i forasteristes', *Ara Balears* (24 May 2013), *www.ara.cat/opinio/mallorquins-forasters-forasteristes_129_2293407. html*.
— *Els carnissers* (Barcelona, Club Editor, 2016 [1969]).
Fuss, Diana, *Identification Papers* (New York and London: Routledge, 1995).
Gabancho, Patrícia, *Sobre la immigració* (Barcelona: Columna, 2001).
Garcia Garcia, Núria, *Percepció dels catalans sobre la immigració* (Barcelona: Centre d'Estudis d'Opinió, 2012).
Geertz, Clifford, *Works and Lives* (Stanford CA: Stanford University Press, 1989).
Gilabert, Joan J., 'Francisco Candel: His Essays and the Catalan National Question', *Siglo XX* 6/1–2 (1988), 10–14.
Ginard, David, 'Pròleg', in Manuela Aroca Mohedano, *Sindicatos y turismo de masas en las Baleares: Del Franquismo a la democracia* (Palma: Documenta Balear, 2018), pp. 9–12.
Jorge Ginieniewicz, 'The Weight of Social Assets: Argentinian Migrants in Spain', *European Review of Latin American and Caribbean Studies*, 92 (2011), 23–38.
Glissant, Édouard, *Poetics of Relation*, trans. by Betsy Wing (Ann Arbor MI: University of Michigan Press, 1997).
Google Streetview, '110 Avinguda Puigmal', *www.google.com/maps/@42.0092357,2.2832488,3a,75y,305.63h,75.33t/ data=!3m6!1e1!3m4!1s1MygJJfdRgqZfrKyJ8veKg!2e0!7i16384!8i8192*.

— '272 Passeig de Sant Joan', *www.google.com/maps/place/Passeig+de+Sant+ Joan,+272,+08560+Manlleu,+Barcelona,+Spain/@42.0088586,2.27925 81,3a,75y,176.63h,86.17t/data=!3m6!1e1!3m4!1sfiUN4li4aixW-Lq5W J00Bg!2e0!7i16384!8i8192!4m5!3m4!1s0x12a525a303ffdb2d:0xf 4593234487c0fc7!8m2!3d42.0082863!4d2.2799916.*

Graset, Xavier, 'Entrevista a Julià Guillamon, escriptor: Ens presenta el seu darrer llibre, El Barri de la Plata', *Més 324*, Canal 3/24, Televisió de Catalunya (16 October 2018), *www.ccma.cat/tv3/alacarta/mes-324/ entrevista-a-julia-guillamon-escriptor-ens-presenta-el-seu-darrer-llibre-el-barri- de-la-plata/video/5792166/.*

Guia Conca, Aitana, 'Molts mons, una sola llengua: La narrativa en català escrita per immigrants', *Quaderns de Filologia: Estudis literaris*, 12 (2007), 229–48.

Guillamon, Julià, 'El sistema murciano en Cataluña', *La Vanguardia* (18 November 1994), 33.

— *La ciutat interrompuda: De la contracultura a la Barcelona postolímpica* (Barcelona: La Magrana, 2001).

— 'La novel·la catalana de la immigració', *L'Avenç*, 298 (2005), 46–9.

— 'Las dos culturas', *La Vanguardia* (27 April 2011), 11.

— *El barri de la plata* (Barcelona: L'Avenç, 2018).

— *El tren de la bruixa* (Barcelona: L'Avenç, 2018).

— '*L'atzar i les ombres*, novel·la total: L'atzar i les obres (II)', *La lectora* (20 December 2022). *https://lalectora.cat/2022/12/20/latzar-i-les-ombres- novella-total-latzar-i-les-obres-ii/.*

Hall, Jacqueline, 'La bena i la mordassa: Els catalans davant la immigració de l'època franquista', *Treballs de sociolingüística catalana*, 5 (1983), 71–92.

Hamilton, Sarah R., 'Environmental Change and Protest in Franco's Spain, 1939–1975', *Environmental History*, 22/2 (2017), 257–81.

Harvey, David, *Justice, Nature, and the Geography of Difference* (Cambridge MA: Blackwell, 1996).

— 'The Right to the City', *New Left Review*, 53 (2008), *https://newleftreview. org/issues/ii53/articles/david-harvey-the-right-to-the-city.*

Heidegger, Martin, 'Building Dwelling Thinking', in David Farrell Krell (ed.), *Basic Writings from Being and Time (1927) to The Task of Thinking (1964)* (London and San Francisco CA: Harper Perennial, 2008), pp. 343–64.

— *Carta sobre el humanismo* (Madrid: Alianza, 2009).

Hirsch, Marianne, *Family Frames: Photography, Narrative and Postmemory* (Cambridge MA and London: Harvard University Press, 1997).

Hita, Victoria, '"Ho he publicat tot, he publicat massa": Entrevista a Paco Candel, escriptor', *Capçalera* (July 2005), 23–7.

Holston, James, 'Spaces of Insurgent Citizenship', in James Holston (ed.), *Cities and Citizenship* (Durham NC and London: Duke University Press, 1998), pp. 157–73.

Hron, Madelaine, *Translating Pain: Immigrant Suffering in Literature and Culture* (Toronto, Buffalo NY and London: University of Toronto Press, 2009).
Institut d'Estadística de Catalunya (Idescat), *Població a 1 de gener: Total i estrangera* (28 February 2022), *www.idescat.cat/poblacioestrangera/?b=0*.
Jablonka, Ivan, *History Is a Contemporary Literature: Manifesto for the Social Sciences* (Ithaca NY: Cornell University Press, 2018).
Jacobs, Jane, *The Death and Life of Great American Cities* (New York: Random House, 1992).
Janer, Maria de la Pau, *Mallorca, l'illa de les mil i una nits: Carta a un estranger que ens visita* (Barcelona: Columna, 2011).
Jòdar, Julià de, *L'àngel de la segona mort* (Barcelona: Quaderns Crema, 1998).
— *El trànsit de les fades* (Barcelona: Quaderns Crema, 2001).
— *El metall impur* (Barcelona: Proa, 2006).
— 'Notes sobre memòria col·lectiva i identitat literària', in *Literatura, territori i identitat: La gestió del patrimoni literari a debat* (Girona: Curbet, 2011), pp. 127–44.
— *Els vulnerables* (Barcelona: Comanegra, 2018).
Jordà, Joan-Pau, Joan Colom and Gabriel Mayol, *Somnis compartits: La identitat mallorquina a debat* (Palma: Documenta Balear, 2016).
Junta Directiva de la Casa Regional de Murcia y Albacete, 'Carta abierta a Carlos Sentís', *Solidaridad Obrera* (27 January 1933), 4.
King, Stewart, 'Inmigración y literatura nacional en Cataluña. Una lectura periférica', *Journal of Iberian and Latin American Research*, 27/2 (2021), 357–63.
Kristeva, Julia, *Strangers to Ourselves*, trans. by Leon S. Roudiez (New York: Columbia University Press, 1991).
Lacan, Jacques, *Anxiety: The Seminar of Jacques Lacan: Book X*, trans. by A. R. Price (Cambridge: Polity, 2018).
Laufer, Laurie, *L'énigme du deuil* (Paris: Presses Universitaires de France, 2006).
Leader, Darian, *The New Black: Mourning, Melancholia and Depression* (London: Hamish Hamilton, 2008).
Leersen, Joep, and Manfred Beller, *Imagology: The Cultural Construction and Literary Representation of National Characters: A Critical Survey* (Amsterdam and New York: Rodopi, 2007).
Lejeune, Philippe, 'El diari com a antificció', in Joan Borja, Joaquim Espinós, Anna Esteve and M. Àngels Francés (eds), *Diaris i dietaris* (Alicante and Valencia: Denes, 2007), pp. 13–25.
López-Pampló, Gonçal, 'L'assaig català en l'època postmoderna: Funció social i especificitat estètica' (unpublished PhD thesis, Universitat de València, 2015).
Lorde, Audre, *Zami; Sister Outsider; Undersong* (New York: Quality Paperback Book Club, 1993).
Losada, Jordi, 'Mor Carles Sentís', *El Punt Avui* (20 July 2011), 30.

Löwy, Michael, *Walter Benjamin: Avís d'incendi* (Barcelona: Flâneur, 2020).
Madriarga, Rafa, Joan Carles Martori and Ramon Oller, 'Renta salarial, desigualdad y segregación residencial en las ciudades medianas de Cataluña', *Scripta Nova*, 24/640 (2020), 1–25.
Magnússon, Sigurður Gylfi, 'The Singularization of History: Social History and Microhistory within the Postmodern State of Knowledge', *Journal of Social History*, 36/3 (2003), 701–35.
Magris, Claudio, 'Desde el otro lado: Consideraciones fronterizas', *Utopía y desencanto: Historias, esperanzas e ilusiones de la modernidad* (Barcelona: Anagrama, 2001), pp. 55–70.
Maiol, Roger, 'La fricció amb la immigració és una crònica social del nostre país', *El País*, supplement *Quadern* (24 October 2014), 8.
Manera, Carles, 'Història del creixement econòmic a Mallorca, 1700–2000', *Anuari de la Societat Catalana d'Economia*, 19 (2011), 77–84.
Marçal, Maria-Mercè, *La germana, l'estrangera (1981–1984)* (Barcelona: Edicions 62, 1995).
— *Llengua abolida: Poesia completa 1973–1998* (Barcelona: Edicions 62, 2017).
Marcillas-Piquer, Isabel, 'Veus de frontera: Els *altres catalans* d'ara', *Caplletra*, 65 (2018), 177–89.
Marín, Martí, 'Ritmes i composició migratoris: Les xifres d'un fenomen complex', *L'Avenç*, 298 (2005), 24–31.
— *Història del franquisme a Catalunya* (Vic: Eumo Editorial, 2006).
Martínez, Francisco, 'Habitatge, habitatge social, especulació', in Josep Maria Solé i Sabaté (dir.), *El franquisme a Catalunya (1939–1977)*, vol. 2: *Catalunya dins l'Espanya de l'autarquia (1946–1958)* (Barcelona: Edicions 62, 2005), pp. 156–62.
Martínez-Gil, Víctor, 'Els escriptors com a intel·lectuals postmoderns', in Ramon Panyella and Jordi Marrugat (eds), *L'escriptor i la seva imatge* (Barcelona: L'Avenç, 2006), pp. 299–322.
Masferrer, Mariona, *Origen: Tambakunda* (Figueres: Brau Edicions, 2013).
Milian, Àlex, 'Valencians a Catalunya: La invisible migració interior', *El Temps* (10 March 2015), *www.eltemps.cat/article/4716/valencians-a-catalunya-la-invisible-migracio-interior*.
Minca, Claudio, and Nick Vaughan-Williams, 'Carl Schmitt and the Concept of the Border', *Geopolitics*, 17 (2012), 756–72.
Mokhtari, Fizia Hayette, 'Autobiographie et transgression générique dans *Les homes qui marchent*, *La Transe des insoumis* et *Mes hommes*, de Malika Mokeddem', *Lublin Studies in Modern Languages and Literature*, 40/2 (2016), 82–103.
Molinero, Carme, and Pere Ysàs (eds), *Construint la ciutat democràtica: El moviment veïnal durant el tardofranquisme i la transició* (Barcelona: Icària, 2010).
Montero Cartelle, Enrique, 'Omne animal post coitum triste: De Aristóteles a S. Freud', *Revista de Estudios Latinos*, 1 (2001), 107–19.

Moskowitz, P. E., *How to Kill a City* (New York: Bold Type Books, 2018).
Mouffe, Chantal, *The Democratic Paradox* (London: Verso, 2009).
Mudde, Cas, *The Far Right Today* (Cambridge: Polity, 2019).
Mueller, Stephanie, 'Jordi Puntí's *Els castellans*: Reshaping Catalan Narratives of Immigration and Integration', *Romance Quarterly*, 67/4 (2020), 214–28.
Muñoz, José Esteban, *Disidentifications: Queers of Color and the Performance of Politics* (Minneapolis MN: University of Minneapolis Press, 1999).
Muñoz, Josep Maria, 'Julià de Jòdar o la construcció literària de la memòria', *L'Avenç*, 284 (2003), 57–65.
Muñoz Carrobles, Diego, 'Xenografías femeninas en la literatura catalana contemporánea: Laia Karrouch y Najat El Hachmi, integración e identidad', *Revista de Lenguas y Literaturas Catalana, Gallega y Vasca*, 22 (2017), 207–20.
Muñoz Jofre, Ferran, 'Més enllà del Pijoaparte: La ciutat dels marges', *L'Avenç*, 485 (2021), 47–52.
Murray, N. Michelle, 'Migration and Genealogies of Rupture in the Work of Najat El Hachmi', *Research in African Literatures*, 48/3 (2017), 18–32.
Nancy, Jean-Luc, 'La existencia exiliada', *Archipiélago: Cuadernos de crítica de la cultura*, 26–7 (1996), 34–40.
Nopca, Jordi, 'Jordi Puntí: M'indigna el que és políticament correcte', *Ara* (17 March 2011), https://llegim.ara.cat/actualitat/jordi-punti-mindigna-que-politicament-correcte_1_2996513.html.
Nora, Pierre (dir.), *Essais d'ego-histoire* (Paris: Gallimard, 1987).
Oliver, Maria Antònia, *Cròniques d'un mig estiu* (Barcelona: Club Editor, 2006 [1970]).
Ollé, Manel, 'Els de Can Garcia', *L'Avenç*, 367 (2011), 56.
Oyón, José Luis, and Borja Iglesias, 'Les barraques i l'infrahabitatge en la construcció de Barcelona, 1914–1950', in Mercè Tatjer i Cristina Larrea (eds), *Barraques: La Barcelona informal del segle XX* (Barcelona: Ajuntament de Barcelona, 2010), pp. 23–36.
Pagès Jordà, Vicenç, 'Una mirada convincent', *El Periódico de Catalunya* (28 September 2016), 59.
Panera Martínez, Pedro, '"Endavant, catalans!": Voluntarios de Cataluña para la guerra de África (1859–1860)', *Revista Digital Guerra Colonial*, 1 (2017), 89–107.
Parés i Cuadras, Betlem, 'El Pla de Millora del Barri de l'Erm, una oportunitat per a la cohesió social', in *Osona: La cohesió social* (Manlleu: Fundació Antiga Caixa Manlleu, 2020), pp. 51–62.
Parés i Cuadras, Betlem, and Mariona Casas Deseures, 'L'Experiència del barri de l'Erm de Manlleu', *Ausa*, 22/159 (2007), 59–71.
Parramon, Clara Carme, '*Els altres catalans*: Entusiasme i pertorbació a la Catalunya dels anys seixanta', in Andreu Domingo (ed.), *Recerca i immigració VII: Migracions dels segles XX i XXI: Una mirada candeliana* (Barcelona: Generalitat de Catalunya, 2015), pp. 219–35.

— 'El debat català sobre la immigració durant el franquisme: Integració social i adaptació cultural', *Cercles: Revista d'Història Cultural*, 18 (2015), 43–60.
Pàmies, Teresa, 'El reportatge triomfant', *Avui* (14 November 1994), 72.
Peñarrubia, Bel, *Mallorca davant el centralisme (1868–1910)* (Barcelona: Curial, 2006).
Pernau, Gabriel, *El somni català* (Barcelona: La Campana, 1997).
Picornell, Mercè, *Discursos testimonials en la literatura catalana recent* (Barcelona: Publicacions de l'Abadia de Montserrat, 2002).
— *Sumar les restes: Ruïnes i mals endreços en la cultura catalana postfranquista* (Barcelona: Publicacions de l'Abadia de Montserrat, 2020).
Piquer, Eva, 'Qui m'ha robat el mes d'abril?', *Ara* (10 September 2016), 45.
Pitarch Calero, Kenneth, 'Anàlisi sociodemogràfica de la migració valenciana a Catalunya i altres destinacions' (unpublished PhD thesis, Universitat Autònoma de Barcelona, 2018), *www.tdx.cat/handle/10803/663903#page=1*.
Pla, Xavier, 'Reparar el món: La literatura catalana i el procés', *Revista de Catalunya*, 301, (2018), 5–11.
— *El soldat de Baltimore: Assaigs sobre literatura i realitat en temps d'autoficció* (Palma: Lleonard Muntaner, 2022).
Pomar-Amer, Miquel, 'Voices Emerging from the Border: A Reading of the Autobiographies by Najat El Hachmi and Saïd El Kadaoui as Political Interventions', *Planeta Literatur: Journal of Global Literary Studies*, 1 (2014), 33–52.
Pons, Margalida, 'El discurs testimonial: Memòria compromesa, pràctica lectora, creació crítica', preface to Mercè Picornell, *Discursos testimonials en la literatura catalana recent* (Barcelona: Publicacions de l'Abadia de Montserrat, 2002), pp. 5–14.
Pons, Pere Antoni, 'Jordi Puntí, escriptor: Vull explicar la immigració afrontant-ne els tabús', *Diari de Balears* (21 May 2011), 3.
Puig, Jordi, 'Catalans i castellans ara fan front comú contra la nova migració', interview with Jordi Puntí, *El 9 nou* (26 March 2011), *https://el9nou.cat/osona-ripolles/cultura-i-gent/catalans-i-castellans-ara-fan-front-comu-contra-la-nova-immigracio/*.
Puig, Valentí, 'Del tracoma a la FAI', *ABC Cataluña* (25 November 1994), x.
Pujol, Jordi, *La immigració, problema i esperança de Catalunya* (Barcelona: Nova Terra, 1976).
Puntí, Jordi, *Maletes perdudes* (Barcelona: Empúries, 2010).
— *Els castellans* (Barcelona: L'Avenç, 2011).
Radatz, Hans-Ingo, '*Castellorquín*: el castellano hablado por los mallorquines', in Carsten Sinner and Andreas Wesch (eds), *El castellano en las tierras de habla catalana* (Madrid: Iberoamericana, 2008), pp. 113–32.
Rancière, Jacques, *Le partage du sensible* (Paris: La Fabrique, 2000).

—— *The Philosopher and His Poor* (Durham NC, and London: Duke University Press, 2003).
—— *The Lost Thread: The Democracy of Modern Fiction* (London: Bloomsbury, 2017).
Ricci, Cristián H., 'The Reshaping of Postcolonial Iberia: Moroccan and Amazigh Literatures in the Peninsula', *Hispanófila*, 180 (2017), 21–40.
Rich, Adrienne, 'Compulsory Heterosexuality and Lesbian Existence', *Signs: Journal of Women in Culture and Society* 1980, 5/4 (1980), 631–60.
Richardson, Nathan, *Constructing Spain: The Re-imagination of Space and Place in Fiction and Film, 1953–2003* (Lewisburg PA: Bucknell Unversity Press, 2011).
Riera, Carme, *Te deix, amor, la mar com a penyora* (Barcelona: Columna Jove, 2005 [1975]).
Rodríguez, Ileana, 'Hegemonía y dominio: Subalternidad, un significado flotante', *Estudios: Revista de Investigaciones Literarias*, 14–15 (2000), 35–50.
Römhild, Regina, 'Beyond the Bounds of the Ethnic: For Postmigrant Cultural and Social Research', *Journal of Aesthetics and Culture*, 9/2 (2017), 69–75.
—— 'Postmigrant Europe: Discoveries beyond Ethnic, National and Colonial Boundaries', in Anna Meera Gaonkar, Astrid Sophie Øst Hansen, Hans Christian Post and Moritz Schramm (eds), *Postmigration: Art, Culture, and Politics in Contemporary Europe* (Bielefeld: Transcript, 2021), pp. 45–55.
Roniger, Luis, 'Changing Cultural Landscapes under the Impact of Exile, Diasporas and Return Migration', *Araucaria*, 20/40 (2018), 185–208.
Rothstein, Richard, *The Color of Law* (New York: W. W. Norton, 2017).
de Sagarra, Josep Maria, 'Poesia murciana', *Mirador* (10 August 1933), 2.
Said, Edward, 'Representing the Colonized: Anthropology's Interlocutors', *Critical Inquiry*, 15/2 (1989), 205–25.
—— 'The Politics of Knowledge', in *Reflections on Exile and Other Literary and Cultural Essays* (London: Granta, 2000), pp. 372–85.
Sala, Toni, *Un relat de la nova immigració africana* (Barcelona: Edicions 62, 2004).
Santandreu, Jaume, *Camí de coix* (Palma: Moll, 1980).
Schmidt, Susana, 'Migraciones y exilios en la historia reciente de Argentina: Una interpretación a la luz de la teoría de espacios transnacionales', *Studia Historica: Historia contemporánea*, 28 (2010), 151–80.
Schmitt, Carl, *The Concept of the Political* (Chicago IL: University of Chicago Press, 2007).
Segarra, Marta, 'Literatures migrants: *Jo també soc catalana* de Najat el Hachmi', *Mètode: Science Studies Journal*, 4 (2014).
Sendra Ferrer, Olga, *Barcelona, City of Margins* (Toronto: University of Toronto Press, 2022).
Sentís, Carles, *Viatge en Transmiserià* (Barcelona: La Campana, 1995).

Serés, Francesc, *La pell de la frontera* (Barcelona: Quaderns Crema, 2014).
Serres, Michel, *The Parasite* (Minneapolis MN: University of Minnesota Press, 2007).
Sinca, Genís, *La providència es diu Paco: Biografia de Francesc Candel* (Barcelona: La Magrana, 2008).
Škrabec, Simona, 'El repte d'acceptar la diferència', in Gabriella Gavagnin i Víctor Martínez-Gil (eds), *Entre literatures: Hegemonia i perifèries en els processos de mediació literària* (Lleida: Punctum, 2011), pp. 43–59.
Sloterdijk, Peter, *Foams: Spheres III* (South Pasadena CA: Semiotext(e), 2016).
Som identitaris, 'Manifest Ideològic (I)', 14 March 2017, www.somidentitaris. cat/index.php/layout-1/layout-2/layout-3/layout-4/style-2/style-4/style-6/ columns--com-left-right/columns--left-com-right/columns--right-left-com/ columns–right-com-left/regions-1234/regions-1324/regions-1423/regions-4123/root/layout/manifest-idiologic-1.
Song, H. Rosi, 'Narrating Identity in Najat El Hachmi's *L'últim patriarca*', in Lucia Aiello, Joy Charnley and Mariangela Palladino (eds), *Displaced Women: Multilingual Narratives of Migration in Europe* (Newcastle: Cambridge Scholars Publishing, 2014), pp. 45–58.
Spencer, Robert, 'Contented Homeland Peace: The Motif of Exile in the Work of Edward W. Said', in Adel Iskandar and Hakem Rustom (eds), *Edward Said: A Legacy of Emancipation and Representation* (Berkeley CA, Los Angeles CA and London: University of California Press, 2010), pp. 389–413.
Spivak, Gayatri Chakravorty, 'Can the Subaltern Speak?', in Cary Nelson and Lawrence Grossberg (eds), *Marxism and the Interpretation of Culture* (Urbana IL: University of Illinois, 1988), pp. 271–313.
— *A Critique of Postcolonial Reason* (Cambridge MA.: Harvard University Press, 1999).
Steedman, Carolyn, *Landscape for a Good Woman: A Story of Two Lives* (London: Virago, 1986).
Tatjer, Mercè, 'Barraques i projectes de remodelació urbana a Barcelona, de l'Eixample al litoral (1922–1966)', in Mercè Tatjer i Cristina Larrea (eds), *Barraques: La Barcelona informal del segle XX* (Barcelona: Ajuntament de Barcelona, 2010), pp. 37–60.
Tomàs, Gabriel, *Corbs afamegats* (Palma: Nova Editorial Moll, 2020 [1972]).
Torras, Isabel, 'Emigrar: l'única sortida', *Foc nou* (January 1995), p. 32.
Traverso, Enzo, *Passats singulars: El 'jo' en l'escriptura de la història*, trans. by Gustau Muñoz (Catarroja and Barcelona: Afers, 2021).
Turner, Victor, *The Anthropology of Performance* (New York: PAJ Publications, 1988).
Vallvé i Diaigües, Xavier, *La discriminació, el racisme i la xenofòbia contra els immigrants estrangers i les minories ètniques a Catalunya* (Barcelona: Gabinet d'Estudis Socials, 2005), www.fundaciobofill.cat/publicacions/ la-discriminacio-el-racisme-i-la-xenofobia-contra-els-immigrants-estrangers-i-les.

Vandellós, Josep Antoni, *La immigració a Catalunya* (Barcelona: Altès, 1935).
— *Catalunya, poble decadent* (Barcelona: Edicions 62, 1985 [1935]).
Vargas Castro, David Andrés, 'El odio en la clínica del duelo', *Desde el jardín de Freud*, 19 (2019), 159–74.
Vázquez Montalbán, Manuel, *Barcelones* (Barcelona: Empúries, 1990).
Vicens, Antònia, *39° a l'ombra* (Barcelona: Edicions 62, 2002 [1968]).
Vicens Vives, Jaume, *Notícia de Catalunya* (Barcelona: Edicions 62, 1999 [1954/1960]).
Vilarós, Teresa, 'The Passing of the *Xarnego* Immigrant: Post-Nationalism and the Ideologies of Assimilation in Catalonia', *Arizona Journal of Hispanic Cultural Studies*, 7 (2003), 229–46.
Villatoro, Vicenç, *Un home que se'n va* (Barcelona: Proa, 2014).
Vogt, Silvana, *La mecànica de l'aigua* (Barcelona: Edicions de 1984, 2016).
Wamba Graviña, Graciela, 'Emigración e identidad cultural en la reciente narrativa argentina', *Puertas abiertas*, 6 (2010).
Waldren, Jackie, 'Crossing Over: Mixing, Matching and Marriage in Mallorca', in Rosemary Breger and Rosanne Hill (eds), *Cross-Cultural Marriage: Identity and Choice* (Oxford and New York: Routledge, 1998), pp. 33–48.
Wells, Caragh, 'The Freedom of the Aesthetic: Montserrat Roig's Use of the City in *Ramona, adéu*', *Catalan Review*, 21/1 (2007), 87–99.
Winnock, Michel, *Jeanne et les siennes* (Paris: Seuil, 2003).

Index

A
aesthetics 48–55, 131
Africa xv, xxvi
Agboton, Agnès xxviii
　Més enllà del mar de sorra xxviii
agency 120–1, 127n33
Ahmed, Sara 156, 158–9
　Strange Encounters 158–9
Ainslie, Ricardo C. 208
Akhtar, Salman 208
Al-Andalus 160
Albacete 61
Alexandre, Víctor 23
　Nosaltres, els catalans 23, 28
Algeria 184
Alibek, Pius xxviii
　Arrels nòmades xxviii
Al Jabri, Mohammed 196, 198
Almería 11
Alt Millars 107, 111, 122
Amazigh culture xxxv, 155, 156, 160, 165, 167, 171
　see also Berber; Morocco
Amazigh language 157, 160, 167, 169, 171–3, 176
　see also Berber
ambiguity 12, 14–16, 17–18, 20, 38
ambivalence 166, 176, 206, 207, 209, 214–16, 218–19, 222, 225, 228–9
　see also mourning
anarchism 36, 42

Andalusia xv–xvi, xxi, xxix, 33, 59, 145
　immigration from 99n3, 141
Andratx 62
Anzaldúa, Gloria 173, 179n38, 181
　Borderlands/La Frontera 181
Apocalypse Now 144, 145
Aragon xv–xvi, xxi, 25
　immigration from 84, 99n3
　see also Franja de Ponent
Arbúcies 22, 122, 128n37
architecture 131, 134, 136, 142
archive 47, 107, 116
Arellano-Torres, Ignacio Dionisio 229n2
Argentina xvi, xxxv, 206, 207, 214, 215, 218
　and *corralito* xxxvi, 204–5, 206, 211–12, 218
　immigration from 204–5, 218, 229n2
　military dictatorship 204
Arkoun, Mohamed 196, 197
Arnau, Pilar 4, 59, 72, 194
Aroca Mohedano, Manuela 62, 71
Arxiu Municipal Contemporani de Barcelona 107
Arxiu Municipal de Sant Martí (Barcelona) 107
Asia xv
assimilation 39, 110–11, 166, 208
asymmetry 88–9

Aub, Max 65
Audoin-Rouzeau, Stéphane 116
   Quelle histoire: Un récit de filiation 116
authority xxxi, 3–32
authorship xxxi, xxxii, 3–32
autobiography xxxiv, 5, 17–22, 107–24, 135, 142, 199, 205
autofiction 108, 119, 182, 190, 199
L'Avenç 16, 106, 107, 131

B
Badalona 33–56
   see also   Bon Pastor; Gorg-Progrés; Pont del Petroli
Balearic Islands xviii, xx
   see also Majorca
Bar Roure 122
Barbal, Maria xxviii–xxix
   Carrer Bolívia xxviii–xxix
   Pedra de tartera xxviii
Barberà del Vallès 186
Barcelona xxi, xxx, 33–4, 36, 37, 38, 73, 88, 89, 97, 99n3, 110, 120, 121, 141, 148n8, 151n33, 157, 160, 163, 204, 205–6, 213, 215, 217, 224
   Plan Comarcal de 1953 100n8
   see also Barceloneta; Camp de la Bota; Can Tunis; Canyelles; Ciutat Vella; Els Encants; Gràcia; Nou Barris; Poblenou
Barcelona Universal Exposition (1929) 33, 36
Barceloneta (Barcelona) 106
Barri de la Plata (Barcelona) 106, 109
Batista, Analía 232n27
Batista i Roca, Josep Maria 8
Bauman, Zygmunt 28
Be Negre, El 11
beginning 207
being 93, 193
   see also subjectivity

Belbel, Sergi xxix
Beller, Manfred 193
belonging xix, xxiii, 58, 76, 88, 91, 96–7, 110, 142, 172–3, 190
   and Moroccan migrants xxviii, 172–3, 189, 199
   to literary tradition xxxi, 166
Benet, Josep 12
Benigànim 115–16
Benjamin, Walter xxxiii, 41, 43–6, 52, 53
   'The Storyteller' 44, 45
   Theses on the Philosophy of History 41, 43–4, 45, 52
Berber *see* Amazigh culture; Amazigh language
Besòs river 33, 36, 37, 38, 42, 46, 47
Bhabha, Homi 16, 67, 91, 93–4, 95, 168
   The Location of Culture 67, 93–4
Bildungsroman 35, 142
biopolitics xxxv, 130, 131, 142–3, 147
   see also immunity
blood 174
Bon Pastor (Badalona) 36
Boothby, Richard 231n26
border xxviii, xxxiv, xxxvi, 25–6, 38, 81, 84, 88, 89–90, 95, 130, 134, 136, 139, 141–2, 143, 176, 179n38, 181–201
Bordetas, Ivan 141, 151n33, 152n42
Boulanger, Ghislaine 208
boundaries *see* border
Bourdieu, Pierre 135
Bourland Ross, Catherine 165
Braidotti, Rosi 25
Bromley, Roger xix
Brunet, Manuel 7
Buenos Aires 205–6, 213, 214, 223
Bulgaria 26
bullfighting 3, 109, 122, 126n16, 127n26

Index

C
Cabot, Just 7, 8
Cabré, Anna xv–xvi, xxv, xxvii
  El sistema català de reproducció xv–xvi, xxv, xxvii
Cabrera, Lluís xxxixn26
Cairo 197
Camp de la Bota (Barcelona) 40, 46, 47, 56n15
Campalans, Rafael 149n11
Canadell Rusiñol, Roger xxxvi
Candel, Francesc xxx, xxxiv, 81–101, 119–20, 125n14, 133–4, 144
  and Catalan identity 14–15, 82–4, 85, 88–90, 92, 95–9, 133
  and Catalan language 85–6, 89, 90, 92
  and citizenship 97, 98
  and community 88, 89, 95–6, 98, 102n23
  Els altres catalans xxi, xxiii, xxxii, 6–7, 12–16, 28, 73, 81–101, 132–4, 144–5, 149n14
  Els altres catalans, vint anys després 15
  'El amazacotamiento' 103n30
  'Barraques de la Riera Comtal' 103n28
  Barrio 91, 93, 98, 103n29
  ¡Dios, la que se armó! 102n26, 103n28
  Donde la ciudad cambia su nombre 81, 82, 85–6, 89, 89, 90, 91–2, 93, 95, 98, 102n19, 103n29
  Han matado a un hombre, han roto un paisaje 81, 89, 93, 102n29
  immigrants as protagonist 84, 90, 92
  subjective vs. objective style 13–14, 90–2, 98
Can Garcia (Manlleu) 129, 130, 135, 136, 137, 138–40, 141, 143, 144, 146–7
Can Mateu (Manlleu) 135
Can Tunis (Barcelona) 102n26
Canyelles (Barcelona) 148n8
Cañete, Carlos 179n18
capitalism 39, 43, 54, 97, 137, 144, 145–6, 147, 147n5
Cardús, Salvador xvii, xxi, xxvi–xxvii, xxxviii
  immigration as a memory place 47
  metaphor of grafting 194
  roots as metaphor of identity xxvi, xxxviii, 194, 229
  skin as a metaphor of identity xxvi–xxvii
  'The Memory of Immigration in Catalan Nationalism' xvii, xxi, xxvi-xxvii, 65, 75, 98, 121, 132
  Tres metàfores per a un país amb futur xxvi–xxvii, xxxviii, 194, 229
Carolingian Empire 160
Carranza, Ernest xln34
Carrère, Emmanuel 125n10
Cărtărescu, Mircea 125n10
Casa Regional de Murcia y Albacete 8, 11
Casademont Falguera, Xavier 152n42
Casas Altas 89
Castellano, Margarida xln34, 4, 30n4, 127n27
  Les altres catalanes 127n27
castellans 135–6, 139–40, 142, 144, 145, 148n8
  see also Puntí, Jordi; Spanish-speaking immigration
Castelló 107, 110, 111, 116
Castile 135
Castile-La Mancha xviii, 58
Catalan culture 101n10, 124
  subordinate position of xvi–xvii, xxxi, 120–1, 167
Catalan Eugenics Society 8

Catalan identity xvii, xxi–xxiii, xxiv, 14–15, 83, 84, 88, 95–8, 99n3, 122, 147, 167, 224, 288–9
  ambivalence towards 166
  as threatened 21, 84, 101n13, 229
  definitions of xxiv, xxvii, 102n14, 132–3, 148n11
  Majorca 57–78
  metaphors of xxvi–xxviii, 194, 229
  Valencia 107, 116
Catalan language xvi–xviii, xxiv–xxv, 57–8, 59, 72–6, 120–1, 124, 166
  and identity 58, 73–4
  bilingualism 112
  diglossia 72
  status 160
Catalan literature 157
  and Argentine immigration 205
  and definitions of authorship xxxi
  and Spanish-speaking immigration xx–xxii, xxiii, xxv–xxvi, xxviii–xxx, 57–76
  canon 155, 156, 166, 169, 177
  critical responses to immigration xxx-xxxi, 4–5
  documentation of the past 121–2
  lack of representations of immigration xvi–xvii, xxv, 121–2, 123, 170, 205
  linguistic boundaries 3–4
  representations of the city 121–2
  vitality of xxxi
  writers of foreign origin xxviii, xxxi, 157, 205, 206
Catalan nationalism xxiv, xxvii–xxviii, 75, 81, 100n10, 132, 137, 150n20
Catalonia 73, 81, 106, 132, 134, 160, 167, 206, 214
  as land of passage xxii–xxiii
  as nation xvi
  as stateless nation xix–xx
  country of immigrants xvii, xxvi, 98, 122, 124, 134, 194
  impact of immigration xv–xviii, 132, 134
Cela, Camilo José 63
censorship 93
Centre d'Arts Santa Mònica 106
Centre de Cultura Contemporània de Barcelona (CCCB) 106
Centre d'Estudis Demogràfics 105
Cercas, Javier 108
Chambers, Iain 189
childhood xxxv, 16–21, 22, 23, 27, 131, 135–9, 140, 142
Choukri, Mohamed 196
Chraïbi, Driss 196, 198
  The Simple Past 198
Christianity 43
Círculo de Lectores 118
citizenship xxxvi, 39, 81, 95, 95–8, 122
city 82–99, 93n3, 131, 140–1, 217
Ciutat Vella (Barcelona) 150n24
class 33–5, 39, 42, 52, 55, 61–4, 66–7, 70, 135, 143, 146
Codina, Núria 167
Cold War 137, 145
collage 125n13
Col·legi de Periodistes de Catalunya 11
Colom, Antoni 68
Colom, Joan 76
  Somnis compartits: La identitat mallorquina a debat 76
Colom-Montero, Guillem xviii, xxv, xxxviii, 78n28
Comissions Obreres (CCOO) 135, 143, 150n20
commodification 114, 122, 145
community 83, 88, 113, 130, 136, 143, 158, 208

Index

Company, Flavia 205
Confederación Nacional del Trabajo (CNT) xxi, 42
conflict xvii, xix, xx, xxviii, xxix, xxxi, xxxvii, 3, 20, 23–4, 29, 35, 38, 84, 98, 120, 134–5, 145, 184–5, 187, 200, 207, 215, 223
  see also immigration; representations of immigration
Córdoba xxix, 21
Cornellà de Llobregat 132, 148n8
Coronil, Fernando 6
cosmopolitanism 39
COVID-19 147
Crameri, Kathryn 149n11
Cruells, Manuel 12
  Els no catalans i nosaltres 12
Crumbaugh, Justin 65, 68
Cuito, Amadeu 4, 22

D

Darici, Katiuscia 4, 30n4
Dasca, Maria xxiii, xxxi, xxxixn19, 4, 52n2, 127n28
death 224, 226, 232n26
death drive 221
debt 216, 218, 220
Deer Hunter, The 144
dehumanisation 64
Deleuze, Gilles 6, 145, 152n44
  The Fold 152n44
Delgado, Manuel 85, 86, 93, 94
demography xv–xvii, xxv, 58–9, 105–6, 134
depersonalisation 162
Derrida, Jacques 39
  Of Hospitality 39
desarrollismo 58, 132, 136
  see also Francoism
desire xxix, xxxvi, 159, 165, 169, 170, 178, 185, 189, 207, 208, 210–11, 212, 213, 219, 220, 223–5, 228–9

  see also homosexuality; lesbianism; sexuality; subjectivity
detachment 226
deterritorialisation 145
Díaz, Miguel 7–8
difference 20–2, 67–8, 71, 92, 136, 159, 165, 178, 181
  see also differentiation
differentiation 165, 181
discontinuity 43, 99n4
disidentification xx, xxxv, xxxvi, 155, 165–7, 168–78, 207, 215
  see also identification
dislocation xxxi, xxxv, xxxvi, 99n4, 182, 199, 208
dissociation 162–3, 208, 227
Domingo, Andreu xv–xviii, xxvi, xxvii–xxviii, 4, 12, 84, 100n10, 102n15, 105, 148n11
  Catalunya al mirall de la immigració xv–xviii, xxvi, xxvii–xxviii, 12, 148n11
Dowling, Andrew 150n20

E

eastern Europe xv, xxvi
EFE 11
ego 209
  see also identification; mourning; subjectivity
ego-history xxxiv, 108, 110, 113–19, 121, 122, 124
Eivissa 64
El Hachmi, Najat xxviii, xxx, xxxiv, 81, 82, 83, 84, 99n4, 102n14, 127n27, 134, 149n14, 155–80, 191, 194
  and Catalan identity 166–7
  and Catalan language 157–8
  and Catalan literature 166, 168–78
  and disidentification 165–77, 168–78

and intertextuality 158, 165, 168–78
and mother-daughter relationship 169–77
and rewriting 169
and writing 158, 162, 164–5, 172–3, 174, 176–7, 178
as immigrant writer 157
Jo també soc catalana xxviii, 191
La filla estrangera xxxv–xxxvi, 127n27, 155–80
L'últim patriarca xxviii, 127n27, 157, 166
Mare de llet i mel xxviii, 163–4
see also Amazigh culture; Amazigh language
El Kadaoui, Saïd xxviii, xxx–xxxi, 181–203
and autofiction 182, 190, 195, 199
and dialogics 184
and Catalan identity 190
and European identity 184, 187–8
and literature 192, 193, 196–8
and Moroccan identity 189, 197
and North African literature 196–7
and sexuality 125–6
and transgression 182
and writing 183, 192–3, 200–1
Cartes al meu fill xxviii, 190–1, 192–3, 195
Límites y fronteras 190–1, 192
No xxxvi, 181–203
see also Morocco
emotion 116–18, 119, 122
emptiness 185, 207, 225, 228–9
Encants, Els (Barcelona) 46
encounter 158–9
l'Erm (Manlleu) 129, 130–1, 138–9, 141, 143, 144, 145, 150n30
Ernaux, Annie 119, 125n10
eroticism 175

see also desire; sexuality
Esposito, Roberto xxxv, 130, 131, 136, 140, 146
Esquerra Republicana de Catalunya (ERC) 129–30
estrangement 167, 172
eugenics 84
everyday life 82
exile 34, 181–2, 190, 193, 204–5, 228
Extremadura xviii, 57, 58

F
Fabra, Pompeu 8
false consciousness 135
family 136, 200, 207
Fanon, Frantz 168
fascism 44
fatherhood 188–9, 191
Federación Anarquista Ibérica (FAI) 42
feminism 120, 156, 169
Fernàndez, Josep-Anton xvii, xxxvi–xxxvii, xxxixn18, xxxixn27, xln35, 4, 100n4, 101n12, 123, 132–3, 166
El malestar en la cultura catalana xvii, xxxvi–xxxvii, 123, 132–3
Fernández Parrilla, Gonzalo 179n18
Ferran de Pol, Lluís xxiii
Ferrando, Mireia 206
Feu Gelis, Jordi 152n42
fiction 17, 119–23, 134, 135, 139, 183, 192, 193, 198–201
fixity 215, 217, 219
Flesler, Daniela 159–60
Folkart, Jessica 100n4
Football Club Barcelona 18, 137, 145
forasters xviii, xxxiii, 57–78
foreigners 38–9, 58, 158, 173
foreignness 156, 159
see also otherness
forgetting 107, 166, 176

see also memory
Forns, Albert 221, 230n5
Forns, Josep Maria 160
   La piel quemada 160
Foucault, Michel 6, 50–1
   'Of Other Spaces' 50–1
   The Order of Things 51
Fraga, Manuel 65
France xv, 184
Francès, Josep M. 127n28
   Retorn al sol 127n28
Franco, Francisco xxiii
Francoism xviii, xxiii–xxiv, xxxv, 12, 34, 35, 37, 42, 47, 52, 58–9, 62, 65, 71, 72, 74–5, 81, 83, 89, 93, 99n3, 100n9, 117, 118, 120, 124, 132, 144
   urban planning under 140–1, 152n42
Franja de Ponent (Aragon) 25
Freud, Sigmund xxxvi, 136, 207, 208–9, 225
   'Beyond the Pleasure Principle' 231n24
   'The Ego and the Id' 231n15
   'Mourning and Melancholia' 208–9
Frontera, Guillem xxx, xxxviii, 60, 66
   Els carnissers 60, 68–9
Fuss, Diana 209
Fuster, Joan 12, 75
   Nosaltres, els valencians 12, 75

G
Gabancho, Patrícia xxviii, 150n24, 205
   La neta d'Adam xxviii
   Sobre la immigració 150n24
Garrido, Àlex 130
gaze 82, 187
gender xxv, xxix, xxx, xxxii, xxxv, 68, 116–17, 120, 124, 127n28, 127n33, 155–78

genealogy 96, 166
Ghulam, Nadia 127n27
   El secret del meu turbant 127n27
Gilabert, Joan J. 102n15
Ginard, David 71
Ginieniewicz, Jorge 230n2
Girona 183
Glissant, Édouard 158
Global South 145
Gorg-Progrés (Badalona) 23
Goytisolo, Juan 65
Gràcia (Barcelona) 22, 107, 108, 113, 122
Grass, Günter 53
Great Replacement theory 131, 147n5
   see also immigration
Greenwich Village (New York) 141
Guia Conca, Aitana xxxi, xln34, 4, 30n4
Guillamon, Julià xxiii, xxix, xxx, xxxiv, xxxixn19, 4, 7, 17, 21, 22, 28, 106, 107–24
   and autobiography 107–24
   and autofiction 119
   and ego-history 113–24
   as narcissistic historian 110, 115, 123
   El barri de la Plata 21–2, 32n39, 107–24
   El tren de la bruixa 107, 122
   La ciutat interrompuda 121
Guinea 26

H
habitus 135–6, 137
Hall, Jacqueline 101n13
Hamilton, Sarah R. 152n42
Harvey, David 131, 144
Heidegger, Martin 93, 193
heterotopia 51
hierarchy 168, 178
Hirsch, Marianne 108, 116
   Family Frames 108

historical materialism 42–4
historicism 38, 44, 47, 52
historiography xxxii–xxxiii, xxxiv, 108, 113–19
  see also ego-history
history 42–5, 52, 113–15, 119–23, 207
  see also ego-history
Hita, Victòria 13
Holston, James 96, 97
homophobia 168
homosexuality 64, 167–8
  see also lesbianism; sexuality; subjectivity
homosociality 155
L'Hospitalet de Llobregat 8, 145
  see also Torrassa, La
housing 99n3, 131, 137, 140, 143, 146, 149n14, 151n33, 152n42
  see also tower block; urban planning
Hron, Madelaine 208
humiliation 186–7

I
identification xx, xxxv, xxxvi, 123, 139, 165, 167–8, 207–9, 215, 216, 228–9
  see also disidentification
identity 83, 88, 98, 182–5, 228–9
  and biopolitics 130
  and space 85–9, 89–95, 100n8
  and time 95–6, 99n4
  forgetting of 107
  metaphors of xxvi, xxxviii, 194
  see also Catalan identity; immigration; representations of immigration
ideological State apparatuses 142
Iglesias, Borja 99n3
Iglesias Amorín, Alfonso 179n21
Imazighen people *see* Amazigh culture
immigrant nostalgia 208

immigration
  ambivalence towards xxii–xxiv, xxxviii, 16
  and agency 85, 90, 95
  and assimilation 110–11, 113, 137, 166, 208
  and Catalan language xvi–xvii, xxiii–xxv, xxvii, 58–9, 72–6, 85–6, 90, 101n13
  and Catalan identity 14–15, 66–7, 83–4, 90, 97–8, 101n13, 122, 132–3, 148n11, 194, 224, 228–9
  and Catalan nationalism xxii, xxiv, xxv, 75, 81, 100n10
  and class 33–5, 39, 52, 55, 62–4, 66, 135, 146
  and citizenship 39, 81, 95, 95–8
  and conflict xix–xx, xxii, xxiv, xxxi, 17, 71, 84, 95–8, 134, 184
  and demography xvi, xxv, 58–9, 134–5, 160
  and gender xxv, 116–17, 155–78
  and hybridity xxii–xxiii, 92, 25, 92
  and identity xxxiv–xxxviii, 66–7, 83, 85, 90, 91, 122, 187, 194, 208, 228–9
  and industrialisation xv
  and integration xxiii–xxiv, xxv, xxviii, xxix, 38, 52, 76, 84, 88, 92, 106–7, 121–2, 124, 128n37, 137–8, 148n11, 194
  and loss xxxvi–xxxviii, 206, 214–15, 216–29
  and memory xxvi, xxviii–xxx, xxxiv, xxxviii, 16, 20, 21–2, 35, 43, 44–6, 83, 106, 107, 110, 121–2, 137
  and mourning xxxvi–xxxviii, 206, 207–9, 228–9
  and national identity xvii, xx, xxii, xxiv, xxvi–xxviii, 75–6

and nationalism 160
and nostalgia 208
and segregation 132, 137–8, 140, 142, 147, 150n24, 150n30
and sexuality xxix, xxxvi, 68–9
and social change xxxiii, 59, 67, 137
and social exclusion 57–78
and suffering 208
and time 99n4
and urban space xxxiii–xxxv, 33–5, 81–2, 83, 85–8, 89–95, 96–7, 131–3, 135–6, 137
and vulnerability 61–3
as foundational myth xvii, xxii–xxiii, xxvi, 98
as hereditary condition 138
control of 100n9
dehumanisation of immigrants 64
discourses on xxi–xxx, xxxvii–xxxviii, 75–6, 84, 88, 94, 100n10, 134
history of xv–xviii, xx–xxi, xxx, 111, 159–60
invisibility of xxvi, 91, 95–6, 109–10, 123, 132
metaphors of contamination and infection xxi, 66
mixed marriages 120–1, 124
prejudices against 17–18, 59, 62–3, 66, 94, 101n10, 127n28
seen as invasion xxii, 67, 84, 101n13, 130–1, 134, 143–4, 145, 147n5, 160
see also biopolitics; immunity; representations of immigration
immunity xxxv, 130–1, 139–40, 142–3, 146–7
see also biopolitics
incest 157, 169
inculcation 135–6, 146
individuation 114
inheritance 168, 174

Institut du Monde Arabe 197
integration 38, 76, 84, 88, 92, 94, 106–7, 110, 121–2, 124, 128n37
interstice 81, 82, 84, 89–95, 103n29
intertextuality xxxv–xxxvi, 155–80, 190–8
intimacy 156, 174
Iribarren, Teresa xxxiv
Islam 184, 196, 197
Islamophobia 160–1, 166, 170

J
Jablonka, Ivan 114, 117, 122, 124
 History Is a Contemporary Literature 114, 124
Jacobs, Jane 141
Jaén 63
jaeneros 63, 70
Jamal, Salah xxviii
 Lluny de l'horitzó perfumat xxviii
Jirafa, La 12, 144
Jòdar, Julià de xxix, xxx, xxxii–xxxiii, 33–56
and class 33, 42, 54, 55
and history 38, 41, 43–5, 47, 52, 55
and memory 35, 45–6, 52
and narrative coherence 38
and narrative voice 35
and neighbourhoods 33–5, 36–7
and progress 38–9, 42–3, 45, 52
and space 50–2
and time 41, 45–6, 48, 50, 53–4
 L'àngel de la segona mort 33, 34, 36, 39, 42–8, 52
 L'atzar i les ombres 33–56
 El metall impur 33, 34, 42, 46, 47
 El trànsit de les fades 33, 34, 42, 47, 54
 Els vulnerables 36, 37
Jordà, Joan-Pau 76

Somnis compartits: La identitat mallorquina a debat 76
jouissance 213, 221
journalism 7–12, 13

K
Kabbal, Maati 199
Kant, Immanuel 39
Karrouch, Laila xxviii, 127n27, 166, 194
  De Nador a Vic xxviii, 127n27
King, Stewart xln37
Kristeva, Julia 158
  Strangers to Ourselves 158
Kureishi, Hanif 195, 197

L
Laâbi, Abdellatif 196
Lacan, Jacques 16, 225, 231n26
  Anxiety; The Seminar of Jacques Lacan: Book X 231n26
lack 231n26
Laclau, Ernesto xxxviii
language 193, 224
Laroui, Abdellah 198
Latin America xxvi
  immigration from 159–60
  see also Argentina
Laufer, Laurie xxxvi, 207, 210
  L'énigme du deuil 210, 212–13, 216–17, 222–3, 224, 227
Leader, Darian xxxvi, 207, 209–10, 214, 221
  The New Black 209–10, 214, 216, 221, 225
Le Corbusier (Charles-Édouard Jeanneret) 140–1
Leersen, Joep 193
Leibniz, Gottfried Wilhelm 152n44
Lejeune, Philippe 199
lesbian continuum 155
lesbianism 155, 168–9, 170
  see also homosexuality; sexuality

Levi, Primo 198
libido 209
liminality 38, 134, 142, 156
limit xxxvi, 21, 25, 36–7, 82, 89, 171, 181, 187, 199, 201
literalisation 169, 171, 175, 178
literature 157–8, 161, 187, 191–2, 196–9
Lorde, Audre xxxvi, 156, 165, 166, 169
  Sister Outsider 156, 168
Losada, Josep 7
loss xxxvi–xxxviii, 173, 206, 209–10, 214–17, 220–9
  see also mourning; separation; subjectivity

M
Madrid 40, 73, 141, 195
Maghreb 122
  immigration from 137, 138, 140, 158, 160
  see also Morocco
Magnússon, Sigurður Gylfi 119
Magris, Claudio 187
Majorca xviii, xxv, xxx, 57–78
  Majorcan identity 57–78
  Majorcan Generation of the 1970s xxxiii, 57–78
  see also Frontera, Guillem; Oliver, Maria Antònia; Santandreu, Jaume; Tomàs, Guillem; Vicens, Antònia
Maluquer, Concepció G. xxiii
Manent, Marià 118
  El vel de Maia 118
Manlleu xxxv, 21, 129, 131–47
  see also Can Garcia; Can Mateu; l'Erm
Marca Hispànica 160
Marçal, Maria Mercè xxxvi, 155, 159, 164–5, 169, 170–1, 173–4
  Cau de llunes 170

Desglaç 165
La germana, l'estrangera 156, 164, 168–9, 171–2, 173–4
La passió segons Renée Vivien 170
Marcillas-Piquer, Isabel xxxi, xln34, 4, 29n4
marginality 192
Marín, Martí xxiv, 100n9
Marrakech 187
Marsé, Juan 35
Martínez, Francisco 148n8
Martínez-Gil, Víctor 28
Marxism 44, 150n20
masculinity 120
Masferrer, Mariona 23
  Origen: Tambakunda 23
Masoliver Ródenas, J. A. 206
Mataró 134
Matas-Pons, Àlex xxxii
Mayol, Gabriel 76
  Somnis compartits: La identitat mallorquina a debat 76
melancholia 209
  see also mourning
Melià, Josep 75
  Els mallorquins 75
memory xxvi, xxviii–xxx, xxxiv, xxxviii, 16, 20, 21–2, 35, 43, 45–7, 106, 107, 114, 119, 137, 209, 211, 222–3, 228
  see also immigration; mourning; postmemory
Mendoza, Eduardo 35
Mernissi, Fatima 196
metanarrative 138
micropolitics 108, 120, 124
migrant literature xix, xxx
Milans del Bosch, Joaquim 36
Minca, Carlo 149n17
Mirador xxi, 4
Miró, Asha 127n27
  Rastres de sàndal 127n27
miscegenation xxii–xxiii
Miserachs, Xavier 82, 83, 95, 98
misrecognition 136
Mokhtari, Fizia Hayette 196
Mokkedem, Malika 187, 196, 197, 198
  Les hommes qui marchent 198
  L'interdite 184
Molinero, Carme 102n20
Monzó, Quim 115–16
Moors 18, 138, 160
moriscos 159
Morocco xxxv, 156–7, 167, 181, 192, 194, 201
  immigration from 158–61, 162, 166, 181–203
  see also Maghreb, Rif
Morón, Pedro xxxixn26
Moses, Robert 140, 141
Moskowitz, P. E. 148n6
Mossos d'Esquadra 27
mother-daughter relationship 169–77
Mouffe, Chantal 134, 149n15
mourning xxxvi–xxxviii, 206–29, 230n14
  and ambivalence 207, 209, 214–16, 219, 225, 228
  and debt 216, 218, 220
  and desire 223–4
  and identification 209, 218, 228
  and loss 206–7, 209, 220–9, 231n26
  and memory 211, 222–3, 228
  and representation 214, 221, 220–9
  and sacrifice 216–17, 225
  and temporality 21–13, 219–20
  and trauma 206, 212
  dialogue of mournings 207, 210, 214–20, 228–9
  Freud on 208–9
  social dimension 207, 210, 216–17
  work of 207, 209, 219, 221, 225

Mudde, Cas 130–1
Mueller, Stephanie 142, 145
multiculturalism xxxi, 94
Muñoz Carrobles, Diego 4, 29n4
Muñoz, José Esteban xxxv, 155, 159, 167–8
Muñoz, Josep Maria 56n15
Muñoz Jofre, Ferran 39
Murcia xv–xvi, xxi, 7–11, 33, 63, 71, 145
   immigration from 7–11, 99n3, 141
murcianos xxi, 8, 63, 84, 111, 125n14
Murray, Michelle 160, 166
Museu del Ter 147
muslims 159

N
Nancy, Jean-Luc 190
narcissism 114, 225
narcissistic historian 108, 110, 123
narcissistic novelist 108
Narcissus 123, 142
narrative 20, 38, 39, 46, 54, 90, 92, 95, 114, 115, 119, 156, 207, 224, 228
narrative voice 35, 45–6, 108, 114, 211, 227
   see also representations of immigration
nation 81, 87, 88, 94, 96, 139, 145
national identity xxxvii–xxxviii, 81, 94
   see also Catalan identity; Catalan nationalism
nationalism 130, 145, 160
   see also Catalan nationalism; Spanish nationalism
negation 130, 185, 214
negativity xxxviii, 130, 187
neighbourhoods 33–6, 42, 48, 52, 54, 82–98, 106–24, 131–47
   see also architecture; city; urban planning

neoliberalism 114
New York 140
Nigeria 26
Nopca, Jordi 149n16
Nora, Pierre 108, 114
normalisation xvii, xxiii, xxv, xxxii, 138
Nou Barris (Barcelona) 148n8

O
objet petit a 225
Occitania xv
Olid, Bel xxix
   Una terra solitària xxix
Oliver, Maria Antònia xxx, xxxiii, 60, 72
   Cròniques d'un mig estiu 60, 72–3
Ollé, Manel 138
Olot 152n42
Onda 122
opacity 158
oral language *see* orality
oral tradition *see* orality
orality 166, 172, 178
origin xxvi, xxx, xxxi, xxxii, xxxvii–xxxviii, 5, 12, 88, 91, 94, 124, 194, 229
othering *see* otherness
otherness xix, xxi, xxiii, xxxi, 5–6, 12, 16, 19–20, 24–6, 57–8, 62–3, 66–72, 130, 138, 140, 142, 159, 173, 181, 185–9, 225
   and language 72–6
outside 130, 131, 136, 137, 143, 145, 152n44, 156, 162–3, 167, 182
Oyón, José Luis 99n3

P
Pagès Jordà, Vicenç 206
Pakistan 140
Pàmies, Sergi 125n10
Pàmies, Teresa 7
Panera Martínez, Pedro 179n21

parasitism xxxv, 139, 146
Parés i Cuadras, Betlem 140, 151n30
Parramon, Clara Carme 101n3, 102n15, 102n19
participation 97–8, 102n20
past xix, xxvi, 17, 21–2, 29, 41, 43, 96, 107–8, 114–15, 116, 118, 121–3, 163, 177, 194, 211, 214, 215, 217
patriarchy 166
performance 155
Pernau, Gabriel 23
　El somni català 23, 28
Picornell, Mercè xxi–xxii, xxxii, 32n40, 199
　Discursos testimonials en la literatura catalana recent 199–200
pilota 110
Piquer, Eva 230n5
Pitarch, Kenneth 105, 106, 107, 122
Pla, Josep 4
Pla, Xavier 108, 122, 124, 125n10, 128n34
　El soldat de Baltimore 108, 125n10
place xxxviii, 93, 109, 123, 140, 146, 147, 190, 191–3, 210, 225, 228
Plan Nacional de Estabilización Económica 58, 136
　see also Francoism
Planes de Desarrollo Social y Económico 136
　see also Francoism
Poblenou (Barcelona) 22, 34, 47, 106–24, 125n10
　see also Barri de la Plata
Pomar-Amer, Miquel 4, 30n4, 178n4
Pons, Margalida 200
Pons, Pere Antoni 19, 20
Pont del Petroli (Badalona) 50
populism 131
Porcel, Baltasar 125n10

Porcioles, Josep Maria de 99n3
postcolonialism xxxi, 156, 159
postmemory 108, 116
postmigration xviii–xix, xxviii, xxxv
postmodernism 119
power 67, 131, 135–6, 145, 169, 178
Premi Ciutat de Barcelona 127n27
Premi Ciutat de Palma de novel·la 62, 64, 66
Premi Columna Jove 127n27
Premis Gaudí de Cinema 127n27
Premi Joan Fuster d'assaig 127n27
Premi Prudenci Bertrana 127n27
Premi Ramon Llull 127n27, 157
Premi Sant Joan 127n27
Premi Sant Jordi de novel·la 60
presence 93, 98
Primo de Rivera, Miguel 36
progress 42–3, 48, 52, 54
psychoanalysis 198, 199, 207, 208–29
Puig, Jordi 17, 151n30
Puig, Valentí 7
Pujol, Jordi xxiv–xxv, 102n14, 132, 146n11
Puntí, Jordi xxix, xxx, xxxv, 7, 16–22, 131–52
　and autobiography 135, 142
　and *Bildungsroman* 142
　and childhood 135–9
　and otherness 130, 135–6, 138, 139–40, 142, 144
　Els castellans 16–22, 28, 131–52
　Maletes perdudes 148n8
Pygmalion xxv

Q
queer see homosexuality
Qur'an 197

R
racism xvii, 31n19, 156, 157, 160–1, 162, 166, 170, 178, 183, 208

Radatz, Hans-Ingo 73, 75
Ràdio Barcelona 11
Raimon (Ramon Pelejero) xxxviii, 229
Rancière, Jacques xxxiii, 51, 52, 53–5
  The Distribution of the Sensible 51, 54
  The Lost Thread 51
  The Philosopher and His Poor 54, 55
Rapoport, Amos 86
Real Madrid 18, 137
recognition 122, 123, 208
reconciliation 165, 176
Rendé, Joan 115
reparation 108, 114, 116, 120, 121
repetition 206, 207, 221–3
  see also mourning; subjectivity
representation 6, 51, 88, 95, 193, 210, 214, 220–9
representations of immigration xxx–xxxii
  and aesthetics xxxii–xxxiii, 63, 82, 138
  and authorship xxxii, 108–24, 115, 124, 166
  and authorial point of view 7–12, 82, 108, 115, 124
  and autobiography 107–24, 135, 196, 205
  and autofiction 181–2, 190, 195
  and class 39, 42, 52, 60, 61–4, 66, 70, 135
  and conflict xxviii, xxix, 20, 22, 35, 84, 98, 113, 120, 134–5, 145, 184, 187, 200
  and difference 20–2, 70–1, 72–3, 92
  and intertextuality xxxv–xxxvi, 155–80, 184, 190–8
  and literary form 220–1, 227
  and literary genres 5–29, 35, 91, 107, 108, 113–19, 126n17, 142
  and marginality 192
  and memory xxxiv–xxxv, 35, 43, 45–9, 83, 107, 109–10, 119, 137, 142
  and mourning 214–29
  and political correctness 18–19, 134
  and sexuality 163, 169, 188
  and space xxviii, xxxiii–xxxv, 33–5, 82, 83, 85–6, 95–6, 135–6, 139, 142, 146–7, 161
  and stereotypes 9–11, 18, 35, 60, 66, 88, 94, 166, 184–5, 186–7, 206
  and time 38, 43–4, 51–2, 95–6, 99n4, 118
  and transgression 182, 206, 213, 217
  and visibility 91, 95–6, 170
  as invasion 134, 143–4, 145
  as parasitic 139, 143–4
  author as mediator of migrants' voices 21–2, 82, 91–2, 113
  mixed marriages 119–20, 124
  narrative voice 35, 45–6, 72–3, 82, 90–2, 107–8, 118, 142, 146, 184, 189, 191, 227
  narratives of integration 70–2, 75–6, 84–5, 92–3, 121–3, 124, 128n37, 137–8
  progressive narratives 38–9, 42–3
  verisimilitude 10–11, 21–2
  labels to categorise literary texts 4
return 201
Ricci, Cristián 157, 166–7, 180n22
Rich, Adrienne 155
Richardson, Nathan 100n9
Riera, Carme 156, 178
  'Te deix, amor, la mar com a penyora' 156, 168–9, 174–7, 178
Riera, Marta xxxivn26
Rif (Morocco) 156
Río de la Plata 223

Index

Ripoll, Maria 127n27
   Rastres de sàndal 127n27
Rodoreda, Mercè 126n18, 155
   La plaça del Diamant 126n18, 155
Rodríguez, Ileana 29
Roig, Montserrat xxv–xxvi
   L'òpera quotidiana xxv–xxvi
   Ramona, adéu 156
Römhild, Regina xviii–xix
Roniger, Luis 230n2
roots *see* Cardús, Salvador; identity
Rotger, Agnès 127n27
   El secret del meu turbant 127n27
Roth, Philip 198
Rothstein, Richard 148n6

S
Sabadell 134
sacrifice 216–17, 225, 226
Sagarra, Josep Maria de 7, 8, 11
Said, Edward 16, 182, 185, 196
   Reflections on Exile 182
Sala, Toni 23, 28, 125n10
   Un relat de la nova immigració africana 23, 28
Saladrigas, Robert xxiii
Sansal, Bouamel 196
Sant Adrià del Besòs 38, 46
Santa Coloma de Gramenet 37, 38
Santa Eugènia 57
Santandreu, Jaume xxxiii, 60, 64
   Camí de coix 60, 64–5, 66, 71, 73
Schmitt, Carl 134, 149n15, 149n17
Sebald, W. G. 108
Schmidt, Susana 204–5
Second Spanish Republic 37, 89, 118
Segarra, Marta 4, 30n4
self-referentiality 110, 114, 123
Sendra-Ferrer, Olga xxi, xxiii, xxxiv, 100n6
Sentís, Carles xxi–xxii, xxx, xxxii, 6–12, 28
   critical reception 7

contemporary reactions 8
racism 31n19
   Viatge en Transmiserià xxi–xxii, xxxii, 6–12, 31n19
separation 226–9
Serés, Francesc xxix, xxx, xxxiii, 7, 22–8, 32n39, 125n10
   La pell de la frontera 7, 23–8
Serra d'Or 15
Serres, Michel xxxv, 131, 146
sexuality xxxvi, 11, 64, 67, 68–70, 155, 163, 169, 185–6
Sevilla 126n16
shame 163
Sinca, Genís 92
singularity 185
skin 25, 28, 194
   see also Cardús, Salvador
Škrabec, Simona 191–2
Sloterdijk, Peter xxxv, 143–4, 146
social space 136
Soler-Pont, Anna 127n27
   Rastres de sàndal 127n27
Solidaridad Obrera 11
Som Identitaris 129, 130–1, 147n5
Song, Rosi 157–8
sorority 173
Spain xv–xvi, xxxi, 11, 36, 58–9, 62, 63, 65, 68, 71, 84, 139, 144, 160, 204, 206, 207, 217
   internal migrations xvi, xviii, xxx, 7–20, 33–4, 99n3, 134–5
Spanish civil war xxiii, xxix, 21, 33, 34, 35, 40, 56n11, 118
Spanish identity 81
Spanish language 160
Spanish nationalism xxvii, 75, 81
Spanish-speaking immigration xx–xxi, xviii, xxv, xxviii–xxx, xxxiii, xxxv, 12–16, 16–22, 86, 134–5, 148n8
   in Majorca 58–9, 61–4, 66–9, 72–6
   see also castellans
Spencer, Robert 182

Spivak, Gayatri 5–6
Star Wars 136, 137, 138, 145
Steedman, Carolyn 116
　Landscape for a Good Woman 116
storytelling 44, 224
strangeness 158–9, 173
subalternity xvii, xxxi, 6, 29, 113–14
subjectivity xxxv–xxxviii, 25, 95–6, 108, 114, 118, 136, 142–3, 146, 174, 176, 178, 184–5, 191, 196, 199, 207, 216–17, 224, 227–8
　see also ambivalence; desire; identification, disidentification; loss; mourning; otherness; sexuality; time; transgression; trauma
Szpunberg, Victoria 205

T
Tamazight *see* Amazigh language
Tanna, Natasha xxxv–xxxvi
Tatjer, Mercè 99n3
Tele/eXprés 11
Temps, El 105–6
Terrassa xxiv, 21, 134
time 38, 41–4, 50, 51–2, 53, 95–6, 99n4, 114, 118, 210–13, 217, 219–20
Toga 107
Tomàs, Gabriel xxxiii, 60, 62
　Corbs afamegats 60, 62–4, 65, 66–7, 69–70
Torras, Isabel 7
Torrassa, La (l'Hospitalet de Llobregat) 9, 15, 145
tourism xviii, xxxiii, 58–77
tower block 96, 132, 137, 138, 140, 143
　see also housing; urban planning
trachoma xxi, 9
tradition xx, xxxi, xxxv, 46, 75, 166, 198, 215, 222

transgression xxxiv, xxxvi, 81, 88, 98, 182, 195–6, 206, 207, 213, 217
trauma xix, xxxvi, 75–6, 115, 156, 162–3, 181, 184, 206, 211–12
Traverso, Enzo xxxiv, 113–15, 116, 119, 121, 122, 124
　Singular Pasts 108, 113–15, 124
Tree, Matthew xxviii
tremendismo 63
trinquet 110
Turner, Victor 142
　The Anthropology of Performance 142

U
unconscious 210
United States of America 131, 144, 145, 167
Universitat de Barcelona 196
Universitat Autònoma de Barcelona 105
urban planning xxxv, 86–7, 96, 99n3, 100n8, 131–3, 139–42, 146, 151n33, 152n42
　see also architecture; housing; tower block

V
Valencia xv–xvi, xxi, xxx, 106
　immigration from xxxiv, 22, 84, 99n3, 105–28
Vall d'Albaida 115–16
Vandellós, Josep Antoni xxi–xxiv, xxvii, 8, 16, 84, 94, 100n10, 148n11
　Catalunya, poble decadent xxi–xxiv, 100n10, 148n11
　La immigració a Catalunya 100n10
Vanguardia, La 106
Vargas Castro, David Andrés 230n14

Vaughan-Williams, Nick 149n17
Vázquez Montalbán, Manuel 65, 102n20
Vic 156, 163, 166, 176
Vicens, Antònia xxx, xxxiii, 60
  39° a l'ombra 60–2, 65, 66, 67, 68–9
Vicens Vives, Jaume xxii–xxiv, 31n21, 84, 94
  Notícia de Catalunya 31n21
Viestenz, William xxxv
Viet-cong 144
Vietnam 144, 145
Vilarós, Teresa 101n13, 137, 145, 146, 150n20
Villatoro, Vicenç xxix, 21, 28
  Un home que se'n va xxix, 21
violence 39, 117, 121, 127n28
visibility 91, 95, 96, 132
Vogt, Silvana xxviii, xxx, 205–32
  and ambivalence 207, 214–16, 218–19
  and Argentine identity 214, 215, 218, 220, 228
  and Catalan identity 214, 215, 218, 220, 228
  and dialogue of mournings 214–20
  and literary form 206, 211, 215, 218, 220–1, 223, 227–8
  and literature 220, 222
  and loss 207, 211–12, 214–15, 219–20, 220–9
  and mourning 206–7, 208, 212–29
  and trauma 211–12
  critical responses 206, 221
  La mecànica de l'aigua xxxvi–xxxvii, 205–32
Vuillard, Éric 108

W
Wamba Graviña, Graciela 230n2
Wells, Caragh 157
Winnicott, Donald W. 208
Winnock, Michel 116
  Jeanne et les siennes 116
witnessing 227–8
writing xxxvi, 13, 158, 162, 164–5, 168, 172, 174, 177–8, 183, 192–3, 200
  scene of 211, 227

X
xarnego 14, 94, 103n34, 137
xenophobia xvii, xx, 9–11, 17

Y
Ysàs, Pere 102n20

Z
Zambrano, Paco 129, 130, 131